www.routledgesw.com

An authentic breakthrough in social work education . . .

New Directions in Social Work is an innovative, integrated series of texts, website, and interactive cases for generalist courses in the social work curriculum at both undergraduate and graduate levels. Instructors will find everything they need to build a comprehensive course that allows students to meet course outcomes, with these unique features:

- All texts, interactive cases, and test materials are **linked to the 2008 CSWE Policy and Accreditation Standards (EPAS).**

- **One web portal with easy access** for instructors and students from any computer—no codes, no CDs, no restrictions. Go to **www.routledgesw.com** and discover.

- **The series is flexible and can be easily adapted for use in online distance-learning courses as well as hybrid and bricks-and-mortar courses.**

- Each text and the website can be used **individually** or as an **entire series** to meet the needs of any social work program.

TITLES IN THE SERIES

Social Work and Social Welfare: An Invitation, Second Edition by Marla Berg-Weger

Human Behavior in the Social Environment, Second Edition by Anissa Taun Rogers

Research for Effective Social Work Practice, Second Edition by Judy L. Krysik and Jerry Finn

Social Policy for Effective Practice: A Strengths Approach, Second Edition by Rosemary K. Chapin

Contemporary Social Work Practice, Second Edition by Martha P. Dewees

Human Behavior in the Social Environment

Second Edition
by Anissa Taun Rogers, University of Portland

In this book and companion custom website you will find:

- An **overview of the issues** related to human behavior and the social environment that are important to understand for practice, **updated with current and relevant information** on important topics in social work practice and **expanded to clarify complex issues**.

- Careful organization of chapters to first present **theoretical perspectives on the human condition**, and then provide information on **basic facets of human development**, encouraging students to use conceptual lenses to inform their practice with individuals at different stages of life.

- Particular emphasis on the ways in which **poverty and diversity** affect human development and behavior.

- The opportunity to **see how the concepts fit into social work practice** using case examples that open each chapter and are referred to throughout the chapter.

- **Interactive case studies** at www.routledgesw.com/cases: Three easy-to-access fictional cases with dynamic characters and situations that students can easily reach from any computer and that provide **a "learning by doing" format unavailable with any other text**. Your students will have an advantage unlike any other they will experience in their social work training.

- A wealth of **instructor-only resources** at www.routledgesw.com/hbse that provide **full-text readings** that link to the concepts presented in each of the chapters; a complete bank of objective and essay-type **test items, all linked to current CSWE EPAS standards; PowerPoint presentations** to help students master key concepts; annotated **links to a treasure trove of social work assets on the Internet**; and a forum inviting all instructors using books in the Series to communicate with each other and share ideas to improve teaching and learning.

- Ideal for use in *online* as well as *hybrid* course instruction—in addition to traditional "bricks and mortar" classes.

Human Behavior in the Social Environment

Second Edition

Anissa Taun Rogers
University of Portland

Routledge
Taylor & Francis Group

NEW YORK AND LONDON

First published 2010
by Routledge
711 Third Avenue, New York, NY 10017

Simultaneously published in the UK
by Routledge
2 Park Square, Milton Park, Abingdon, Oxon OX14 4RN

Routledge is an imprint of the Taylor & Francis Group, an informa business

© 2010 Taylor & Francis

Typeset in Stone Serif by RefineCatch Limited, Bungay, Suffolk

Library of Congress Cataloging in Publication Data
Rogers, Anissa.
Human behavior in the social environment / Anissa Taun Rogers. – 2nd ed.
p. cm. – (New directions in social work)
Includes bibliographical references and index.
1. Social service—Psychological aspects.   2. Human behavior.   3. Developmental psychology.   4. Social psychology.   I. Title.
HV40.R664 2010
302—dc22   2009048679

ISBN10: 0–415–80310–1 (hbk)
ISBN10: 0–415–80311–X (pbk)
ISBN10: 0–203–86886–2 (ebk)

ISBN13: 978–0–415–80310–6 (hbk)
ISBN13: 978–0–415–80311–3 (pbk)
ISBN13: 978–0–203–86886–7 (ebk)

To all social workers, both students and those in the field, who helped to shape my ideas and inspired me personally and professionally.

BRIEF CONTENTS

DETAILED CONTENTS

CHAPTER 4

PREFACE

MAJOR CHANGES TO THE SECOND EDITION

Like the first edition of *Human Behavior in the Social Environment*, this edition provides students with an overview of the issues related to human behavior and the social environment that are important to understand for practice. This information has been updated to offer students current and relevant information on important topics in social work practice and expanded to help students understand the complexity of the issues they will face in the field, including how poverty and diversity affect human development and behavior.

For the new editions of all five books in the New Directions in Social Work series, each addressing a foundational course in the social work curriculum, the publisher has created a brand-new, uniquely distinctive teaching strategy that revolves around the print book but offers much more than the traditional text experience. The series website www.routledgesw.com leads to custom websites coordinated with each text and offering a variety of features to support instructors as you integrate the many facets of an education in social work.

At www.routledgesw.com/hbse, you will find a wealth of resources to help you create a dynamic, experiential introduction to social work for your students. The website houses companion readings linked to key concepts in each chapter, along with questions to encourage further thought and discussion; three interactive fictional cases with accompanying exercises that bring to life the concepts covered in the book, readings, and classroom discussions; a bank of exam questions (both objective and open-ended) and PowerPoint presentations; annotated links to a treasure trove of articles, videos, and Internet sites; and an online forum inviting all instructors using texts in the series to share ideas to improve teaching and learning. You may find most useful a set of sample syllabi showing how *Human Behavior in the Social Environment*, 2nd ed., can be used in a variety of course structures. A master syllabus demonstrates how the text and website used together through the course satisfy the 2008 Council on Social Work Educational Policy and Accreditation Standards (EPAS).

The organization and content of this book and companion website are such that students at the bachelor's and master's levels of their social work education can utilize the knowledge gained from studying the material; specifically, this knowledge can be applied to both generalist and specialized practice. The second edition can be used throughout a two-semester sequence as well as a one-semester course, and the integrated supplements and resources on the Web make the text especially amenable for online distance-learning and hybrid courses.

For example, a supplemental online chapter on the autism spectrum can be used to help students learn more about the disorder, spark in-depth discussions about the causes and treatments for autism, and help students understand the ways in which it might impact their practice. Readings (and accompanying questions) have been specifically added to offer more breadth and depth to selected topics, giving students and instructors options about which topics to explore more thoroughly and to provide opportunities to explore the diversity and complexity that are associated with the social issues with which social workers grapple. These readings can also be used to help students with more self-directed learning in areas about which they are particularly interested and may want to explore further beyond the scope of the material that is normally covered in the course.

ORGANIZATION OF THE BOOK

The chapters of this book are arranged first to give students an overview of the content, next to offer brief discussions of theoretical perspectives on the human condition, and then to provide information on basic facets of human development. Chapters 1 through 5 expose students to theoretical thinking and why it is important in social work as well as how it can help them to organize their thinking about clients and the issues they present in practice. Chapters 6 through 12 introduce students to important developmental, social, and cultural issues related to specific phases of life that are often relevant to practice. These chapters present developmental information beginning before conception into old age and encourage students to consider how development on biological, psychological, social, and cultural levels can impact individuals, families, communities, and social institutions. Exploring the various dynamic interactions that occur between the individual and the environment will help students to understand these interactions from theoretical and practice perspectives.

The following paragraphs serve to briefly introduce each of the chapters included in this book, with emphasis on the updated content.

Chapter 1

Theory: The Foundation of Social Work offers a detailed discussion about why thinking about human behavior within the social environment is so important to social work education and to the profession. It will give students a sense of why they were asked to learn all those theories that were presented to them in other classes as well as all the other information that did not seem relevant to their major. The goal of the first chapter is to answer for students the questions, How does all this fit together, and why is it relevant to my work with clients? It also helps students understand how this knowledge base fits with CSWE's education policies. Finally, the first chapter will set the context for the rest of the book and help students to think about how to approach the information. The next four chapters give students an overview of the theoretical concepts often used by social workers to help them make sense of the interactions between human behavior and the social environment.

Chapter 2

Lenses for Conceptualizing Problems and Interventions: The Person in the Environment presents broadly based, comprehensive theoretical models—for example, the biopsychosocial approach, systems theory, and the strengths perspective—that tend to be used frequently in generalist practice. These theories, though often borrowed from other disciplines, lend themselves well to social work because they address constructs of problem conceptualization and intervention that are unique to the profession. Chapter 2 is designed to give students a base on which to incorporate more specific theories discussed in the following chapters.

Chapter 3

Lenses for Conceptualizing Problems and Interventions: Biopsychosocial Dimensions provides an overview of some specific theories that come out of psychology and related fields. These theories help students to think about how and why we become the people we are. Students will encounter theories related to physical, emotional, and cognitive development as well as ways to think about how we learn in both individual and social contexts.

Chapter 4

Lenses for Conceptualizing Problems and Interventions: Sociocultural Dimensions takes a look at how societies function and how individuals are affected by the order and purpose of various social institutions. Each of the theories discussed in this chapter have distinctive "slants" on the way in which they attempt to explain society, which in turn affects the way the social worker explains personal problems. Learning about the theories covered in Chapter 4 will give students an opportunity to think about larger society and the ways in which its structure affects the work you do in the profession. Additional material on theories and related issues was added to this chapter to expand students' thinking in these realms.

Chapter 5

Lenses for Conceptualizing Problems and Interventions: Social Change Dimensions continues the discussion on the broader context of human lives and problems. It explores theories that address the social context in which we live and ways in which we can effect change to better our lives. Chapter 5 explores the problems of social injustice that affect people individually but that are often rooted in larger social contexts. These theories help students to think about how personal issues are often intertwined with social and political issues, and why addressing them often requires social action to change lives on the individual level.

Chapter 6

Pre-Pregnancy and Prenatal Issues offers students information on fetal development and some of the issues that clients may present with during a pregnancy and after birth. For example, students explore topics of low birth weight, planned and unplanned pregnancies, and hazards to fetal development. Students also explore familial and environmental issues such as access to health care, workplace policies, and international issues affecting family planning, with a focus on some of the ethical dilemmas posed by prenatal testing and other related health care situations. Students will find updated research on various topics and an expanded discussion on abortion.

Chapter 7

Development in Infancy and Early Childhood exposes students to physical, psychological, and emotional developmental issues in early childhood and some of the issues that can affect clients and their families during this stage of development. It discusses theoretical perspectives on attachment that are pertinent to this stage of life as well as recent research in areas such as parenting, child abuse, child care, and policies affecting children and families. A section on autism has been added to this chapter.

Chapter 8

Development in Middle Childhood exposes students to developmental processes of children in this age range and presents information on related individual, familial, and social issues pertinent to this age range. Debates and updated information on areas such as intelligence and intelligence testing, learning disabilities, parental discipline, gay and lesbian parenting, divorce and remarriage, and the effects of media are included. Students are also introduced to theory on play in this chapter.

Chapter 9

Development in Adolescence covers developmental considerations of this life stage and the various issues that clients are likely to deal with at this age. Issues such as eating disorders, self-esteem, pregnancy, sexual identity development, substance abuse, and suicide are discussed as are issues around sex education, violence, and heterosexism and homophobia. Students are introduced to theories on moral and sexual identity development, which are likely to be pertinent to their work with clients at this age.

Chapter 10

Development in Early Adulthood covers the continued physical and cognitive development into adulthood and issues people at this life stage are likely to face such as mental illness, disability, and problems with spirituality. Theory around spirituality development and expanded discussion on spirituality are included in this chapter as it applies to work with young adults. Other issues pertaining to domestic violence, sexism, sexual harassment, and related social policies are discussed.

Chapter 11

Development in Middle Adulthood explores continued development as we age and explores in depth some of the physical and cognitive changes that can occur as well as issues these changes may raise. Topics such as the menopause and the andropause, health care and chronic illness, and marriage and love are explored. A section on health disparities has been added to highlight problems that some minority groups face with regard to chronic illness. Retirement and theories surrounding retirement are discussed as are issues around ageism.

Chapter 12

Development in Late Adulthood discusses developmental issues in older age and continued physical and cognitive changes that take place as we age. In this chapter, students are exposed to various theories of aging and how they can be used to conceptualize work with older clients. Expanded and updated discussion on spirituality, depression, sexuality, grief and loss, and issues for gay and lesbian elders are included as are topics surrounding grandparenting, caregiving, living situations, and social policy issues impacting older adults.

INTERACTIVE CASES

The website www.routledgesw.com/cases presents three unique, in-depth, inter-active, fictional cases with dynamic characters and real-life situations that students can easily access from any computer and that provide a "learning by doing" format unavailable with any other text. Your students will have an advantage unlike any other they will experience in their social work training. Each of the interactive cases uses text, graphics, and video to help students learn about engagement, assessment, intervention, and evaluation and termination at multiple levels of social work practice. The "My Notebook" feature allows students to take and save notes, type in written responses to tasks, and share their work with classmates and instructors by email. Through the interactive cases, you can integrate the readings and classroom discussions by acquainting the students with:

The Sanchez Family: Systems, Strengths, and Stressors. The 10 individuals in this extended Latino family have numerous strengths but are faced with a variety of challenges. Students will have the opportunity to experience the phases of the social work intervention, grapple with ethical dilemmas, and identify strategies for addressing issues of diversity.

Riverton: A Community Conundrum. Riverton is a small midwest city in which the social worker lives and works. The social worker identifies an issue that presents her community with a challenge. Students and instructors can work together to develop strategies for engaging, assessing, and intervening with the citizens of the social worker's neighborhood.

Carla Washburn: Loss, Aging, and Social Support. Students will get to know Carla Washburn, an older African-American woman who finds herself living alone after the loss of her grandson and in considerable pain from a recent accident. In this case, less complex than the Sanchez Family, students will apply their growing knowledge of gerontology and exercise the skills of culturally competent practice.

This book takes full advantage of the interactive element as a unique learning opportunity by including exercises that require students to go to the Web and use the cases. To maximize the learning experience, you may want to start the course by asking your students to explore each case by activating each button. The more the students are familiar with the presentation of information and the locations of the individual case files, the Case Study Tools, and the questions and tasks contained within each phase of the case, the better they will be able to integrate the text with the online practice component.

IN SUM

When presented as separate issues, all of the aforementioned developmental topics can seem overwhelming to students, particularly when they realize they have to keep handy their knowledge about each when working with clients. However, all of these topics, as well as other topics that are discussed, are set in a framework that will help students to think about the types of problems their clients might be likely to face at different phases in life. Students will also learn that organizing their knowledge about these areas into a theoretical context that "makes sense" to them will help them to manage the seemingly endless stream of information at their disposal. Ultimately, then, students will become more and more proficient at applying concepts to client problems. Meanwhile, students can enjoy the process of learning about them.

Being an effective social worker means being able to understand the complexities of human behavior, the societies and cultures in which we live, and the interplay between them. Being an effective social worker also means having a solid grounding in various disciplines, such as psychology, sociology, and human biology. It means possessing a well-rounded education and an ability to apply this knowledge to the myriad client problems and situations that students will face in the profession. This edition is intended to help students understand this complexity in the field and to help them gain the knowledge and critical thinking skills they will need to practice social work.

ACKNOWLEDGMENTS

I owe my gratitude to all the social work students I have known since the beginning of my career, for their questions, musings, and insights, and for pushing me to think about what it means to be a social worker. They are the inspiration for this book. I would like to extend my thanks to Kirsten Norris and Maren Andres, graduates of the Social Work Program at the University of Portland, who gave a great deal of their time and energy to help me research this book. Similarly, Rayne Funk, administrative assistant to the Social Work Program, was extremely helpful in the production of this book. Without her, most of my work would be impossible. I would also like to give a heartfelt thank you to Dr. Joseph Gallegos, my colleague at the University of Portland, for all his support and mentorship. And for their support, I would like to thank Dr. Bob Duff, former Chair of the Department of Social and Behavioral Sciences and Fr. Stephen Rowan, Dean of the College of Arts and Sciences.

The project coordinator, Alice Lieberman, and the other authors of the book series, Rosemary Chapin, Marla Berg-Weger, Jerry Finn, and Judy Krysik have been great sources of inspiration and motivation. I have appreciated their feedback and insights throughout the process of writing this book. I am grateful to the reviewers of the book as well as to the editors and staff at Routledge, whose input was invaluable in helping me to move the book forward in a meaningful way.

Finally, I want to thank Tammy Rogers for her unwavering show of enthusiasm and encouragement for my work, and my family, Jim Koch, Olivia, and Grady for their support, patience, and tolerance for my endeavors.

ABOUT THE AUTHOR

Anissa Taun Rogers, PhD, LCSW, MA, is Associate Professor of Social Work at the University of Portland in Portland, Oregon. She also serves as the director of the Practicum Program. She teaches courses across the social work curriculum as well as courses on the body, human sexuality, and interviewing and counseling.

Before finding her way to social work, Dr. Rogers studied psychology, in which she earned undergraduate and graduate degrees. After receiving her MSW and PhD in social work, Dr. Rogers began her career in undergraduate social work education and clinical practice. In addition to teaching, her main clinical and research interests are in sexuality, gerontology, and mental health.

CHAPTER 1

Theory: The Foundation of Social Work

Janice is a single, 21-year-old mother of two. She is talking with her case manager at the local Department of Human Services office about her welfare benefits, which will be cut if she doesn't find steady work. Janice is having trouble finding and keeping jobs, and she is struggling to pay for rent, food, and day care for her children. Although Janice wants to work, she finds it difficult because of the depressed economy in her town, her lack of job skills, and several health problems. Among other symptoms, Janice suffers from severe migraine headaches, and she has trouble sleeping and concentrating. The stress caused by unemployment and health problems has also made parenting more difficult, and Janice finds herself becoming depressed because she is unable to meet her responsibilities as a parent. Although Janice receives Medicaid, she is unable to follow through with recommended diagnostic tests for her health-related symptoms because of transportation and child care issues. Janice frequently feels overwhelmed with all of her responsibilities, and she often wishes she had only herself to support, which would give her time to go out with her friends and experience life.

JANICE'S STORY EXEMPLIFIES THE COMPLEXITY OF HUMAN problems. Rarely in social work will you find yourself working with people whose problems are straightforward. When you carefully examine Janice's situation, you will probably identify several major issues: health and parenting problems, potential mental health issues, developmental issues associated with Janice's age, program policies (such as welfare policies), cultural expectations of parenting and self-sufficiency, access to affordable housing and day care, and employment availability and policies. Regardless of the type of agency in which you work or the population with which you work, you will find people's problems to be multifaceted and interconnected on many different levels. Because the human condition is so complex, social workers need to understand human behaviors in their social environment.

DEFINING HUMAN BEHAVIOR IN THE SOCIAL ENVIRONMENT

No single definition for "human behavior in the social environment" exists. Nevertheless, the social work profession agrees on the importance of understanding how individuals interact both with other people and with their environment as well as how individuals are affected by these interactions. For this reason, the Council on Social Work Education (CSWE), the body that accredits undergraduate and graduate social work programs, requires that programs prepare students to apply knowledge of human behavior and the social environment. Specifically, this policy articulates that, "social workers are knowledgeable about human behavior across the life course; the range of social systems in which people live; and the ways social systems promote or deter people in maintaining or achieving health and well-being. Social workers apply theories and knowledge from the liberal arts to understand biological, social, cultural, psychological, and spiritual development" (Council on Social Work Education, 2008, p. 6). Social workers use this knowledge in their work with clients—from assessment to evaluation of intervention—and they have the ability to critique knowledge that is applied to practice (Council on Social Work Education, 2008). Further, this knowledge is based in and supports a core value system of the profession, which promotes such things as social justice, dignity and worth of people, and scientific inquiry to help promote effective and ethical practice (National Association of Social Workers, 1996). So, students of accredited social work programs must learn about the interrelationships between individual behavior and larger social environments. This includes content on various theories that explain human behavior and social dynamics; ways in which developmental factors affect people in their environments; how these factors play out on different levels, including the individual, family, small group, community, and societal levels; and promote social justice and the dignity and worth of people.

Exhibit 1.1 illustrates the concept of human behavior in the social environment. Each circle represents a level of practice on which social workers might focus. This visualization also shows you how the different areas of people's lives and environments can intersect. The intersections are those areas in which social workers generally focus their assessments and interventions. Depending on the agency or population, though, social workers sometimes move outside the overlapping areas to focus on issues related to a specific circle or realm. For example, a social worker might be employed to conduct mental health assessments for children. Her main focus thus would be on the individual level, specifically, each child's mental health issues. Nevertheless, she would probably still consider issues in the realms of family and small groups and society and larger forces. For instance, she may attend to issues relating to the child's family, peers, school, economic status, cultural background, and so on. Moreover, she might consider other factors on the individual level besides mental health, such as the child's coping skills and physical health. The

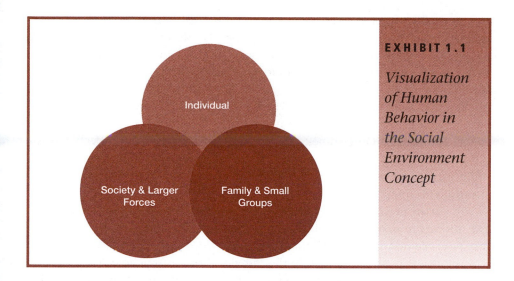

EXHIBIT 1.1

Visualization of Human Behavior in the Social Environment Concept

Individual

Society & Larger Forces

Family & Small Groups

complexities and intricacies of this conceptualization should become clearer to you as you move through this chapter and the remainder of the book.

Learning about human behavior in the social environment will help you to place your knowledge into a meaningful and coherent context as you work with clients, organizations, and communities. It will challenge you to use your existing knowledge of human behavior and social environments while incorporating it into new ideas and perspectives on the human condition. It will give you more complex ways to think about assessment and intervention, which in turn will help you to become a more creative and effective social worker.

Knowledge, Theories, and Social Work

While the core value system of social work means that, as a profession, it tends to generate, draw from, and apply knowledge based in strengths, empowerment, and social justice tenets, it is also inclined to incorporate knowledge from many different disciplines that may not explicitly adhere to these tenets. *Knowledge* in this context refers to a wide range of information such as theories, empirical research, and practical experience that might be generated from different disciplines. Given the complexity of individuals' lives and the multifaceted nature of the problems that clients bring to the working relationship, social workers need to have a broad knowledge base in many different areas—such as politics, biology, psychology, sociology, and economics—and they need to understand how aspects from these different realms interact with and influence one another in ways that affect the well-being of individuals, families, and communities. In other words, social workers must be able both to think comprehensively and creatively and to access their knowledge and "pull it all together" to assess and intervene with client problems. Further, because social work is concerned with social justice and the dignity and worth of people, among other values, social workers must also understand how to incorporate strength-based and empowerment concepts into their work. This is why a strong liberal arts base in your education is so helpful. The more you know about different areas such as history, government, and philosophy, for example, the better the foundation you will have for conceptualizing and intervening with client problems. You can be more helpful when working with a client if you are familiar with some basic facts or updated research on the particular problem with which the client is struggling. Other times, you can use your knowledge to offer a client a different viewpoint on a particular problem, no matter how technical or philosophical, to give the client a new way to think about the problem. These are situations in which your familiarity with different theories will be useful.

To see the benefits of drawing on a broad knowledge base, let us consider how practitioners from other disciplines might approach Janice's situation. A physician may be concerned only with identifying and alleviating Janice's physical symptoms. A psychologist may attend only to the individualistic or psychological aspects of Janice's case. These might include her potential for developing depression or other mental illness, her emotional and cognitive development, her issues of self-esteem and self-efficacy, and the quality of her attachments with her children. After pinpointing these problems, the psychologist might focus on improving Janice's functioning in these areas. An economist may concentrate on employment prospects, economic conditions of the community, and the costs of maintaining Janice on welfare. Economic interventions would include activities to improve employment conditions in the community and to curb costs by reducing the amount of time that Janice spends on welfare rolls. A sociologist may be more interested in examining the larger social and cultural dynamics that contribute to poverty for single mothers. Interventions might include helping Janice adapt to cultural expectations of employment and parenting, or working to change societal attitudes toward poverty and single mothers. Although all of these perspectives are important, considering them in isolation contributes little to understanding the scope and complexity of Janice's problems and, consequently, to the effectiveness of the interventions.

Use of Theories and Empirical Knowledge in Social Work   To help pull sources of information together when working with clients, social workers need to understand basic theories in different areas, how theories can be applied to problems, and how theories' limitations can affect their explanations of problems. A **theory** is a set of ideas or concepts that, when considered together, help to explain certain phenomena and allow people to predict behavior and other events. Theories differ from other types of knowledge in that they allow you to organize knowledge on a particular issue or topic. If theories are well developed, they provide a blueprint for testing hypotheses or hunches about behavior and other phenomena, predicting certain events, and validating assumptions and knowledge about certain issues. Without theories, knowledge about human behavior and social issues would remain unwieldy; you would not be able to make connections among related facts and information to form ideas that could help you advance your knowledge about human behavior and social issues. A variety of theories can help social workers organize information and make sense of certain problems. Theories can offer social workers contexts from which to approach problems with the confidence that interventions are sound. Of course, some theories are more valid than others, but part of being a skilled social worker is knowing how to evaluate theories for their strengths and limitations and how to apply them responsibly.

Theories are often developed and refined through the process of empirically based (or experimentally generated) research and investigation. Beyond its use for theory development, **empirically-based knowledge** is often used to provide the most updated, valid, and reliable information on issues to help guide practice. Keep in mind that the idea that social work practice should be informed by (1) theory and (2) empirically based knowledge is relatively recent. Historically, social work was rooted in charity and volunteerism, and only recently did it become more rationalized and scientific (Fischer, 1981). As the disease model emerged and other disciplines such as psychology, sociology, and economics began using more scientific methods to advance knowledge and theory, social work moved away from relying solely on **practice-based knowledge**, or practice wisdom, which is knowledge generated from practice experience. Practice-based knowledge tends to be anecdotal and ambiguous and cannot always be generalized to new situations. Though practice-based knowledge can be based on theoretical foundations, it often is not subjected to controlled tests to verify how valid and reliable it may be for work with clients outside of a particular practice context. However, it certainly has its value; throughout practitioners' careers, they may work with thousands of people, giving them rich insights into various issues and problems. And, practice-based knowledge can lead to hunches, questions, and curiosity about various problems, which can lead to scientific exploration that can generate science-based knowledge and the development of theories about particular issues.

Science-based knowledge relies more on empirical or experimental research and theoretical tenets on which to base ideas about certain issues. It is knowledge that is developed over time using objective methods to test hypotheses that allow practitioners, with some degree of reliability and accuracy, to generalize their knowledge beyond single-client cases. It also allows people to modify existing theories about certain issues as well as develop new ones that might explain issues more accurately. The movement among social workers to use more scientific approaches has also been driven by **evidence-based practice**, or an increased responsibility by social workers to document that their interventions are effective.

The Debate over Theory in Social Work   Despite this trend toward science-based knowledge, there has been and currently is considerable debate about how much the social work profession can and should rely on empirical and theory-based knowledge—particularly as it relates to some entrenched, classic theories of human development—given the complexity of human behavior (Osmond & O'Connor, 2006; Parton, 2000; Sheppard, 1998). On one end of the continuum is the idea that theory, or some guiding set of principles about certain phenomena, is needed to help social workers organize concepts and offer principles from which intervention outcomes can be tested. This line of thinking supports the belief that social workers need some kind of guiding conceptualization of client problems, which can support empirical testing of interventions, which can lead to the modification of theoretical conceptions and ideas and, ultimately, to better and more effective interventions (Simon & Thyer, 1994).

On the other end of the continuum is the argument that many of the theories from which social work borrows are outdated and ineffective for social work practice. This line of thinking suggests that many theories taught in social work curricula have no utility when students begin their practice. Those arguing from this standpoint posit that many constructs or concepts in these theories have not been (and probably cannot be) supported through empirical research. They point to various limitations in the development of many theories, making them biased and inappropriate for use with people who come from diverse situations. For instance, Freud's theory of psychosexual development and Piaget's theory on cognitive development were developed in specific time and cultural contexts. This issue and others call into question the appropriateness of using these theories in work with clients who come from backgrounds and generations different from the people who were studied to develop these theories. At best, such theories need additional testing to understand how well they help to explain problems of clients who come from contexts other than the typical Eurocentric ones in which these theories have been developed and often are employed. Further, because of the sheer number of theories that could be related to social work practice, this argument points out that these theories cannot be taught in sufficient depth for students to understand them well enough to apply them effectively in practice (Simon & Thyer, 1994).

The reality is that because of the scope of problems with which social workers grapple, theories do come in handy. Moreover, because social work is such a broad field, social workers can rely on a vast number of theories when working with clients. Regardless of your particular view on the usefulness or appropriateness of theories in your work, you are likely to deal with them. Thus, you will find it helpful to think about theories in broad categories based on which aspects of human behavior they address. For example, does a theory explain personality development or economic development? Does it explain causes of racism or causes of obsessive-compulsive behavior? You will see by looking at this book's table of contents that Chapters 2 through 5 are organized on this basis. Chapter 2 discusses broad organizing theories used in social work, while Chapters 3, 4, and 5 focus on theories that are more specific to other disciplines. Each set of theories offers a different lens through which to view problems.

Of course, this is just one way to organize the many theories with which social workers are likely to come in contact. Another way would be to group theories in

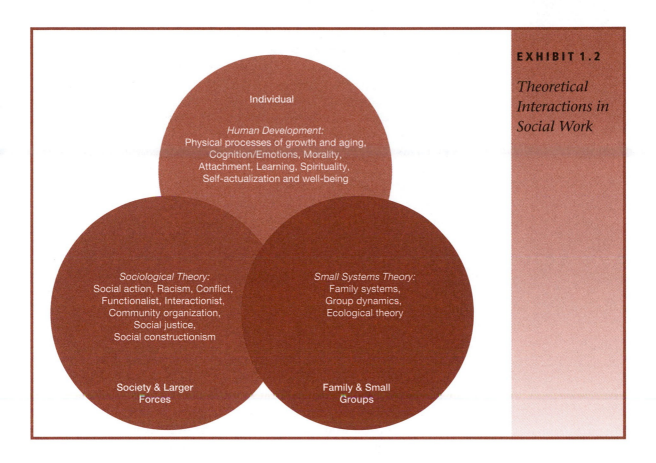

EXHIBIT 1.2

Theoretical Interactions in Social Work

terms of whether they address individual, familial, or larger social issues or some combination of these. Alternatively, theories can be grouped into subcategories according to the specific area or problem that they address. For instance, some theories explain personality development while others address social development. Some theories explain how social change occurs while others explain why social dysfunction is resistant to change.

As you can see in Exhibit 1.2, sometimes concepts from different theoretical frameworks overlap; theories can explain aspects of problems in different realms. For example, theories that address how children and their caregivers establish attachments to one another might be informed by theories that explain how people in a relationship interact with one another, how they perceive these interactions, and how attachments impact these interactions. Attachments and interactions can also be explained by broader family system dynamics. Social workers' understanding of learning processes can be augmented by understanding how family systems may impact the development of their members. Family systems might be improved by theories addressing social justice (for example, to improve access to resources that support families), which can indirectly impact the nature and quality of attachments, interactions, and learning that take place within families. Of course, these are only a few of the many ways in which theories might be used in combination to help explain various problems that occur at individual, familial, and social levels.

As another example of how theories might overlap, the case manager who is working with Janice could rely on various theories that explain not only individual development and functioning but also social problems and change. Because some of Janice's problems surrounding unemployment are interrelated with problems such as parenting, physical health, and larger social forces like the economy, the case manager can incorporate theoretical concepts from all of these areas to better explain how problems on different levels contribute to Janice's situation as well as to develop interventions that will help to alleviate these problems.

For many social workers, the sheer amount of knowledge that is available for use with clients can seem overwhelming at times. Keep in mind that many disciplines have established and well-known theories whose concepts tend to be used more than others. One approach is to learn these theories well and then expand your knowledge base on other theories depending on the type of agency and problem with which you will be working. Further, to augment theoretical knowledge, social workers acquire a lot of knowledge about problems (such as facts, statistics, new research findings) from their experience, education, and other sources that can inform their thinking. Thus, problem conceptualization and intervention in social work are part of a dynamic process. Social workers' thinking needs to be flexible as they work with clients because there can be many different ways to work toward problem solving. As you read about theories in the next several chapters, think about different aspects of social work for which these theories might be useful. You may come up with better ways to group or conceptualize theories that are more meaningful to you and that you can use in practice.

What It Means to Be Eclectic

As we have been discussing, social work is naturally informed by multidisciplinary knowledge. For example, social work with children and families might borrow from psychological theory that deals with aspects of development and behavior change. Social work with communities might rely on sociological theory that addresses group dynamics and social change. Administrative social work might be heavily informed by economic or organizational theory. Perhaps it is not surprising, then, that some social workers describe themselves as **eclectic practitioners**; that is, they borrow ideas and constructs from several theories when working with clients.

Nevertheless, some social workers, regardless of the population or problems with which they work, adhere to a particular theory. For instance, some social workers might describe themselves as behaviorists, psychoanalysts, or family system theorists. These theoretical preferences tend to be influenced by the political and philosophical climate in which social workers received their training (Saltman &

Greene, 1993) as well as the contexts in which they work. Naturally, social workers' tendencies to use some theories more than others influence the ways they conceptualize clients' problems, the ways in which they move through assessment, and the types of interventions they choose.

To study the ways in which social workers' theoretical biases might play out in practice, Saltman (2002) surveyed 175 social workers in Jewish Family and Children's Agencies in the United States and Canada. She administered questionnaires and case vignettes to explore workers' theoretical orientations and interventions in practice. Based on self-report, the results indicated that respondents tended to show flexibility between their personal theoretical orientation and the types of interventions they chose to use in the case vignettes. Specifically, respondents did not necessarily choose interventions whose theoretical underpinnings were the same as their stated orientation. A majority (87.5 percent) of respondents reported having a psychosocial orientation, for example, but they applied a family systems intervention to the case in the vignette. According to Saltman, it may be that respondents were using theories that best "fit" clients' problems rather than forcing the problems to fit respondents' favored theories. In other words, respondents probably were relying on practice knowledge, empirical knowledge, or both, rather than their personal preferences, to guide their decisions about which theoretical approaches to use in their interventions.

Although results from studies like this one cannot tell us whether all social workers would respond to client situations in the same way, especially when faced with real versus contrived situations, they do help us to understand the reality that social workers often rely on multiple theories when working with clients. The results also suggest that other forces from sources such as the client, the agency, the political sphere, and even popular opinion might influence the theories that social workers use in their interventions with clients. For example, a social worker might use a particular theory for a specific problem because of recent empirical research that supports its effectiveness in explaining that problem. Similarly, an agency or funding source may only pay for the use of treatments based on a particular theory or set of theories. In these cases, social workers may be dealing with outside pressures to pick one theory over another, or even to use certain constructs from multiple theories, regardless of the social workers' personal orientations or biases.

The Single Theory Argument   There is considerable debate about how effective social workers (or any professionals who work with people) can be if they are "pure theorists" as opposed to eclectic. One side of the argument posits that to thoroughly understand the essence of a theory and to apply its constructs effectively and appropriately, social workers must study and adhere to only that particular theory when working with clients. For example, a social worker who uses behavioral theory to assess children's behavior problems needs to have a deep understanding of the underlying tenets of behaviorism (its history, developers, applications, constructs, and limitations) to use it appropriately when working with clients.

Proponents of adhering to a particular theory maintain that social workers who try to borrow constructs from many theories can never really know each one sufficiently or thoroughly enough to use parts of it correctly. Proponents also argue that in order to remain valid, theories must be used as a whole; they become invalid when only parts of them are used in isolation. Using just one behavioral technique, for example, such as time-outs, in work with children should not be done without using other related techniques supported by behavioral theory. This is especially true when the person using the technique does not adequately understand the underlying assumptions of behavior as explained through behavioral theory. Other arguments along this line of thinking include the following (Payne, 1997):

- Social workers get their training early in their careers and are likely to stick to the ways of thinking and practice that they learned in school. Thus, they are unlikely to be familiar with new knowledge across a range of theories and therefore cannot integrate this knowledge into their practice.

- There are no guidelines or rules about how to choose concepts from one theory or another, making the use of different theories rather haphazard and unsystematic.

- Social workers are unlikely to get needed supervision on using multiple theories and techniques, so relying on multiple techniques in practice can be risky.

- The underlying philosophies about human behavior tend to differ from one theory to the next; trying to integrate their concepts may lead to disjointed practice or even contradictory applications.

The Argument for Eclecticism   The other side of the argument states that because social work is concerned with people and problems on many different levels, the need to be flexible and comprehensive is inherent in the work. The nature of the work is such that if social workers try to use one theory for all types of populations and problems, they will inevitably be ineffective. Proponents of this argument state that social work should not adhere to a "one theory fits all" policy. In fact, some might argue that rigidly adhering to only one perspective can be oppressive to clients, forcing the unique characteristics of clients and the human condition into a uniform mold. Further, because uncertainty is a constant in the social sciences, particularly when it comes to human behavior and social issues, relying on a single theory to explain all problems will cause social workers to miss the bigger picture. Consequently, they will be more likely to misinterpret problems and apply inappropriate interventions, potentially doing more harm than good for clients. Being eclectic, flexible, and comprehensive allows social workers to be creative and resourceful in finding solutions to their clients' myriad problems. Indeed, some social workers argue that doubt, ambiguity, and uncertainty are hallmarks of the profession. Thus, social workers should be equipped with a broad "toolbox" of theoretical knowledge to work effectively with clients.

This line of thinking supports the idea that clients should benefit from all of the theoretical knowledge available to social workers. And because every theory has its limitations with regard to what it explains, social workers need additional resources when working with clients. Social work processes such as intake (initial client interviews and information gathering), relationship building, assessment, planning, intervention, evaluation, and follow-up are commonplace in many agency settings and working relationships. To guide these processes, social workers tend to rely on theories to inform the way they approach client situations. Because client problems and situations are complex, just one approach from one particular theoretical orientation might not be all that social workers need in certain circumstances or at different places in the working relationship (Payne, 1997).

Regardless of which perspective you take on this debate, it is obvious that to be an effective social worker, you must have at least a working knowledge of various theories that explain human development and behavior. Without this knowledge, you will not be able to make informed decisions about how to use theory, whether that means taking the eclectic approach or the pure theorist or single theory approach. Moreover, it is likely that the educational and work settings in which you find yourself will dictate, to some extent, how theories get used in practice. For example, some treatment programs for children with behavioral problems only use behavioral theory in their interventions, while some social workers in private practice may only use Freudian psychoanalysis. To be adaptable, as well as to serve clients ethically and responsibly, you need to understand multiple theories as well as how to use them in the appropriate context.

Evaluating the Quality of Knowledge and Theory

Previous sections discussed the need for social workers to use a broad range of knowledge, including empirical and theoretical knowledge, in their work with clients. You also learned about some of the debates regarding how to apply this knowledge, particularly theoretical knowledge, to work with clients. In this section, we will turn our attention to evaluating knowledge to determine how appropriate it is for use with clients.

With regard to how we know what we know, there are many ways in which we gain knowledge and develop theories. One way to do this is through experience. This is similar to the ideas of practice-based knowledge and practice wisdom discussed earlier. It also refers to the experiences that we gain as we live life. How we construct our reality and perceptions of things is often based on the types of experiences we have. These experiences allow us to feel that we "know" things. Alternatively, knowledge can be constructed through what we have been told to be true. This includes knowledge that is transmitted through (1) *tradition*—our culture and what we learn from others—and (2) *authority*—what we are told by experts.

Knowledge transmitted through authority is akin to the idea of empirical or science-based knowledge, also discussed earlier.

Unfortunately, these avenues of transmitting knowledge are full of pitfalls. For instance, how do you know that you can rely on information given to you by those you know? How might your culture influence various facts and ideas? Do you consider celebrities, athletes, and the media to be experts? How do your own values and beliefs bias the knowledge that you seek or the way in which you interpret it? To make matters more complicated, there are yet more debates within the social work discipline about what kinds of knowledge are appropriate for practice. Should you rely on experts, even if what they say does not seem to fit with the problems of your clients? Alternatively, should you rely on practice or experiential knowledge, even if its effectiveness cannot be proved? What role should social work values, which are difficult to measure and observe, play in applying knowledge to your work? If some of the knowledge used in practice is potentially biased or suffers from other problems, is it ethical to use it in work with clients? All of these questions have implications for the effectiveness of social work and the policies and funding that support it.

Given the myriad theories from which to learn and choose when practicing social work as well as the ongoing debates about the utility of learning one or more theories (or even learning any theory at all), where do you go from here? One place to begin to tackle these issues is to think about how to arm yourself with skills to understand what knowledge, theoretical and otherwise, is valid and what is not. An understanding of the characteristics of a useful theory (and well-designed empirical research that assists in theory development) can help you to wade through the flood of knowledge that you will encounter as you move through your career.

There are a lot of ways to judge the accuracy and applicability of knowledge, particularly theoretical and empirically based knowledge. And there are a lot of ideas about what makes knowledge "good," or valid for practice. Box 1.1 displays some basic guidelines for evaluating theoretical knowledge. These guidelines are generally accepted in many disciplines as the standards by which to determine the quality, usefulness, and applicability of theories in explaining certain phenomena (Homans, 1967; Lenski, 1988; Popper, 1959). Based on these guidelines, a theory should be able to offer information that allows you to reasonably predict and explain behavior in a way that will help you develop appropriate and effective interventions for your clients.

You should also be aware that people make all kinds of judgments when they conduct research to develop theories and generate knowledge about social and other issues. Consequently, there is a lot of room for bias, error, and misinterpretation, which can affect the quality of research and its outcomes. When you evaluate research, you need to be clear about factors such as which variables are being manipulated and controlled and which have not been accounted for. You also need to recognize how researchers' biases, values, methods, and motives for doing research can influence outcomes. A number of human errors can affect the way

---

When judging the usefulness of a theory, think about the following criteria:

- **Is it functional?** Does it clearly explain how concepts are related to one another and to the phenomenon it is trying to explain?

- **Is it strong?** Is it able to make certain predictions about behavior that can be confirmed through empirical observation?

- **Is it parsimonious?** Do the theory's concepts explain a lot about the phenomenon in clear, simple, and straightforward terms?

- **Is it falsifiable?** Can it be tested and refuted by empirical observation?

- **Does it make practical sense?** Does it inform your work with clients and relate to what you already know about various phenomena?

- **What are the philosophical underpinnings of the theory?** Does it fit with and promote social work values and ethics?

BOX 1.1

Evaluative Criteria for Theory

---

research is developed, carried out, interpreted, and applied to human situations. Here are some of the more common ones:

- *Problems with observations:* Human beings have notoriously faulty memories, and our own experiences of events can be very unreliable. Moreover, we tend to look for evidence to support our assumptions about certain phenomena, ignoring evidence that contradicts what we think we know.

- *Overgeneralizations:* We tend to assume that what we experience can be generalized to other people and circumstances.

- *Biases and value judgments:* We often impose our own values, inclinations, expectations, and experiences onto an event to help make sense of it.

- *Lack of inquiry:* We stop asking questions about an event because we think we understand it or have pursued it sufficiently.

Any of these pitfalls can result in the development of faulty knowledge, which in turn can lead to problems with accurately assessing and intervening with clients. For instance, many feminist scholars and others working in minority research argue that, historically, a great deal of empirical and theoretical knowledge that has been generated in social and other sciences has focused on the concerns of white males. Knowledge and theoretical developments coming from this research really only apply to people who have been studied (usually white men), but this knowledge is often applied to minority groups (such as women and ethnic and sexual minorities). This does not take into consideration biological, cultural, economic, and other

BOX 1.2

Evaluative Criteria for Research

Some criteria to consider when evaluating research:

- **How current is the information?** If it's not current, is it likely to still be valid? Is there a good reason why it hasn't been updated?

- **Who is the intended audience?** Is the research conducted for the purposes of a particular interest group? Are the results biased to serve the needs of a particular group?

- **Who is the author?** What is the author's expertise and affiliation?

- **Are original sources of information listed?** Can you locate original works cited by the author? Are you given other sources where you can check facts and statements or do further research?

- **Is the information peer reviewed?** Have other experts in the field reviewed the information?

- **Is the information biased?** Does the language seem biased or slanted to suit particular purposes?

- **What is the purpose of the information?** Is it to inform, teach, entertain, enlighten, sell, persuade?

differences that might invalidate the use of this knowledge with diverse groups (Reinharz, 1992; Solomon, 1976). Thus, many classic theories and empirical research on human behavior have been criticized because of the pitfalls listed earlier.

When evaluating empirical research that is being used to support or discredit a theory or that might be used for practice, there are other questions to ask yourself; Box 1.2 outlines some of them. Keeping these criteria in mind and posing some well-thought out questions as you read through the mounds of information you will find in newspapers, on the Internet, in agency and government reports, and even in scholarly journals will help you to avoid the pitfalls just discussed as well as to make some educated decisions about which information is appropriate to use in your practice. The complexity of information about human behavior and social issues makes this sort of scrutiny essential.

In thinking about how this information might be useful in Janice's case, the case manager may want to think about whether the theories and other knowledge used to work with Janice's problems are appropriate. For instance, some theories and other knowledge may be biased toward their applicability to men, or they may focus solely on individual responsibility while overlooking social contributions to the problem. The latter might happen if the case manager has extensive training in mental illness. She or he may focus more on Janice's physical and mental issues and not attend as much to broader issues, such as a poor economy, which are outside of Janice's control but still may add to her problems.

RELATING KNOWLEDGE OF HUMAN BEHAVIOR TO OTHER SOCIAL WORK CONTENT AREAS

You can see how having a broad knowledge base in human behavior and the social environment can be useful for social work practice. Social workers can never know enough about the many facets of human life. Fortunately, the core courses in social work, as well as the electives, offer a foundation on which to apply knowledge of human behavior and to build new knowledge that is more specifically related to various aspects of your work. The following are a few of the courses you will encounter in the social work curriculum:

- Policy courses prepare you to develop, interpret, analyze, and apply social policies, which in turn influence the well-being of individuals, families, and communities on varying levels. You need to understand the interrelationships between policy and human behavior and how to apply perspectives on social policy to client problems.

- Research courses are an important facet of social work education because they teach you how to conduct research to evaluate practice as well as how to incorporate research into practice for more effective results. Research skills are the key to building theory and to ensuring that the approaches and outcomes built on theory are effective. Moreover, social workers need to keep themselves up to date on research in various fields that relate to their practice. New data or research on certain disorders or programs, for example, are constantly being produced, and social workers must be able to evaluate this research to ensure that it is valid, reliable, and sound and to understand how it can be used to inform practice.

- Practice courses rely heavily on theory to teach you empirically based practice methods in working with clients. Depending on the level of the program (undergraduate or graduate), you will learn either generalist or specific theories to help guide your assessments, planning, and interventions with clients, agencies, and communities. Often, these courses are paired with your field experiences and related seminars, which give you opportunities to apply your knowledge of human behavior and various theoretical approaches to your work and to integrate your knowledge with your practical experiences.

In addition to the core courses in the curriculum, social work programs also must incorporate certain content into courses throughout the curriculum. These areas deal with diversity, populations at risk, and values and ethics. All of these areas are crucial components of human behavior and the social environment because, when you consider human development and social problems that affect development, you run into ethical issues, questions of how diversity influences people and their surroundings, and how people can be marginalized by personal and social problems and situations.

USING THIS BOOK TO THINK ABOUT HUMAN DEVELOPMENT AND SOCIAL WORK PRACTICE

This book is organized to help you think about how theory and other knowledge relate to human development and social problems that affect people. It presents information sequentially, discussing theory first as a base on which you can build your knowledge about specific issues relating to human development. This chapter sets the stage for thinking about knowledge and how it is applied to social work practice. While you keep in mind the debates about how knowledge of human behavior in the social environment should be evaluated and used, you will be able to use this information to think about practice applications.

Chapters 2 through 5 present some of the many theories that are commonly used in practice or whose concepts serve as a foundation for interventions. The discussion in these chapters reviews popular theories that can inform practice and describes some of the limitations to using these theories.

Once you have a handle on theory, you will be better prepared to read the remainder of the book. Chapters 6 through 12 take you through common human developmental processes across the life span. Along with developmental information, these chapters introduce issues that tend to present themselves during various life stages and discuss specific theories that help explain these issues. To help you conceptualize the issues within the practice context, they are presented as they relate to different levels—individual, families and small groups, and society and large groups. These chapters will also improve your understanding of how theory, research, and practice inform one another. The goal is to learn to think critically about the debates discussed in this chapter and to develop your own opinions regarding the role of theory and other knowledge in practice.

CONCLUSION

Understanding human behavior in an environmental context is a crucial aspect of good social work. To be an effective social worker, you need a broad knowledge base that incorporates information on theories of human behavior, basic human development, and social issues that affect people in various stages of life.

There are many debates in the social work discipline about what kind of knowledge is needed to be an effective practitioner. Most social work scholars would agree, however, that social workers should be able to evaluate the quality of the knowledge they encounter and to determine whether it is appropriate to use in practice.

As a social worker, you also need to be aware of how your own values, experiences, and training have influenced your perceptions of people and social problems. These biases and preferences for certain ways of perceiving social issues affect the work that you undertake and how you interpret and use information. Having a solid and broad knowledge base as well as consistently questioning and evaluating knowledge and motivations for pursuing certain avenues when working with clients will help to ensure that you are doing all you can to be an effective social worker.

MAIN POINTS

- Human behavior in the social environment is a core content area in the social work curriculum that includes content on human development and various theories that explain interactions between behavior and social dynamics.

- More so than other disciplines, social work requires a broad knowledge base in many different areas such as politics, biology, psychology, sociology, and economics. Moreover, social workers need to understand how aspects from these different disciplines affect the well-being of individuals, families, and communities.

- Theories should allow you to reasonably predict and explain behavior in terms that are as clear and straightforward as possible. They should also be testable through empirical observation, and they should make practical sense.

- There is debate among social workers regarding whether practitioners should adhere to one theory when working with clients or whether they should rely on components of several theories.

- Knowledge comes from many sources, including experience, tradition, and authority.

- There are many pitfalls to logical thinking, including problems with observations, overgeneralizations, biases and value judgments, and lack of inquiry.

- Elements for judging the validity of knowledge include the currency of the information, the intended audience, the expertise and affiliation of the author, the availability of original sources and other related information, agreement by other experts on the validity of the information, and the purpose of relaying the information.

- Policy courses, research courses, and practice courses within the core curriculum in social work offer a foundation of knowledge that informs the conceptualization of human behavior in the social environment.

EXERCISES

1. Using the Sanchez Family interactive case (go to www.routledgesw.com/cases), review the major issues involving the Sanchez family. After giving this information thorough review, answer the following questions:
   a. What would you say are the three most crucial problems facing the family? Briefly justify your choices.
   b. In what ways might the way you've attained your knowledge affect your choices? For example, has your culture influenced the way you think about certain problems, and thus the importance you place on them?
   c. In what ways might theory help you in conceptualizing the family's situation?
2. Using the Riverton interactive case (go to www.routledgesw.com/cases), review the situation and the issues presented in the case and answer the following:
   a. What would you say are the three most pressing problems facing this community?
   b. How do you think you could use theory to help you conceptualize the situation in this case?
   c. In what ways do these two cases differ with regard to the problems they face, the complexity of the situations, and the ways in which you might approach intervention with the problems?

Lenses for Conceptualizing Problems and Interventions: The Person in the Environment

Juan is a 16-year-old Latino whose parents migrated to the United States from Mexico before he was born. Recently, Juan has been struggling in school. His grades have been dropping over the past two years, his attendance has been poor, he frequently falls asleep or gets bored in class, and he fights frequently with other students. Juan doesn't have many friends, but he does get along with several of his teachers. Juan's home life has also been in turmoil over the past several years. His mother was diagnosed with cancer about a year ago, and his father, who had been laid off from his job at a manufacturing plant, is still unemployed. Juan's mother wasn't working, so the family lost their health care and other benefits when Juan's father lost his job. Since then, Juan's father has been drinking heavily, and when he is drunk, he gets violent with Juan. Juan spends a lot of time away from home, mostly wandering the neighborhood or spending time at his church. Juan has a good relationship with the priest at his church, and he likes to volunteer when he's not in school. Juan has been referred to the school social worker regarding his academic problems.

EVEN IN THIS BRIEF SCENARIO, YOU CAN PROBABLY SEE THAT A lot is happening in Juan's life. If you were to explore his situation further, you would probably uncover more information that would potentially help you in your work with Juan. Where should you begin? How could you conceptualize Juan's situation to make some decisions about the way to approach his problems? This is the sort of situation in which theories can be applied, and in this chapter, we explore some of the most common theories and perspectives used in social work.

In Chapter 1, the discussion focused on understanding what theories are. This and following chapters introduce theories as well as various models, approaches, and perspectives that help social workers conceptualize and work with client problems. The terms *model*, *approach*, and *perspective*, as discussed in this book, can be used interchangeably. Like theories, these terms refer to ideas, structures, and conceptualizations that help social workers organize information. They provide ways to visualize and think about problems and issues. However, unlike theories, they lack some of the necessary elements that allow for empirical testing of hypotheses and constructs. Specifically, models, approaches, and perspectives may be functional and make practical sense, but they often do not possess specific tenets that are falsifiable, parsimonious, and that can predict behavior, as discussed in Chapter 1 (refer back to Box 1.1).

The theories and perspectives discussed in this chapter adopt a comprehensive approach to describing human behavior and problems in relation to their inter-action with the environment—what social workers often refer to as the **person-in-environment approach**. This approach views client problems within the environmental context in which they occur, and it is the cornerstone of social work practice (Gordon, 1969; Richmond, 1920). These theories and perspectives tend to be broad, dynamic ways of conceptualizing work with people. They also tend to focus on client **systems**, which are the interrelated aspects of clients' lives that when considered together, function as an integrated whole. To think of it another way, your body and the physiological processes that support it can be considered a system. The body is made up of parts that work together to allow it to function. Families and communities are also systems; they each have members who contribute to those systems through the relationships that they share and the various roles that they play. Similarly, a workplace, a school, and a church also function as systems. Each consists of individuals, processes, and interrelationships that keep it organized and running and that contribute, in turn, to the lives of the individuals who are part of it.

The theories and perspectives presented in this chapter address how different systems in clients' lives operate independently and interdependently and how this affects clients' well-being. Table 2.1 summarizes all of the theories and perspectives discussed in this chapter for purposes of review and comparison.

MICRO, MEZZO, AND MACRO LEVELS OF CONCEPTUALIZATION

The micro-mezzo-macro approach exemplifies the person-in-environment idea. Although it does not provide testable constructs that help to predict behavior, it does offer a visual framework that is useful when thinking about, assessing, and intervening with client problems. Social work education and literature often use the terms *micro*, *mezzo*, and *macro* when describing the different levels at which people can experience problems. These terms also provide a helpful way to organize a great deal of information about a client and to think about how various aspects of a person's life and environment can interact with one another. Rather than focusing

TABLE 2.1

Characteristics of Theories, Approaches, and Perspectives on the Person in the Environment

		MICRO-MEZZO-MACRO	BIOPSYCHOSOCIAL	SYSTEMS	ECOLOGICAL	STRENGTHS
Type		Approach	Approach	Theory	Theory	Perspective
Focus		Individual & environment	Individual & immediate environment	Individual & environment as part of various systems	Individual & environment	Individual & environment
Assumptions		People are active in their environment.	Some emphasis is placed on people's active involvement in their immediate environment.	Systems are interactive.	People are active in their environmental settings.	People are active agents in the change process.
Strengths		• Comprehensive approach to problems. • Looks for causes of problems at individual and environmental levels. • Considers dynamic interaction between person and environment. • Useful in assessment of client problems.	• Some focus on biological aspects of behavior and problems. • Helpful in guiding assessment and intervention process.	• Comprehensive approach to problems. • Concepts are useful and easy to apply to practice. • Considers dynamic interaction among systems.	• Comprehensive approach to problems. • Concepts are useful and easy to apply to practice. • Considers dynamic interaction between person and environment.	• Positive, empowering approach to work with clients. • Concepts are useful and easy to apply to practice.

TABLE 2.1
continued

	MICRO-MEZZO-MACRO	BIOPSYCHOSOCIAL	SYSTEMS	ECOLOGICAL	STRENGTHS
Limitations	• Too broad. • No consistent set of constructs that can be applied to client situations. • Concepts can be difficult to define and test empirically. • Because of its breadth, it cannot easily predict behavior.	• Narrow focus only extends to immediate environment. • Too problem oriented. • Definition of constructs can vary among clinicians, making them difficult to test empirically and predict behavior.	• Too broad. • Can be difficult to test empirically and predict behavior. • Too problem oriented. • Not enough focus on biological aspects of behavior and problems.	• Too broad. • Can be difficult to test empirically and predict behavior. • Not enough focus on biological aspects of behavior and problems.	• Present oriented; could be a problem in some agency settings. • No consistent set of constructs that can be applied to client situations. • Difficult to test empirically and predict behavior.

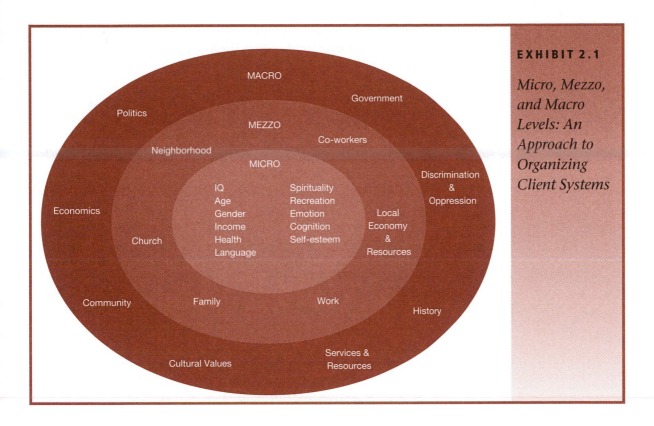

EXHIBIT 2.1

Micro, Mezzo, and Macro Levels: An Approach to Organizing Client Systems

solely on the individual, the **micro-mezzo-macro approach** helps social workers to view people as active agents whose lives, relationships, and environments are interdependent. In many ways, this approach is similar to the other approaches and theories described in this chapter, and as you will see, they are often used interchangeably in social work practice. Indeed, Chapters 6 through 12 of this book organize issues based on the micro-mezzo-macro conceptualization. Exhibit 2.1 illustrates this approach and the different aspects that make up each level.

- The **micro level** incorporates facets of the individual such as biological, psychological, developmental, spiritual, emotional, cognitive, recreational, and financial aspects of personality and individual functioning considered vital to a person's well-being. This level also includes factors such as age, gender, income, and ethnic background.

- The **mezzo level** consists of elements in a person's immediate environment. Family, friends, co-workers, neighborhood, work environment, church activities, local resources and services, and transportation could all fall into the mezzo level.

- The **macro level** includes larger social forces that might affect an individual, such as governmental policy, discrimination, oppression, social policy, economic conditions, societal values, and even historical events.

When assessing and developing an intervention with a client, social workers would consider these and many other aspects on all three levels that seem relevant to the client's particular problem and situation. Further, the micro-mezzo-macro approach can be used to explore how past issues on different levels have affected clients as well as how they are affecting clients' current functioning. Often social workers use this conceptualization as a jumping-off point to explore other facets of their clients' behavior and environment.

Applying the Micro, Mezzo, and Macro Levels of Conceptualization

Let us look at how the micro-mezzo-macro conceptualization could be applied to Juan's situation. As the social worker in his case, you would pay attention to Juan's situation on all three levels. You would explore facets of Juan's individual, or micro, system, such as his spirituality, impulse control, progress in school, physical and mental health, and cognitive and emotional development.

At the mezzo level, you would consider small groups and aspects of the immediate environment that impact his functioning, such as family dynamics, relationships with peers and teachers, his connection with his church, and resources in his neighborhood. Finally, you would assess how components of the larger social environment impact Juan's situation. A macro-level analysis might include looking at school policies, issues of discrimination, cultural factors that may be impeding the efforts of Juan and his family to fit into the community, and lack of access to resources such as health care and employment opportunities. Based on this assessment, you would identify the major problems and then design interventions to address them.

Given that all three levels of analysis work together to define a person's situation, intervention on one level should impact Juan's functioning on other levels. For example, you could decide that based on a physical exam, Juan has some health problems that need to be addressed. Theoretically, improving Juan's health would likely enhance his performance in school, which in turn might improve his feelings of social and academic competence. Specifically, as his health and academic performance improve, he is likely to feel more motivated and self-assured, which may give him more confidence in his interactions with peers. These improvements may also help him cope more effectively with the problems he faces at home. If Juan has areas in his life in which he feels successful, he may be less likely to blame himself for problems such as his father's violence or his mother's illness. In essence, his feelings of competence at school and with his peers will act as a buffer against other problems over which he has little or no control.

Similarly, you could intervene on the mezzo and macro levels by helping the family to access resources such as unemployment and health benefits and resources (such as Medicaid or health services in the Latino community). As the family's situation improves, the members' relationships with one another are likely to improve as well. For instance, Juan's father may become more motivated to work on his drinking and his violent behavior, which in turn will have a positive impact on Juan's physical and mental well-being. Improvements in these areas may help Juan to improve his academic performance, and he may feel more confident in his interactions with his peers. Increasing these feelings ultimately might help him to address his problems at school and at home. Because the micro-mezzo-macro levels are interrelated, there is a ripple effect throughout all three when intervention takes place at one level in one particular area.

Critiquing the Micro, Mezzo, and Macro Levels of Conceptualization

Obviously, the micro-mezzo-macro approach enables a social worker to obtain vast amounts of information about a client. This is actually one criticism of this approach: It is easy for clients and practitioners to become overwhelmed. There is an endless list of things that social workers could explore with their clients, and gathering too much information may paralyze clients as well as their social workers. Specifically, social workers and clients may have difficulty identifying and prioritizing problems in a way that will make client goals seem achievable. Indeed, social workers want to help clients feel that problems are not insurmountable. If the micro-mezzo-macro approach is not used skillfully, clients (and their social workers) may get a sense that they are facing too many problems, which may leave them feeling defeated before any work gets started. Moreover, many social workers will probably not have time to fully explore the range of issues that may be impacting clients. This is especially true if social workers wish to obtain an extensive history of these issues.

Further, as discussed earlier, because the micro-mezzo-macro approach is not a theory, it cannot be empirically tested. Ideas about which concepts should be assessed at each level may vary from one social worker to another; so interventions based on this approach can vary a great deal. Moreover, this approach does not have a consistent set of constructs that can be applied to client situations, which means that there is really no valid or reliable way to measure how effective it is when used with clients.

Nevertheless, the micro-mezzo-macro approach is useful when thinking about the complexities of clients' lives, and it helps social workers to consider the myriad factors that can affect clients, particularly on the sociocultural level. For this reason, this approach tends to take the focus and "blame" off the client and instead looks for causes of problems in the client's environment. Though social workers are likely to assess individual problems, they tend to consider these problems along with problems on other levels. Thus, they do not consider individuals to be the sole "cause" of problems. Consequently, they frequently target their interventions at larger forces such as unresponsive governmental institutions that fail to provide adequate support for clients.

THE BIOPSYCHOSOCIAL APPROACH

Several disciplines, including social work, conceptualize human behavior from a **biopsychosocial approach**, which breaks down human behavior into several components that involve a person's biological, psychological, and social functioning. Unlike the micro-mezzo-macro model, the level of functioning in these areas is usually assessed on the individual level; that is, each area is assessed as it relates to the client or person with the presenting problem. Clearly the biological and psychological facets of this model are inherently individualistic. However, the social realm, which some people might interpret as very broad influences, also tends to be defined rather narrowly as those issues that affect the individual directly. In fact, it is usually limited to the immediate social environment, particularly friends, family, and workplace.

Some of the areas on the biological level that a social worker might consider include the client's diet, health (both past and present), exercise patterns, sexual functioning, medication and substance use, and family health and genetic history. In fact, the worker might explore any factor that relates to the client's biological functioning to assess how it affects the client's well-being. On the psychological level, a social worker might explore the client's self-esteem, coping skills, mental health (both past and present), personality characteristics, family history of mental illness, spiritual development, and cognitive and emotional development. On the social level, a social worker might collect information on the client's work stability, engagement with social activities and recreation, and relationships with family, friends, and co-workers. In essence, all of the levels included in the biopsychosocial approach are encompassed in the micro and mezzo levels of the micro-mezzo-macro model discussed previously. This is one reason why the latter approach is viewed as more comprehensive than the biopsychosocial approach.

Many social service agencies use the biopsychosocial model to assess client problems, particularly in their intake processes. Governmental programs, hospitals and health care clinics, community mental health care agencies, and nonprofit organizations often rely on this approach when collecting information on clients and developing interventions. Even when social workers and other practitioners use other perspectives in their work, the biopsychosocial approach can often be found as part of their agency's infrastructure. Some social workers use only this information to begin work with clients, whereas others use it as one part of a more comprehensive approach to assessment and intervention.

Applying the Biopsychosocial Approach

Despite its seemingly limited scope, especially when compared to the micro-mezzo-macro approach, there are many ways that social workers can incorporate the biopsychosocial perspective into practice. Again, let us look at how Juan's situation might be viewed from this perspective. Some of Juan's problems involve absenteeism, falling grades, sleepiness in the daytime, lack of interest in school activities, and fighting with peers. He also seems to be having problems with his relationships with his parents, which directly and indirectly could affect him physically, emotionally, and financially. His father's drinking, violence, and unemployment as well as his mother's illness all have potential ramifications for Juan's overall functioning.

On the biological level, you might look at Juan's physical health and functioning. You might examine his nutrition and general health habits, assess his overall physical development in comparison to his peers, and refer him to a doctor for a physical exam. It could be that poor nutrition, lack of sleep, or hormonal imbalances are contributing to some of Juan's symptoms such as aggression and poor concentration. You might also want to assess whether Juan is getting enough exercise or is using drugs or other substances, as these issues can exacerbate some of his problems.

On a psychological level, you might assess Juan's emotional and cognitive development. You could refer him to a psychologist for intelligence (IQ) and other tests to determine whether he has any learning disabilities or related problems that might account for his low academic performance. You can assess various emotional and psychological realms to determine whether his problems with academics or peers might be caused by problems in functioning in these areas. For instance, you might look for signs of depression that could be impacting all aspects of his life or assess factors like impulse control that could be causing his aggressive behavior.

On a social level, you might focus on family issues and dynamics, the quality of Juan's peer relations, and his interactions and relationships with others, such as his teachers and his priest. In addition, you would rely on information from theories that address specific developmental processes to help assess Juan's level of psychosocial development. Many of these theories are discussed in the following chapters. Depending on the outcomes of these assessments, you would prioritize Juan's problems and choose interventions that best target them.

Critiquing the Biopsychosocial Approach

Although biopsychosocial information is vital in working with clients, there are some criticisms of this particular conceptualization of problems. Some social workers argue that the focus of this approach, when used by itself, is too narrow. That is, conceptualizing clients' functioning from these three realms fails to acknowledge both the complexity of clients' lives and clients' interactions with larger social forces. Thus, social workers could miss a great deal of information, particularly on a broader social level, about clients' lives that could be exacerbating their problems. For example, social workers run the risk of overlooking economic, political, and cultural influences as well as problems of racism and discrimination. By missing out on some pertinent information, social workers are at risk of implementing only partial interventions; there could be many other problems that if not addressed could undermine any potential gains made in working with clients.

The biopsychosocial approach has also been criticized for being too problem oriented and not sufficiently focused on people's strengths. This criticism is related to the idea that the biopsychosocial perspective focuses entirely on the individual who is experiencing problems. Not only does it define a person's problems as "limitations" or even failings in her or his life, but it views the individual having the problems as being responsible for causing them. Therefore, the individual is also responsible for fixing them. Some social workers complain that this treatment of individuals is too short-sighted and that it can perpetuate an individual's problems by ignoring larger social issues that can contribute to individual problems and make them more difficult to overcome. For instance, a person may begin drinking after experiencing difficulties in finding a job, particularly when the economy is weak. If a social worker focuses only on the person's drinking, she or he would underestimate or miss entirely the importance of the influence of the economy on the person's behavior. Thus, an intervention focused on the drinking behavior may be ineffective, or its gains might be short-lived. Further, the social worker would miss the opportunity to target and address the root of the person's problem—the lack of jobs and the poor economy. Although the social worker may not be able to do much, at least immediately, about the availability of jobs, she or he could facilitate access to training or unemployment benefits, which may, indirectly, alleviate the person's destructive drinking behavior. The social worker could also become involved politically, or otherwise, to help improve the economy or bring more jobs to the community.

There is some debate in the social work discipline about whether social workers know enough about biological aspects of human behavior to effectively assess various problems and to incorporate alternative interventions into their work. One group of researchers (Johnson et al., 1990) has argued that social workers need more knowledge and training in the biological bases of behavior to work effectively with other practitioners such as health care professionals and to meet the challenges in working with various populations such as elderly people and individuals with mental illnesses. Because many people in these populations are experiencing problems and illnesses that are based at least in part in biology—for example, schizophrenia, substance abuse, and Alzheimer's disease—social workers need to be well versed in biological processes that can contribute to symptoms and disease progression. Thus, the biopsychosocial approach can help social workers focus on biological issues that may be affecting clients' lives. Using this approach may encourage social workers to acquire and incorporate biological knowledge into their work with clients.

By using the biopsychosocial approach, social workers can obtain a lot of information about their clients that can be useful in their work. Aspects involving biological, psychological, and social functioning are crucial building blocks to clients' health and well-being, and being knowledgeable about these aspects will affect social workers' approaches to their clients' situations.

SYSTEMS THEORY

Although systems theory has been heavily influenced by many disciplines, particularly sociology, it is discussed in this chapter because of its utility in social work and its comprehensive approach to human behavior. Systems theory is widely used in social work as a way to understand human interactions within the environment; it is also popular in social work with families.

The term "general systems theory" was first used in 1949 by biologist Ludwig von Bertalanffy (Bertalanffy, 1972). However, many other scientists in disciplines such as physics, mathematics, psychology, and engineering were also exploring ideas of interactions within systems.

Social workers became more interested in systems theory in the 1960s during a movement away from a psychiatric focus toward greater inclusion of environmental factors. Systems theory fit well with this philosophical shift. Social workers tended to rely heavily on the influence of scholars such as Talcott Parsons, Kurt Lewin, Urie Bronfenbrenner, and of course, Ludwig von Bertalanffy. The use of systems theory in family therapy was also influenced by these scholars, but social workers and other family therapists relied heavily on other theorists (see Bateson, 1972; Hoffman, 1981; Jackson, 1957; S. Minuchin, 1974).

Systems theory views human behavior as the result of active interactions between people and their social systems. The idea of "systems," then, is central to this theory. Recall that systems consist of interdependent parts that when combined, make up an organized whole (Goldenberg & Goldenberg, 2004; P. Minuchin, 1985). To describe this process, systems theory uses several key concepts; these are listed in Box 2.1.

Systems can include any formal or informal grouping of people or facets of organizations, including couples, families, schools, communities, governments, and social service agencies. All of these systems are made up of smaller, interdependent parts that contribute to the entire system. For example, a school is made up of administrators, teachers, and students. Each contributes to the functioning of the school system as a whole. Each of these parts could also be considered a *subsystem*. Administrators make up a smaller, organized system within the school, and they often have their own way of functioning with the larger system. This is true of teachers and students as well.

For each subsystem, and for the system itself, there are *boundaries* that define its roles, rules, and identity and inform those outside the system or subsystem as to

BOX 2.1

Key Concepts in Systems Theory

- *Boundaries:* Patterns of behavior that define relationships within systems and give systems their identity.

- *Differentiation:* A system's movement from a simple existence toward a more complex form of functioning.

- *Entropy:* A system's movement toward disorganization and death. Negative entropy is a system's movement toward growth and development.

- *Feedback:* A form of input, which informs a system about its performance. Feedback can be positive or negative; this tells a system what it's doing correctly or incorrectly with regard to functioning.

- *Homeostasis:* The tendency that systems have to work toward and maintain stability and equilibrium.

- *Input/Output:* Input is the information, communication, or resources coming into a system from other systems. Output is what happens to this information, communication, or resource after it has been received by a system.

- *Roles:* Socially or culturally sanctioned patterns of behaviors expected of individuals within a system.

- *Subsystem:* Secondary, smaller systems within a larger system.

- *System:* Set of parts that are interdependent and make up an organized whole.

Source: Adapted from Bertalanffy, 1972; Brandell, 1997; Goldenberg & Goldenberg, 2004.

how open or closed it is to interaction, communication, relationships, and the like. A subsystem of teachers might have boundaries that let students know how and when to approach teachers for help or personal matters and what to expect from teachers in the school setting. Furthermore, teachers' boundaries also inform the boundaries of the students. Based on how they perceive the roles of the teachers, students quickly learn their own roles. For instance, students learn when they are permitted to talk in class, how they should behave around teachers, and what is expected of them academically.

Systems are always striving to maintain status quo with regard to their functioning, whether this functioning is seen as positive or negative. That is, systems hum along in their daily routine, and members of systems usually know what to expect and how to behave to keep them running as usual. Members assume *roles*, such as teacher or student, that ensure that systems run smoothly. Sometimes a subsystem or a member of a system does something different that upsets the status quo. According to the concept of *homeostasis*, others within the system will adjust their behavior or try to influence the wayward member to restore the system to its original state of functioning.

An example of this process is a family in which one member has an alcohol problem. If the problem has been present for many years, each member of the family has probably learned how to behave during different situations so as not to "rock the boat." That is, each member has become adept at reading verbal and nonverbal cues in the environment and can therefore alter her or his behavior to ensure stability in the family. Now, suppose that the member with the alcohol problem decides to get help. Even though this decision can be viewed as positive, the system will still be upset, because this member is changing her or his behavior. Other family members will need to adjust to this new behavior and find other ways of interacting with one another. Some family members might need to work on communicating openly with one another, or they may need to alter their own drinking behaviors to support the member who is getting help. Making such adjustments is often challenging, especially if the system has been functioning in a particular way for a long time. However, once members of the family learn and become used to new ways of interaction, they can establish a new, and hopefully better, level of homeostasis.

Systems are continually receiving information about how they are performing. *Input*, also referred to as energy, information, communication, or resources, comes to systems from sources outside of itself. For example, schools receive input about educational goals and standards from parents, students, and communities. Based on the nature of the input, schools develop curricula and programs to serve students. These latter actions constitute a form of *output* by the schools. That is, output refers to the ways in which a system responds to input. A special form of input is *feedback*, which informs the system about its performance. A school could receive positive feedback on programs and policies from these same sources, causing the school to believe that it is functioning as it should be. Conversely, negative feedback on a particular aspect of the school might cause the school to undertake an evaluation to determine effectiveness of a program, or to change a policy that does not seem to be working for parents or students.

Over time, systems tend to become more and more complicated. Interrelationships within systems develop and change; roles and rules become more complex as people and ways of doing things change; and subsystems, boundaries, and homeostasis all shift. This tendency toward greater complexity is referred to as *differentiation*, and it is a natural part of a system's life. For example, as children in a family grow older and gain experience, they change as individuals. As a result, relationships within the family change, as does the way the family system itself functions.

Similarly, systems have a tendency to move toward disorganization, or *entropy*. In a school, for example, teachers leave, administration changes hands, programs are cut, and funding dries up. However, schools can also improve and become better organized. A school can recruit better-qualified teachers, develop improved programs, and secure a constant, stable source of income. This movement toward growth and development is referred to as *negative entropy*.

Applying Systems Theory

Imagine that you are the school social worker using systems theory to make sense of Juan's situation. First, you would want to define Juan's systems. You could look at his family system, his school system, and his church system. Within each of these systems, Juan will belong to various subsystems, have different roles, relationships, and boundaries, and receive different forms of input and feedback. For the sake of space, let us focus on Juan's family system, because he seems to be experiencing many problems at home that are probably impacting other aspects of his life.

Family Subsystems and Boundaries   Juan's family system consists of Juan and his parents. The main subsystem in Juan's family consists of his parents, although it is possible that Juan is in a subsystem with one parent as well. You would need to assess the boundaries of the family system as well as boundaries of the subsystem of the parents and each individual within the system. For the family system, you would want to know how open the family is to outside help, support, and feedback; how private the family keeps its affairs; and how rigid or flexible the family seems to be about allowing interaction with other systems. You would determine whether the family's boundaries seem flexible enough to allow for outside interaction yet firm enough to give the family a sense of identity. In addition, you would consider whether there could be cultural differences that dictate boundaries that might not seem appropriate in terms of U.S. culture but that are very appropriate in the context of Juan's parents' culture. For instance, Juan's parents may insist that the family's problems be solved within the family unit. In some Hispanic or Latino cultures, family problems are viewed as private matters; thus, taking private concerns to a stranger, such as a social worker, is not viewed as appropriate. Conversely, in mainstream U.S. culture, many families deem it appropriate to seek outside help when they experience problems. If you do not take issues such as this into consideration, you may incorrectly assume that Juan's family is not open to help or is denying their problems.

As mentioned previously, you would also need to assess boundaries for Juan's parents as a subsystem of a couple. For example, Juan's father might have some trouble with boundaries, as indicated by his violence and drinking. When he's drunk, Juan's father appears to have trouble maintaining not only his father and husband roles but also his personal space, both physically and emotionally.

This blurring of boundaries will likely affect Juan: His father's behavior seems inconsistent, and Juan lacks a good role model for appropriate behavior. Juan also may be learning that violence is an appropriate response to personal troubles. You would also want to find out how Juan's mother is responding to her illness. It could be that his mother is shutting herself off from her family and friends, choosing to handle her illness on her own. Further, Juan may be taking sole responsibility for caring for his mother, assuming more than his share of the mental and emotional burden for her illness.

Looking at Juan's personal boundaries, you can see that Juan seems to pull away from his peers, and he often responds with violence when he has problems. However, Juan seems to maintain positive boundaries with some of his teachers, his priest, and the social worker. Further, you need to explore the patterns of Juan's interactions with his parents to determine whether the boundaries between Juan and his parents are appropriate for a teenage boy and his parents. Here again, you would want to take into consideration what appropriate boundaries are for parents and children in Juan's and his parents' particular cultural context.

Roles and Homeostasis   In addition to exploring boundaries, you would want to assess the roles that each family member assumes. Given Juan's age, you could expect him to perform certain developmental tasks that are normal for a teenage boy. Similarly, you would expect his parents to carry out certain roles and responsibilities, although these might differ slightly from those normally expected in North American society, given his parents' cultural background. Assessing roles is particularly important in Juan's case because so much has happened to the family. For example, Juan might have assumed a parental role because of his father's drinking and his mother's illness. This disruption in the family system's homeostasis may be disrupting roles and responsibilities. Because the stability of the family has been shaken up considerably, you may even choose to begin intervention here, helping the family find ways to achieve a new level of stability given the circumstances.

Input and Output   Juan's family does not seem to be receiving much input, other than negative feedback from Juan's teachers. The family's income has dropped due to his father's unemployment and his mother's illness, and the family does not seem to be getting much emotional or other financial support. The family also does not seem to be receiving much positive feedback. Juan may be receiving input from his interactions with his church, which results in output through Juan's volunteer work. You might want to help Juan and his family find ways to receive positive input and feedback, leading to positive outputs from the family. They are certainly receiving a great deal of negative feedback about their functioning, which may be eroding their sense of self-efficacy as a family.

Entropy   Under present circumstances, Juan's family seems to be moving toward entropy. Juan is continually doing worse in school, and his interactions with most people seem to be poor. Further, his father's drinking and his mother's illness seem to be moving the family toward depletion and death. It also does not appear that anyone in the family is working toward growth, development, or differentiation; rather, all family members seem "stuck" in their personal development because of their circumstances. It may be that as you intervene in other areas of the family's life, the process of entropy will reverse itself, leading to negative entropy.

Critiquing Systems Theory

As with the micro-mezzo-macro approach, systems theory can be a little unwieldy to use when working with clients. Identifying the many systems in a client's life and assessing how these systems interact and impact a client's functioning is not an easy task. Systems theory seems to be more appropriate for working with family or other identifiable systems like an organization or workplace. Applying the concepts from this theory can be more straightforward in those situations.

As with the other approaches discussed so far, this broad focus on systems as well as concepts that seem somewhat abstract can make the theory difficult to articulate and test empirically, especially when attempting to predict behavior. However, many social workers and other professionals succeed in applying the theory consistently enough to support its validity and reliability across client situations. Some social workers also argue that this theory is too problem oriented, ignoring positive areas of functioning in clients' lives. Further, the focus on family and other systems in this theory makes it less likely that social workers will attend to individual biological aspects that could be contributing to clients' problems. Thus, this information may be overlooked in assessment and intervention. Further, because this theory tends to concentrate on current functioning of clients and their systems, social workers may overlook important information about past functioning that could be relevant to current problems.

At the same time, systems theory provides a broad look at client problems, and it considers people as active, living beings who are an integral part of a dynamic environment. The concepts used in this theory are effective at explaining behavior and problems, and they go a long way to inform work with clients. For example, concepts such as boundaries or homeostasis can be easy to use for assessment and intervention, particularly when working with families or organizations. However, these concepts can be difficult to explain to clients.

A growing body of literature explores these concepts and uses of systems theory in social work. This research provides an empirical foundation for social workers who want to apply this theory to their work with clients and who want to better understand its effectiveness when used for intervention.

ECOLOGICAL THEORY

Originally developed by psychologist Urie Bronfenbrenner (1979), **ecological theory** explains human development by describing aspects of the individual, the environment, and the interaction between the two. Ecological theory argues that people are actively involved in their own development (versus some developmental theories that argue that people are passive—they do not play an active role in their development) and their environments and that both development and environments are always changing. People are born with both negative and positive tendencies, and they are influenced equally by nature and nurture. Development, then, is influenced by the actions of the individual, occurrences within the individual's environment, and the interactions between the two.

A fundamental tenet of ecological theory is that the way people *perceive* their environments and experiences significantly affects their well-being. Specifically, the meaning that people place on the things that happen to them and the way they interpret these events in the context of their environments have a major impact on how these events influence their well-being. For example, two people living in the same community may have different reactions to economic downturns that cause both of them to lose their jobs. One person may view unemployment as a crisis in which he will be unable to pay bills and support his family. This prospect may leave him feeling depressed and hopeless, which may mean that he needs mental health support to cope with the situation and to find the motivation to look for employment. Conversely, another person may view her unemployment as an opportunity to return to school or develop new skills, which will lead to a job that is more enjoyable or profitable. She may feel relieved, or even liberated, by being "forced" to take a new direction in her life.

Clearly this example oversimplifies the situation of unemployment and people's reactions to it. However, it does highlight the importance of people's perceptions of their circumstances, a key tenet of ecological theory. Indeed, this concept is central to social work and is discussed throughout this book: Regardless of how problems may appear to social workers, they need to explore how clients view their situations before assuming that certain situations are problematic.

The organization of ecological theory is very similar to the micro-mezzo-macro conceptualization. Exhibit 2.2 displays the four levels of the environment described by the theory: microsystem, mesosystem, exosystem, and macrosystem. As with the micro-mezzo-macro approach, ecological theory contains several levels that describe factors within a person's environment that are significant in development. Ecological theory treats these levels a little differently from the micro-mezzo-macro approach, though, in that there is an additional level, and the dimensions of the environment that fall within each level are slightly different. Ecological theory also places more emphasis on the physical settings in which people live as well as on how two or more settings interact with one another to affect people and their experiences. The arrows in the diagram represent the dynamic interactions between different levels.

- In ecological theory, the **microsystem** consists of all the roles and relationships that a person has in the immediate environment. This level contains physical places such as home, school, work, and the neighborhood; these are places where people have daily face-to-face contact with one another.

EXHIBIT 2.2

Ecological Theory: Examples of Factors at Each Level and Their Interactions with One Another

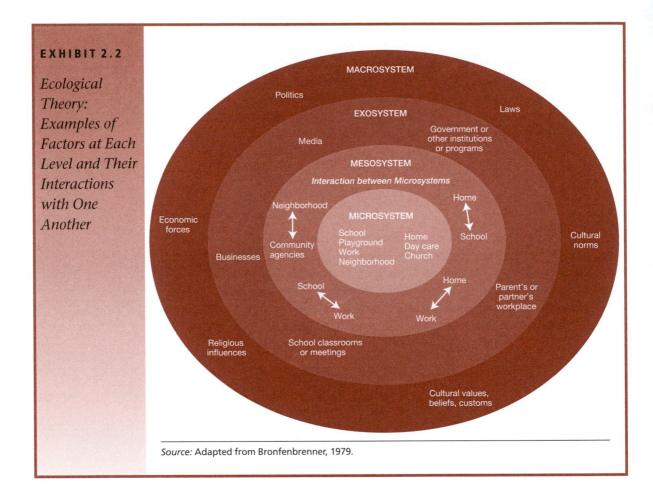

Source: Adapted from Bronfenbrenner, 1979.

- The **mesosystem** focuses on the interactions among two or more environmental settings in which people live. To put it another way, the mesosystem comprises a system of microsystems. For example, the dynamics in a person's work and home lives often impact one another; this is exemplified when a person brings home the tensions from her work.

- The **exosystem** consists of all of those social settings (for example, child's school, parent's workplace, neighborhood community center) in which things happen that affect people. Although the person is not necessarily an active participant in these settings, what happens in them will impact the person directly or indirectly. An example is policy decisions about school closures in a community. Though residents of the community are not involved in making these decisions, their children and families are affected by them. Some families may decide to move to another school district or bus their children to a school that is far away. Residents who do not have

Source: Scott Vandehey

EXHIBIT 2.3

Common mesosystem interactions take place between home and work realms

children will experience the impact of community change created by the decisions.

- The **macrosystem** refers to all the ways in which larger cultural factors affect the other levels of a person's environment and, consequently, how they affect a person's development. This includes aspects such as laws, political philosophy, and cultural beliefs. Societal attitudes against gay marriage, laws prohibiting it, and resulting discrimination in benefits (such as health care for a partner) are examples of how issues in the macrosystem can play out and affect individuals.

In addition to conceptualizing individuals and their environments based on different systems or levels, ecological theory employs several constructs to help describe how interactions among systems or levels take place and how individuals react to those interactions. Some terms used in ecological theory are similar to those in systems theory, but others that are specific to ecological theory are presented in Box 2.2.

According to ecological theory, all people have *transactions*, or positive and negative exchanges, with others. For example, a positive exchange would be when a person receives praise or money for doing good work. A negative exchange might occur when a child is scolded for not sharing toys.

Because people are actively engaged in their environments, they receive and expend *energy* in the form of inputs and outputs. Recall that these last two terms

BOX 2.2

*Key Concepts
in Ecological
Theory*

- *Adaptation:* The ability of individuals to adjust to their environments.

- *Coping:* The ways in which individuals deal with negative events and situations.

- *Energy:* The active engagement of people with their environments. Energy can take the form of input or output.

- *Interdependence:* The reciprocal and mutually reliant relationships that people have with one another and with their environments.

- *Transactions:* Communication, interactions, or exchanges that occur between people and their environments. These can be positive or negative communications or exchanges.

Source: Adapted from Brandell, 1997; Bronfenbrenner, 1979.

were introduced earlier in the discussion on systems theory. Another way to think about inputs and outputs, according to ecological theory, is to consider all aspects of information, communication, or resources that add something to or take away from an individual's life. Education, services, or health benefits are examples of inputs. Spending time or money on a family member's care or putting efforts into a neighborhood renewal project are examples of outputs. Keep in mind that even though outputs imply that energy is being spent, it can be spent on activities that are rewarding, which can be viewed as an input. In this sense, inputs and outputs have a dynamic relationship.

To maintain health and well-being, people must be able to *adapt* to changes in their environments. Because, according to ecological theory, people and their environments are always changing, adaptation is a significant issue. A key role for social workers is to help people adapt to changes that take place in their environments as well as to adapt environmental circumstances to the changing needs of individuals. For instance, people must adapt to events such as moves, marriages, and job promotions. Similarly, environmental issues such as housing, transportation, and social policies need to be adapted to meet the needs of individual members of society.

Social workers are also concerned with how well people cope with various situations. *Coping*, similar to adaptation, deals with how people adjust to the negative events that occur in their lives. For example, people have different ways of coping with death, stress, or crises. Coping styles can either add to or detract from people's ability to function.

Finally, ecological theory is concerned with the *interdependence* of people with others and their environments. In the context of their environments, people have a mutually reliant relationship in which each depends on the other for growth and development. Similarly, people have dynamic relationships with their environments and vice versa; each maintains a balance with the other to sustain life and growth. When one is out of balance, so is the other. Many of these concepts are similar to those used in systems theory. These similarities are discussed in more detail later in the chapter.

Ecological Theory

s look at Juan's situation from the point of view of ecological theory. Juan's microsystem, you could assess his developmental status as a teenager, all the settings with which Juan interacts, and the roles he plays in each. These areas might include his physical, emotional, and cognitive development; the physical environment of his home, school, church, and neighborhood; his interactions with his family, teachers, peers, social worker (you), and priest; and his roles of son, student, friend, and parishioner. You would also want to explore how Juan perceives his roles and interactions within each of these settings.

In Juan's mesosystem, you would want to consider how two or more of the systems within Juan's environment interact to influence his development as well as how Juan interacts with people and situations within these settings. For example, you could examine the interplay between Juan's home and school life and between his home and church life. You could also look at how Juan's neighborhood affects all the other settings in which he is involved.

Juan's exosystem would consist of facets like the manufacturing plant where his father worked, his mother's physician and the health care system where she receives care, bars or other places where his father goes to drink (if his father leaves the home to drink), and community agencies that could provide support for Juan. You would assess various factors in Juan's environment that affect him indirectly but that could potentially impact his development.

The macrosystem would involve issues such as local, national, and international economic pressures; school policies regarding educational standards; societal attitudes about families, teenagers, and minority groups; tenets within the Hispanic or Latino culture and its interface with the majority culture; societal expectations about roles, norms, and expectations of individuals; and other factors such as laws and social policies that can affect individual lives.

In addition to assessing the levels on which Juan is experiencing problems, you would need to assess the ways in which Juan is dealing with his problems and how his interactions with others and his environment are affecting his functioning and development. In doing this, you would assess how Juan's transactions with others and his environment are affecting his well-being, how well Juan seems to adapt and cope with problems and new situations, how energy is expended and replenished in his life, and how Juan's interdependence with others and his environment both supports and hinders his well-being.

Given all of this information, you would need to make some decisions about which factors in Juan's environment are exerting the greatest influence on his development and functioning. These factors would then serve as the point at which to develop interventions for improving Juan's situation. Because of the interactive nature of this theory—as with the micro-mezzo-macro approach—it is likely that as you intervene on one level or with a few facets of Juan's environment, this intervention will have a ripple effect. That is, intervention at one point will have an impact on other areas of Juan's environment to create change in his situation.

Critiquing Ecological Theory

Perceiving client problems from the ecological theory can be daunting, as you saw in the discussion of the micro-mezzo-macro perspective. There are, potentially, an endless number of areas in each level that could be assessed, which can seem overwhelming. Two practitioners working with the same client and using the ecological theory could end up choosing two completely different realms on which to focus, making it seem as if the theory lacks validity and reliability. The scope of the theory also makes it difficult to test empirically and to predict behavior. These limitations are especially true if social workers attempt to gather historical information on these levels in addition to current information. Another criticism of ecological theory is that it does not pay enough attention to biological aspects of clients. However, social workers could choose to incorporate biologically related information into an assessment and intervention. For example, social workers could request information from a client's physician about that client's health status, results of various tests, and medications that the client is using.

Conversely, the ecological theory has some compelling strengths. First, it is comprehensive. It goes beyond the psychological and attends to the larger environment in which clients live. The theory takes a balanced approach to human nature (it considers the interaction between an individual and the environment); therefore, it is less likely to place "blame" for problems in functioning entirely on the individual or the environment. Rather, solutions to problems can be sought from both realms. Also, ecological theory attends to the interactions that occur within and between systems, which underscores the complex and important dynamics that exist in clients' lives.

Finally, the constructs that make up ecological theory, particularly coping and adaptation, can be relatively easy for social workers to apply to client situations and for clients to understand, which can facilitate the helping process. And it is possible to standardize definitions for many of these constructs, which means that they could be applied and evaluated in ways that add to their empirical value in social work practice.

Combining Ecological and Systems Theories: An Ecosystems Approach

From the earlier discussions on systems and ecological theories, you have probably noticed many similarities among concepts and ideas in the two theories. Indeed, in social work and other literature, concepts from the two theories have been combined to explain and work with client problems. Because these two theories share similar ideas relating to systems and the interactions between individuals and their environments, many scholars and practitioners combine them to create an even more comprehensive way to approach work with clients (Beckett & Johnson, 1995). Specifically, both theories look at the interactions and interdependence between person and environment. Both view these interactions and relationships as dynamic, changing processes. Both theories focus on systems and how these systems maintain themselves, influence other systems, and how they work together to function as a whole system.

Alone, each theory provides a comprehensive way to view people in their environment. Each offers slightly different ways to think about how systems impact one another and how people adapt to their changing circumstances and surroundings. Taken together, these theories build on each other to explain more fully how various processes might affect individual functioning. For example, systems theory focuses on the roles that people assume to help bring order to their systems. Ecological theory takes a slightly broader view by looking at the settings in which people play out those roles and how aspects of these settings might interact to impact people's functioning. Systems theory offers ideas about how systems maintain homeostasis. Ecological theory contributes to this idea by considering how people adapt to their environments and cope with problems, which are ways to maintain homeostasis in their environments.

Keep in mind, however, that some critics argue that combining concepts from two theories undermines the validity and effectiveness of each. Recall from Chapter 1 that pure theorists or single theory advocates would question the use of these two theories in combination because, although they share similar characteristics, they differ slightly with regard to definitions and approaches. Others would argue that the utility of combining the theories far outweighs any compromises in the theories' reliability and validity that might result from doing so.

THE STRENGTHS PERSPECTIVE

Another approach that is widely used in social work is the strengths perspective. The **strengths perspective** is based on the assumption that all human beings have the capacity for growth, change, and adaptation (Weick, Rapp, Sullivan, & Kisthardt, 1989). All people, regardless of the severity of their situation or problems, possess skills, capabilities, and strengths. To put it another way, people are much more than their problems. Using the strengths perspective in social work means examining clients' skills, goals, talents, abilities, and resources, as well as the strengths and resources found in their environments, and then incorporating these strengths into the processes of assessment and intervention.

In addition, the strengths perspective asserts that people are experts on their situations and problems, which means that they are naturally well positioned to develop solutions to those problems. People have usually survived both troubling and successful times in the past, so they have insight into which approaches to problems have worked and have not worked for them.

An important tenet of the strengths perspective is that people are resourceful and resilient, characteristics that should be used when clients seek help from social workers. Even so, social workers recognize that oppression, discrimination, and other forces beyond the individual's power also contribute to client problems. Therefore, social workers need to assess their clients' abilities while evaluating the environment for potential barriers that may be beyond the control of even the most resourceful client (Early & GlenMaye, 2000; Saleebey, 1992).

The strengths perspective requires that the client and the social worker be collaborators in the change process. Social workers begin "where the client is," relying on the client's interpretation of the situation and trusting the client to accurately state her or his needs and desires about how to make changes and which goals to achieve. The social worker is responsible for creating opportunities for clients to use their strengths in the change process and to help clients learn new skills that will support them in achieving their goals. Social workers also may need to provide education about the larger environment if there are conditions that the client may not be able to change. This education process is viewed as empowerment: The social worker is arming clients with information that they can add to their set of skills (Early & GlenMaye, 2000; Saleebey, 1992).

When working with clients from the strengths perspective, social workers do not focus on labeling the problem or identifying its causes. Rather, they spend time assessing clients' strengths and resources to change their situations. The focus on strengths is a way to empower clients and divert attention from obstacles that might be impeding clients' progress. This does not mean that social workers ignore their clients' problems. Rather, they view these problems as catalysts for change. The fact that a client has a problem means that there is opportunity for her or him to do something differently and to learn or use skills that will help to achieve the established goals (Early & GlenMaye, 2000; Saleebey, 1992).

This idea of taking the focus off problems is central to the strengths perspective. Some social workers argue that typical social work assessment and intervention place too much emphasis on client problems. This problem-focus orientation tends to view the client as helpless and unable to resolve problems. It also presents the social worker as the expert, because only a professional with the right expertise can solve the client's problems. This problem orientation encourages social workers to find the precise cause of the problem, leading to a specific solution, and focuses on the individual (she or he "has" a problem) rather than on socioenvironmental issues that contribute to problems. Focusing on the problem leads to several assumptions about the helping process:

(1) The problem invariably is seen as a lack or inability in the person affected, (2) the nature of the problem is defined by the professional, and (3) treatment is directed

toward overcoming the deficiency at the heart of the problem. (Weick et al., 1989, p. 352)

The strengths perspective directs the social worker and client away from the problem to focus on the expertise of the client in understanding her or his situation. This focus enables the client to use skills to deal more effectively with the problem, which can improve feelings of competence in dealing with other problems.

Social workers often identify client strengths as part of an initial assessment. Many social service agencies include a section in client records where social workers can list client strengths. However, using the strengths perspective involves much more than writing down a list of client strengths (Early & GlenMaye, 2000). Rather, the social worker consistently focuses on the client's strengths and skills throughout her or his work with the client and helps the client mobilize resources to achieve goals. The social worker has to use these strengths in the helping process from beginning to end, with the main focus being on empowering clients to use their own resources to make changes. The social worker's job is to help the client reframe negative situations to find the skills and resources needed to move forward.

Applying the Strengths Perspective

As Juan's social worker, how would you apply the strengths perspective to his case? One of the first places to start is to identify his strengths, skills, and resources. Juan seems to have many resources, including his positive relationships with several teachers and his priest. The background information suggests that Juan might have some positive relationships with students at the school and in the neighborhood; so you could explore those resources. Also, it is possible that Juan has a good relationship with his mother and other family members, but more information on these relationships needs to be gathered. You can help Juan apply the positive aspects of these relationships to other relationships that may not be functioning as well.

Juan seems to have several interests and abilities that include his volunteer work and his involvement with his church. You could begin with these interests and build on them to find other activities in which Juan is interested. For example, you might want to find out if Juan enjoys sports, art, or music. More involvement in activities that Juan enjoys may help to build his self-confidence, which could help improve his performance in other academic areas. Related to academic performance, Juan's grades and attendance are described as worsening over the last several years. What were these areas like a few years ago? It is possible that Juan was doing well before his family situation worsened. You could also explore what Juan's relationships with his peers and parents were like before things started to deteriorate. For example, has Juan always had a problem with behaving violently? If Juan had performed well before his parents' problems developed, then you would only need to tap into his previous successes to help him find ways to deal with his current situation. For example, you could start with building his skills at school. Thus, Juan could work on his grades, behavior, and relationships and then use his skills to improve relationships at home.

You could also educate Juan and his family about resources in the community that could target his father's unemployment and his mother's health care needs. By focusing on education instead of the family's "lack of ability" to find work and health care, you take the focus off what seems like individual "problems" and put it onto the family's efforts to develop skills that will allow them to problem-solve effectively now and in the future. Similarly, rather than making Juan's problems the central focus for intervention, you would consider his strengths and skills as the starting point for intervention. By adopting this approach, Juan is more likely to feel empowered and hopeful that things can improve rather than focusing on his many problems, which could feel overwhelming to him. Through this process, you consistently identify the family's existing skills and strengths and use these as the basis on which to develop further skills and solve problems.

Critiquing the Strengths Perspective

An obvious benefit to the strengths perspective is that it is a very positive framework in which to conceptualize clients' issues. Working with client strengths can be empowering for the client and the social worker. This is congruent with the value of dignity and worth of the person outlined in the *Code of Ethics* (National Association of Social Workers, approved 1996, revised 2008). Specifically, the strengths perspective allows social workers to support the dignity and worth of clients by concentrating on their strengths; as clients' strengths develop, their problem-solving skills can be enhanced, which ultimately can lead to deeper feelings of dignity and self-worth.

Another benefit is that the strengths perspective diverts the focus from the client's problems, thereby removing sole responsibility for problems from the client. Also, because the social worker is not spending time identifying problems and looking for causes, she or he can spend more time identifying resources that the client already has to solve problems. This last point is related to the idea that the strengths perspective is "present oriented." Very little time is devoted to collecting client histories other than to identify skills that the client has used in the past to solve problems. A focus on the present can make working with the client easier than approaches that call for a lot of history taking and information gathering. Finally, the concepts that underlie the strengths perspective are fairly straightforward and can be easily applied to work with clients.

One major limitation to the strengths perspective is that many agencies probably would not be amenable to using only this approach. Because of governmental mandates and funding issues, many agencies rely on and are required to collect extensive background information on their clients. Further, many agencies operate from a problem-focused perspective, which naturally dictates that social workers delve deeply into the circumstances surrounding the client's problems.

Social workers can incorporate elements of the strengths perspective to augment approaches based on other theories and perspectives, but this might not be sufficient to use the strengths perspective effectively.

Although the strengths perspective seems straightforward and its concepts appear simple, different social workers will probably define the meaning of *strengths* very differently. Therefore, defining and measuring the concepts from this perspective could be difficult, making empirical testing difficult as well. That being said, some empirical evidence does exist on the effectiveness of strengths-based social work interventions, pointing to the feasibility of testing concepts from this perspective (e.g., Vanderplasschen, Wolf, Rapp, & Broekaert, 2007). Also, because of the current popularity of problem-focused models, social workers who want to use the strengths perspective may not be taken seriously by other professionals, and the methods that these social workers employ may not be considered as valid as other, more accepted methods—although, again, as empirical evidence increases on the effectiveness of this perspective, these attitudes and views may change.

CONCLUSION

Although social work relies on many theories, the theories and perspectives discussed in this chapter can be viewed as bases on which to conceptualize client problems in the context of client environments. Social workers often use these theories and perspectives as guiding concepts, while also incorporating knowledge from other areas to enhance their understanding of client situations. Using these comprehensive theories and perspectives helps to ensure that social workers consider different areas of a client's situation, not just the areas that are particular to the client's immediate environment.

The theories and perspectives presented in this chapter get at the essence of social work; that is, they help to view clients as dynamic, active beings who interact with their environment. Although these theories and perspectives have their limitations, they help to ensure that social workers consider a broad range of factors that could influence their clients' problems and well-being. These considerations include factors that might perpetuate problems of discrimination and oppression, which are key issues addressed by the social work profession. Indeed, these theories and perspectives serve as the foundation to which other theories, models, approaches, perspectives, and supporting knowledge can be added when working with clients. All of the theories and approaches discussed in this chapter are similar in that they move from the individual to the environment to explore complex characteristics that are part of a client's life. Although some are more inclusive and far-reaching than others, they all offer a template on which social workers can begin to assess and intervene with clients. Look back at Table 2.1 to review and compare the characteristics of the theories discussed in this chapter.

MAIN POINTS

- Social work tends to use a comprehensive approach to conceptualizing client problems, often referred to as person in environment. This means that client problems are viewed within the environmental context in which they occur.

- The micro-mezzo-macro approach provides a helpful way to organize a great deal of information about a client and to think about the ways in which various aspects of a person's life can interact with one another. Rather than focusing solely on the individual, the micro-mezzo-macro approach views people as part of a system of individual, immediate social, and larger social systems with which they interact.

- The biopsychosocial approach is used by several helping professions and is useful in conceptualizing client problems from a multidimensional perspective. It tends to view the client's situation from an individualistic perspective; that is, it assesses the client's biological, psychological, and immediate social environment to identify problems and areas in need of intervention.

- Systems theory describes the active interactions between people and their social systems. It is used in social work as a way to comprehensively understand human interactions within the environment. It is also used to work with families when trying to understand family dynamics and interactions.

- Ecological theory separates the factors within a person's environment that are important to development into four distinct levels. This theory emphasizes the physical settings in which people live as well as how two or more settings interact to affect people and their experiences.

- Many scholars and practitioners combine ecological theory with systems theories to create an even more comprehensive way to approach work with clients. However, some critics argue that combining concepts from more than one theory undermines the validity and effectiveness of each.

- The strengths perspective conceptualizes people as much more than their problems. It is based on the assumption that people have the capacity for growth, change, and adaptation, and that people possess skills, capabilities, and strengths to improve their situations. An important tenet in the strengths perspective is that people are resourceful and resilient, characteristics that should be used in the intervention process.

EXERCISES

1. Using the Sanchez Family interactive case (go to www.routledgesw.com/cases), study the Sanchez family and its makeup. After getting acquainted with the family, apply concepts from systems theory to assess their situation. Below are questions to guide your analysis; refer to Exhibit 2.2 to review concepts from the theory.
   a. What are the subsystems in this family?
   b. What are the boundaries like between subsystems and for the family as a whole?
   c. In what ways does the family maintain homeostasis?
   d. What roles does each family member take? Would you say these are age and relationship appropriate?
   e. What inputs and feedback (positive and negative) are the family receiving? What are the family's outputs?
   f. Is the family moving toward differentiation, entropy, negative entropy? Why or why not?
   g. Given your assessment, are there areas that might be of concern with regard to the well-being and functioning of this family? At what points might you want to intervene?
   h. What are the strengths and limitations to using this theory to assess and intervene with this family?

2. Using the Carla Washburn interactive case (go to www.routledgesw.com/cases), study the situation presented in her case. After getting acquainted with her situation, apply concepts from the biopsychosocial approach to assess her situation. Below are questions to guide your analysis.
   a. What are some of the biological issues you might want to attend to?
   b. What are some of the psychological issues you might want to attend to?
   c. What are some of the social issues you might want to attend to?
   d. How would the assessment of the three areas above help guide your intervention with Carla? In what ways?
   e. What are some of the limitations to using this approach in Carla's situation?

CHAPTER 3

Lenses for Conceptualizing Problems and Interventions: Biopsychosocial Dimensions

Carlos is a 61-year-old Cuban immigrant whose family came to the United States when he was 15. After 20 years of marriage, Carlos's wife died five years ago, and he hasn't been in a serious relationship since. Carlos retired from his job in sales two years ago after he noticed that he was experiencing problems remembering client names and orders. Shortly after noticing these symptoms, Carlos was diagnosed with Alzheimer's disease. Carlos has three children, all of whom live at least 100 miles away. Carlos misses his children, and he hasn't been able to spend much time with his grandchildren because of the distance and his children's busy schedules. Carlos also has two siblings, both of whom moved back to Cuba 10 years ago, and he doesn't get to see them much, either. Carlos describes his relationships with his children and siblings as "close," and he feels lonely because of his lack of contact with them. He misses the strong family ties that characterized his life in Cuba. Carlos has a few close friends in his church and his neighborhood, but he's afraid that he will lose these connections if he moves into a care facility when his symptoms get worse. When he thinks about having to move, Carlos gets depressed over losing his independence and his sharp intellect, which he has always prized. Moreover, Carlos is worried about how he will pay to live in a care facility, particularly if he is there for a long time. Lately, Carlos has been feeling depressed, and he finds himself struggling with the meaning of life. He's not sure what all his hard work was for, and he feels as though all that he's done for his family has been in vain, especially because he knows how he will "end up" in the final stages of the disease. Carlos has been referred to a social worker at the health clinic where he receives care.

CARLOS'S STORY, ALTHOUGH SEEMINGLY STRAIGHTFORWARD, can quickly become complicated due to the many factors that may be affecting his well-being. On the surface, it seems as if many of Carlos's problems are psychological.

Indeed, many social workers might begin by exploring psychological or even biological issues that appear to be causing these problems. Chapter 2 discussed how social workers could use a biopsychosocial conceptualization for client problems. In this chapter, we will explore specific biopsychosocial theories and models that social workers often use to explain client problems. As in Chapter 2, the theories, models, and perspectives discussed in this chapter are summarized and their various characteristics compared in Table 3.1.

THE DISEASE MODEL

The disease model is rooted in physiological processes that affect behavior and development. It is concerned with individual illness and dysfunction, which contributes to its problem-oriented focus. The disease model maintains that there is a clear and identifiable relationship between "dis-ease" and people's functioning and behaviors and problems. Therefore, according to this model, if interventions are targeted toward dysfunctional behaviors or physiological processes, the resulting problems can be "cured."

The disease model tends to be popular among health care and other helping professionals, including social workers. Indeed, regardless of the setting, much of social work involves assessment and intervention related to biological processes. Although many social workers may use other types of theories or approaches when working with clients, aspects of physiological functioning or biological processes are often relevant to the problems that clients present in practice. Moreover, social workers often collaborate with other health professionals in their work with clients. Thus, social workers need to understand how to assess and intervene with clients based on the disease model as well as how to communicate to other professionals about physiological and biological concerns related to their clients' issues. As you will see as you move through this book, the disease model can be used not only to inform many aspects of assessment and intervention, but also to augment other theories and more effectively explain client problems.

The Medical Model

Probably one of the most fundamental disease-based models for conceptualizing problems and interventions in social work and other professions is the **medical model**. This model emerged from Freud's ideas about the roots of psychological problems as well as from advances in medicine and in our understanding of physiological processes. Indeed, Freud's work on psychosexual development and increasing knowledge of disease processes had a profound effect on the way many disciplines conceptualized problems. After decades of relying on interventions based on morality and charity, social work adopted this more "scientific" model.

TABLE 3.1

Comparison of Selected Characteristics for all Theories, Models, and Perspectives

	MEDICAL MODEL	COGNITIVE DEVELOPMENT	PSYCHOSEXUAL DEVELOPMENT	PSYCHOSOCIAL DEVELOPMENT	LEARNING*	HUMANISTIC
Type	Model	Theory	Theory	Theory	Theories	Perspectives
Focus	Individual	Individual	Individual	Individual & limited focus on the environment	C/O: Individual SLT: Individual & environment	Individual & environment
Assumptions	People are passive agents in their development.	People are passive agents in their development.	People are passive agents in their development.	People take an active role in their development.	C/O: People are passive agents in learning. SLT: People are active agents in learning.	People are active agents in their development.
Strengths	• Places emphasis on biological issues that can cause problems, which often get overlooked in assessment. • Physiological problems and their interventions can be empirically tested. • Diagnostic criteria offer clinicians a common language to use when working with clients. • Pinpointing problems can offer clients hope for a cure.	• Many constructs can be tested empirically and used to predict behavior. • Many constructs are consistent with knowledge on biological aspects of cognitive development. • Practical for use with clients. • Behavior can be predicted in the context of stage development.	• Credited with bringing sexual issues to the forefront. • Constructs such as defense mechanisms are widely used in practice. • Used in practice with clients who want to explore psychosexual development. • Behavior can be predicted in the context of stage development.	• Places some emphasis on interactions between individuals and their environments. • Explains development across the life span. • "Normalizes" some developmental crises and struggles that might otherwise be considered dysfunctional. • Practical for use with clients. • Behavior can be predicted in the context of stage development.	• Concepts are useful and easy to apply to practice. • Constructs can be tested empirically and can be used to predict behavior. • SLT, and to a certain extent C/O, can be empowering for clients if they are taught or made aware of tenets behind behavior change. • SLT addresses people's active role in learning to influence behavior.	• Positive, empowering approach to work with clients. • Interventions are client focused, allowing clients to guide process. • Focuses on strengths rather than problems. • Some specific interventions based on these perspectives can be applied in a systematic manner, which lend themselves to empirical testing.

Limitations					
• Diagnostic information is contained in health records, so appropriate and ethical use of model is important. • Use of diagnostic criteria for mental illnesses can be unreliable among clinicians. • Reduces clients to a set of symptoms, which may leave them feeling powerless to change. • Not enough focus on how environmental issues affect client problems.	• Explanation of development stops at adolescence. • Theory was developed on a small, nonrepresentative sample. • Isn't very flexible to allow for individual variations in development. • Doesn't consider sociocultural influences on development.	• Use with clients may not be practical. • Constructs cannot be tested empirically. • Doesn't consider environmental influences on development. • Theory was developed on a nonrepresentative sample. • Some constructs such as penis envy are considered sexist and outdated.	• Isn't very flexible to allow for individual differences in development. • Constructs can be difficult to test empirically. • May lack relevance for different minority groups.	• C/O theories may give too little credit to people and their roles in learning. • C/O theories do not place emphasis on the environment and its influence on learning and behavior.	• Concepts are vague and difficult to define from person to person. • Broad constructs cannot be tested empirically or predict behavior.

* C = classical conditioning; O = operant conditioning; SLT = social learning theory.

The emergence of the medical model promoted doctors to the level of experts who could diagnose and cure the ills that plagued their patients. It also introduced a new language that influenced how social workers thought about problems. For example, the medical model turned people into "patients," who were said to suffer from "disorder" and "disease." (Social workers use "client" as opposed to "patient" to demedicalize the client–worker relationship.) The model posits that (1) diseases can be identified through a list of symptoms, and (2) these symptoms can be alleviated through logical and scientific examination of the patient. Thus, problems and ills are viewed as being a part of the patient: Something about the person is causing the problem, and this cause can be treated.

A common tool based on the medical model and used by social workers and other helping professionals is the *Diagnostic and Statistical Manual of Mental Disorders*, currently in its fourth edition and abbreviated DSM-IV-TR (American Psychiatric Association, 2000). This manual describes the symptoms, etiology (causes), prevalence, and other aspects of most major mental health problems. Box 3.1 describes the areas of assessment, referred to as axes, which are used by the DSM-IV-TR.

Before a diagnosis can be made, the client has to meet a certain number of criteria described under each disorder in the DSM-IV-TR. Most insurance companies

BOX 3.1

DSM-IV-TR Multiaxial Assessment

Axis I: Clinical disorders or other conditions that may be a focus of clinical attention. Disorders such as dementia; substance abuse; schizophrenia; and mood, anxiety, sleep, eating, and adjustment disorders are recorded on this axis.

Axis II: Personality disorders or mental retardation. Here, personality disorders such as paranoid, antisocial, narcissistic, and borderline are recorded. Also, any disorder related to mental retardation is included.

Axis III: General medical conditions. This axis describes current medical conditions that are relevant to disorders recorded on axes I and II. These might include diseases of the blood; the skin; or nervous, respiratory, digestive or circulatory systems.

Axis IV: Psychosocial and environmental problems. This axis describes problems in the client's life that may be relevant to the diagnoses recorded on the previous three axes. These could include problems with the primary support group, social environment, health care system, legal system, or problems with education, housing or employment.

Axis V: Global assessment of functioning. On this axis, the social worker assigns a number to reflect the client's overall level of functioning. The scale that the social worker uses ranges from 1 (persistent danger of severely hurting self or others) to 100 (superior functioning in a wide range of activities).

Source: Adapted from American Psychiatric Association, 2000.

and social service agencies require that clients presenting with mental health issues be assessed using the DSM-IV-TR. Further, this assessment often dictates how the social worker will intervene with the client.

Applying the Medical Model

Using the medical model as Carlos's social worker, you would focus on the biological and disease-based issues impacting Carlos's problems and affecting his well-being. Because of Carlos's age and his diagnosis of Alzheimer's disease, you would concentrate your efforts on how these factors may be causing problems as well as how to prevent further problems from developing as Carlos ages and his disease progresses.

You could begin by assessing Carlos's symptoms using the five axes of the DSM-IV-TR. To do a thorough job, though, you would need to spend some time asking Carlos about his symptoms and other problems affecting his functioning. Because Carlos has already been diagnosed with Alzheimer's disease, this fact would likely be recorded on Axis I. You do not have enough information on Carlos to formulate opinions for use on Axis II or Axis III, but you could request medical information from Carlos's physician to ascertain whether health issues are complicating the Alzheimer's disease or vice versa. You could also request information from other professionals, such as a psychiatrist, who might have treated Carlos in the past. This additional information would offer a historical view of his problems and help to inform the current diagnoses. Several psychosocial and environmental problems might be recorded on Axis IV, such as problems with Carlos's primary support group, social environment, and potentially with housing, as his disease progresses. Finally, you would want to determine to what degree Carlos's problems interfere with his daily functioning, which would be represented by a number on Axis V. After making an assessment, you would develop an intervention based on Carlos's diagnoses. The intervention would most likely focus mainly on his Alzheimer's disease and the problems associated with it.

In addition to problems related to Alzheimer's disease, you may choose to examine Carlos's physical health to determine whether he has any problems associated with his age or general health status, such as diabetes, heart disease, or high blood pressure. Ensuring that he is as healthy as possible can help prevent or minimize some of the complications that may result from Alzheimer's disease. Moreover, improving or maintaining Carlos's physical health will add to his overall well-being and functioning as he ages.

Critiquing the Medical Model

Because DSM-IV-TR criteria are so widely used and are often a part of clients' permanent health care records, any use of the manual needs to be taken seriously. Professionals need extensive training and supervision before using the manual in clinical settings to ensure its ethical and appropriate use. Further, even though criteria for the disorders are generally based on research, there is still much room for speculation and error; so keep in mind that the process of diagnosis is not an exact science and that diagnoses can lack reliability from clinician to clinician.

Besides being subject to error, the research that supports the diagnostic criteria in the DSM-IV-TR is open to criticism. Although this research is empirically based, it still suffers from weaknesses associated with the inability to control and account for all of the possible biopsychosocial factors that could influence symptoms of mental illness. Even with the increasing knowledge about the biological etiology of some mental disorders, the question of how much these disorders are influenced by environmental and other factors remains. This question is the reason why conducting empirically based research in this area can be so difficult, much more so than research that is conducted on purely biological processes where variables can be identified and controlled. Regardless of how well developed the studies are that support the diagnostic criteria in the DSM-IV-TR, there will probably always be some doubt surrounding the validity, reliability, and applicability of diagnoses in some circumstances.

Another concern is that if clients learn of their diagnosis, the symptoms or disorder might become a self-fulfilling prophecy. That is, clients may come to believe that because they have been labeled with a disorder, they have no control over the symptoms or its "cure." For this reason, the DSM-IV-TR and the medical model in general have been criticized for reducing clients to nothing more than a set of symptoms, a process that ignores larger issues and undermines clients' power to solve their own problems (Katz, 1983). Specifically, some professionals argue that this approach may give clients an excuse not to attempt to solve their problems.

Another limitation to the medical model is that it tends to focus exclusively on the individual. This focus views the problem as coming from inside the individual, which minimizes ways in which the person's environment might contribute to or exacerbate problems. Even though Axis IV describes psychosocial and environmental problems, this information is generally limited in scope to clients' immediate environment, and it is usually not the primary consideration in assessment and intervention. Finally, the medical model focuses on clients' problems, ignoring their strengths and resources. This problem-focused approach can be discouraging to clients, particularly those clients who have multifaceted problems that seem overwhelming and impossible to solve.

These criticisms notwithstanding, the medical model does have certain strengths. A major strength is that it emphasizes the physiological processes that can cause problems. Decades of research and medical advances have revealed a great deal about the etiology of many diseases that can interfere with daily living. Many symptoms can be controlled through diet, medication, and behavior modification, and many diseases and disorders can be cured and even prevented. Further, the knowledge about physical diseases and disorders can usually be empirically tested with some accuracy. There are usually a finite number of variables associated with physical diseases and processes, which means that they can be easily controlled and tested, making it easier to develop theories and hypotheses that can predict outcomes of interventions.

Another benefit of the medical model is that the use of diagnostic criteria, whether it is in the form of a DSM-IV-TR diagnosis or a set of symptoms that make up a physical disease, gives clinicians across disciplines a common language to describe problems. This ensures that clinicians have the same basic understanding of clients' problems, which increases the likelihood that interventions originating from different clinicians will complement each other in a way that will maximize the benefit of the clients for which they are developed. Finally, some clients who suffer from physical or mental health problems may experience relief just by receiving a diagnosis. Specifically, putting a name to a problem can help some people by validating the fact that the problem exists and by offering hope that it can be treated.

THEORIES OF COGNITIVE DEVELOPMENT

Several theories focus on the development of **cognition** (or mental processes) and how this development can impact behavior. The next section covers one well-known approach to explaining cognitive development and some of the ways it can be applied when working with clients. This chapter discusses a general theory of cognitive development, while Chapters 6 through 12 present more specific information on cognitive development as it relates to different stages and growth processes across the life span.

Piaget's Theory of Cognitive Development

One of the best-known theories of cognitive development was introduced by the Swiss psychologist Jean Piaget in the 1950s. Piaget's theory describes how people develop their capacities to think, learn, and process information from birth through their teenage years. Piaget proposed that people actively develop their cognitive skills in relatively fixed and universal stages that are qualitatively different from one another.

Cognitive development from birth to about the late teen years is characterized by increasing complexity and flexibility. Development begins with children's use of basic reflexes to get needs met and progresses to their being capable of abstract thinking and examining multifaceted relationships among many variables. According to Piaget, by the age of 16 or 17, young people should possess the skills necessary to operate in the adult world (Piaget & Inhelder, 1969).

Piaget's theory consists of several substages that include key concepts or skills developed at each stage. Though the substages are not presented here, we will look at the main developmental tasks that occur in each stage (Piaget, 1952).

Within the **sensorimotor stage** (birth to age two years), the major accomplishment is *object permanence*. This is when children learn that even if objects and events are out of the range of their senses, they continue to exist (for example, when Mom leaves the room, she hasn't disappeared). Children begin to coordinate their actions through reflexes such as sucking and rooting, and they learn that they can get pleasurable results by performing certain actions, such as crying when they are hungry or want to be held. Additionally, a child's preoccupation moves away from the self toward the outside world. Eventually, children learn to combine and coordinate actions and to manipulate objects to get novel results. By the end of this stage, children have attained primitive symbolic capacities that allow them to hold rudimentary pictures of objects, or words for objects, in their minds.

During the **preoperational stage** (two to seven years), children continue to exhibit many limitations in their cognitive abilities. A major characteristic of this stage is *egocentrism*, which means that children cannot take into account the perspectives of others when thinking about objects or events. Children also tend to show characteristics of *animism*, the belief that inanimate objects have lifelike qualities. They also display a tendency known as *centration*, which means that they can focus on only one aspect of an object at a time. Children at this stage also lack a sense of *conservation*, meaning that they cannot understand that an object remains the same even if its characteristics change, such as its shape or the way it is contained. For example, if a child were shown a cup of juice, she would think that the amount of juice was different if it were poured into a different-shaped container. Finally, children demonstrate *irreversibility*, or the inability to think about events in reverse order. For example, a child might understand that John is his cousin but not that he is therefore John's cousin.

At the same time, however, children in the preoperational stage undergo a great deal of development. Two major examples of this development are classification and seriation. *Classification* means that children can differentiate between two objects based on their differences and unique properties. By the end of this stage, children should be able to separate blocks into groups based on their color and shape, for example. Children should also be able to differentiate among objects based on their size, weight, or length, which is known as *seriation*. This means, for instance, that a child can put pebbles in order from smallest to largest or from lightest to heaviest.

During the **concrete operations stage** (7 to 11 years), children develop the cognitive skills that were lacking in the previous stage. Children become adept at understanding events from the perspective of others and appreciating the more complex relationships among variables. In addition, they master all of the skills associated with classification, conservation, and seriation. Finally, they learn to use symbols effectively to represent objects and events in the real world. This skill improves children's performances at certain activities, such as math and the use of language.

Finally, in the **formal operations stage** (11 to 16 years), children learn to use *hypothetical-deductive reasoning*. They can engage in abstract thinking, consider multiple aspects of an object or event at one time, formulate hypotheses about what might happen if certain variables were manipulated, and analyze the properties of an object or event to derive conclusions about its nature or behavior. It is at this stage that children develop the ability to use logic and to systematically work through a problem to come to viable solutions.

For cognitive development to take place, we need to organize new information and adapt it to our existing knowledge. We also have to be able to adapt our thinking to new information and ideas. Central to Piaget's theory, then, are the ideas of schemas, accommodation, and assimilation. **Schemas** are the internal ideas and representations we hold about the world. They result from our efforts to systematically process and store information to make sense of what happens around us. According to Piaget, this happens in two ways. One way is through **accommodation**, which is when we *change* our schema about something because new information we receive about it does not fit our preexisting ideas about how that something should be. In other words, sometimes we have to change our ideas about something because we learn something new about it that is contrary to or different from what we originally thought. **Assimilation** occurs when we bring in new information about something to *fit* our existing schema. In this case, we incorporate or integrate new information into what we already know about something without altering our schema (Piaget, 1952).

Applying Piaget's Theory

As Carlos's social worker, you would probably only be able to use Piaget's theory in a limited way to help understand what is happening in his situation. This is one of the criticisms of Piaget's theory: It does not explain continued development into adulthood. In contrast, many psychologists and other professionals argue that development progresses well into older age. You could try to ascertain whether Carlos successfully moved through the formal operational stage and how that development has affected him since. You could assess how his level of cognitive development may be affected by Alzheimer's disease and come up with interventions to maximize his functioning as the disease progresses.

It would probably be more useful, though, for you to look at Carlos's schemas for older age and Alzheimer's disease. What thoughts and attitudes about aging does he hold? Does he define Alzheimer's disease, isolation, and loneliness as "normal" components of aging? It may be that Carlos's schema of aging and disease is not helping him to cope well with the inevitable changes that he will experience.

One approach to altering Carlos's schema is to look at how he assimilates and accommodates information about aging and disease. For example, let us say that Carlos has a schema about aging that includes characteristics of misery, disability, and isolation. He is familiar only with older people who have these characteristics, so these observations get assimilated into his existing schema about aging, thus reinforcing his negative views. One of your goals might be to get him to alter his schema to include other ideas of aging. To accomplish this you need to show Carlos different examples of aging, perhaps by exposing him to elderly people who are active, happy, and functioning well. According to Piaget, this last experience would be an example of accommodation: Carlos would have to change his schema about aging to incorporate new ideas, which in turn might improve his attitude about the possible outcomes of his own aging process.

Critiquing Piaget's Theory

We have already encountered one major limitation of Piaget's theory, namely, that his model of the development process stops in adolescence. Another major criticism is that he developed his ideas based on observations of his own children. Some critics therefore contend that his methods biased his work and did not offer a large enough sample from which to generalize his results to other children. Further, his theory tends to focus on what is "normal" or "average" for development, leaving little room for individual deviations in development that may also be "normal." The stagelike progression of development also tends to underestimate the variations that take place in development: Does everyone really follow these stages in precise order and in the time frames proscribed? Many critics would argue that development is too individualistic to fit into neat stages.

Still others criticize Piaget's theory for not paying enough attention to socio-cultural factors that affect cognitive development. Piaget does not offer much explanation for how personality, stimulation, social interaction, cultural context, and other related factors promote or detract from development, although he attempted to incorporate these ideas into his theory later on (Piaget, 1972). Recent research based on Piaget's theory suggests that he may have underestimated children's abilities, lending credence to the idea that children may develop skills earlier than Piaget originally thought possible. For example, some researchers argue that if you alter the methods used to test skills, the test results demonstrate that children are capable of understanding and performing various skills at earlier ages than those proposed by Piaget (Baillargeon, 1987). Research has also found that skills that Piaget assumed to be mastered in the formal operations stage, which takes place during adolescence, do not develop predictably or universally at any specific time. Rather, it is likely that there are many individual differences related to skill development in formal operations that are influenced by neurological changes based on individualistic experiences (Kuhn, 2008).

On the positive side, Piaget's theory provides relatively sound and usable guidelines for thinking about children's cognitive development. Many of the theory's concepts are, indeed, consistent with current knowledge concerning various aspects of biological development such as neuron growth and synapse connections. For example, we now know that it takes time for children to fully develop neuron connections to perform certain mental tasks, which corresponds with many of Piaget's ideas on how skill development occurs. This fact can help explain the occurrence of separation anxiety among young children, which fits well with the idea of object permanence. What child would not be frightened when his mother leaves the room if he does not have the physiological capability to keep a mental picture of her in his mind? It takes time for young children to develop neural pathways and mental capabilities that allow them to retain these mental pictures. And, there is substantial evidence to support the idea that a great deal of cognitive development takes place in the teen years, leading to skills articulated in formal operations (Kuhn & Pease, 2006). Finally, many of the constructs in Piaget's theory are testable. Thus, the theory has been subject to replication and modification based on research conducted since it was first proposed.

PSYCHODYNAMIC THEORIES

This section discusses two theories of personality development that are psycho-dynamic in nature and have been influential in social work and other helping professions. Sigmund Freud and his ideas on psychosexual development are well known, as is Erik Erikson's theory of psychosocial development. Though some of the ideas from these theories, particularly Freud's, are considered outdated or controversial, concepts originating from these theories still contribute to many facets of social work practice.

Freud's Theory of Psychosexual Development

Sigmund Freud, a physician, was a leader in developing psychoanalytic theory. This philosophy underscores the importance of unconsciousness and early experiences in shaping personality. His stage theory of psychosexual development is based on the psychoanalytic tradition, and it describes three concepts or mental structures thought to be at the crux of personality: the id, the ego, and the superego.

- The first of these concepts is the **id**, an element of our unconscious, which is made up of our basic needs and drives such as sex, thirst, and hunger. The **pleasure principle** governs the id to ensure that needs are satisfied. When needs are not met, the id creates tension until the drive or need is satisfied. For example, many infant behaviors such as sucking and crying are driven by the id; these behaviors help to ensure that the need for food is met.

- The second concept is the **ego**, which Freud described as the rational aspect of the mind. When children gain experience, their ego develops, which helps keep the id in check. Thus, a child learns to decide rationally how to meet the id's needs in ways that are socially acceptable. The **reality principle** governs the ego by ensuring that actions are evaluated according to their consequences. Neither the id nor the ego has moral components. They are not concerned with what is right or wrong, just with what is needed (in the case of the id) or what is reasonable (in the case of the ego).

- The third concept is the **superego**, or conscience. It is based on society's morals and values, which Freud believed are incorporated into the superego between the ages of three and five. The superego tells the person what is right and wrong. So, if the id wants something that the superego does not approve of, the superego creates anxiety or guilt, forcing the ego to suppress the drive. The ego would then find a way to meet the need that is in accordance with the superego (or with societal values). In this sense, the ego is the mediator between the id and the superego, ensuring that neither dominates (Freud, 1920a).

In addition to these ideas, Freud delineated five stages through which personality develops: the oral, anal, phallic, latency, and genital stages. These stages are summarized in Box 3.2. Freud believed that within each stage, a person must resolve a conflict to successfully move on to the next. That is, a person must deal with the tensions between satisfying needs or seeking pleasure and the reality or morality of satisfying those needs or achieving pleasure. If this does not happen, the person can become **fixated** at a particular stage, leaving the person's development halted or incomplete.

A person who is fixated would either resolve the conflict or construct a defense mechanism to deal with the conflict. **Defense mechanisms** are unconscious attempts to hide, suppress, or otherwise control the conflict. Some common defense mechanisms are described in Box 3.3.

BOX 3.2

Freud's Stages in Psychosexual Development

ORAL STAGE (BIRTH TO 18 MONTHS)
Pleasure centers on activities of the mouth, including feeding, sucking, chewing, and biting. Child focuses on receiving and taking.

ANAL STAGE (18 MONTHS TO 3 YEARS)
Pleasure centers on anal activities such as toileting. Child focuses on giving and withholding.

PHALLIC STAGE (3 TO 6 YEARS)
Pleasure centers on the genitals and self-manipulation. In this stage, children experience the Oedipus and Electra complexes, resulting in castration anxiety.

LATENCY STAGE (6 YEARS TO PUBERTY)
Sexual instincts are unaroused, and the child focuses on play, learning, and socialization.

GENITAL STAGE (PUBERTY ON)
Pleasure centers on love, work, and maturing sexually.

Source: Adapted from Freud, 1920a.

- *Denial:* Avoidance of unpleasant realities by ignoring or refusing to acknowledge them; probably the simplest and most primitive defense mechanism.

- *Identification with the aggressor:* Increasing feelings of worth by taking on the attributes of people or institutions of greater power, strength, or importance.

- *Intellectualization:* Creating emotional distance through rationalizing or using logic.

- *Projection:* Blaming others for one's own shortcomings and mistakes; unconsciously ascribing to others one's own unacceptable impulses and desires (for example, a person with a tendency to be lazy criticizes others for laziness).

- *Reaction formation:* Developing attitudes and behaviors that are the opposite of repressed and unconscious dangerous or unpleasant impulses and desires (for example, expressing abhorrence of homosexuality when one has repressed homosexual feelings).

- *Regression:* Retreating to behaviors that were appropriate in earlier stages of development (for example, temper tantrums) that bring easy satisfaction of desires or needs.

- *Repression:* Unconscious process whereby painful or dangerous thoughts and desires are excluded from consciousness. These can be revealed through dreams, jokes, or slips of the tongue.

- *Sublimation:* Consciously satisfying socially unacceptable needs and desires through socially acceptable activities (for example, playing football to satisfy aggressive impulses); probably the most advanced defense mechanism.

- *Withdrawal:* Retreating into solitude to avoid painful emotions and situations.

Source: Adapted from Freud, 1909, 1914, 1920a.

BOX 3.3

Common Defense Mechanisms in Psycho-analytic Theory

Defense mechanisms have many forms, some being more productive and sophisticated than others. For instance, sublimation is considered to be a more highly developed and constructive defense mechanism than projection or denial because it allows a person to satisfy needs through productive and socially accepted activities instead of avoiding them. One goal of psychoanalysis is to bring a conflict to the person's conscience, break down defense mechanisms that are maintaining or perpetuating it, and help the person resolve the conflict that is keeping her or him fixated in a particular stage (Freud, 1909, 1914, 1920b; Rickman, 1957).

To exemplify how conflicts and defense mechanisms work, let us turn our attention to the phallic stage, where Freud argued that boys and girls deal with Oedipus and Electra complexes, respectively. Freud described the *Oedipus complex* as a dilemma or conflict in which boys fall in love with their mothers. At the same time, boys feel antagonistic toward their fathers because of the rivalry for their mother's attention. Boys fear that their fathers will find out about this attraction, which leads boys to have castration anxiety, or the fear that their father will remove their genitals. To successfully resolve this conflict, boys must repress their sexual feelings for their mother, develop a reaction formation in which they have positive feelings for their father, and eventually identify with their father by taking on their father's behaviors. In essence, this is how boys learn to become men and take on gender-specific roles.

The female equivalent of the Oedipus complex, according to Freud, is the *Electra complex*. Girls' love for their fathers also results in castration anxiety, but this anxiety is different from that experienced by boys. Specifically, this anxiety forces girls to realize that they do not have penises, so they conclude that they were castrated in infancy by their mother. Consequently, because they "lack" penises, girls feel inferior to boys, which is the foundation for girls' submissiveness and other gender roles later in life. Freud never described the process for successful resolution of the Electra complex. As with boys, defense mechanisms are used to help girls successfully resolve conflicts so that they can move on to the latency stage, without being fixated in the phallic stage.

Many theorists who subscribed to Freud's ideas broke away to form their own theories on development. Most neo-Freudians believed that Freud placed too much emphasis on sexual drives, so they constructed theories that incorporated many of Freud's ideas but moved away from the sexual focus. Some of the better-known neo-Freudians are Carl Jung, Alfred Adler, and Harry Stack Sullivan.

Applying Freudian Theory

If you wanted to apply Freud's theory to Carlos's case, you would need a lot of time! Psychoanalysis can take several years. But putting time issues aside, you could delve into Carlos's past, examining his relationships with his parents and the process of his psychosexual development. You may find areas in which he has become fixated, and you would help him resolve conflicts he may have at various stages.

One way to find areas for work is to explore Carlos's defense mechanisms, such as denial, to ascertain whether he is avoiding issues by blocking them out of his consciousness. For example, he may be denying the painful reality of the losses he has faced (for example, his wife's death and the loss of family ties) and will face in the future (the loss of his health, independence, and social networks, for example). This may be hindering his free expression of feelings such as grief. Through the expression of his feelings, Carlos may be able to come to terms with his situation and find productive ways of dealing with it. Carlos's cultural background may dictate that it is unacceptable for a man to express his feelings, which could be contributing to denial about his situation. Perhaps his superego, which has been shaped by the values, norms, and mores of his culture, is successfully repressing his id's need to express his grief about his situation.

If Carlos finds it unacceptable to express his feelings about his situation, a better approach might be to help him find more productive ways to satisfy his needs, such as through the use of sublimation. You could help Carlos find more culturally relevant ways to work through his feelings, such as through art, music, or writing. In essence, you would help Carlos replace one defense mechanism that may be destructive to his well-being with another, more industrious one. Because you don't know how quickly his cognitive capacities will diminish, trying to rid Carlos of his defense mechanisms altogether may not be useful. Rather, the more prudent approach is to find ways to work with defense mechanisms that will maximize his well-being.

In addition to helping Carlos get rid of or work with his defense mechanisms, you may also explore with him how and why his defense mechanisms were constructed in the first place. For instance, perhaps in the phallic stage, rather than resolving the Oedipus complex through the defense of reaction formation, Carlos denied his feelings toward his parents. Thus, as he moved through later stages and into adulthood, he employed denial in his romantic and intimate relationships to protect himself from unwanted feelings.

You would have to spend a great deal of time exploring Carlos's past and current issues to arrive at some conclusions about how his problems may relate to defenses or fixated development. Given the reality of Carlos's disease, he may not be able to participate cognitively in this kind of exploration, and depending on how quickly his disease is progressing, he may not have the luxury of time to do so. You may be more successful if you were to focus on problematic defense mechanisms and attempt to begin an intervention at that point.

Critiquing Freudian Theory

One obvious limitation to Freud's theory is that it frequently does not seem applicable to client situations. Sometimes it can be a stretch to relate problems of daily living to psychosexual development. In addition, as discussed in Carlos's situation, psychoanalysis can take a lot of time, which is not practical in many social service agencies. Given the budget constraints that many agencies face, spending a great deal of time delving into clients' pasts is impractical. Moreover, the constructs in this theory are almost impossible to define, measure, and test, which makes it even more unlikely to be used in many agencies that insist on outcomes that can be quantified and proven to be effective.

Another criticism of Freudian theory is that like the medical model, it focuses solely on the individual, ignoring the impact of outside forces on client problems, such as economics or social policies. Thus, interventions based on this theory may be irrelevant for many clients who are facing environmental barriers. Freud has also been criticized for basing his ideas on the experiences of his patients, who were almost exclusively wealthy Caucasian women seeking therapy during the Victorian age, when sexual repression was the norm. His ideas surrounding the

Oedipus complex and castration anxiety that supposedly occur in the phallic stage have been criticized for being male centered and sexist. Specifically, some critics argue that this theory places too much emphasis on the importance of male genitalia and women's supposed envy of them.

On the positive side, Freud can be credited with bringing sexual issues to the forefront of psychological thinking. Moreover, many of Freud's concepts are still widely used today. For example, many social workers refer to clients' use of defense mechanisms such as denial, projection, and repression. Work with defense mechanisms can be useful (for example, focusing on a client's denial of various problems or withdrawal from painful situations can be helpful), and this type of work does not necessarily require a lot of time to do. So, many agencies may be amenable to incorporating such interventions into work with clients. Also, for some client situations, the application of this theory to problems may be desirable if the client is open to exploring relationships and psychosexual developmental processes.

Erikson's Theory of Psychosocial Development

Erik Erikson's theory of psychosocial development incorporates many of the basic tenets of Freudian theory, though it places greater emphasis on social versus sexual influences on development. Erikson's theory proposes that a person progresses through eight stages of psychosocial development, which extend throughout the life span. Box 3.4 describes these stages.

Erikson (1950) argued that we move through each stage in a consistent manner, dealing with developmental tasks and resolving crises unique to each stage. Developmental tasks are healthy, normal activities that help promote growth. Within each stage, there are periods in which people are highly susceptible to learning age-appropriate tasks that help them adapt to and gain mastery over their environments. *Crises* are psychological efforts to adjust to the demands of the social environment. These are "normal" stressors that can be anticipated at each stage to help people develop (versus rare, extraordinary events or trauma that are unanticipated). The goal at each stage is to resolve crises by developing positive qualities that allow for growth and support the exploration of self and the environment. If people successfully negotiate the tasks and crises in each stage, they gain and process new information that helps them maintain control over their emotional states and their environments. Even if particular tasks and crises at a stage are not learned or resolved, people still move on to the next stage, but they will probably face problems due to the unresolved crises experienced at earlier stages. According to Erikson, we can reach the end of our lives without having fully resolved crises from earlier stages of development.

Erikson's theory focuses on the continual interaction between the individual and the social environment. Erikson based his theory on the **epigenetic principle**, which states that people have a biological blueprint that dictates how they grow and reach maturity. Although people's growth and development are guided by this

BOX 3.4

Erikson's Theory of Psychosocial Development

STAGE ONE: TRUST VS. MISTRUST (BIRTH TO 18 MONTHS)
In this stage, children learn to trust others, particularly their caregivers. Infants learn that they can count on their caregivers to give them food, shelter, and love, and to meet their needs. If their needs are not met, infants learn to mistrust others.

STAGE TWO: AUTONOMY VS. SHAME AND DOUBT (18 MONTHS TO 3 YEARS)
Children learn to do things, such as eat and dress, independently. Through accomplishing various tasks, children gain a sense of self-confidence. If children's independence is not encouraged, or if they are punished for acting on things independently, they can develop a sense of self-doubt.

STAGE THREE: INITIATIVE VS. GUILT (3 TO 6 YEARS)
Children are active in their environment. They need to take initiative to learn, explore, and manipulate their surroundings. Children who are encouraged to do so will develop skills that allow them to pursue goals and interests in the future. Children who are discouraged will lack confidence to act on their interests and will not take the initiative to shape their lives.

STAGE FOUR: INDUSTRY VS. INFERIORITY (6 TO 12 YEARS)
Children need to be productive and have successful experiences. Children are busy playing and learning, giving them opportunities to master various tasks. Children who are able to find ways to succeed will learn to be industrious. Those who experience repeated failures will develop feelings of inferiority, hampering their chances of success in the future.

STAGE FIVE: IDENTITY VS. IDENTITY CONFUSION (ADOLESCENCE)
Adolescents are exploring who they are and developing their sense of identity. They try out roles for the future and integrate these into their sense of self. Adolescents who have difficulty integrating their roles into their identity will experience confusion about who they are.

STAGE SIX: INTIMACY VS. ISOLATION (YOUNG ADULTHOOD)
Young adults are looking for intimacy and closeness in their relationships. They learn to give and take with a significant other without sacrificing their identities. If they are unable to establish intimacy, they are at risk for isolation as they move into adulthood.

STAGE SEVEN: GENERATIVITY VS. STAGNATION (ADULTHOOD)
Adults are involved in investing in their work, families, communities, and future generations. They begin to look past their own lives to the well-being of those around them. Adults who are unable to do this never move past investing in themselves and are self-absorbed. They become stagnated and are unable to be productive for the sake of others.

STAGE EIGHT: INTEGRITY VS. DESPAIR (OLD AGE)
People in older age reflect on their lives and take inventory of their successes. People who are satisfied with what they have accomplished have a sense of well-being and peace. Those who are not satisfied have a sense of despair, and they mourn for lost opportunities.

Source: Adapted from Erikson, 1950.

biological blueprint, social forces and expectations also influence growth and development and help to determine how well people adapt and adjust to their environments.

Applying Erikson's Theory

There are several ways in which you could apply Erikson's theory to Carlos's situation. You could begin by exploring the tasks Carlos faces given the stage he is in, which, based on his age, is integrity versus despair.

According to Erikson, Carlos will be reflecting on his life and determining whether he has accomplished all that he has wanted. Indeed, in many ways, Carlos seems to be doing just that. It is a normal developmental task for Carlos to question the value of his past activities and the course that his life is taking. Not only may Carlos be reflecting on the quality of his relationships with his wife, children, and friends, but he may also be reviewing the contributions he has made through his work. He may be contemplating how the progression of Alzheimer's disease will impact his relationships and contributions to society in the future. You may want to help Carlos explore other areas, such as his identification with his culture, his investment in his community, and his perceptions of his own growth and development. You could also help him to articulate how his perceptions of himself and his relationships with others might change as his health deteriorates.

The crisis with which Carlos must contend relates to the results of his contemplation on the issues just stated. Specifically, if Carlos's exploration leads him to confirm his speculation that his work, relationships, and personal development have been wasted, then he will likely feel despair. Helping him to gain a sense of integrity despite his current challenges might be one goal in your work. For instance, you might encourage him to reflect on the successes of his life and identify the ways in which these successes have been fulfilling. You could also help him find positive ways of coping with his disease and his changing environment. In doing so, Carlos may be able to relieve some of the stress he may feel because of his deteriorating health and the uncertain future that it represents.

If Carlos takes steps to secure comfortable housing and assistance as his disease progresses, he may feel that he has some control over his environment, which can lead to a sense of integrity. Likewise, he may want to find ways to work through his grief over the loss of relationships in his life, or he could explore how to reconnect with his cultural roots, if he feels this is an issue. If Carlos is successful, he will avoid feeling despair and will be able to face his disease and other problems with a renewed sense of hope.

Other possibilities are that Carlos has some unresolved conflicts or that he did not successfully complete certain developmental tasks from earlier stages. For example, he may feel that during the previous stage (generativity versus stagnation) he did not contribute enough to the well-being of his children or that he was not a significant part of his community. Consequently, he is experiencing a sense of stagnation rather than generativity. You would want to explore these areas as well to identify barriers to Carlos's current developmental tasks that could be hindering his growth, making his disease and aging more troublesome.

Critiquing Erikson's Theory

As with many of the other theories discussed in this chapter, Erikson's emphasis on stages of development can be limiting. Because there are so many individual differences in development, trying to place people in a particular stage based on their age can be problematic. Moreover, the constructs of this theory can be very abstract and therefore difficult to measure and test. For instance, practitioners and clients may have different interpretations of constructs such as "integrity" or "inferiority," making a common definition of them difficult.

Another limitation of Erikson's theory is that societal norms and expectations about the developmental processes that should occur at various ages are always changing. You can see an example of this in the traditional activities of marriage and having children that seem to characterize Erikson's stages of intimacy versus isolation and generativity versus stagnation. Because of economic conditions, technological advances, expanding employment opportunities for women, and changing attitudes about marriage, many young people may put these activities off until later years. Similarly, people may find alternative ways to achieve intimacy or generativity that do not include traditionally accepted activities. Moreover, this theory may lack relevance for some ethnic and other minority groups. It does not account for how developmental tasks may be different for gay and lesbian youth, for example, or how people develop ethnic identity.

Nevertheless, Erikson contributed a great deal to the understanding of development because he placed more emphasis on the social dynamics of human behavior than many other early theorists did. Also, unlike other theorists such as Piaget and Freud, Erikson described development into old age, which assists practitioners' work with clients of all ages.

Erikson's theory also provides a useful developmental guide for social workers and other professionals when working with clients. By helping people understand some of the struggles that are a "normal" part of development, it can promote tolerance and patience with certain behaviors. For example, parents may be more patient and willing to work with their children's temper tantrums if they can view these behaviors as a normal way that children develop autonomy and test limits and boundaries. In essence, this theory views some seemingly problematic behaviors and stressors as necessary in the process of development and growth. It also highlights the resilient nature of people and the capabilities they have to cope with their problems and adapt to their social environment. Although this theory emphasizes individual development more than the influences that the social environment has on that development, it still considers the interaction between the two and acknowledges the importance of that interaction on human development.

BEHAVIORAL AND LEARNING THEORIES

Now that we have considered a number of theories related to development, we shift our focus to several ideas relating to learning that have been incorporated into many social work interventions. Concepts from these theories describe, among other things, how people learn and modify their behaviors. "Pure" behaviorists argue that personality development occurs through learning and shaping behaviors. Social workers tend not to take a pure behaviorist stance on personality development, but many will incorporate behavioral and learning tenets into their work with clients. Indeed, many concepts associated with behaviorism and learning lend themselves well to interventions that involve behavior change. We look at three theories: classical conditioning, operant conditioning, and social learning theory. Because so many of the tenets in behavioral and learning theories are similar, their applications and strengths and weaknesses are discussed under the general heading of "learning theory."

Classical Conditioning

Ivan Pavlov (1927) is the theorist most commonly associated with **classical conditioning**, which focuses on how people respond to stimuli in their environment. In his classic experiment, Pavlov noted that dogs naturally salivate at the sight of food. Pavlov thus labeled the food an **unconditioned stimulus** and the salivation an **unconditioned response** because the dogs learned this behavior "naturally"; that is, the dogs did not need any training or conditioning to salivate at the sight of food. When Pavlov subsequently paired the food with another stimulus—in this case, he rang a bell when the food was presented—he was able to train the dogs to salivate at the sound of the bell. The bell thus became the **conditioned stimulus**, and the salivation to the bell became the **conditioned response**. Thus, Pavlov concluded that the dogs' natural salivation response could be elicited through training simply by presenting an alternative stimulus with their food.

John B. Watson (1925) generalized this work to humans. He conducted an experiment with Albert, a little boy who was conditioned to fear white rats. Before the experiment, Albert showed no fear (unconditioned response) of white rats (unconditioned stimulus). Watson then created a loud noise (conditioned stimulus) while Albert played with a white rat, startling Albert (conditioned response). After a while, Albert associated the loud noise with the white rat, and when Watson showed Albert the rat, Albert became startled. Thus, Albert's fear of white rats was conditioned. Though this type of experiment is considered unethical now (who knows what kind of psychological consequences this experiment had on Albert!), it is a powerful example of how behavior can be learned.

Operant Conditioning

Building on the ideas of classical conditioning, B. F. Skinner (1938) developed the concepts underlying operant conditioning. In **operant conditioning**, it is the consequences of behavior that result in behavior change (either an increase or decrease in behavior). So, if a child scribbles on the wall with a crayon (the behavior) and is punished (the consequence), the child's behavior of scribbling on the wall will decrease. Conversely, if the behavior is rewarded, the behavior will increase. Skinner argued that behavior could be shaped through this type of interaction.

Reinforcement, a primary component of operant conditioning, refers to a consequence that occurs immediately after a behavior that increases the strength of that behavior. Reinforcements can be *positive*, which means that something positive is *added* to strengthen a behavior. For example, after a child cleans her room, she may receive praise or get to watch her favorite movie. These positive consequences strengthen the behavior of cleaning. Reinforcements can also be *negative*, meaning that something negative is *taken away* to strengthen a behavior. An example of negative reinforcement is when you get into your car and hear a buzzer. That buzzer is annoying, and the only way to get it to stop is by latching your seat belt. Once you do that, the buzzing sound stops. The annoying buzzer stops, or is taken away, every time you put on your seat belt. The desired behavior, wearing your seat belt, is negatively reinforced, or strengthened, by the buzzer turning off. The important thing to remember is that positive and negative reinforcement both strengthen a behavior, they just do so in slightly different ways.

Let us take a look at another example of how positive and negative reinforcement work together. A mother has taken her son to the grocery store. While they are shopping, the child begins to cry because he wants chocolate. At first the mother refuses to give him the candy, and the child continues to scream while they move through the store. Finally, the mother, becoming really annoyed at his screaming, breaks down and gives him the chocolate, which quiets him down. In this scenario, the crying behavior of the child and the chocolate-giving behavior of the mother both have been reinforced. The mother's behavior is negatively reinforced because the child's screaming stops as soon as she gives him chocolate. The child's crying behavior is positively reinforced because he learns that he will be given chocolate when he cries.

Another component of operant conditioning is **punishment**, which involves the application of something negative or the removal of something positive to *weaken* or *reduce* the frequency of a behavior. This is different from negative reinforcement, which aims to increase the frequency of a behavior. An example of punishment is when a child misbehaves and her mother tells her that she must take time out in a quiet room, without her toys, for 15 minutes. Placing the child in this situation removes something positive: The child loses the stimulation of being with others, and she loses her toys. Hopefully, the removal of these positive things will decrease the frequency of the child's misbehaving. In another scenario, the mother could scold the child for misbehaving, which is adding something negative, or unpleasant (in this case, scolding), to decrease the frequency of the inappropriate behavior.

Social Learning Theory

A theory related to classical and operant conditioning is **social learning theory**, or social cognitive theory. Albert Bandura (1977), a leading proponent of social learning theory, posits that people are active agents in their learning. His theory supports the ideas put forth by the learning theorists just discussed; however, it goes further by maintaining that people use cognition and social interactions in learning. People do not simply respond automatically to stimuli; rather, they are able to think about processes in learning, and they actively interact with their surroundings, which often results in learning. Specifically, people think about the ramifications of their actions and make decisions about whether to act based on the outcomes of those actions.

Social learning theory suggests that people can learn vicariously, or through watching others. This type of learning is called **modeling**. That is, we can learn behaviors by watching how others do things and then imitating those behaviors. Moreover, we often watch what others do to see what the consequences will be for their behavior. If we observe someone being punished for a particular behavior, we are less likely to engage in that behavior ourselves. Conversely, if we observe some-one being rewarded for a behavior, we are more likely to imitate that behavior to receive the same rewards. Therefore, according to social learning theory, people do not actually have to perform a behavior themselves to learn from it. Rather, simply by watching what happens to others, people learn by others' successes or failures (Bandura, 1965).

Bandura identified one important aspect of learning as **self-efficacy**, which he defined as people's expectations that they can perform a task successfully. According to social learning theory, successful experiences are necessary to build self-efficacy. Further, when people have high levels of self-efficacy, they are more likely to per-form well in school, work, and other areas of their lives, which helps to build and reinforce their feelings of competence (Bandura, 1997). In essence, the development and maintenance of self-efficacy involves a cyclical process, whereby the more successful experiences people have, the more likely they are to seek other opportun-ities that lend themselves to successful outcomes, which helps to further build a sense of competence.

Applying Learning Theory

In Carlos's situation, you could use concepts from social learning theory or combine them with concepts from classical and operant conditioning to help him deal with his current situation. For example, let us say that Carlos has a fear of care facilities.

Every time he sees one, he becomes anxious and cannot step inside. To help him overcome this, you could use **systematic desensitization**, which builds on concepts of rewards and self-efficacy. You could begin by talking to Carlos about care facilities while teaching him relaxation techniques. Eventually, you would show Carlos pictures of facilities, then take him on a drive or walk past one, and then finally help him to physically walk into one. The idea is to expose Carlos to these facilities gradually while helping him to calm his anxiety. Simultaneously, Carlos will gain intrinsic rewards through feeling pride in his successes, which will reinforce his behaviors of approaching facilities. After some work, he should be able to enter a facility without any fear or anxiety.

You could also use the concept of modeling by introducing Carlos to other people who have Alzheimer's disease but who are coping well with the symptoms. Through modeling, Carlos may be able to learn new ways of coping and functioning. This exposure may also help to reduce some of his fears about having the disease. You could also use his past successes and high level of functioning to tap into his self-efficacy. Carlos seems to have performed well in the past: He was successful at his work, he has close relationships, and he has shown that he can cope with adversity. Carlos may need to be reminded of his successes to help him transfer this self-efficacy to his current situation and to future challenges.

You may also find it useful to explore with Carlos how learning has shaped his perceptions of certain characteristics such as intimacy, independence, and display of emotion. Because these issues seem to be relevant in his current situation (and they are likely to be relevant in the future), you may want to explore whether behaviors that could be beneficial to Carlos, such as expressing feelings, have been punished or not reinforced. For example, because of gender role stereotypes or cultural context, Carlos may have been punished for crying or talking about feelings. Or, he could have been positively reinforced for stereotypical masculine behavior such as holding in feelings. You could help Carlos by extinguishing behaviors that are detrimental to his well-being. For instance, you could help him "relearn" that expressing feelings is acceptable by positively reinforcing any efforts on his part to talk openly about his fears, regrets, or other feelings associated with his situation.

Critiquing Learning Theory

Social workers have found many ideas from learning theories to be effective for a wide range of client problems. One reason for this is that the concepts underlying these theories are fairly easy to define, measure, and evaluate. Thus, they can be applied to interventions, and the outcomes can be tested empirically. Many of these interventions can be applied quickly, making them popular in settings that mandate short-term work with clients. Further, the ideas about learning incorporated in these theories can be empowering for clients. They offer a straightforward approach to changing behavior that, with some guidance from social workers, helps to put control into the hands of clients. Specifically, social workers can help clients understand how to change undesirable behaviors, which can be generalized to other situations in which clients wish to change behaviors.

Because—as social learning theory recognizes—people can gain insights into their behavior and ultimately can take an active role in changing behavior based on these insights, some critics take issue with some of the tenets behind classical and operant conditioning. For example, they argue that conditioning theories treat people as passive agents who sit back and allow things to "happen" to them. These theories fail to address innate cognitive processes that may be motivating people's behaviors. However, there is some debate about how much these theories do acknowledge the influence of active cognitive process in the individual (Jensen & Burgess, 1997; Swann, 2009). Classical and operant conditioning also do not consider the ways in which the environment influences people's decisions and behaviors. Conversely, social learning theory takes into account the interactions between people and their environment. Although social learning theory incorporates some of the basic learning concepts, it augments these ideas with more complex processes that affect how people learn and behave.

HUMANISTIC AND EXISTENTIAL PERSPECTIVES

There are many other biopsychosocial theories that could influence your work with clients. The last type that we will look at in this chapter are humanistic and existential theories, which deal with the effects of people's worldviews or the meanings they place on life and on their behavior. These theories have a strong base in philosophy and are tied to Eastern beliefs of Zen Buddhism, Hinduism, and Islam (Payne, 1997). Existentialist and humanistic perspectives assert that people are capable of developing their spiritual selves, although aspects of spirituality may be defined differently by social workers than they are within organized religion.

Existentialism focuses on the meaning of life and people's views on existence. It teaches that people have control over their lives; people act on their environments, yet they are still influenced by their environments. Specifically, people are cognitive beings who can think critically about who they are and who they would like to be, but society also influences these thinking processes by "selling" stereotypes and images of success and happiness. Although people often understand that these are stereotypes, they have a tendency to allow these images to dictate how they view themselves as well as how they perceive happiness and well-being. So, a dynamic process occurs between people and their environments. Because of this, predicting human behavior is different—people are constantly growing and making choices that can change their lives, and these choices are influenced by their social surroundings (Payne, 1997). Existentialism addresses the human motivation to live lives that can sometimes be painful and unrewarding.

Like existentialism, the **humanistic perspective** focuses on the ways people view life and being. This perspective emphasizes people's role in shaping their own experiences. Essentially, it posits that each person has the potential for healthy and creative growth. There is no predetermined pattern to personality development; rather, people's subjective views on life help to shape their personality and experiences. These experiences, along with the feelings, values, and perceptions surrounding them, are important factors in shaping development. The humanistic perspective is rooted in the belief that people are active agents in their lives; people have the ability to reason, make choices, form their experiences, and control their destiny (Payne, 1997). Humans are resourceful, purposeful, and independent beings who are motivated to achieve love, growth, success, and acceptance.

These two perspectives are very similar with regard to their underlying tenets and view of human development and behavior. In social work, they tend to be grouped under the humanistic model. To better articulate their views on human development, we will look at specific therapeutic interventions that have been developed based on these perspectives.

Person-Centered Therapy and Transactional Analysis

One of the most famous humanistic theorists is Carl Rogers. Rogers is best known for client-centered or **person-centered therapy**, which is based on a person's self-concept. Rogers agrees that people are the product of their experiences and how they perceive those experiences. His theory states that people have a natural inclination toward self-actualization: We strive to develop our ideal self or the person we would like to be. We achieve self-actualization when (1) our self-concept is congruent with our experiences and (2) we have positive regard (for example, respect, esteem) from others and positive self-regard (we value ourselves). Similarly, a lack of well-being results from an incongruence between our self-concept and experiences. Rogers proposed that psychological maladjustment occurs when a person denies or distorts her or his experiences and is unable to deal with incongruence. From this perspective, the crux of social work with clients is to establish warmth, respect, empathy, genuineness, and positive regard in the working relationship. According to Rogers, these factors must be present for change to occur (1951).

Other theorists who fall into the humanistic category are Fritz Perls, who developed gestalt therapy, and Eric Berne, who founded transactional analysis. **Gestalt therapy** is based on psychodynamic theory. It posits that people go through life with "unfinished business" (for example, unresolved feelings or conflicts with others) that affects behavior and relationships. People naturally attempt to avoid this unfinished business because they erroneously believe that experiencing it will bring catastrophe. As people avoid the powerful feelings associated with unfinished business, they disown essential parts of themselves and do not fully experience life. Gestalt therapy is geared toward helping people work through this unfinished business and fully "own" the self. People work toward making the past and hidden aspects of themselves fully known, and they are encouraged to live in the present (Perls, Hefferline, & Goodman, 1973).

Transactional analysis is also based on psychodynamic theory, and it shares the notion that maladaptive behavioral patterns established in childhood often get in the way of well-being in later life. However, unlike psychodynamic theory, transactional analysis states that people are active, responsible beings who have the capacity to solve problems. This theory posits that in infancy, people have a need for physical contact. As people age, they satisfy this need through conversation and verbal contact with others. Transactional analysis focuses on people's transactions with others, especially on the problems that occur in these transactions that can hinder positive behavior and development. This therapy uses different types of analyses to work with clients in promoting well-being. One technique used in this therapy is *structural analysis*. It looks at people's ego states, or the structures that make up personality. These ego states are thought to be associated with people's behavioral patterns. Structural analysis examines the interactions of ego states among two or more people. Another technique, *game analysis*, examines specific patterns of interactions and behaviors among two or more people (Berne, 1961).

Applying and Critiquing Humanistic and Existential Perspectives

Given the broad philosophies found in humanistic and existential perspectives, there are many ways in which you could approach your work with Carlos. However, the basic approach would be to better understand how Carlos perceives his situation. You would want to know how his subjective views of the world and of the meaning of life are shaping his experiences. While acknowledging the need to recognize that Carlos has the capacity to shape his future experiences and to control his own destiny, you will want to keep in mind that these considerations might not apply to Carlos in a literal sense since his physical problems will take much control out of his hands. You could still help Carlos find meaning in what is happening to him or at least help him come to some sense of peace with his situation.

Working from person-centered therapy, you would strive to establish a working environment with Carlos that promoted warmth, empathy, genuineness, and positive regard. You would then work with him to explore his views of his self-concept and his ideal self. Your goal would be to ensure that Carlos experiences congruency between his self-concept and his experiences, which may be a problem given his diagnosis and impending loss of independence. Carlos might be in denial about his situation, which means that he could be distorting his experiences and maintaining a state of incongruence. His diagnosis is also likely to be in conflict with his view of his ideal self.

One of the main limitations to humanistic approaches, some critics argue, is that they are not based on a coherent theory of personality. Rather, they espouse vague ideas and concepts that are not easily defined. Thus, evaluating whether these approaches are effective in creating change with clients is difficult. Further, depending on the philosophy of the social worker, these ideas can be applied very differently by different workers.

Proponents of these theories assert that they are positive and strengths based (as opposed to problem-based theories) and can help to empower clients. Some social workers like these approaches because they put the client at the center of the working relationship, allowing the client to guide the process. Indeed, concepts in Rogers's theory such as respect, empathy, and positive regard are seen as crucial components in the working relationship regardless of the theory used to guide the process. And, the use of these skills has been empirically shown to be more effective in producing positive client outcomes than the use of any specific theory (Gurman, 1977; Orlinsky and Howard, 1986; Patterson, 1984). Finally, some approaches, such as transactional analysis, can be applied to work with clients in a somewhat systematic manner. Many agencies have developed therapeutic programs that use these concepts as guiding facets of work with clients. For example, social workers can employ structural or game analysis in their interventions. Social workers can be trained in the use of transactional analysis, which helps to ensure that it is used consistently and accurately across clients and agencies.

CONCLUSION

The theories, models, and perspectives discussed in this chapter tend to focus on the individual and how various problems and processes affect development and behavior on an individual level. To review their main characteristics, look back at Table 3.1. Although some of the theories and approaches discussed here do take into account environmental influences, these influences tend to be limited to those within a person's immediate environment. Many social workers argue that these types of considerations are too limited, and that larger environmental forces outside of clients' control must be considered in assessment and intervention. Still, the ideas presented in this chapter influence social work in general, and they contribute a great deal to social work practice. For social workers in many settings, the underlying tenets of these theories, models, and perspectives need to be understood in order for social workers to communicate and work with other helping professionals.

As discussed in Chapter 1, these theories and approaches can be used in combination with other theories and approaches that address larger social forces to offer a more comprehensive view of client problems. Moreover, tenets of the theories and models discussed in this chapter, particularly some of the constructs used in disease-based models, can be used to inform person-in-environment conceptualizations of client problems. Keep in mind that with technological advances and an increasing need for social workers to stay abreast of biological knowledge, disease-based and other micro-focused theories and models are an integral part of social workers' knowledge base.

MAIN POINTS

- One of the lenses for conceptualizing client problems and considering interventions is the biopsychosocial lens. Social workers may use several models, theories, and perspectives within this dimension, including the medical model, learning theory, and humanistic perspective.

- The medical model is a disease-based model that focuses on the symptoms of problems, which can be cured by an expert. When applying this model, social workers may begin by assessing the client's problems using the DSM-IV-TR.

- Piaget's theory of cognitive development consists of four main stages that describe cognitive development from birth to about age 16 as becoming more complex, flexible, and capable of abstract reasoning.

- Freud's theory of psychosexual development, based on the concepts of the id, the ego, and the superego, consists of five stages that explain personality development. People can become fixated in each stage, and they use defense mechanisms to suppress conflicts that may occur at each stage.

- Erikson's theory of psychosocial development consists of eight stages that describe development across the life span. He proposed that people face crises in each stage that must be resolved; otherwise, they take unresolved crises into the next stage, which affects development and the ability to face new crises.

- Learning theories focus on how people respond to stimuli in their environment. Some theories, such as classical conditioning, view people as passive learners, while others, such as social learning theory, view people as actively involved in their environments, which means that they are actively involved in learning.

- Humanistic and existential perspectives, which focus on how people view life and meaning, emphasize the abilities of people to make decisions and shape their own experiences. Although critics argue that the ideas in these perspectives are vague and outcomes difficult to evaluate, person-centered therapy and transactional analysis are two well-used concepts in social work.

EXERCISES

1. Using the Sanchez Family interactive case (go to www.routledgesw.com/cases), review the Sanchez family and the issues facing each member. Pick a family member or two on whom you'd like to focus for this exercise. You will also need to choose three different theoretical perspectives discussed in this chapter to apply to the problems of the family member(s). When you've chosen your clients and perspectives, answer the following questions:
   a. Briefly describe the problems you see with the family member(s) you've chosen.
   b. Describe how you would perceive the family member(s) and their problems through the lens of each theory you chose. Make sure you are being detailed enough to capture the essence of the theory.
   c. Briefly discuss how you would develop an intervention that is based on each theory.
   d. Discuss how the family member, problems, and interventions differ from one another from the perspective of each theory.
   e. Discuss some of the strengths and limitations to working with the family member from each perspective.
   f. Based on your discussion thus far, which approach would you take with the family member and why?
2. Using the Riverton interactive case (go to www.routledgesw.com/cases), review the situation and the problems faced by that community and answer the following questions:

a. Based on your assessment of the situation in this case, could you use any of the theories discussed in this chapter to help you conceptualize the problems faced by this community and to help guide your intervention? Why or why not? Be specific and give examples to justify your thoughts.

Lenses for Conceptualizing Problems and Interventions: Sociocultural Dimensions

The Smith family has just adopted Aisha, a 10-year-old African American girl who has been in the foster care system for six years. Aisha was placed in foster care after her mother was arrested for shoplifting; Aisha's father hasn't been involved with her since she was two years old, and her other family members were unable to care for her. Before Aisha was placed in foster care, she lived in poverty with her family. However, despite these difficulties, she seemed to be thriving in her environment, and her mother was able to provide the necessities for her family. After her mother's arrest, Aisha was placed briefly with an African American family and had been adjusting well to school, peers, and her new family. Aisha's new adoptive family are devout Catholic, upper-class Caucasians with three other children who are all older than Aisha. For the past several weeks, Aisha has experienced trouble adjusting to her new family. She won't talk or eat, and she has encountered problems in school. Aisha told the social worker at the foster care agency that she misses her family, church (her family of origin is Baptist), friends, and neighborhood. She feels out of place with her new family and school, and she isn't sure how she will fit into her new environment.

W ITH REGARD TO SOCIAL WORK, AISHA'S SITUATION RAISES many ethical, practical, and philosophical questions. Some of these questions relate to Aisha's adjustment and well-being as a new family member. Others involve the adjustment of the family as they attempt to accommodate a new member. Still other questions focus on the utility of institutions such as family, religion, adoption, and foster care and how institutions support or undermine individual functioning and the integrity of cultural diversity and ethnic differences. To look for answers to some of these broad philosophical questions, social workers often turn to sociological, feminist, and cultural theories to conceptualize larger social issues.

As in Chapters 2 and 3, the theories and perspectives discussed in this chapter are presented in Table 4.1 for purposes of comparison and review.

SOCIOLOGICAL THEORIES

The discipline of sociology focuses on the study of social behavior and groups. Sociologists develop theories to explain how social forces affect people on a large scale. For example, sociological theory might explain how unemployment affects a community or why a group of people would follow a leader of a religious sect to the point of committing suicide. Most sociological theories reflect the **sociological imagination**, a term coined by C. Wright Mills (1959) to describe the relationship between the individual and the wider society. According to Mills, this awareness allows us to better understand the connection between our personal lives and larger social forces that influence us. An important component of the sociological imagination is the need to view outside social forces from an objective perspective and not just from our own culturally biased point of view.

Based on the topics discussed in the previous chapters, you can see how well sociology fits with social work. Many of the theories, models, and perspectives that we have reviewed are rooted in the idea that social workers need to understand individuals within their environmental context. The first part of the chapter discusses some fundamental theories in sociology and how they can be applied to social work practice.

Conflict Theory

One of sociology's first theoretical orientations was **conflict theory**, an approach that views social behavior from the perspective of conflict or tension among two or more groups. This theory provides a framework from which conflict between superordinate and subordinate groups in society can be systematically analyzed (Turner, 1998).

Marx and Conflict Theory   Conflict theory can be traced to the writings of Karl Marx, who believed that struggle or conflict among classes was an inevitable feature of capitalism (Marx, 1987; Marx & Engels, 1977). Marx argued that various groups, or social classes, in society are perpetually fighting and competing for resources and power—he viewed resources primarily in terms of economics—and that groups remain polarized against one another. As resources become scarcer and are more unequally distributed—with the upper classes accumulating an increasing proportion of them—this conflict increases. In addition, as subordinate groups become aware that they are being treated unfairly, they are more likely to question and fight against the status quo. Finally, as groups become increasingly polarized,

TABLE 4.1

Characteristics of Sociocultural Theories and Perspectives

	CONFLICT	FUNCTIONALISM	SYMBOLIC INTERACTIONISM/SOCIAL CONSTRUCTIONISM	FEMINISM	CULTURALISM
Type	Theory	Theory	Theory	Theory	Perspective
Focus	Social groups	Social groups	Society & the individual	Society & the individual	Society & the individual
Assumptions	Tensions among groups shape social structures.	Aspects, or functions, of a society work together to maintain stability.	Ways in which people and systems interact, and the meaning that people attach to those interactions, shape individual experiences and society.	Interactions of individuals and social forces affect development, oppression and discrimination, and institutional structure and functioning.	Individual experiences help give structure to experiences and shape society.
Strengths	• Can be used to conceptualize interventions in community-based practice. • Helps social workers understand the complexity of client problems. • Focuses on how power can be misused to create inequality and to disenfranchise clients.	• Offers clients an alternative viewpoint to problems. • Understanding manifest and latent functions of social institutions can help social workers target interventions. • Tenets of theory fit well with ideas from systems and ecological theories.	• Provides a useful way to assess problems. • Focus on the meanings clients place on their experiences can be empowering. • Approach to assessment fits well with humanistic perspectives and can be combined with other theories. • Tenets have been useful in postmodern research.	• Focuses on equality and the role of the dominant structure in causing and perpetuating client problems. • Tenets have helped guide postmodern research. • Has raised awareness of multiple points of view on issues.	• Offers ways to articulate, organize, and understand cultural elements of clients' lives. • Helps social workers to be more culturally competent in practice.

TABLE 4.1
continued

	CONFLICT	FUNCTIONALISM	SYMBOLIC INTER-ACTIONISM/SOCIAL CONSTRUCTIONISM	FEMINISM	CULTURALISM
Limitations	• Focus is limited to the macro level. • Interventions based on conflict can be difficult to carry out. • Can be difficult to define and empirically test constructs.	• Focusing on changing dysfunction within a system could be an empowering approach for clients. • Little attention given to the complexity of interactions that take place among systems. • Does not address the inequity that may result from a system's manifest and latent functions. • Can be difficult to use for developing interventions. • Can be difficult to define and empirically test constructs.	• Does not offer a clear way in which to intervene with clients. • Too micro focused. • Lacks a solid, consistent theoretical base from which to examine relationships. • Can be difficult to define and empirically test constructs. • Difficult to predict behavior.	• Focuses on women at the expense of other minority groups. • Can be difficult to define and empirically test constructs. • Cannot predict behavior.	• There is no single, coherent theory of culture. • Concepts may be difficult to define, apply, and test empirically. • Cannot predict behavior.

the conflict becomes more intense and ultimately leads to change in the status quo (Marx, 1994; Turner, 1998).

Significantly, Marx argued that conflict is not necessarily violent. Rather, it can take the form of struggle within business or political negotiations, religious or philosophical ideologies, or personal attitudes and beliefs (Lefebvre, 1968; Marx, 1973; Mills, 1994; Sayer, 1989; Turner, 1998). For instance, conflict can be represented in differing opinions between two religious groups or in the competition for resources between two political parties.

Conflict Theories since Marx   Marx's views sparked a great deal of thought and debate. Numerous sociologists, including Max Weber, Georg Simmel, W. E. B. Du Bois, and various feminist thinkers, developed and modified Marx's views. Their efforts contributed to the development of sociological research and conflict-based theory.

One of the biggest critics of Marx's ideas was Max Weber (1958, 1968), an economist, who argued that Marx's theory was too focused on the inevitability of conflict in society. Although Weber agreed with Marx that conflicts among groups can emerge, he maintained that groups need a leader to spur the conflict. These leaders must be able to incite resentment and anger in subordinate groups, which can lead to structural change and a more equal distribution of resources. Weber also disagreed with Marx's views of absolute polarization among groups. Weber posited that groups possess a great deal of variation with regard to class, politics, philosophies, and so on (Turner, 1998; Weber, 1957, 1994). Thus, Weber maintained that groups could be defined by class, status, and party rather than just by social class as Marx had posited. He further argued that membership or identification with a particular group did not automatically assure power.

Many aspects of Georg Simmel's ideas were similar to those of Marx and Weber. Simmel generally concurred with Weber regarding the origins of conflict in society. Specifically, he argued that as the levels of emotional involvement and solidarity increase among group members, the level of violence also increases. He further argued that conflict serves to centralize power, establish clear boundaries among groups, and restrict deviance among group members. Simmel also proposed that conflict can be beneficial for society if it is not too inflammatory. That is, conflict that is not intense or violent and whose ground rules can be agreed upon can encourage coalition building and discussion among groups (Turner, 1998). For example, political parties in the United States tend to have clear ideological boundaries and goals, which tend to decrease deviancy among their members so that members tend to be loyal to their chosen party. Conflict between parties, which is not often overly emotional, tends to spur debate, which can lead to social and other change, including the shift of power from one group to the next. Conversely, pro-life and pro-choice groups have clear ideological boundaries regarding abortion, but the conflict between the two tends to be very emotional, which can lead to violence such as the bombing of abortion clinics or the murder of physicians who provide abortions. This emotionally laden conflict and the fierce loyalty of group members to a certain ideology decrease the likelihood that the two groups will come to an agreement on abortion policies.

W. E. B. Du Bois is another thinker associated with the conflict perspective. Du Bois (1911, 1970) focused primarily on racial and ethnic inequality. He argued that sociologists should pursue scientific knowledge to help overcome bias and prejudice in society. To pursue this objective he supported various social groups and organizations that questioned the status quo. For example, he helped found the National Association for the Advancement of Colored People (NAACP) in 1909. Du Bois's push for more concentrated research on conflict and its effects on minority groups helped to increase sociological knowledge of racial and social inequality, much of which has benefited the African American community. For instance, a great deal of knowledge has been generated that informs unique health issues of African Americans such as sickle-cell anemia.

Many other theorists have developed ideas that have been integrated into conflict theory. Indeed, various events of the 1960s and 1970s such as the women's and civil rights movements as well as riots, demonstrations, and confrontations over such issues as the Vietnam War and governmental scandals increased the support for conflict theory. Sociologists have expanded conflict theory by building on the tenets of earlier theories to include struggles that occur in many different aspects of social and personal life. These later theories examine which groups either benefit or suffer from the established order and the distribution of resources. They focus on who has power and how this power is used to perpetuate inequality. These perspectives explore conflicts among gender, ethnic, religious, and cultural groups as well as conflicts that occur within social institutions such as the media, family, and government. In addition, these approaches examine how power and resources can be distributed among groups more equitably to benefit everyone instead of just a few (Dahrendorf, 1958). Some proponents argue that conflict approaches encourage sociologists to examine issues from the perspective of people who enjoy fewer privileges and influence than others in society.

Applying Conflict Theory

This section offers specific examples of how conflict theory can be applied to some common institutions. These examples take a contemporary look at conflict theory and its relevance to social issues. We will also consider the relevance of conflict theory to social work in general and to Aisha's situation in particular.

The Family   You can apply conflict theory to many different realms in people's social and personal lives. As an example, let us analyze the family through the lens of conflict theory. The conflict perspective views families as institutions that both reflect and perpetuate the unequal distribution of power and resources within the larger society. In other words, families serve as the means through which wealth, power, poverty, privilege, and inequality are passed from one generation to another, thereby contributing to economic injustice. For example, children inherit the poverty or privilege of their parents. Children born to wealthy, educated, well-connected parents benefit from quality housing, education, health care, and access to opportunity. These children are at an advantage as they grow older due to their quality of life. Conversely, children born to poor and uneducated parents inherit debt and a lack of exposure to equal education, health care, and other opportunities that can help them get ahead in life.

Families also pass on to their children other characteristics besides economic and related opportunities. The social class and economic status of families influence the ways in which children are socialized, which impacts the children's views, values, beliefs, attitudes, and behaviors. Children carry these values and perspectives into their adult lives, which in turn influences the ways they vote, make policy, and believe that society should distribute resources.

In addition, according to conflict theory, the family legitimizes male power and dominance, which in turn validates and perpetuates the lower status of women and children. This unequal power distribution affects women and children in realms outside the immediate family such as education, economics, child care, workplace policy, health care, reproductive choices, and freedom from violence. For example, women are still more likely than men to leave their jobs and relocate when they get married, when the man receives a promotion, or when child or elder care is needed. Women are also more likely to postpone their education or career goals after marriage. In addition, domestic violence remains a serious problem. Though the feminist movement has helped women and children to achieve broader rights, men are still viewed as dominant within the family unit.

Health Care   Another example of how conflict theory can be applied to a sociological issue is health care. From the perspective of conflict theory, medicine and medical professionals hold a great deal of status in U.S. society. The medical institution has the power to define wellness and illness as well as acceptable treatments for people who are ill. This power enables the medical establishment to exert a certain amount of social control and to define and reinforce many social values.

Sociologists have coined the term **medicalization of society** to describe the influence of the health profession in shaping societal values and exerting social control in many arenas, not just health care. As the range of expertise in medicine has grown over the decades, the medical profession has acquired the power to influence knowledge, attitudes, opinions, and even social policy. For example, the opinions of physicians and other medical professionals increasingly influence and shape public opinion and policies regarding such issues as old age, obesity, sexuality, and addiction. Conflict theory further argues that the enhanced power of the medical establishment also reflects the perception among the lay public that medical professionals possess special knowledge and expertise that make them uniquely qualified to evaluate health-related issues. As a result, the medical profession has achieved unchecked jurisdiction over policies and procedures that would otherwise be open to public scrutiny, including those related to abortion, childbirth, child care, drug costs, and nationalized health care.

One prominent example of the medicalization of society is childbirth. Formerly the realm of female midwives, childbirth had been turned over to a mostly male medical profession, which forced onto women unnatural childbirth practices and undermined the credibility of midwives by creating a perception that their practices were "unscientific" and therefore questionable. Only recently have midwives begun to recapture their reputation and their hold on childbirth practices, a process that, according to its proponents, restores power to those individuals who provide more natural childbirth practices (Schoen, 2000). Additionally, women (and physicians) have rediscovered the benefits of breastfeeding after the experts had shunned breast milk as inferior to scientifically engineered formula.

Conflict Theory and Social Work   By now you probably recognize that the application of conflict theory to family and health care has many ramifications for social work. Because conflict theory fits so well with the underlying values and ethics of social work, including empowerment and social justice, social workers can find many uses for it. Social workers who work with victims of domestic violence, for example, can use conflict theory to conceptualize the power differential that exists between men and women and the ways in which patriarchal society supports and maintains this inequality. This conceptualization, in turn, can help social workers to understand the obstacles that discourage or prevent many women from leaving their situations. Many of these obstacles are embedded in the fabric of societal values, which makes leaving for some women extremely difficult. For example, the expense of child care, women's struggle to earn wages that will support themselves and their families, and the court system's slow and often ineffective response to domestic violence can all create barriers to women's successful exit from violent situations. Further, some social workers may choose to intervene against domestic violence on a larger societal level by dealing with policies and value systems that perpetuate current thinking about the unequal roles of men and women in society.

With regard to health care, social workers can use conflict theory to better understand how medicine as an institution affects clients. If the medical establishment possesses the ability to influence people's lives, as posited by conflict theory, then social workers need to be educated about how organized medicine uses this power to determine policies and services that directly affect clients. In addition, social workers frequently intervene with clients whose values conflict with those of the medical establishment. For example, what if a client's beliefs dictate that she seek alternative medicine or refuse all medical treatments? Conflict theory can help social workers to understand how hospitals can exert pressures on people that might conflict with their personal values and beliefs. Social workers must act as mediators between hospitals and clients to ensure that clients' rights are not undermined by the policies and mandates of hospitals.

As another example, the current state of privatized and managed care, soaring health care costs, and ever-advancing technology have created a two-tiered health care system: One tier is for the wealthy and gainfully employed who can afford private health insurance, and the other is for people who are poor, unemployed, and underemployed. This second group is increasingly being forced out of the system, leaving them without quality care. Because of costs and other issues, many qualified physicians are abandoning their communities and practices for safer and more lucrative positions, leaving many poor people, particularly in rural areas, without care. This phenomenon is occurring worldwide. It is clearly occurring in the United States, where infant mortality rates are higher than in many other countries, reflecting unequal access to care (World Bank, 1999). Conflict theory offers one perspective from which to view these problems, which can be used as a springboard for devising interventions that will lead to system change. Indeed, it is often social workers who bring attention to ethical, cultural, and other issues that may clash with the predominant medical model, thereby helping to initiate changes that can benefit clients.

Aisha's Case Revisited   Let us look at how Aisha's situation might be viewed from the perspective of conflict theory. As the social worker, you might be inclined to focus on the broad issues that forced Aisha into this situation in the first place, which can then help you focus on specific areas appropriate for intervention. One place to begin would be to look at the poverty in which Aisha's family was living. You might question why Aisha's mother was unable to secure employment that paid enough to support the family. Based on conflict theory, you might argue that unequal distribution of resources and access to opportunities are causing poverty for Aisha's family. Further, this inequality is being maintained by societal values and a status quo that keep families like Aisha's in poverty. For Aisha's mother, discrimination in the workplace is a likely barrier as are more insidious factors such as unequal access to quality education that provides employment skills; lack of a livable wage (being African American and female probably contributes to low wages as well); lack of opportunities to "network" with those who might provide opportunities; lack of access to resources such as child and health care that could free up time for work; and lack of access to reliable and affordable transportation to get to work. You could also assess other areas of Aisha's situation such as institutional policies in education, foster care, and criminal justice that seem to be further disenfranchising Aisha and her family.

Critiquing Conflict Theory

Though you might find many areas to assess from the conflict perspective in Aisha's situation, from a strictly micro-oriented standpoint, it is unlikely that you will be able to develop any immediately effective interventions. Although the conflict perspective allows social workers and clients to analyze societal problems that contribute to clients' situations, it often does not identify time- and cost-effective strategies for dealing with these problems, though these can be developed over time. Because many agencies, including foster care agencies, must focus on efficient interventions, unfortunately they usually do not have the luxury of pondering issues involving social change. However, social workers who focus on community action and change may find conflict theory more applicable to their work, which can then inform work done on the micro level.

As reflected in Aisha's situation, the main limitation of conflict theory is that it tends to lend itself only to the macro level of conceptualization of problems. Besides the difficulty of developing interventions based on this theory—especially within the realm of practice with individuals—carrying out these interventions after they are developed is also problematic. Issues of inequality are often firmly institutionalized and embedded in the fabric of societal values. Of course, this assertion does not suggest that you should not focus your attention on social issues that create problems for your clients or try to address these issues on a global level. It does recognize, however, that some social workers are not in a position to devise interventions on this level. As we saw earlier, one exception to this generalization is social workers who focus on community- or organizational-based interventions, which are more amenable to perspectives like conflict theory.

Conflict theory is useful for understanding the different levels of social work and of the environment that may be the source of many client problems. It can help you grasp the complex and varied relationships that occur within and among groups at these levels and the ways in which power can be used and misused to create inequality. Finally, the focus on how individuals and groups can become disenfranchised by unequal power distribution is congruent with the values and ethics of the profession, which serves as a reminder that the causes of problems are often out of the hands of the individuals facing them.

Functionalist Theory

Another of sociology's original theories is functionalist theory. In contrast to conflict theory, **functionalist theory** attempts to explain how various aspects, or functions, of a society work together to maintain stability. Specifically, functionalist theory is concerned with the ways in which values, norms, institutions, and organizations contribute to the overall good of society. Like the systems and ecological theories discussed in Chapter 2, the functionalist approach views society as a living organism that consists of parts functioning as a whole. All systems coexist and are dependent on one another; and they work together to ensure the smooth functioning of the whole. Aspects of society that are functional and contribute to society will be maintained and passed on from one generation to the next. In contrast, dysfunctional systems will be changed or thrown out all together.

Manifest Functions, Latent Functions, and Dysfunctions   Functionalist theory proposes that various functions of society work together to ensure the well-being of society as a whole. These functions can express themselves in different ways, some of which are more observable and obvious than others. Theorist Robert Merton (1968) has distinguished between manifest and latent functions. **Manifest functions** are those whose purposes are readily discernible. For instance, many students would agree that the purpose of course grades is to give students feedback on their performance and to provide a report to outsiders (such as parents, employers, and graduate schools) that reflects the student's abilities. The purpose of giving grades, then, seems apparent and straightforward.

Conversely, **latent functions** are those whose purpose is not necessarily what it seems to be on the surface. Again using grades as an example, although grades do offer students feedback, they can perform a number of less obvious functions as well. For example, they can discourage students, they can misrepresent a student's true capability, they can be given arbitrarily without a fair or uniform standard, and they can be used to discriminate against students. In other words, whether intended or not, latent functions often serve purposes that can either promote or undermine an institution or an aspect of society, depending on the viewpoint of the person being helped or hurt by them.

Finally, **dysfunctions** can be described as those parts of society that do not contribute to the well-being of the larger system. Dysfunctions may actually add to instability and chaos in a system, sometimes causing the system to disintegrate. For example, most people perceive crime as dysfunctional. Criminal acts such as fraud, theft, arson, and murder all disrupt the order of the personal lives affected by such acts, and they can create chaos for communities and society. Depending on the crime, they can cause physical, financial, emotional, and psychological instability that can cause problems for people and communities in other areas. Sometimes criminal acts can cause total disintegration of systems; for example, a person may commit suicide in the wake of losing all her money due to fraud, or riots may break out in a community because of a murder.

Functionalist Theorists: Durkheim and Parsons   Emile Durkheim (1933, 1938), a pioneer in the field of sociology, made many contributions to functionalism through his work on biological processes and their application to social systems. He also promoted the idea that behavior must be considered within its social context. Based on this assertion, he concluded that society must be considered as a functioning whole; its parts cannot be viewed separately. He posited that these parts serve a function, purpose, or role that contributes to the whole. For society to function well and to maintain homeostasis, it must meet various needs (such as social, physical, emotional, and economical) of its members and institutions (Turner, 1998).

Durkheim was particularly interested in how industrialization affected people, especially the workers, who were increasingly exposed to specialized labor, isolation from the institutions that employed them, and other changes that accompanied this process. He became convinced that when society undergoes dramatic change such as industrialization, people lose their sense of meaning in life and feel directionless in their activities. He coined the term **anomie** to describe this process. Ultimately, if anomie goes unchecked, society as a whole loses its sense of purpose and becomes unable to control individual behavior (Durkheim, 1933, 1938). Through his analyses and ideas, Durkheim influenced other sociologists who were developing functionalist theory.

Talcott Parsons, another prominent functionalist theorist, was influenced by the work of Weber and Durkheim. Parsons (1951, 1994) supported the ideas behind functionalism throughout much of the 20th century, and he helped shape the field during this time. Parsons agreed with Durkheim that society is the sum of its parts. If a particular part is not contributing to the operation of society, it will "die off" or become obsolete. Parsons offered an in-depth and scholarly analysis of society through the lens of functionalist theory, and this analysis helped to place emphasis on larger social systems and their effect on individual behavior.

Applying Functionalist Theory

As with conflict theory, functionalist theory can be applied to many social realms. This section offers specific examples of how functionalist theory can be applied to problems and issues and looks at the relevance of functionalist theory to social work.

Education and Language   In the case of education and language, the functionalist perspective looks for ways in which these cultural elements contribute to the homeostasis of society. How does education do this? First, education as an institution contributes to society by imparting knowledge to children. Schools teach children many skills, from reading and writing to understanding complex mathematical equations. Schools also impart social status to children. Depending on the school that children attend (for example, poor, wealthy, private, public, curriculum focus), they become a reflection of the type, quality, and reputation of the school's instruction. Imparting knowledge and status would be considered manifest functions of education. Schools also serve many latent functions. They intentionally or unintentionally pass along social norms, values, beliefs, and philosophies, and they "train" children to control their behavior and obey authority.

Functionalist theory can also be applied to language. Manifest functions of language include the transmission of wants, desires, needs, and ideas from one person to another. We need language to communicate and to ensure that things run smoothly. Latent functions of language include reinforcing social status and roles, transmitting and perpetuating values and beliefs, and instigating social change. For instance, aspects of language such as nuances in vocabulary, nonverbals, and vernacular can be used to reinforce social class, to isolate or solidify groups, and to incite rage or encourage pride among group members.

Functionalist Theory and Social Work Social workers who adopt a functionalist perspective might look at the ways in which various social institutions help to maintain order in clients' lives. For instance, as a school social worker, you might focus on the ways in which the educational system benefits society through educating and socializing children. You may want to work toward improving these functions to ensure that all children benefit from them. You may also see the value of certain latent functions (for example, providing social control), in which case you might encourage teachers and parents to support this aspect of education.

Of course, conflicts can arise between social workers who support functionalist theory and those who don't "buy into" the functions of various institutions such as education. For example, how might you intervene with parents who choose to educate their children at home? Does home schooling undermine the functions of established educational systems? As another example, what should you do when parents or a community disagree with the school's curriculum? These questions pose challenges for social workers who attempt to view client issues through the functionalist lens.

Aisha's Case Revisited Let us look at another example of how functionalist theory might be applied to a client situation. How might you view Aisha's problems from this perspective? There are actually many angles from which this situation can be analyzed. One place to start is by looking at the foster care and adoption systems in which Aisha has been involved. You might see these systems as a way to provide stability for children whose biological families have broken up. They act as substitutes for families to provide basic needs, love, socialization, and so on. Although Aisha's family seemed to be fulfilling her needs before her mother was arrested, it was not able to continue doing so after the arrest. Therefore, placement with an African American family would seem to be the most functional way to meet Aisha's developmental needs. Not only could this family meet her basic needs, but they could also help to socialize her into a specific ethnic and cultural environment. Based on this approach, you could advocate Aisha's return to an African American foster or adoptive family.

Aisha's adoption by a Caucasian family could be viewed in several different ways. On the one hand, the family is able to provide for Aisha's needs, which is functional. On the other hand, the family may not be providing for other needs such as a feeling of belonging to an ethnic and cultural group. And, because this family practices Catholicism, it would be providing the basic needs or manifest functions through organized religion (for example, transmission of morals, beliefs, and ideology), but the latent functions of this particular religion might be different from those provided by Aisha's Baptist religion. You might think in terms of what types of role models this particular church would provide for her, and what beliefs about herself and her heritage she might develop in this environment. Because Aisha is not doing well in school or at home since her placement with the Caucasian family, this placement could be dysfunctional; that is, it is not effectively performing the functions of a family that Aisha needs.

From this perspective, you would want to ensure that the functionality of the placement is maintained. Accomplishing this objective might involve assessing where dysfunction in the system is occurring and helping the family to make adjustments to better suit Aisha's needs. It might also involve removing Aisha from the home and placing her in one that is a better fit.

Critiquing Functionalist Theory

Given the examples we have looked at thus far using the functionalist approach, you might see some obvious strengths and limitations to relying on this theory in practice. One main limitation is that functionalist theory views the interactions among systems as closed; that is, it does not place emphasis on the complex interactions that take place among systems, which can create a great deal of conflict. Moreover, it does not address the inequity that can result from a system's manifest and latent functions, which is an important ethical consideration. It treats these functions as rather benign and one-dimensional: As long as they help a system run smoothly, the problems that they can cause for individuals and groups are not addressed. For example, although Aisha's needs seem to be met according to the functionalist theory, she is not doing well in her new placement. What accounts for the underlying problems that seem to be creating stress for Aisha? What if Aisha were placed with an African American family and she still had problems? What would account for those problems? The functionalist theory does not necessarily explain these issues.

In addition, like conflict theory, functionalism does not lend itself well to developing interventions for clients. For example, although you could proceed by finding ways to make Aisha's current situation more functional, this intervention may not be the most culturally appropriate for Aisha. Indeed, anything short of returning Aisha to her biological mother may not be the most functional approach to her situation. On the positive side, using functionalist theory to explain issues to a client may offer the client an alternative way to think about problems and provide insight into why social institutions function in the ways they do. (This approach could help clients to make some sense out of the seeming madness that often characterizes our bureaucratic institutions!) If clients and social workers understand the manifest and latent functions of social institutions, they can work toward eliminating those functions that are contributing to clients' problems as well as to inequity and disempowerment. Overall, the functionalist theory fits well with ideas from systems and ecological theories, so it could be used in conjunction with these approaches in work with clients. Focusing on changing dysfunction within a system could be an empowering approach for clients.

Symbolic Interaction Theory and Social Constructionism

Symbolic interaction theory refers to the unique ways in which people and systems interact and communicate with one another as well as the essence and characteristics of that interaction and communication. An important tenet of symbolic interaction theory is that we all attach meaning to our communications with others within the context in which the interaction takes place. So, even though several of us might experience an interaction in the same place and time, we might interpret that interaction very differently, depending on the meaning we place on it. Symbolic interaction theory maintains that we are not just passive receivers of information. Rather, we filter and interpret the information based on our culture, cognitions, experiences, and so on, and we respond to this information based on how we interpret it (Blumer, 1969).

There are three main premises to symbolic interaction theory. The first is that we act on our world based on the meanings that we attach to our experiences. The second is that the meanings we attach to our experiences stem from our interactions with others. The third is that these meanings are affected by our interpretations of our interactions. Thus, our experiences, interactions, and interpretations of our experiences and interactions constitute an ongoing, dynamic process. People make meaning of their experiences and the nature of society as they interact with others, which in turn shapes how society develops and is structured (Blumer, 1969).

Symbolic interaction theory is very similar to **social constructionism**, which asserts that we construct our reality based on our experiences. Social constructionism argues that there is not a single reality, but rather, multiple realities, because each of us perceives the world around us differently. We are active in our world, and how we perceive our interactions is a reflection of our culture, history, language, and experiences as well as how these things have impacted our interpretations of the world. Social constructionism focuses on the *process* of how we go about constructing our reality. In other words, this perspective is not so much concerned with the results of interactions as with what happens within and among people *during* interactions. The emphasis is on people as actors and how they make sense of interactions to form their individual realities.

The term *social constructionism* is probably used more than symbolic interaction in social work; though again, they espouse the same ideas, and we will use the two terms interchangeably for the remainder of this discussion. *Social constructionism* better reflects the ideas of diversity that social workers support, and it fits well with recent discussions on postmodern theory and practice. You will probably find *social constructionism* used widely in the literature and practice to describe how social workers need to "deconstruct" the prevailing realities in social institutions and client thinking in order to initiate change. Social constructionism is valued by the social work profession because it provides a basis for **deconstruction**—the analysis of how one group's construction of reality has become the accepted reality, justifying and reinforcing that group's power over social values, beliefs, and institutions.

Once a group's reality becomes accepted by a majority, it acquires the power to shape subsequent beliefs, policies, behaviors, and other aspects of society. That reality becomes the "right" way to do things. One example of this process involves patriarchy and the norms, beliefs, and values about women's roles that it espouses. For instance, in a patriarchal society, men, in large part, exercise power and control over various forms of media such as music videos.

Men have the power and money to decide what types of stories and images are depicted in music videos, and they usually make decisions about these depictions based on what will sell, resulting in more money that men can use to perpetuate their power. Many music videos portray women as sex objects, with men manipulating women for their own pleasure. These images perpetuate the gender role stereotypes of women as sex objects. Because women have to overcome obstacles to breaking through these stereotypes and generating the type of money and power needed to control this form of media, the likelihood of producing and airing images that contradict typical patriarchal gender stereotypes is slim.

Social constructionism also offers social workers a framework in which to view humans as active beings who interact in a world full of meaningful objects. These objects can be things, people, behaviors, animate or inanimate symbols, and so on. All of these objects help members of a society find common ground that binds them together, help them make sense of the world, and help society to run more smoothly. By understanding how people make sense of their world, social workers can better understand how individual meaning, collectively, affects the way society—including its laws, norms, values, and social institutions—is developed and maintained through human interactions (Schaefer, 2001). These approaches are similar to the humanistic and existential approaches discussed in Chapter 3 in that they focus on clients and their interpretations of their situation. Clients are the experts on their situation and must articulate how they view their problems, a belief that is congruent with social work values and ethics.

George Herbert Mead   One of the founders of the interactionist perspective was George Herbert Mead. Mead's contribution to this perspective was the focus on the self. He saw the self as an active player in society that maintains the process of shaping experiences versus a mere structure that is acted upon, such as we saw in Freud's and others' theories (for example, self as ego). Because people are active, they can act toward themselves as well as others, which affects the ways in which they deal with the world. For example, people can use introspection to help guide their actions, make decisions, and place meaning on the outside world. In other words, people do not simply respond to their environment; rather, their "self" is constantly changing as it encounters new experiences and attaches meaning to them (Blumer, 1969; Mead, 1934, 1956).

Mead identified two types of interaction: nonsymbolic and symbolic.

Nonsymbolic interaction describes how people respond directly to the actions of others. For example, we respond to cues such as tone of voice, language, and hand gestures while we interact with others. **Symbolic interaction** refers to the ways in which we interpret these actions. For example, we can interpret another person's tone of voice as threatening or sarcastic, depending on the context in which the interaction takes place and the meaning that we assign to it. Similarly, we can perceive a pointing hand gesture as either informational or challenging. Both symbolic and nonsymbolic interactions play a part in the ongoing process of developing meaning and reality (Blumer, 1969; Mead, 1934, 1956).

Erving Goffman   Another major player in the development of the interactionist perspective, Erving Goffman espoused an interactionist method known as the **dramaturgical approach**, which likens everyday life to the drama of theater and stage. In other words, we go through our lives acting and projecting images that we want others to see. We have rules, rituals, and props, and we create settings to ensure that our interactions project an image that is important to us. All of these things help to define our environment and guarantee that behavior is predictable and that social order is maintained. Without them, we might not know how to react or interact with others in given situations (Goffman, 1959).

Charles Horton Cooley   Finally, the concept of the **looking-glass self**, coined by Charles Cooley (1902), is closely related to the ideas behind symbolic interactionism and social constructionism. The looking-glass self refers to the idea that we learn who we are through our interactions with others. We develop our sense of self through our social interactions and our impressions of how others view and perceive us. So our views of ourselves stem from our *perceptions* of what others think of us—which are not necessarily based in reality or fact. The process of self-identity development generally takes place in three phases: (1) we have a perception of how we present ourselves to others around us; (2) we then have a perception of how others evaluate us based on this presentation; and (3) we develop feelings about ourselves based on these perceived evaluations. For example, a young child may think she is a good big sister to her little brother because she helps feed and bathe him, but based on her parents' negative response to her "helpfulness"—for instance, their comments about how she is getting in the way, she develops a self-perception that she isn't a good big sister. However, this self-perception can change if she overhears her parents telling others that she is, indeed, a huge help with her little brother.

Applying Symbolic Interaction Theory

As with the previous sections on applying conflict and functionalist theories, this section provides a discussion on the application of symbolic interaction theory and its relevance to social work practice.

Body Piercing How might the symbolic interactionist perspective explain certain behaviors? Let us examine the practice of body piercing and tattooing. In previous decades, Western society generally defined piercing and tattooing as deviant (and in some contexts and groups, they still are). Therefore, in most contexts it was rare to see someone with a nose ring or tattoo. If someone with a tattoo were seen at an expensive, elite restaurant, for example, he would be viewed as going against social norms and might be asked to leave—at the very least people would stare at him. However, if this same person were observed on a Navy boat, he would be seen as fitting into the dominant culture of those who serve in the Navy.

This situation demonstrates how our interpretation of certain events, the contexts in which they occur, and the meanings we place on them influence our views of what is appropriate. Over time, as more and more people get tattoos and pierce different body parts, we are increasingly exposed to these practices and eventually come to accept them. Our interpretations of these behaviors change as we see that people other than sailors, in this case, engage in these types of behaviors. The meanings behind such practices change, our experiences and interactions with people who engage in these behaviors change, and the contexts for such behaviors change. This ongoing process continually shapes the norms, meanings, and acceptance level for such behavior in larger society.

Aisha's Case Revisited How might you view Aisha's case from this perspective? You would most likely focus on how Aisha perceives her situation and how her daily experiences help her to construct her reality. Her reality would include her relationships with her mother, family, and foster and adoptive families; her experiences in the Baptist and Catholic churches; and her perceptions of her new school and peers. You would pay particular attention to the meanings Aisha places on all of these elements and how these meanings might be contributing to her problems. Although symbolic interaction theory does not guide you in developing an intervention, assessing Aisha's situation from this perspective would give you some indication as to where Aisha believes her problems lie. This insight would then give you a place to begin intervention.

Critiquing Symbolic Interaction Theory

The last point in Aisha's situation suggests both a strength and a limitation of symbolic interaction theory. This perspective can help you assess and examine a client's situation, but it does not offer a clear intervention strategy. A major strength of symbolic interaction theory is that it provides an empowering way to examine clients' problems. More specifically, it empowers the client to guide the working relationship (versus the social worker guiding the process), and it focuses on the meanings that clients place on their experiences, lending validity to their points of view. Thus, it is also an ethical approach to work with clients. Moreover, this approach to assessment fits well with humanistic perspectives on working with clients, and it can easily be combined with other theories in practice.

At the same time, however, symbolic interaction theory is more micro focused, emphasizing individual experiences; whereas the conflict and functionalist approaches, which tend to be more macro focused, emphasize broader social factors that affect people. For this reason an interactionist focus might fail to take into account larger social forces that are impacting clients. Still, social workers who use the symbolic approach might think that the meanings that clients place on forces are more important than the forces themselves.

Another criticism is that the interactionist perspective lacks a solid, consistent theoretical base from which to examine relationships. In other words, the constructs that make up this approach can be vague and difficult to define, apply, and measure consistently across different contexts. However, many social workers and other professionals have used the philosophy behind interactionism to guide research methodology and to empower participants in research studies. In fact, social work researchers have increasingly conducted studies that employ deconstructive methods to explore perspectives of those on whom the research is focused. That is, the research aims to better understand the worldview of the participants, which guides the analysis and the application of the results. The research process includes deconstructing the dominant view of reality by exploring the perspectives of the research participants and reconstructing reality from different viewpoints.

Symbolic interaction theory focuses attention on individualistic thinking, which can be useful when trying to move beyond the majority mind-set. At the same time, the theory has been criticized for ignoring the power of majority group members to impose their construction of reality on the broader society. This criticism is highly relevant to social work because it cautions that any intervention that disregards the realities of the larger society might be ineffective.

FEMINIST THEORY

Although feminist theories are not inherently sociological, we will discuss them here because they are helpful in analyzing societal processes. Feminist thought can be applied to many different levels of social assessment, including those that examine psychological development, oppression and discrimination, and institutional structure and functioning. As its name suggests, feminist theory is based on the ideas of **feminism**, which can be defined as the advocacy of social, economic, and political equality between men and women. Many social workers take this definition a step further by applying it to all minority groups, advocating for equal rights in all arenas. Clearly, then, feminist theory provides an avenue for examining various personal and social issues as they relate to inequality, oppression, and disenfranchisement.

In reality, there is not a single feminist theory or founder (indeed, feminists can differ considerably on certain ideas), and feminist thinking is influenced by many different disciplines and theorists. Nevertheless, all feminist theories share certain basic tenets. Van Den Bergh and Cooper (1986) identify nine tenets that are fundamental to all feminist theories. Many of these tenets are similar to the philosophy behind social constructionism, and they question how reality as it is generally accepted in U.S. culture was established. These nine tenets are listed in Box 4.1. As you review them, consider how you could apply them to social work practice.

As noted at the beginning of this section, no one is recognized as the founder of feminism, but many influential people have contributed to feminist theory and have been instrumental in promoting its ideas well into the 21st century. During the Enlightenment period of the 18th century, women like Mary Wollstonecraft, Judith Sargent Murray, and Abigail Adams played key roles in espousing the idea, which was radical for its time, that women are equal to men. Later, other women like Sarah Grimké, Margaret Fuller, Harriet Taylor Mill, and Simone de Beauvoir contributed to the analysis of social inequality and promoted views that laid the foundation for more recent feminist thinkers. Simone de Beauvoir's book *The Second Sex* (1949) articulated theoretical views that closely resembled those discussed in symbolic interactionism but reflected a very different and pointedly female perspective. For example, she asserted that the ideas of "self" have been written and exemplified by males and that historically males did the acting, thereby creating the majority reality (Donovan, 1994). As another example, you will see in Chapter 9 that Carol Gilligan responded to Lawrence Kohlberg's male-oriented theory of moral development by constructing her own theory concerning different—yet equally valid—moral development. There is a rich history behind the development of feminism, and feminist thought has encouraged many lines of thinking and theories that continue to influence social work.

Branches of Feminist Theory

As mentioned earlier, several branches of feminist thought exist. These perspectives differ in their views on equality and social change, which affect social work in different ways. One main branch is **liberal feminism**, which was the first to support the ideas of equal rights and equal treatment for women. Liberal feminism developed during the 18th century, when women like Mary Wollstonecraft demanded that such Enlightenment principles as equality and self-determination be applied to women. Like their historical counterparts, contemporary liberal feminists believe that biological differences between men and women are not important, and they fight to achieve equal rights for women in all social realms, including politics, economics, and education. Social workers who support this ideology can pursue equality on a macro level by advocating for policies and laws designed to change the structure of society. On a micro level, they can educate or empower clients to fight for their rights.

- *Challenge false dichotomies:* This tenet asks us to challenge the social practice of creating mutually exclusive categories (dichotomies) to describe various behaviors and characteristics, which in turn create expectations for behavior and characteristics. For example, Western society places much emphasis on the differences between men and women, rich and poor, and young and old. These categories prescribe behaviors for those who fit into a particular category.

- *Rethink established knowledge:* This tenet asks us to reevaluate and critically analyze what we know, how we know it, and where this knowledge comes from. As an illustration of this point, consider that until recently, research topics and methods excluded issues that are particularly important to and beneficial to women and ethnic minorities.

- *Examine different patterns of socialization:* A third premise involves examining the differences between men and women based on differing socialization and experiences. Men and women adhere to different gender roles and expectations, which ultimately influence behaviors and development.

- *Deconstruct patriarchal hierarchies:* This premise relates to examining patriarchy as it exists in society and influences the experiences of people. By implementing this strategy, feminist theory challenges the power and domination by men over women in all social institutions.

- *Increase opportunities for empowerment:* This tenet focuses on ways in which women can be empowered to instigate social change. For instance, empowerment might come through women's active involvement in policy development and implementation that concerns reproductive rights, which places more control over women's bodies in women's hands. This involvement ultimately gives women more control over health care procedures such as birth control and childbirth, which can directly affect women's and children's physical, economic, and emotional well-being.

- *Value process orientation:* Feminism often focuses on the different ways in which men and women work and think. Women tend to be more process oriented, which refers to the ways in which people interact and relate to one another when they work on and solve problems. Conversely, men tend to be more product oriented, which places emphasis on the end result of the problem-solving process. In Western society, product is often valued more than the process through which the product is made.

- *Understand that the personal is political:* This tenet reflects the belief that all personal behaviors are influenced by political actions; what we might traditionally classify as the personal realm can also be political. For example, a woman's decision to become pregnant is influenced by health care and other policies that will affect her during and after her pregnancy.

- *Respect diversity:* Feminist theories emphasize the need to maintain solidarity while simultaneously respecting individual differences. Women, especially, need to find common ground to effect change without losing individual diversity in the process.

- *Promote awareness of interactions between the individual and social forces:* A final tenet relates to promoting awareness of the larger social forces that affect women and their personal and social lives. Once awareness is raised, change can take place.

BOX 4.1

Fundamental Tenets of Feminist Theory

Another branch of feminist thought, **socialist feminism**, charges conservative viewpoints with undermining social change and supporting the unequal status quo, and it criticizes liberalism as being too focused on politics. The socialist perspective views economic equality as paramount to true equality and freedom for women. Perpetuation of traditional societal values and the right to vote are not sufficient to truly promote equality. Social workers who support socialist feminism focus on economic justice and equality. For example, they may work with international agencies to help communities establish self-sustaining economic systems.

A third branch is **radical feminism**, which argues that oppression and inequality are supported through male hierarchy and domination. A basic tenet of radical feminism is that men construct reality for all of society. Not surprisingly, this reality includes the notion that men are superior, forceful, aggressive, and intellectual, whereas women are weak, emotional, and irrational. To challenge these stereotypes, radical feminism espouses the idea that dominant values should be reestablished to include the realities of women (Hunter College Women's Studies Collective, 1995). A social worker using a radical feminist perspective might help clients to gain insight into traditional values and social systems, thereby empowering them to reframe their reality and change their situation.

Applying and Critiquing Feminist Theory

As Aisha's social worker, there are several different ways that you could conceptualize her situation from the feminist perspective. The particular strategy that you adopt will depend, of course, on which branch of feminism you choose to apply. In general, though, you would begin by analyzing how systems (family, foster care, adoption, education, and religion) are perpetuating inequality, and therefore problems, for Aisha. You may want to deconstruct dominant social values regarding what is "appropriate" for Aisha in order to gain a better understanding of what Aisha wants in her life. Going further, you might need to advocate for Aisha in negotiating various systems to ensure that her welfare, as she sees it, is addressed. Even though Aisha is young, respecting her wishes is essential. Finally, as Aisha matures and becomes independent, you may help her to become her own advocate as a female and ethnic minority.

Among the obvious strengths of feminist theory are its focus on equality and its questioning of the dominant structure. These strengths uphold the basic ethical tenets of the social work profession. Although feminist theories focus primarily on inequality between the sexes, many social workers use these theories to examine inequality for other groups. This last point is significant because some critics have charged feminist theory with focusing exclusively on women and thereby ignoring the plight of other minority groups. Going further, some critics contend that this exclusive focus on women actually perpetuates the oppression of women by highlighting their special circumstances, thereby making them "separate" from men and suggesting that they require special treatment. However, more recent research using feminist perspectives has applied its tenets to the general study of oppression for many disenfranchised groups.

Regardless of a person's standpoint on the appropriate focus for feminist theory, this perspective clearly has drawn attention not only to predominant cultural values and structures but also to the ways in which we generate knowledge. Many social workers and scholars in other disciplines have relied on feminist theory to guide their research. One result of this process has been the creation of a body of literature that is qualitatively different from past work.

Feminist theory has validated the use of alternative research methods such as inductive reasoning, employment of qualitative methods, the equal treatment of research participants (for example, they are often called "co-investigators" in this type of research), and the ways in which results are interpreted and applied. Further, feminist theory has played a major role in raising awareness of multiple points of view on issues. As with symbolic interactionism, feminist theory teaches that people construct their own realities. In the case of women and other minority groups, this reality is often based on history and past experiences of discrimination and oppression.

CULTURAL PERSPECTIVES

Although no single theory explains culture and its effects on human behavior—in fact, there is no universally accepted definition of culture—we need to consider cultural theories, particularly in the context of social work. Ideas, concepts, and applications of culture are inextricably linked with social aspects that affect clients. Of all the disciplines, social work is probably the most concerned with understanding the complexities of culture, especially when working with people.

So far in this book, I have talked a lot about culture, but what does that term mean? What do you think of when you think of your culture? Culture can mean different things to different people. In fact, definitions vary depending on the discipline and theory from which they originate. Even within the field of social work, the meaning of culture will differ depending on the context, problem, client, and social worker.

Defining Culture

From a sociological standpoint, **culture** is the result of all human endeavors. Culture can be viewed as including all things human such as norms, values, customs, symbols, thoughts, traditions, politics, religions, languages, philosophies, and material objects (Barker, 2003; Turner, 1998). Culture consists of both external and internal components. External components are things that can be observed or quantified, such as behaviors, products, artifacts, and other tangible objects. In contrast, internal components are not readily observable. Examples are ideas,

EXHIBIT 4.1

Cultural perspectives are important to effective social work practice

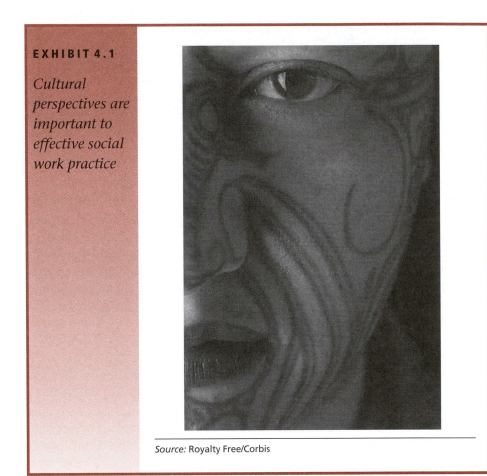

Source: Royalty Free/Corbis

interpretations, perceptions, and the meanings that people attach to the external components. Culture, then, is created through experiences, but it also helps to give structure to the experiences. This is a dynamic process that continually develops and changes as the experiences of people in a society change. Even the meaning of the word *culture* changes over time.

Over the years, social work has developed theories and models of culture and its effects on behavior as well as incorporated many ideas and terms from models coming out of related disciplines. Box 4.2 highlights several terms that are important to social work practice. These terms all help to define the essence of culture and the various ways in which culture affects people in their environment. Some of these terms, such as ethnicity and social class, can help social workers understand how society perceives clients, however biased this view might be. Other concepts, including ideology, ethnic identity, and worldview, can provide insight into how clients view themselves relative to their culture. These terms refer to the cultural construction of a client's reality. Without this knowledge, it would be difficult for a

- *Cultural relativism:* The idea that different cultures should be treated equally; cultures cannot be ranked based on which is better or superior.
- *Ethnic identity:* How people form their identity in relation to their ethnicity.
- *Ethnicity:* How people associate themselves with a group through the use of aspects such as values, traditions, customs, language, and religion.
- *Ethnocentrism:* The belief that one culture is superior to others and that culture serves as the norm by which others should be judged.
- *Ethos:* The moral, ethical, and aesthetic tone of a person's life; the emotional aspect of the worldview.
- *Ideology:* One's dominant ideas about what is correct and how things should be.
- *Social class:* A category for groups of people who share similar economic stratification.
- *Worldview:* The way in which people perceive their world that gives them a frame of reference; a personal philosophy about how things are and the way things should be.

BOX 4.2

Cultural Concepts in Social Work Practice

social worker to understand a client's experience in the context of her or his immediate and larger community environment. Consequently, any intervention that the social worker develops will be ill informed at best and harmful at worst.

The concept of ethnocentrism helps to explain how a dominant ideology can perpetuate cultural values that help or hinder clients. Understanding the effects of ethnocentrism can help social workers to grasp how clients may view their own culture as superior, which can create problems for clients in interfacing with other cultures, particularly if their culture is not the dominant one. Maintaining a sense of cultural relativism can assist social workers in their assessment of all of the potential cultural variables that come into play when working with clients. Beyond simply recognizing that different cultures cannot be ranked as superior or inferior to other cultures, social workers can better understand that each client will bring her or his own reality to the working relationship, which will contribute to the qualities of the client, the client's problems, and her or his approach to solutions. All of these ideas come into play when you actually work with clients. They are also critical to understanding the issues of racism, discrimination, and oppression, which are discussed in the next chapter.

Cultural Perspectives and Social Work

To be effective practitioners, social workers must understand how a client's culture affects the client's behavior, perceptions, and life. To achieve this understanding, social workers must recognize how values, beliefs, philosophies, experiences, and social structures vary from one society to another. They should be able to separate stereotypes that define cultures and the people who live within them from individual client realities. Clients are more than the culture with which they identify. Thus, social workers need to be skilled at identifying how people function as active agents within their culture. They must realize that clients are both recipients and shapers of culture and that both of these roles impact their clients' behaviors.

According to the National Association of Social Workers (NASW) *Code of Ethics* (approved 1996; revised, 2008), social workers should

> understand culture and its function in human behavior and society, recognizing the strengths that exist in all cultures, . . . demonstrate competence in the provision of services that are sensitive to clients' culture and to differences among people and cultural groups, [and] obtain education about and seek to understand the nature of social diversity and oppression with respect to race, ethnicity, national origin, color, sex, sexual orientation, gender identity or expression, age, marital status, political belief, religion, immigrant status, and mental or physical disability. (p. 9)

Further, in 2001, NASW approved 10 standards for culturally competent social work practice that include: recognizing how personal and professional values impact work with culturally diverse clients; continually developing knowledge around cultural diversity; using culturally appropriate methods in work with clients; being knowledgeable about culturally appropriate services for clients; understanding how policies and programs affect culturally diverse clients; supporting efforts that advocate for professional diversity in social work education and practice; working toward eliminating service barriers for culturally diverse clients; and providing leadership in cultural competence for the profession (NASW, 2001).

These standards define social workers' responsibilities to become culturally competent with clients and familiar with the broad, complex definition of *culture* held by the profession.

To capture this complexity, social workers often use the term **multiculturalism**, which refers to the idea that all cultures should be recognized, respected, and treated equally. Similarly, **cultural pluralism** refers to the recognition and accommodation of a variety of cultures that have different values and norms. Often social workers focus on multiculturalism as it applies to groups who are at risk of marginalization and oppression (Fellin, 2000). This last reference probably best defines how the concepts of culture and multiculturalism are currently used in social work, as is reflected in the quotation from the *Code of Ethics*.

In addition to cultural concepts and terms that social workers use in practice, several perspectives help social workers think about cultural diversity in the context of human development. For example, the **dual perspective** (Norton, 1978) gives context to the ways in which people from minority groups experience different systems throughout development and how these experiences impact development. The primary or *nurturing system* consists of people and circumstances close to an individual—for example, immediate and extended family and local environments with which the individual is connected (e.g., church, the neighborhood, etc.). The *sustaining system* consists of larger systems that impact an individual, such as political and economic dynamics and educational and social service systems. According to the dual perspective, culturally relevant values, beliefs, customs, and behaviors are instilled in individuals within the nurturing system. As individuals grow and increasingly interact with sustaining systems, they may find that the values of their nurturing system clash with those of the sustaining system and are devalued by the sustaining system. This is when members of minority groups may experience racism, prejudice, and discrimination. Further, conflicts in values between the two systems may cause developmental problems, such as low self-esteem, for members of minority groups.

Other perspectives and models that address acculturation, socialization, and identity development also help social workers conceptualize how members of minority groups may experience development differently than the majority group. For example, the concept of bicultural socialization refers to the idea that members of minority groups not only receive extensive enculturation and socialization from their cultural group (e.g., through language, customs, and traditions), but they also receive socialization from the majority culture. Models of bicultural socialization (Chau, 1991; de Anda, 1984; Lum, 1995; Robbins, 1984) help to explain developmental tasks (e.g., formation of self-esteem and identity) for minority group members as well as some of the bicultural tensions that may exist between two cultures of which a person is a member. Within the process of bicultural socialization, some people may develop coping skills that allow them to effectively function in the context of two cultures while others may experience problems that negatively affect their development. Viewing development from these perspectives helps social workers conceptualize issues from a more culturally competent standpoint. For instance, these perspectives make it less likely that social workers will view client problems from a dominant group ideology, blaming clients for "lacking" the ability to adapt to the majority culture or somehow being "deficient" because clients haven't adopted larger cultural values. Thus, social workers can use these perspectives to conceptualize development within a cultural context, making assessment and intervention techniques with minority clients more effective and culturally appropriate.

Applying and Critiquing Cultural Perspectives

In Aisha's case, there are many cultural factors that you will need to consider. Recall from Chapter 2 that cultural factors can be placed into macro, mezzo, and micro levels. In Aisha's case, some of the macro issues involve the ideology and ethos of the social institutions with which she is involved. These are reflected in the policies and procedures of the foster care and adoption agencies working with Aisha and her family. On a mezzo level, you need to consider these aspects in relation to Aisha's school and church as well as her peers and her two family structures. On the micro level, you need to explore Aisha's worldview and her construction of her cultural reality. All of these cultural factors interact to create the dynamics unique to Aisha's situation.

You also need to be aware of ethnocentrism and other cultural dynamics that could be creating problems for Aisha. For example, the adoption agency could be operating from the value that family is crucial to the well-being of children, regardless of whether that family is ethnically similar to the child being placed. From Aisha's perspective, similar ethnic background may be more important to her well-being than belonging to an intact family.

As another example, Western society tends to view poverty as a culture, which places responsibility onto the people who are living in poverty. This perspective, termed the **culture of poverty**, argues that poor people's worldviews and ethos work toward maintaining them in poverty. Poor people develop an identity that is congruent with those who live in poverty, which makes it difficult for them to move up the economic ladder. For example, a cultural view on poverty posits that poor people pass on from generation to generation characteristics of laziness and a poor work ethic, which validates the reliance on public assistance. Children learn from their parents that laziness is a way of life, as is receiving food stamps every month; children never gain the motivation to work their way out of poverty. However, in attributing poverty to people's cultural values, the culture of poverty perspective denies that societal forces and dominant culture play a significant role in perpetuating poverty.

In conclusion, then, as Aisha's social worker, you need to assess many cultural factors on many levels. The outcomes of this assessment will help guide you in developing an intervention that addresses cultural issues that are creating problems for Aisha.

Obviously, developing methods to articulate, organize, and understand cultural elements is important to social work. A natural strength of cultural conceptualization is that it offers tools to help social workers incorporate the conceptualizations into the assessment process, which enhances their understanding of clients and clients' situations. Viewing clients in the context of their culture ensures that social workers will grasp some, if not all, of the complexities in their clients' lives and reduces the risk of working with clients from an ethnocentric perspective. They will be better able to empower clients and advocate for larger social change. Though cultural perspectives do not necessarily inform intervention directly, when they are combined with other theories, they contribute to more powerful and effective interventions.

On the negative side is the absence of a single, coherent theory of culture. Instead, there is a collection of ideas and definitions of culture from many disciplines. As a result, the application of cultural perspectives to social work is difficult to define, apply, and measure. For example, determining whether interventions are as effective as they could be, as well as whether social workers are including all relevant aspects of culture, is difficult. How do social workers know if they are applying cultural relativism to their clients? Can they be sure they are not responding ethno-centrically to certain situations? Can they truly understand their clients' world-views? There is still much work to be done to further develop and define culture and its place within the social work profession.

CONCLUSION

In this chapter, we have looked at many sociological theories and perspectives that relate to social work practice. To review and compare them, look back at Table 4.1. Sociological theory focuses on broad aspects of society and how these affect human behavior. Many of these theories and perspectives help social workers to think about clients' problems from a broad perspective and to develop interventions that will target issues on a macro level. As you have seen in previous chapters, this macro focus can be helpful because it takes the focus off the individual, which tends to be the emphasis of biopsychosocial approaches. In essence, sociological theories and perspectives offer social workers a balanced approach to their work.

All of the theories, models, approaches, and perspectives discussed thus far in this book have applications to issues of social and economic justice, but sociological theories and perspectives are especially useful for supporting the ideas espoused in the *Code of Ethics*. For instance, societal causes of oppression and discrimination are more fully explained by sociological models than by micro or mezzo approaches, and these models help guide social work interventions on a macro level where problems of oppression and discrimination can be eradicated. Moreover, socio-logical models allow social workers to think more comprehensively, including in their assessments and interventions cultural and ethnic issues that can affect and perpetuate client problems.

MAIN POINTS

- The sociological imagination is a term coined by C. Wright Mills to describe the relationship between the individual and wider society.

- Conflict theory, which can be traced to Karl Marx but has had many more contributions all the way into the 1970s, views social behavior from the perspective of conflict or tension among two or more groups. Although it fits well with the underlying values and ethics of social work, it often does not offer practical interventions.

- Functionalist theory—through the use of manifest and latent functions—explains how aspects of society work together to maintain stability. Social workers can use functionalist theory to explain how social institutions maintain order in clients' lives.

- Symbolic interaction, which is similar to social constructionism, describes the unique ways in which people and systems interact and communicate with one another as well as the essence and characteristics of that interaction and communication. Social constructionism better reflects ideas of diversity that social workers espouse and helps explain how one group's construction of reality can become accepted reality.

- Feminist theory is based on the ideas of feminism and provides an avenue for examining various personal and social issues as they relate to inequality, oppression, and disenfranchisement. Several branches of feminism guide social work in different ways with regard to how equality and social change are viewed.

- Culture involves the "complex pattern of living that directs human social life, the things each new generation must learn and to which eventually they may add" (Stark, 1998, p. 36). According to the National Association of Social Workers *Code of Ethics*, social workers should strive to be culturally competent practitioners.

EXERCISES

1. Using the Sanchez Family interactive case (go to www.routledgesw.com/cases), review the Sanchez family and the issues facing each member and the family as a whole. Using the theories presented in this chapter, answer the following questions:
   a. How might the Sanchez family's problems be explained through conflict theory? Give specific examples.
   b. How might some of the problems experienced by the family and individual members be explained through symbolic interaction theory?
   c. How might culture be defined for the Sanchez family? What aspects might you want to take into consideration when trying to understand this family's culture?
   d. In what ways might a cultural perspective be applied when working with this family?
2. Review the Carla Washburn interactive case (go to www.routledgesw.com/cases), and reacquaint yourself with her situation. Review the concepts discussed in the chapter on culture and in Box 4.2, then answer the following questions:
   a. What elements presented in Box 4.2 might be important to consider in Carla's case and why?
   b. In what ways might Carla's culture help or hinder her situation?
   c. How could you use Carla's culture to help guide your assessment and intervention with her problems?

Lenses for Conceptualizing Problems and Interventions: Social Change Dimensions

In a western state, there is a small, rural town with a population of about 200. It is surrounded by larger towns that offer some variety in banks, grocery stores, clothes shops, entertainment, and other services, but the closest one is 20 miles away. The town itself does not have a bank, school, or large grocery store. Instead, it has only a small post office and a very small convenience store where items are limited and expensive. The town's population consists mostly of Hispanic/Latino elderly individuals and young families who work at nearby farms or mills or who commute at least 50 miles to towns with more industry. Children must take a bus into the next town to go to school, a trip that usually takes more than an hour each way because it picks up students whose homes are spread out geographically. Many teens in this town have problems with unintended pregnancy, alcohol and drug abuse, and a lack of recreation and other opportunities. In fact, the suicide rate among the young people is higher than the state and national average. The school that the children attend lacks money, qualified teachers, good programs, and a competitive curriculum that will help its students get into college or land well-paying jobs. In fact, the school has a graduation rate of 70 percent. Many students drop out of high school to help their families run the farms, so they never escape the poverty that has characterized past generations. Public transportation is nonexistent, and there is a lack of social services, including those that address domestic violence, which is a problem for many families. The town has been unable to secure resources or services, primarily because of a lack of leadership. Residents are not well represented in the state legislature, and they struggle to get their concerns heard by policy-makers. The sheriff, who is also the mayor, has tried a few times to rally the townspeople to confront their problems, but he has been unsuccessful. He lacks the necessary knowledge and skills to help people with their problems or to initiate change for the community. He has been referred to a social worker in a nearby town to express his concerns and to enlist her help in solving the town's problems.

———————————————————————————————————

THIS SCENARIO IS A COMMON ONE AND COULD REPRESENT MANY rural towns in the United States. Many social workers are interested primarily in working with individuals, but as this situation brings to light, many individual problems are the result of or are aggravated by larger social problems. If a social worker were to intervene with an individual or family from this small town, she or he would quickly find that skills in macro assessment and intervention would be necessary.

This chapter discusses some of the models used in social work to conceptualize and address macro-oriented issues that affect clients. Although not an exhaustive discussion, it examines several fundamental perspectives that are frequently used in the field and that can be combined with other theoretical approaches. These perspectives deal with such broad categories as ethnicity, oppression, social change, community organization, and social and economic justice.

As you will see, many of the concepts discussed in this chapter are interrelated. For example, when social workers speak of justice, they are also frequently referring to social change and the instigation of some kind of action that will lead to social and economic justice. Social change and action are also closely related to community development. Despite such overlaps, we will look at each concept separately to focus on its unique attributes. Keep in mind, though, that in many ways these concepts are inextricably linked in social work practice. We begin by examining prominent theories that focus on the macro-level forces of race, discrimination, and oppression. As in previous chapters, Table 5.1 compares and contrasts the theories discussed in this chapter.

THEORIES OF RACISM, DISCRIMINATION, AND OPPRESSION

Race, as a contemporary term, refers to biological differences among groups of people. The term was developed in the 18th century to describe blood lineage and then to differentiate among people and groups based on skin color and other visible, physical characteristics. With the growth of biology and science in the 19th century, race became associated with biological factors and evolution. Race as a biological construct became the basis on which to judge people's social status and to classify members of certain races as superior to other races. Members of one group of people who deemed certain racial characteristics objectionable used these characteristics to justify separating themselves from those groups who possessed them (Payne, 1997).

Currently, there is ongoing debate regarding the question of whether race is a socially constructed, rather than a biological, category (Goodman, 2000; Harris & Sim, 2002; Kim, 2004; Shih & Sanchez, 2009). Traditional thinkers argue that race

TABLE 5.1
Characteristics of Theories and Perspectives on Social Change

	RACISM, DISCRIMINATION, AND OPPRESSION	SOCIAL & ECONOMIC JUSTICE	SOCIAL CHANGE & ACTION	COMMUNITY ORGANIZATION
Type	Theories	Perspectives	Perspectives	Theories
Focus	Individual & environment, depending on the theory	Society	Society & the individual	Society & community members
Assumptions	Varied: Some view behavior as influenced by psychological factors; others view behavior as influenced by external forces.	Varied: Some view society as "owing" its members; others view social institutions as having limited roles in providing resources to members.	Varied: Some view interactions among people as important instigators of change; others view external sources as important factors in change.	Varied: Some view community members as key change agents; others view "experts" outside of community realms as key change agents.
Strengths	• Concepts are useful for effective and ethical practice. • Considering factors of diversity, such as race, as socially constructed concepts can be useful in understanding and working toward ending oppression.	• Concepts are powerful tools for social change, which is a central charge of the social work profession. • Concepts fit well with other theories used in social work.	• Can provide a useful way to assess problems and guide intervention. • Constructs are amenable to empirical testing. • Can be combined with other theoretical approaches.	• Can provide useful tools for assessing and intervening with community problems. • Constructs are amenable to development and empirical testing. • Can help to predict behavior of communities.
Limitations	• No single theory on racism, discrimination, or oppression exists, making clear explanations of problems difficult. • Because there are a wide range of constructs behind theories, and many theories are not well developed, it is difficult to empirically test constructs and predict behavior.	• No clear organization of concepts, which makes articulating common definitions among practitioners difficult. • Lack of clear definitions in and among perspectives makes empirical testing of perspectives difficult. • Cannot predict behavior.	• Because theories are used in different disciplines and contexts, a consensus on the definition of constructs is difficult.	• Increased numbers of theoretical perspectives have created problems with definitions and applications of constructs. • Number of theories can make comparison of approaches difficult.

defines groups of people who, after many generations of living together or in close proximity, have developed a common gene pool. Over time, these people breed and pass on to their children unique genetic patterns that identify them as a race. In contrast, contemporary thinkers posit that true biological differences among groups do not exist. Though groups of people often live together and breed among them-selves, creating generations of people who share biological characteristics, this does not mean that they have created a unique race that is quantitatively and qualitatively different from others who do not live in the same area. This line of thinking supports the notion that groups of people, even those who have been geographically separated from others over time, still share a basic genetic com-position that makes all groups more similar to one another than different.

Some critics of biological theories of race go even further, arguing that historically, groups of people have intermixed more than they have remained separate, creating an even more complex and diverse genetic lineage. To them, race as a biological phenomenon is an idea that has been constructed by society to justify separating and treating groups differently based on certain characteristics. More specifically, the concept of race as a biological category is reinforced by societal institutions through ideologies and policies that segregate people based on skin color and other distinguishing physical characteristics (Fong, Spickard, & Ewalt, 1995; Montague, 1964). As one example, census forms ask people to designate their race, and this information is used to make funding and program decisions.

Regardless of whether true biological distinctions among groups exist, there are many political and social ramifications associated with race. We still use race in many social contexts: It holds personal meaning for us, we base assumptions about people on it, and we rely on it to make social policy and other decisions. Though it can mean different things to different people, and different groups use it for different purposes, it is still a powerful concept in U.S. society. For this reason, understanding the origins of the term as well as its implications for individuals and for society as a whole is particularly important for social workers.

Racism

One reason why understanding race is so important is because it leads to the potential for racism. **Racism** involves stereotyping people based on their race. Stereotypes tend to be negative (though sometimes they can be positive), and they are generalized to all people in a racial category (Barker, 2003). More specifically, racism refers to sociological and other ideological processes that promote dif-ferential treatment of racial and ethnic groups in interpersonal and institutional interactions (Payne, 1997).

When applying the concept to social work practice, you can think of racism as it occurs on different levels. In some cases racism manifests itself on the micro, or individual, level. **Individual racism** refers to personal or one-on-one actions between two or more people. It involves the negative attitudes and beliefs that people hold about persons from other groups that usually result in actions such as name-calling, ostracizing, or even the violence played out in hate crimes. Because individual racism occurs on a personal level, it is often overt, which makes intervention relatively straightforward. For example, a social worker who hears one child call another child a derogatory name can step in and talk with them about the ramifications of such actions. In more extreme cases, such as in hate crimes, individuals committing the crimes are often caught and brought to trial. Even though racism on this level can be devastating, it is often easier to deal with than more subtle types of racism, which are described next.

On a broader, macro level, social workers often deal with **institutional racism**. This type of racism describes actions that occur in social institutions and, more generally, attitudes that are reflected in the larger society. Examples of institutional racism are policies, programs, and procedures in social institutions (for example, legal, economic, political, and educational realms) that systematically benefit members of certain racial groups more than others. These acts and policies tend to be embedded in various social systems. They are pervasive and persistent ways of functioning in institutions, which can make them difficult to identify and to change, even when they are illegal (Barker, 2003).

One example of institutional racism involves the ways in which African Americans are consistently treated differently by the criminal justice system. Because of stereotyping and poor training, racial profiling by police is an issue in many communities. Some police officers are more likely to stop and arrest African Americans than people from other ethnic groups. Consequently, African Americans tend to be overrepresented in the criminal justice system and are therefore more likely to have criminal records. Because a criminal background can restrict people's employment and other opportunities, this process can contribute to higher rates of unemployment and, ultimately, poverty. Further, many African Americans cannot afford good legal representation, which perpetuates their overrepresentation in the criminal justice system, including their presence on death row. It is this pervasive, consistent process of bias that characterizes institutional racism.

In general, cases of institutional racism present greater challenges for social work intervention than individual acts because transforming an entire system is more difficult than modifying individual behavior. Moreover, as mentioned earlier, institutional forms of racism are often covert and difficult to expose, making them difficult to eradicate.

Discrimination and Prejudice

Two issues with which social workers are concerned that are closely related to racism are discrimination and prejudice. **Discrimination** is the "prejudgment and negative treatment of people based on identifiable characteristics such as race, gender, religion, or ethnicity" (Barker, 2003, p. 123). Discrimination thus involves treating individuals or groups differently based on preconceived notions about them. This treatment is usually intended to create some type of disadvantage for that individual or group (Newman, 1973).

In contrast, **prejudice** tends to be more of a cognitive process than a behavioral one. That is, prejudice refers to the attitudes, beliefs, and stereotypes that a person holds about others. It involves making prejudgments about people based on preconceived ideas about characteristics of certain groups. Although prejudice can be positive or negative (for example, we can hold positive stereotypes about our own group and negative stereotypes about dissimilar groups), prejudice is usually discussed in terms of negative views that we hold about others who have characteristics different from our own.

These prejudices tend to be reinforced by the belief that groups who possess different characteristics also possess different values, morals, skills, and so on (Newman, 1973). For example, a Caucasian person may believe that a person who looks Mexican is lazy and one who looks Asian is industrious. Moreover, if the Caucasian person identifies with industriousness, she is also more likely to see the Asian person in a positive light because she perceives the value of industriousness to be similar to her own, whether or not it actually is.

Once you understand the concepts of discrimination and prejudice, you can examine the interplay between the two. For example, if an individual is prejudiced toward another person, will these attitudes lead to a discriminatory act? The answer is maybe, but maybe not. Not everyone acts upon her or his thoughts or beliefs, especially because many discriminatory acts are illegal; but these beliefs may still be evident in subtle ways. Therefore, it is possible for prejudice to exist in the absence of discrimination. However, some people argue that the opposite condition cannot exist; that is, an act of discrimination means that prejudice must be present. Why, they ask, would an individual discriminate if he did not hold preconceived ideas about the person or group against whom he is discriminating? In this sense, then, prejudice constitutes the thought and discrimination constitutes the act.

Regardless of your views on the relationship between prejudice and discrimination, you need to understand these concepts. Not only do social workers concern themselves with these issues, but they must also be cognizant of how these issues are related to other *isms* such as racism, sexism, ageism, and others that will be discussed in later chapters. Discrimination and prejudice are at the heart of all the isms that social workers encounter.

Theories of Prejudice   As with other phenomena that social workers confront, there is not a single explanation for prejudice. Rather, several theories attempt to explain where prejudice comes from, how it is generated, and how and why it occurs; most of these theories are borrowed and adapted from different disciplinary theories and perspectives. Box 5.1 offers a brief overview of several of these theories.

As you can see from the box, all but two of the explanations—"history" and "competition and exploitation"—describe prejudice from an individualistic

BOX 5.1

Theoretical Conceptualizations for the Origins of Prejudice

- *Authoritarianism:* Rigid, inflexible, conformist, and loyal following of authority figures, which is more likely to lead to discrimination and oppression of others.

- *Belief in the one true religion:* The belief that a particular religion is "correct," which leads to feelings of superiority and the condemnation of others who believe otherwise.

- *Competition and exploitation:* The idea that competitive society creates conditions in which some groups perceive themselves to be superior, leading to the exploitation of inferior groups.

- *Frustration-aggression:* A process by which frustration and anger about a situation are directed at another person or group perceived as a scapegoat.

- *History:* The view that historical occurrences of oppression have consequences for the way in which members of oppressed groups are viewed. For example, African Americans might be viewed as inferior because of their past enslavement.

- *Projection:* A Freudian defense mechanism that results in one person's placing undesirable personal characteristics onto another.

- *Socialization:* The process through which we learn to value some characteristics, ideas, and behavior more than others, leading to prejudice.

Source: Adapted from Freud, 1914; Marx, 1994.

standpoint. These concepts focus on the ways in which individuals learn to value certain characteristics more than others, to develop stereotypes about groups whose characteristics are different from theirs, and, ultimately, to discriminate against others based on prejudgments about them.

For example, projection, in combination with socialization, can help to explain why a self-identified heterosexual man might possess prejudiced attitudes toward homosexual men. U.S. society tends to instill in young boys the characteristics of being male (for example, toughness, aggressiveness, controlled expressions of emotion). Boys who subscribe to these characteristics may learn to view those who do not possess these characteristics as "unmanly," inferior, and "gay," which in and of itself could lead to discrimination. However, at some point in his life, the heterosexual man may discover that he possesses some of the very characteristics that he has been socialized to despise (for example, femininity, emotionality). This realization can lead to anxiety, which may cause him to "project" the unwanted characteristics he sees in himself onto others who are perceived to display them (that is, gay and heterosexual men who have feminine characteristics—they would all be considered "gay" by this particular man). In an extreme case, the heterosexual man may lash out at a man who has feminine characteristics, thereby relieving his anxiety and confirming his "manliness" because he has physically assaulted (a socially acceptable manly expression) a man who does not possess traditional masculine characteristics. Although men, regardless of their sexuality, display a range of feminine and masculine traits, in this scenario those who display feminine characteristics are likely to be targets of discrimination or abuse and be called "gay" because they deviate from the traditional norm of masculine behavior.

Frustration-aggression may work in similar ways, although an individual may lash out at another person for reasons more external to the self than those causing projection. As an example, when economic times become difficult, some groups (those who have some power and status) blame other groups (those who do not have much power or status) for "taking all the jobs," even though those jobs are probably minimum-wage jobs that the more powerful groups would not take under normal (or even extreme) circumstances. However, the more powerful group uses the less powerful one as a scapegoat for their economic woes. The less powerful group is often unable to fight back when accused of stealing jobs, so it constitutes an easy target. The more powerful group is less likely to blame an even more powerful group, like the government or wealthy corporations, for their problems because they are not likely to get very far, even though the government or corporations are probably more responsible for the poor economy and lack of jobs than the less powerful group.

Prejudice and Social Work   Social workers should approach prejudice from several different perspectives, because many of these perspectives can provide insight into clients' problems and situations. For example, some clients may exhibit personality traits that leave them susceptible to projection or authoritarianism, which can contribute to prejudicial attitudes about others. In this case, social workers need to explore these possibilities in some detail before concluding that the client's personality is to "blame" for prejudicial attitudes. Other clients may be a "product" of their social environment in which they unquestioningly subscribe to the values and beliefs of those around them. For still other clients, a combination of personal and social factors might interact in such a way that they develop prejudicial attitudes toward certain groups. In other words, even though you have some ways of explaining how prejudice develops, there is no single concrete or certain explanation, which means that you must use caution when designing interventions to deal with prejudice.

Oppression

A concept related to prejudice, **oppression** can be difficult to define. Its root word, *press*, means to mold, flatten, reduce, or immobilize something (Frye, 1983, as cited in Brittan & Maynard, 1984). Barker (2003) describes oppression as "the social act of placing severe restrictions on an individual, group or institution" (p. 306).

One widely accepted model defines oppression in terms of its primary and secondary natures (Brittan & Maynard, 1984). **Primary oppression** refers to the direct consequences of perceived group differences. An example is any policy that posits that women are biologically inferior to men and therefore should not be afforded the same rights. In contrast, **secondary oppression** refers to a deeper awareness of oppression by those who are oppressed that goes beyond the obvious consequences. For example, an African American who is denied housing probably recognizes the oppressive structure that supports that action, but she does not need this action put into logical or analytical terms to understand it. Rather, this type of oppression has more to do with the experience of being oppressed and all of the emotional, cognitive, and interpersonal interactions that take place to create an oppressive situation.

Another approach to oppression commonly used in social work is the **anti-oppression model**, which explores the ways in which oppression is integrated in social and other systems that impact the individual lives of clients. The goal of this model is to eliminate all oppression by transforming society and all its social structures, creating equity, inclusion, and social justice for everyone, regardless of individual situations. So, rather than just focusing on the micro level, on the experience of oppression for individual clients, social workers using this model would assess how oppression plays out for clients in broader, more pervasive ways, in an effort to identify and eliminate it at the mezzo and macro levels as well (Bishop, 1994; Campbell, 2003; Dominelli, 2002; Mullaly, 1997).

People living under oppressive conditions usually have a deep understanding of these processes because they encounter them on a daily basis. These conceptualizations of oppression are important because too often oppression is analyzed from a primary perspective, which is reductionistic and tends to isolate oppressive actions from the complex nature and various sources from which it can stem. In social work, this complexity is crucial to understand if social workers are to truly help clients and work toward eliminating oppression in different social realms.

Applying Theories of Racism, Discrimination, and Oppression

In what ways might information on race, discrimination, and oppression be applied to the case of the rural town introduced at the beginning of the chapter? One of the best ways to use this information is to consider which diversity factors are affecting the community. On a large scale, the town lacks resources, which directly or indirectly may be contributing to its oppressed situation. Given the lack of effective representation in the state's legislature and access to power that will help community members obtain resources they need to improve their situation, there seems little that can be done to improve their situations. Thus, poverty, domestic violence, low-quality education, teen pregnancy and suicide, and other problems are perpetuated.

With regard to race, prejudice, and discrimination, as the social worker, you could assess and intervene with these issues on many different levels. On a macro level, you might identify some biases attached to the rural nature of the town. For example, some powerful state officials might hold prejudices and stereotypes about rural areas that lead to discriminatory actions with regard to budgets and resource allocation.

On a micro level, officials who implement budgetary and other legislative policies may be acting from preconceived notions about elderly people, Hispanics/ Latinos and Latino Americans, and the needs of Latino American children. Even if these notions are inaccurate, the officials' policy decisions have ramifications for the people in the community, the ways in which the children are reared and the older citizens are perceived, the resources to which community members have access, and the culture to which they are exposed. Moreover, growing up in a rural area with a lack of quality education and other social services, the children will likely encounter stereotypes held by others outside their community as well as those that they might develop about themselves. In turn, these stereotypes will affect their socialization and their long-term chances of improving their situation. Finally, on a mezzo level, members of the community will need to explore their visions for community development as well as the ways in which their values, beliefs, and culture affect their interactions with one another and help or hinder their growth as individuals and as a community.

In general, prejudice and discrimination on different levels seem to be inter- acting in ways that are contributing to the oppression of many members of this community. You must decide at which level you would help the sheriff intervene to begin to solve the community's problems.

Critiquing Theories of Racism, Discrimination, and Oppression

Probably one of the most important reasons to consider theories or perspectives on race, discrimination, and oppression is that attending to these issues is crucial when working with clients. Many facets of assessment rely on information about diversity and need to be considered when developing interventions. Being cognizant of diversity factors as well as having ways to organize diversity information when working with clients is paramount to ethical and effective social work. Because social workers are concerned with pursuing justice and equality, being aware of how issues related to difference can create and maintain oppression is a primary skill they must develop. In fact, any successful efforts toward social change rely on a combination of knowledge and skill that can contribute to ending oppression.

At the same time, however, there is no coherent theory to organize the infor- mation that exists on race, discrimination, oppression, and issues of diversity. Con- sequently, social workers cannot distinctly or consistently define factors of diversity, nor can they empirically test these factors in a way that enables them to create a single theory that can inform practice. The best that social workers can do is to be knowledgeable about the many facets of diversity that might influence their clients' lives and to keep up to date on issues and information concerning diversity. Finally, considering race as a socially constructed concept can be helpful in understanding how society may use it to maintain oppression. This understanding can be advantageous in developing interventions and instigating social change. It can also help social workers to educate clients about how socially constructed concepts are influencing their lives and well-being.

SOCIAL AND ECONOMIC JUSTICE PERSPECTIVES

A central tenet of social work is social and economic justice. In fact, promoting social justice is a core value and ethical principle of the NASW *Code of Ethics*. This principle calls for social workers to "pursue social change, particularly with and on behalf of vulnerable and oppressed individuals and groups of people. Social workers strive to ensure access to needed information, services, and resources; equality of opportunity; and meaningful participation in decision making for all people" (NASW, approved 1996, revised 2008, p. 5). This sentiment is also reflected in the Educational Policy and Accreditation Standards (EPAS) set forth by the Council on Social Work Education (CSWE). In its educational policy, CSWE states that ". . . social work's purpose is actualized through its quest for social and economic justice, the prevention of conditions that limit human rights, the elimination of poverty, and the enhancement of the quality of life for all persons" (Council on Social Work Education, 2008, p. 1). Further, Educational Policy 2.1.5 articulates basic human rights, such as freedom, privacy, and education that social workers should strive to protect, and it stresses the need for social workers to incorporate knowledge and practices related to economic and social justice in their work (Council on Social Work Education, 2008). Thus, the basic premise of **social justice** is that all humans have a right to live fulfilling lives, which requires access to appropriate resources (economic and otherwise), decision-making opportunities, and freedom from fear of persecution (Prigoff, 2003).

Much of the impetus in the development of social and economic justice perspectives has been rooted in efforts to overcome discrimination and oppression. There is a long history of writers and activists from diverse disciplines who have contributed to the development of these perspectives. For example, movements that include voting rights, settlement houses, labor organization, abolition of slavery, and civil and women's rights have all brought heightened awareness to injustices suffered by different groups at the hands of individuals and social institutions. Important figures in this history include Jane Addams, Martin Luther King, Jr., Cesar Chavez, Simone de Beauvoir, Paolo Freire, Nelson Mandela, Frances Fox Piven, and bell hooks, to name a few (Prigoff, 2003).

Dorothy Van Soest (as cited in Swenson, 1998), a well-known scholar in this area, discusses the importance of **distributive justice** in social work. This type of justice is concerned with how a society gives back to its members, or what it "owes" its members. That is, communities should support their members in social, economic, and other important ways that promote their well-being. Similarly, John

EXHIBIT 5.1

Promoting social and economic justice is a central tenet in social work

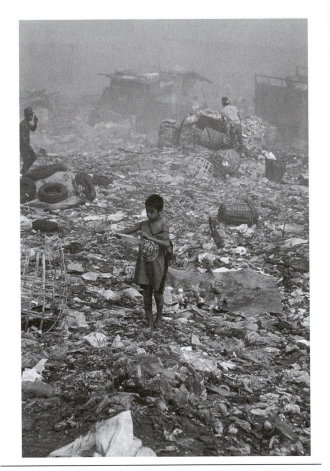

Source: Getty (Digital Vision)

Rawls (1971), another well-known scholar, argues that distributive justice is the essence of equality because every person is considered to be deserving; thus, no one suffers for the "good" of the whole of society. Rawls further posits that for a society to be just, everyone must have equal rights and access to equal opportunities.

Keep in mind, too, that social workers are interested in distributive justice not only as it relates to economic equality, but as it relates to all realms of life—social, sexual, political, educational, spiritual, and so on—that might promote the full development and well-being of people. This philosophy contrasts sharply with the **libertarian perspective** on justice, which argues that government and other aspects of society should have only a limited role in human affairs, including securing people's rights to liberty, property, and personal protection. Distributive justice also

ECONOMIC	POLITICAL	MULTICULTURAL	BOX 5.2
PROMOTE:	**ADVOCATE FOR:**	**SUPPORT:**	*Social Work*
• Local and cooperative economic development.	• Campaign finance reform.	• Diverse perspectives in assessment and intervention.	*Practice Activities to Promote Social*
• Regulated and deprivatized public and other services.	• Inclusive participation in political processes.	• Affirmative action efforts.	*Justice and Equality*

Source: Adapted from Prigoff, 2003.

differs from the **utilitarian approach**, which defines justice as beliefs and policies that support the "greatest good for the greatest number of people" (Van Soest, 1994, p. 714). Though there are some useful aspects to these last two approaches, they tend not to be as widely used in social work as the distributive justice perspective, mostly because tenets of distributive justice seem to fit well with social work values.

Based on justice perspectives, the social work profession has identified several practice activities that promote the goal of equality, listed in Box 5.2. This might appear to be a daunting list of tasks, but they reflect fundamental ideas that are at the heart of social work values. Though these activities tend to be macro focused, they have compelling implications for the lives of individuals. For instance, supporting affirmative action within institutional settings not only has ramifications for entire groups, but also has far-reaching consequences for individuals within those groups. As individuals who benefit from these policies gain status and power within various institutions, they can improve access to these institutions for others.

Applying Social and Economic Justice Perspectives

Let us return to the opening case study and consider how you could assist the sheriff in conceptualizing the town's problems from the perspective of economic and social injustice, suggesting ways to work toward justice. Issues surrounding lack of resources, inadequate representation at the state level, lack of quality education, and a lack of social services to improve the situation of its members are all major issues that contribute to the injustice facing this community.

From a distributive justice standpoint, you could help the sheriff conceptualize how the community might benefit each member, considering each member to be valuable and deserving of equal rights and opportunities afforded to other members in the community and members of other communities. Using activities listed in Box 5.2, you might help the sheriff assess the needs, problems, and strengths of the community and its members, focusing on the unique ethnic and cultural aspects of each. You and the sheriff could work toward finding ways to include each member in political processes to ensure fair representation in budgetary and other issues that affect the community. Moreover, you could help the sheriff and community members to develop the town's employment, education, and other resources to help the community become more self-sustaining. Community members could also strive toward developing coalitions within the community and with other communities to gain more power and representation in government and other entities where decisions about resource allocation are made. Finally, you and the sheriff might want to think about how issues of racism, discrimination, and oppression, as discussed earlier, might be impacting community members' efforts toward change and growth. For example, it may be that state legislators have prejudices about Hispanic/Latino Americans that are causing them to discriminate against community members, leading to their underrepresentation in the state legislature.

Critiquing Social and Economic Justice Perspectives

A great deal has been written on social and economic justice by social workers and theorists from related disciplines, which has helped the profession to make significant inroads with regard to social change. This work has been and will continue to be a powerful resource for social workers and the clients and communities with whom they work. Though these conceptualizations have great potential for larger social change, they have yet to make a significant, long-lasting impact at the macro level or to affect social policy in a concrete way. Other theories and perspectives, discussed in the following sections, have been more successful. On a smaller scale, however, they have heightened awareness of the impact that larger social and international issues have on individual clients and communities. For example, the social work literature contains an extensive discussion about transnational policies and organizations, such as the North American Free Trade Agreement (NAFTA), the International Monetary Fund (IMF), and the World Bank, and how these entities impact workers and communities in the United States and other countries.

As with issues surrounding diversity, perspectives on social and economic justice are not well conceptualized, at least insofar as an organized theory has been developed to help guide actions toward achieving justice. In reality, defining and testing concepts related to justice can be difficult. However, justice perspectives obviously fit very well with the core values of social work practice. They also complement theoretical and other models such as the strengths perspective, multicultural approaches, feminist theories, and humanistic perspectives.

SOCIAL CHANGE AND SOCIAL ACTION PERSPECTIVES

Much of social work deals with change, whether it occurs on the individual, community, or larger social level. It is change on a social level that often sets social work apart from other related disciplines. As you may have noticed, a great deal of our discussion of theories has focused on how they can be used to create some kind of positive change on a broad scale.

Significantly, when social workers talk about social change, they are often also referring to social action, which can lead to change geared toward social and economic justice. Within the social work profession, **social action** is defined as efforts to modify societal institutions to meet needs, resolve issues, achieve social and economic justice, and provide for the well-being of society's members. Generally, social action refers to coordinating activities intended to meet these goals, and it can be used to describe change efforts in the policy, community, or legislative realms. Social action usually involves **advocacy**, which entails representing or defending the rights of clients or those who lack skills or resources to represent themselves. **Social movement**, a term that social workers often use interchangeably with social change, consists of efforts conducted on a large scale to produce changes that affect people's lives (Barker, 2003).

The roots of social change efforts in the United States can be traced back to many great social movements, including abolitionism, women's equality, and the Progressive Era, when great changes were occurring within the country. Beginning in the late 1800s and early 1900s, industrialization and its subsequent social problems spurred efforts at reform. This period saw a shift away from charity work toward methods that involved advocacy skills to abolish poverty and other social problems. Many reformers viewed settlement houses as the best way to accomplish these goals. Located within communities that needed help, **settlement houses** provided organized programs that addressed nutrition, literacy, day care, and other needs. In addition, they enabled workers to learn about social problems directly from the people who suffered from them. The knowledge gained through direct practice was used to change social policy at the legislative level, which affected the lives of millions of people. Some of the professional skills that were developed during this time revolved around the use of scientific research methods (for example, data collection and dissemination) to increase knowledge about social problems. From the advancements made by the settlement house movement, social workers themselves learned more effective methods of successful public relations and use of the media in negotiating the legislative process (National Association of Social Workers, 1987).

During the Great Depression, another round of social action efforts was undertaken. Severe social and economic problems in the 1930s forced millions of Americans to turn to the federal government for help. President Franklin Delano Roosevelt initiated the New Deal, which created many social programs such as Social Security and Aid to Families with Dependent Children. Many social workers were employed to administer these programs using the skills mentioned earlier. In addition, communist ideology fueled the fires for labor movements and discussion of revolution.

Decades later, the 1960s witnessed social change efforts in the form of civil rights and other movements that championed entitlements, racial equality, and local control of community institutions. The Great Society agenda of Lyndon Johnson's administration, especially its War on Poverty, created many new social programs and provided funds that enabled social workers to legitimize their efforts toward social change. Some of the professional skills that were developed during these times were confronting racism and sexism; perfecting fund raising and intra-group processes (for example, meeting and working with organized groups with many agendas); using political skills while working with coalitions (for example, working with the disparate political ideologies of different groups); and understanding political structures and the power that stems from them.

During the conservative era of the 1980s, money began to dissipate, which spurred movements toward community organization, development, and leadership. Because money and resources were scarce, social workers shifted their focus onto one issue at a time, allowing them to raise awareness of the issue and gather information that could be persuasive to constituents and policy-makers. During this time, many social workers became more politically active to effect change at legislative levels (National Association of Social Workers, 1987).

Contemporary Social Action Perspectives

Several perspectives guide contemporary social action and change efforts, though we will look at only a few of them here. As you read the following descriptions, ask yourself how these perspectives can contribute to the social work profession:

- The **political opportunities perspective** views political structures as benefiting only the elites, who have access to power and resources that are needed to maintain or change social institutions. This arrangement disenfranchises other groups with less power, which makes it difficult for them to instigate changes that will benefit them. The political opportunities perspective posits that institutions can be vulnerable and unstable at times, which affords "outsiders" the opportunity to gain access to them. If these outsiders are able to change an aspect of an institution, this success can lead to further changes in other realms (Tarrow, 1994).

- The **mobilizing structures perspective** promotes the idea that disenfranchised groups can organize and use existing resources (for example, power, money, people, and information) to initiate change. This process can occur through informal or formal channels, such as when people gather in a community to take on tasks (informal) or to enlist the help of professionals who are in positions of power (formal). For change to continue, though, groups must be able to continually recruit members to keep energy flowing into the efforts. Coordination of change efforts can take place through formal organizations, or **social movement organizations (SMOs)**. SMOs rely on professionals who possess skills specifically designed for social change. Social movement agencies are often set up under the auspices of these organizations to tackle specific issues through the delivery of direct services. For example, the national Association of Community Organizations for Reform Now (ACORN) could be considered a social movement organization. ACORN's local community chapters and programs could be considered social movement agencies that carry out the organization's philosophy and mission. Other examples of social movement agencies are feminist health clinics and domestic violence shelters. These operate under the auspices of larger social movements. In addition to providing services, these agencies strive for social change through education, advocacy, and raising awareness of the issues they represent (Zald & McCarthy, 1987).

- Finally, the **cultural framing perspective** suggests that social movements are successful only when those in a group striving toward change agree on the purpose or issue behind the movement. Like the interactionist theory discussed in Chapter 4, this perspective emphasizes that people's interactions are crucial in defining the issue and in raising awareness of the problems associated with the issue. It further posits that people must feel a sense of solidarity and commitment to working on the issue (McAdam, McCarthy, & Zald, 1996).

Applying Social Change and Social Action Perspectives

With regard to the rural town discussed in the case study, you may want to help the sheriff assess the community's situation and then choose a model from which to work based on the outcome of the assessment. To accomplish this task you would need to consider several factors. First, can community members agree on the definition of change and the need for it? Some residents may be content with the status quo, making them reluctant to support any efforts toward change. Second, will community members agree on the need for advocacy, which the sheriff is already making use of? Will they be open to continued advocacy? Do they need it? Third, you can help the sheriff decide which model of social change and action best addresses the community's needs.

The political opportunities perspective might be useful in this case, because state power seems to be concentrated in the hands of officials who represent the interests of larger communities. Opportunities may arise for the community to access this power when the existing power structure is vulnerable and unstable. Indeed, because this community rarely makes itself known, it is in a position to "sneak up on" legislators when they least expect it. If community members are able to access existing power structures, they are likely to bring about some modest but permanent changes in policy and budget decisions that will benefit the community.

The mobilizing structures perspective may not be as feasible for this community. Because the community lacks resources such as money and political power, it might not have the local support in place to take advantage of organized efforts.

In contrast, coming at the issues from the cultural framing perspective may be useful. Given the multitude of problems facing the community, it may be advantageous to get a better understanding of how community members view the situation. As we have seen, it is possible that not everyone agrees that problems exist or defines them in quite the same way. If any efforts are to be successful, everyone must be willing to support the change efforts. Finally, you can assist the sheriff in identifying and developing local leadership to help guide the change process.

Critiquing Social Change and Social Action Perspectives

Though difficult to define and measure, ideas surrounding social change and action may be amenable to empirical testing with further development and articulation of the models discussed previously. In fact, the social work profession could probably achieve a consensus both on the definitions of *social change* and *social action* and on strategies for defining and measuring the basic concepts contained in these models. Certainly, practitioners could determine whether change actually took place, although they would have to agree on what constitutes change. However, as with other theories and concepts we have looked at, many of the concepts related to social action and change can be difficult to articulate. In addition, because these concepts are being discussed in so many different contexts and disciplines, consensus on meanings can be difficult to achieve.

All of these problems notwithstanding, the perspectives discussed in this section offer social workers a framework on which to base macro practice, which is a vital part of the discipline's charge. Until recently, a dearth of knowledge in this area afforded social workers little by way of a foundation on which to build their work. However, with continued additions to the knowledge base, social workers can build on this framework by implementing strategies that are time-tested and that are being formed into increasingly sound theoretical concepts. Moreover, these models, in combination with other theoretical approaches, can offer social workers a broad range of strategies and skills from which to choose when developing social change interventions.

COMMUNITY ORGANIZATION THEORY

Many concepts associated with justice and social change can be applied to community organization. Indeed, as discussed at the beginning of the chapter, community organization is closely related to these concepts and, in large part, has developed alongside of them. However, we still want to take a closer look at some of the theories and strategies that social workers use in their practice with communities.

The development of community organization as a practice reflects the development of social action strategies. Because community organization was frequently at the crux of social change activities, its development tended to occur simultaneously with events that called for social change.

Community practice began in the late 1800s with charity organizations and the settlement house movement. Many private organizations provided social services, and the Charity Organization Society (COS) was created to coordinate service efforts and to plan for how to best meet community needs. However, the COS focused on individual casework that sought to "morally uplift" the poor, whereas settlement houses were concerned with self-help and social and political action. As we saw in the previous section, settlement house workers successfully negotiated legislative channels to create social change and recruited community members to join community development efforts. In this sense, community organization became a practice that brought with it a set of defined skills and strategies that could be organized within a theoretical context.

How Social Work Defines and Perceives Community

The term *community* can have many definitions depending on the discipline and the context in which it is being used. Generally stated, though, **community** can be considered as a group of people who are bound together through geography or common ties such as values, beliefs, and culture. Within this definition, two broad themes emerge. One is **territorial community**, which refers to geographical boundaries that bind people together. The other, known as **relational community**, involves the common ties or relations that hold people together as a group. People do not necessarily have to live within close proximity to consider themselves a community. Often, communities develop when common ideas, issues, causes, and struggles bring people together, regardless of whether they live next door to one another or across the globe. Examples of relational communities include the Hispanic/Latino community, the gay and lesbian community, and the social work community (Garreau, 1992).

Generally, there are three contexts in which social workers can view community with regard to macro-based practice (Homan, 1999):

- *Community as the milieu in which practice actually occurs:* This view focuses on the community as a unique, living entity. The dynamics of the community are central to the change strategies that are chosen. This context defines the problems that communities face, and it helps to determine the types of services that will be provided and the interventions that can be used based on those problems.

- *Community as the change target:* This perspective views communities from a more objective stance versus a more subjective one, and social workers devise standardized strategies and interventions to create change within communities. That is, assessment and intervention are typically conducted by social workers and others from outside the community rather than by the community members themselves.

- *Community as a mechanism for change:* This perspective posits that the community itself is responsible for solving its own problems and for using the skills and talents of its members toward the goal of change. Social workers help to support those change efforts by guiding members through the assessment and intervention process.

In addition to the contexts in which community practice can take place, several perspectives describe the ways in which social workers can view communities and the ways they can approach their work with them. For instance, some perspectives analyze communities in terms of their physical and other properties such as geographical location, population distribution, and rules and regulations. Other perspectives analyze communities with regard to the level of commitment shown by members and the relationships that members have with their community. Still other perspectives view communities as systems with unique norms, symbols, cultures, and interactions among members. This last perspective is similar to systems theory discussed in Chapter 2. Other perspectives analyze the power structures in communities and the ways in which community members control assets and compete for resources. All of these perspectives can be used to analyze problems and strengths of communities within the different contexts just discussed (communities as milieus, change targets, or mechanisms for change). These ways of viewing communities give social workers a place to begin in assessing and intervening with community issues.

Community and Social Work Practice

The ways in which social workers define and perceive communities obviously influence the interventions they develop in macro practice. Over time, different theoretical approaches and strategies have been developed to better define the activities involved in community change. For the most part, all community approaches are based on planned change. But how this change is implemented differs from one approach to another. Some approaches emphasize working with traditional institutions and power structures within a community, using gradual and deliberate methods, usually through service delivery, to bring about change. Others emphasize challenging traditional institutions and power structures. Using these methods, social workers attempt to confront issues and use mediation efforts to achieve goals. They also strive to turn control over to community members and to find alternative ways of functioning for communities that will benefit and improve the lives of their members. Still other approaches emphasize strengthening the skills and resources of community members through the use of lobbying, legal maneuvers, and coalition building. Three main models for community work are based on these ideas: the locality development model, the social planning model, and the social action model.

- Also known as community development, the **locality development model** uses the skills of community members to approach problems from the local level. Community members who possess a wide range of talents are recruited to find relevant, broad-ranged solutions to issues. In this model, social workers are not the main change agents. Rather, they support community members and leaders by offering education, information, and guidance. In this way they become participants in the change process, using their skills to support the efforts of community members.

- In contrast, in the **social planning model**, social workers act as experts who take the lead in developing change strategies. This model tends to focus on the process of problem solving, assuming that only social workers or other professionals have the expertise to guide this process. In other words, the social planning model relies on specialized skills and methods to develop interventions, and community members "contract" with outside professionals to plan and intervene on the community's behalf.

- Finally, the **social action model** maintains that community members must be empowered to initiate changes for themselves and their communities. In this model, social workers seek to organize community members, who in turn challenge existing power structures to increase the equitable distribution of resources, create more just institutions, and instigate social reform. Community members are active agents in the change process. The social action model views social workers as activists who work in concert with community members. Social workers act as agitators and protestors to create tension that will lead to change. They can also use their knowledge and skills to engage in activism, lobbying, boycotting, and using the media to help communities achieve their goals (Rothman, 1995).

A well-known person associated with the social action model is Saul Alinsky. Alinsky's concerns center on how community members become oppressed and disconnected from the functions of their communities. He focuses on how institutional and other structures maintain oppression and alienation among community members as well as how institutions determine the distribution of resources. Alinsky posits that these dynamics create learned helplessness and apathy among community members, particularly those who are disenfranchised. Thus, he insists that the disenfranchised persons themselves must instigate change. Through this process, they can become empowered, develop their capabilities, and strengthen their connections with one another to increase cooperation and collaboration.

Alinsky focuses on methods and strategies to organize community members and to develop effective strategies toward change. He maintains that the goal of community change is to empower community members to bring about social and institutional change to create justice and equal distribution of resources. He posits that community change occurs through strategies that (1) contribute to building power among community members, (2) generate methods that are representative of the needs of the group, and (3) contribute to positive conflict resolution (Pruger & Specht, 1969).

Applying and Critiquing Community Organization Theory

Once more, let us return to the vignette at the beginning of the chapter and see how you might help the sheriff develop a plan for community organization. Probably the best place to begin is to assess how invested the community members are in solving problems. If it seems unlikely that the sheriff will be able to mobilize community members in working toward change, you would not want to use the locality development model. Because this model relies on the skills of community members, it may not be the best approach if people lack the skill or desire to organize. The social planning model may be a good approach if community members are willing to accept advocacy from a social worker who is an outsider. In this case, the community might need someone with the expertise to effectively plan for change and to negotiate the various systems that might offer viable resources. Ultimately, however, given the longevity of the problems that confront this community, the best approach might be to empower the community members to solve their own problems. Using, the social action model, you might be able to instill in the community members a sense of self-efficacy from which they could create permanent change. Of course, this approach would require community members to organize and work toward change, but it may be the approach that would best lead to lasting and positive change for the community.

As with social change and action models, approaches to community organization have the potential to develop into coherent theories that can be tested empirically. Over time, the definition of community organization and the ideas behind the practice have been shaped and structured in such a way that they are useful tools for macro practice. At the same time, as the use of community organization strategies in social work has increased, so have the number of theories and perspectives dealing with this aspect of macro practice. Unfortunately, this process has produced increased inconsistency within and among approaches. In turn, this inconsistency has led to problems in fairly and effectively comparing the approaches as well as in evaluating their outcomes. Nevertheless, regardless of the particular approach you adopt in working toward change, you can easily use different aspects of these models in concert with other theoretical approaches in developing community interventions.

CONCLUSION

Dealing with macro-oriented issues is a common activity in social work. Though working with racism, discrimination, oppression, and social change can be included in micro practice, social workers often associate these activities with practice that involves working with institutions and larger societal attitudes.

This chapter has covered some of the basic ideas surrounding social justice and social change. Although there are many theories, perspectives, and ideas about how to achieve social justice and change, social work relies increasingly on coherent, organized perspectives in these areas to guide practice. Look back at Table 5.1 to see how the theories and perspectives presented in this chapter compare.

Overcoming oppression, along with the racism, prejudice, and discrimination that usually lie at the heart of oppression, is a core social work value. No discipline can lay claim to a fully developed theory that includes all of these concepts, but the knowledge that we do have helps to guide assessment and intervention in social work practice. Social workers must be knowledgeable about the history of oppression as well as contemporary issues surrounding it to effectively serve their clients and communities.

Similarly, striving toward social and economic justice is a crucial component of social work practice. Though ideas surrounding justice are rooted in philosophical and other disciplines, social work is the primary profession that attempts to put these ideas into action. These activities are geared toward ending oppression and creating a more equitable distribution of resources throughout society. Over time, several principles to promote justice have been developed that guide social work practice.

Related to the ideas of ending oppression and working toward social and economic justice are activities involving social change and action. Social workers often view social change activities as one way to achieve equity in society. Social change often involves advocacy, and several models or perspectives have arisen over the past several decades to help organize ideas and strategies surrounding social action. Although social change and social action tend to be basic activities that are part of macro practice, social workers' interest in these types of activities tends to ebb and flow depending on the political and economic climate.

Community organization is commonly associated with macro practice, probably because of its well-rooted history in the development of the profession, as well as the existence of established theories and perspectives on community practice. Although community organization tends to include activities that create social change and strive toward social and economic equity, this mode of practice relies on well-established and continually developing strategies to create change.

MAIN POINTS

- Race, as a contemporary term, is defined as biological differences among groups of people. Although the debate over its precise meaning and use goes on, social workers need to understand its origins and implications for individuals and U.S. society as a whole.

- Racism, which involves stereotyping people based on their race, occurs on different levels. Individual racism refers to personal actions such as name-calling or hate crimes; institutional racism refers to practices in social institutions, such as racial profiling, that systematically treat one race differently from another.

- Discrimination generally refers to behavior, whereas prejudice refers to the attitudes, beliefs, and stereotypes that a person holds about others. Oppression can be defined as severely restrictive social acts that affect individuals, groups, and institutions. Although theories of racism, discrimination, and prejudice help to inform social workers' interventions with clients and help to guide social change to end oppression, no specific, coherent theory exists that can be empirically tested.

- A core value and ethical principle in the NASW *Code of Ethics* involves promoting social justice, and it is also a core educational policy set forth by the CSWE. Since social workers are concerned with social change, they often look to social action strategies to work toward social and economic justice for their clients.

- Social action (often used interchangeably with the term social movement) refers to efforts that concentrate on changing societal institutions to meet needs, resolve issues, achieve social and economic justice, and provide for the well-being of society's members. A perspective that originated in the work of settlement houses, social action can be guided by the political opportunities perspective, the mobilizing structures perspective, or the cultural framing perspective.

- A community can be defined as a group of people who are linked geographically (territorial community) or through common ties such as values, beliefs, and culture (relational community). Three main models for community work are the locality development model (community development), the social planning model, and the social action model.

EXERCISES

1. Using the Sanchez Family interactive case (go to www.routledgesw.com/cases), review the issues facing each family member and the family as a whole. Using theories presented in this chapter, answer the following questions:
   a. In what ways might racism, discrimination, and oppression be contributing to the family's problems?
   b. How could social and economic justice perspectives be applied to this family's situation?
   c. How could social change and action perspectives be applied to this family's situation?
   d. In what ways could community organization theories be used to intervene with this family?

2. Review the Riverton interactive case (go to www.routledgesw.com/cases), and reacquaint yourself with the different facets of the community. Review the content discussed in the chapter on social change/action perspectives and community organization theory, then answer the following questions:
   a. Which social action perspective might you want to use to help guide your change efforts with this community and why? What might be some of the limitations to using the perspective you chose?
   b. Describe the territorial community and relational community involved in this case.
   c. Which community practice approach would you pick for your work with this community and why? What might be some of the limitations to using the model you chose?

CHAPTER 6

Pre-Pregnancy and Prenatal Issues

Josie is a 15-year-old Japanese American who has just found out that she is two months pregnant. The father of the baby is Josie's 17-year-old boyfriend of one year. They both are in high school, have a lot of friends, and are doing well in their classes. Josie's parents are first-generation Americans and hold conservative views on family, dating, marriage, religion, and roles for family members. For this reason, Josie is afraid of how her parents will react if they find out she is pregnant. In fact, her parents do not even know she has been dating. At the insistence of her friends, Josie went to a local Planned Parenthood when she didn't seem to be recovering from flulike symptoms. The social worker at Planned Parenthood was not required to get parental permission to run a pregnancy test, but she wants to work with Josie to include her parents in Josie's decisions about how to proceed. Josie is reluctant to tell her parents: She is afraid her parents will disown her, and she is not sure if her extended family will offer any support, regardless of whether she decides to keep the baby. Josie's boyfriend has told her that he will not help her if she chooses to keep the baby. Josie also does not want to drop out of school, so she is trying to explore all of her options with the social worker.

THIS SCENARIO RAISES MANY ETHICAL AND PRACTICE ISSUES ON several different levels. As in previous chapters, imagine that you are the social worker who is helping Josie. You and Josie have many decisions to make, and you must possess not only sound practice skills but also solid knowledge about human development; sensitivity to cultural issues; awareness of your own values and beliefs concerning teen pregnancy, adoption, and abortion; and up-to-date information on legal and ethical issues surrounding working with minors. This chapter explores human development from conception to birth, along with some of the issues, such as those just stated, that may present themselves when working with clients who are pregnant or who have recently given birth.

DEVELOPMENTAL MILESTONES IN THE FETUS

Given the extraordinary process of fetal development as well as the many psychosocial factors related to being pregnant, social workers need a thorough, accurate, and broad knowledge base about pregnancy, childbirth, and postnatal considerations. Clients often rely on social workers for decision-making support and basic knowledge on pregnancy, because social workers are often the first professionals with whom some clients come into contact after discovering they are pregnant. Social workers can provide a great deal of support and education to clients during this crucial time. Although most of the developmental information presented here is couched in medical and biopsychosocial models, social workers often incorporate information from other theories in their interventions to help understand how pregnancy and fetal development can affect clients on individual, interpersonal, and social levels.

Growth Processes from Conception through Birth

Obviously, a great deal of complex fetal growth and development takes place in a short amount of time. Although many women experience pregnancies without complications or problems, arming clients with as much information as possible about fetal development can help to prevent some otherwise devastating problems with their babies. Some of these problems are discussed in more detail in a later section. However, because these problems can occur, social workers must have a basic understanding of "normal" fetal development. This knowledge includes the milestones of development as well as maternal behaviors that should be promoted or discouraged at each stage.

Box 6.1 displays a timeline of fetal development along with the major milestones in growth that take place during each stage. This table breaks up fetal development into trimesters, each of which lasts about 13 weeks. Social workers should become familiar with the developments that occur in each trimester so that they can assist their clients in tracking the progress of their babies' growth.

Keep in mind that medical professionals often track fetal growth by **gestational age**, which means that the age of the fetus is based on the first day of a woman's last menstrual cycle (or about 14 days *before* ovulation, assuming a regular cycle), not on the date of actual conception, which would be around the time of ovulation. Calculated fetal age based on the date of conception is the **fertilization or conception age**. Because many women do not know the actual date of conception, using the menstrual cycle to determine the age of the fetus tends to be more reliable (if the woman's menstrual cycle is regular; many women experience variance in their cycles from month to month) (Murkoff & Mazel, 2008).

However, the gestational dating method can be confusing to parents; it can even become a point of contention for some couples. For example, let us say that a woman is told by her physician that her baby is eight weeks old, based on the timing

BOX 6.1

Milestones in Fetal Development

FIRST TRIMESTER
Weeks 0 through 13 (up to week 10 based on fertilization age) are considered the most critical with regard to prenatal care and fetal exposure to maternal and environmental toxins.

Month One
- Primitive brain, heart, lungs, and digestive and nervous system development by end of month one
- Beginnings of arms and legs

Month Two
- Internal organs become more complex
- Eyes, nose, mouth become identifiable
- Heartbeat is detectable
- Up until eight weeks, the baby is referred to as an embryo, after which it is called a fetus

Month Three
- Formation of arms, hands, legs, feet, fingernails, hair, eyelids
- Fingerprints are established
- Gender is distinguishable (though it may not be seen via ultrasound until around 16 weeks)
- Bone development
- Can smile, frown, suck, swallow
- End of first trimester, baby is about three inches long and weighs about one ounce

SECOND TRIMESTER
Weeks 14 through 27 (up to week 25 based on fertilization age) are marked by continued development and growth.

- All development continues; differentiation of organs and systems proceeds
- Toes and fingers separate
- Fingernails and toenails form
- Has coordinated movement
- Hair, eyelashes, eyebrows are present
- Regular heartbeat is established
- Wake and sleep cycle is established
- End of second trimester, baby is 11 to 14 inches long and weighs 1 to 1½ pounds

THIRD TRIMESTER
Weeks 28 through 40 (up to week 38 based on fertilization age) mark the final stages of development.

- Completed development, organs become functional
- Fatty tissue develops under skin
- Fetus is very active until time of delivery
- Responds to sound
- End of third trimester, baby is 19 inches long and weighs about 6+ pounds

Source: Adapted from Curtis & Schuler, 2004.

of the woman's last period. But the woman insists that this is not correct, because she and her partner did not have intercourse eight weeks ago; her partner was out of town. (You can imagine what kinds of problems this news might cause!) The woman knows, though, that when her partner returned, they had intercourse. So, she cannot figure out why her doctor is telling her the baby is two weeks older than she would expect. Often, when the gestational age is used to determine fetal age, the fetus is said to be about two weeks older than it actually is (based on when it was likely to be conceived due to ovulation patterns). In Josie's case, her physician has told her that her baby is eight weeks old, which means that the baby is actually around six weeks old, based on conception. Social workers who understand these systems of dating can help confused and anxious clients who are not privy to the methods used by physicians.

Referring back to Box 6.1, you can see that the most complex and crucial development in the fetus occurs during the first trimester. For this reason, the first trimester is considered the most critical with regard to prenatal care and fetal exposure to maternal and environmental toxins. Throughout pregnancy, the fetus is vulnerable to the mother's behavior and environment. However, because critical organs and systems such as the heart, eyes, limbs, ears, teeth, and central nervous system develop during the first nine weeks, major structural and physiological damage to these systems can occur during this period. As development progresses past nine weeks, damage can still occur, but it tends to be less severe. The type and extent of damage depend on the type of substances to which the baby is exposed and the timing and amount of exposure (Moore & Persaud, 1998). These issues will be addressed in more detail in a later section.

Low Birth Weight

Generally, a full-term pregnancy lasts between 38 and 40 weeks' gestational age. Babies born three weeks or more before the pregnancy reaches full term (35 weeks or less) are called **preterm**. The age of viability (age at which babies are able to survive) for preterm babies is about 25 to 26 weeks, though babies born as early as 21 weeks have survived; however, babies born this early tend to have many short- and long-term problems. One issue surrounding preterm babies is **low birth weight**, which refers to babies who weigh less than 5½ pounds at birth. **Very low birth weight** babies weigh less than 3 pounds, and **extremely low birth weight** babies weigh less than 2 pounds (Klaus & Fanaroff, 2001).

Low birth weight and premature birth can be caused by a variety of factors, including smoking, disease, maternal age (at both young and old ages), drug abuse, malnutrition, and excessive stress (Murkoff & Mazel, 2008). In Josie's case, she is very young, which puts her at higher risk for having a preterm, low birth weight baby. However, with early intervention that includes good prenatal care, you can help Josie with education and other supportive resources to increase the chances that she will have a healthy baby, should she choose to continue with the pregnancy.

Approximately 1 in 12 babies born in the United States are categorized as low birth weight. Rates for ethnic minority groups tend to be higher than both the rates for Caucasians and the national average. For instance, African American babies are twice as likely as Caucasian or Hispanic babies to suffer from low birth weight (Children's Defense Fund, 2008). Significantly, the United States in general does not fare well compared to other developed countries such as Spain, Canada, Norway, France, and Italy, all of which have lower annual rates of low birth weight babies than the United States. Estimates based on 145 countries suggest that 15.5 percent of all babies born each year (about 20 million) are low birth weight. Southeast Asia has the highest rate: More than half of the low birth weight babies born each year are from this region. Low birth weight babies are also common in sub-Saharan Africa and the Caribbean. Approximately 16.5 percent of all babies born in developing countries are considered low birth weight compared to 7 percent in developed regions (UNICEF, 2004).

In industrialized countries, low birth weight babies tend to survive and eventually thrive. However, as mentioned previously, as birth weight decreases, the number and severity of short- and long-term problems increase. Technology that enables babies who are born at 25 weeks to survive only increases the chances that these babies will develop problems such as brain damage and cerebral palsy. Long-term effects of low birth weight include higher risk of death, asthma, diabetes, malnourishment, heart disease, learning problems, social impairments, impaired immune function, attention deficit hyperactivity disorder, and reduced muscle strength (Klaus & Fanaroff, 2001; Moster, Lie, & Markestad, 2008; UNICEF, 2004).

Of course, all of these problems have other ramifications for children and their families. For example, depending on the circumstances, low birth weight children and their families can face economic problems, increased stress, lack of support, inadequate access to health care, and educational issues throughout life. Moreover, the cost of caring for low birth weight babies is one of the contributors to rising health care costs. This is not to say that there are no positive outcomes to situations involving preterm births. Nevertheless, social workers must be aware of the potential problems, for clients and society, that tend to be correlated with preterm and low birth weight babies in order to provide appropriate, responsible, and effective services.

As discussed earlier, much of the knowledge surrounding fetal development is couched in the medical model, and social workers usually rely on this approach when working with clients who are pregnant or planning to become pregnant. Certainly, information on development is a crucial part of biopsychosocial assessment, which can include other factors that might affect a mother and her unborn baby, such as economics, social support, cultural considerations, and spiritual issues surrounding pregnancy. In Josie's situation, you must have this basic knowledge to help her come to some conclusions about how to proceed in her situation, particularly with regard to prenatal care should she choose to continue with the pregnancy.

PREGNANCY, BIRTH, AND THE INDIVIDUAL

Many social workers have the daunting task of being knowledgeable about and staying current with the many issues surrounding pregnancy, birthing, and post-natal situations. Clients often bring myriad issues and questions to the working relationship. To work effectively with clients, social workers need to feel confident in their understanding both of contemporary issues and of rapidly expanding knowledge created by advances in technology. Given all of the potential scenarios with which clients might be faced, social workers must be ready to take on a variety of helping roles, including advocate, educator, facilitator, and mediator.

Planned and Unplanned Pregnancy

Social workers frequently encounter clients who are dealing with unintended, unwanted, or unplanned pregnancies. Unplanned pregnancies often raise a host of questions, dilemmas, and issues for the clients and their families. Clients confronted with an unplanned pregnancy face decision-making prospects on many different levels, many of which we will consider in later sections. On the individual level, clients must work through personal decisions about the pregnancy, which often involves, among other things, exploring their spiritual and religious beliefs.

An important part of a client's decision-making process relates to the client's right to self-determination. According to the NASW *Code of Ethics* (NASW, approved 1996, revised 2008), social workers have a responsibility to promote clients' desire to set and pursue their own goals unless the social worker determines that those goals may pose an imminent threat to clients or others. This consideration has particular relevance to issues that may arise when working with clients who are faced with an unplanned pregnancy. For example, the prospect that a client may want to pursue an abortion can pose an ethical dilemma for some social workers. Based on personal beliefs, some social workers may feel that this option should not be available to clients, even though it is legal. Social workers in this situation often find them-selves attempting to balance their own beliefs about abortion with the ethical responsibility of client self-determination. Even if social workers support clients' rights to abortion, an ethical dilemma arises if they question the ability of some clients to make reasonable, well-informed decisions about continuing or ending a pregnancy.

Because issues such as these can be so personal, emotional, and value-laden, social workers must be prepared in advance to deal with them. They must explore their own feelings and values about such issues before working with clients; this exercise will decrease the likelihood that the worker's own biases will hinder the working relationship. For example, after engaging in self-exploration, some social workers might choose not to work with clients seeking abortions. Alternatively, some social workers may work toward increasing the options that are available for clients who choose not to keep their babies but who do not want to abort. Social workers also may work toward making social policies more family oriented so that some women do not feel compelled to choose abortion, or they may work toward changing the laws surrounding abortion options on a legislative level. Regardless of the outcome, self-exploration is a necessary part of effective social work practice that helps to ensure that clients are not harmed through the working relationship.

Even when a pregnancy is planned or desired, working with pregnant clients may not be any easier or more straightforward than working with clients whose pregnancies are not planned. Clients experiencing pregnancies face similar challenges, ranging from personal feelings about pregnancy to accessing resources throughout pregnancy and child rearing. Making matters more complex, many women cannot articulate whether their pregnancy was planned or unplanned. That is, many pregnancies fall somewhere in between being planned and unplanned, leaving women with conflicting feelings about their pregnancies (Bachrach & Newcomer, 1999).

Medical researchers have investigated the question of whether planning affects the outcomes of pregnancy and childbirth. So far the results have been inconclusive. Some studies suggest that planning has no effect on the use of prenatal and post-natal care services and is not related to rates of spontaneous abortion or other negative outcomes (Bitto & Gray, 1997; Winterbottom, Smyth, Jacoby, & Baker, 2009). In contrast, other studies conclude that lack of planning places infants at risk for health disadvantages (Blake, Kiely, Gard, El-Mohandes, & El-Khorazaty, 2007; Hulsey, Laken, Miller, & Ager, 2000; Joyce, & Kaestner, 2000; Joyce, Kaestner, & Korenman, 2000; Kost, Landry & Darroch, 1998; Waller & Bitler, 2008). However, outcomes often depend on the use of natural family planning methods and on the woman's philosophy regarding abortion, childbearing, and so on. Thus, social workers need to be cognizant of the diverse variables that may influence pregnancy outcomes and not focus solely on whether the pregnancy was planned.

Pregnancy in Later Life   Increasingly, social workers are working with clients who are waiting until later life to become parents, which again raises many issues. For example, advancing technology is allowing women to wait until their 40s, 50s, and even 60s to begin families. Although on the surface this development might seem liberating for women, social workers must deal with the ramifications of such issues as infertility, emotional aspects of later parenthood, economic challenges to the health care system, potential birth defects and other problems for the baby, and changing societal roles as older people begin raising infants. People who choose to become parents in later life may also face ethical dilemmas about genetic testing and terminating pregnancies if the testing identifies problems. And, because prenatal care is so crucial, social workers can play a role in helping clients obtain care as early as possible.

On a more positive note, women who wait until later life to become parents may have many advantages, such as maturity and economic and emotional stability, and social workers can take advantage of these strengths when working with these clients.

Fertility Issues   Social workers also intervene with clients who would like to become pregnant but cannot because of fertility problems. Approximately 10 percent to 15 percent of couples in the United States present with problems involving conception. Infertility can be caused by many conditions, including fibroid tumors, low sperm count, hormonal problems, and structural problems involving male or female reproductive organs (National Women's Health Information Center, 2006).

Increasingly, people are taking advantage of technology that can alleviate fertility problems. Some of the methods now being used are surgery, medication, sperm donation, hormone therapy, in vitro fertilization, artificial insemination, and the use of surrogate mothers (National Women's Health Information Center, 2006). Technology is even making it possible for egg cells to be extracted, frozen, and stored when a woman is young so that they can be used later in a woman's life. All of these methods have their supporters and critics, and there are many legal, ethical, and economic considerations associated with each method. For example, what are the financial and social ramifications of a 50-year-old woman carrying an embryo that was frozen when she was in her 20s? What are the biological and social ramifications of multiple families using sperm from one donor (though many fertility clinics have regulations restricting the number of families in specific geographical areas that can use sperm donated from one person)? Should all people have access to fertility treatments, regardless of their ability to pay? These are some of the ethical questions with which social workers must grapple in clinical work and in their work on the legislative level. Because of these issues, social workers need to remain current on technological advances in reproductive technology to help clients grapple with the complexity of the situations with which they may be dealing.

Parents' Biological, Psychological, and Emotional Health

Social workers are likely to confront many biopsychosocial issues when intervening with pregnant clients. As we have seen, pregnant clients will face various issues, regardless of whether the pregnancy was planned or unplanned.

First and foremost, some clients must work through the decision of whether to continue with the pregnancy. To assist in working through this decision, social workers can help the client explore her religious and spiritual beliefs, the emotional ramifications to different decisions, and practical considerations in parenting, adoption, or ending a pregnancy.

If the client decides to continue with the pregnancy, the social worker must assess both parents' biological health to help determine the likelihood that the mother will have a relatively healthy and uneventful pregnancy and that postnatal problems can be avoided. This process involves exploring factors such as nutrition, disease, stress, exercise, and substance use with clients. Further, some clients may have family histories of disease or genetic problems that can be assessed through genetic testing. Both the mother and father should be assessed, because paternal factors like substance abuse and exposure to environmental toxins can affect the baby. Social workers can offer a great deal of support to clients by educating them about expected growth throughout pregnancy and client behaviors that can optimize the health of the mother and the baby. Other factors that social workers need to consider with prospective mothers and fathers are their strengths, developmental and emotional levels, cognitive functioning, mental readiness for parenting, spiritual and religious beliefs, economic situation, relationship issues (particularly if domestic violence has been a problem), access to quality supports and other resources, and postnatal and parenting preparation.

Let us consider Josie's case as an example. There are many factors that you will want to address that can increase Josie's chances of having a healthy baby, if that is what she chooses to do. To begin with, you can assess Josie's physical health and psychosocial status by exploring the areas just described. Further, at this point you might decide to use a theoretical perspective (or perspectives) to help guide her assessment and intervention. For example, just by examining the individual factors affecting Josie, you are using both the biopsychosocial and micro levels of conceptualization. Further down the road, you can consider mezzo- and macro-level factors such as family functioning and economic and cultural issues. Ecological theory might also be useful in organizing all of the individual and environmental factors impacting Josie and her situation.

At the same time that you are looking at individual factors, you may want to employ narrower psychosocial theories for ideas about how Josie might cope with her situation. For instance, components of the medical model will come into play as you consider Josie's physical health. In assessing Josie's cognitive and emotional status, you can apply concepts of Piaget's theory to determine how far along Josie is in her cognitive development; this determination will be important in assessing how well Josie will cope with her situation. Perspectives on temperament may also be useful (these are discussed in Chapter 7), particularly if Josie decides to parent her child. Determining the "fit" between Josie and her baby could help Josie deal with potential problems with her baby such as fussiness and excessive crying. Erikson's theory might also be useful to help you think through which developmental tasks Josie might be facing and how a new role of parent might affect Josie's growth in the future. Bringing in aspects of the strengths perspective will help to empower Josie, as will exploring relevant cultural and religious issues. Finally, you may want to consider Josie's current stage of moral development (discussed in Chapter 9), which may affect her decisions about proceeding with her pregnancy.

All of these approaches, whether used in isolation or in combination with other theories, will offer suggestions for how to conduct the intervention with Josie. Depending on the outcome of the assessment, the theories and perspectives used, and Josie's wishes, you can choose from several intervention strategies.

Hazards to Fetal Development

Because of the many problems that can occur with fetal development, prenatal care and maternal health are of primary importance in working with pregnant clients. We already looked at issues surrounding preterm and low birth weight babies. However, many other problems can occur in fetal development, and social workers—in combination with clients' physicians—are often the primary source of information for many clients. Social workers can help clients prevent problems and can support clients who are already expecting problems with their babies.

Box 6.2 lists some common hazards to prenatal development. Hazards that are not naturally occurring are often referred to as **teratogens**; these are substances that can cause birth defects. The timing and amount of exposure to a teratogen, the type of teratogen, and the manner in which the mother's body handles the teratogen greatly influence the kinds of problems these substances might pose for the fetus. Further, genetic abnormalities in the mother or father can also cause problems in fetal development.

In general, the earlier clients access prenatal care, the better the chances that they will avoid problems. Unfortunately, many clients, depending on their circumstances, do not receive adequate prenatal care in a timely manner. This deficiency is often due to lack of knowledge as well as a lack of resources, a topic we will explore

PSYCHOACTIVE DRUGS
- Alcohol
- Nicotine
- Illegal drugs (for example, cocaine, marijuana, heroin)

INCOMPATIBLE BLOOD TYPES
- Rh positive/Rh negative

ENVIRONMENTAL TOXINS
- Radiation
- Pesticides
- Chemicals
- Emissions

MATERNAL AND PATERNAL FACTORS
- Disease (for example, rubella, syphilis, herpes, AIDS, toxoplasmosis)
- Nutrition
- Stress
- Age
- Genetic abnormalities

BOX 6.2

Common Hazards to Prenatal Development

EXHIBIT 6.1

Alcohol consumption and cigarette smoking are teratogens that can negatively impact fetal development

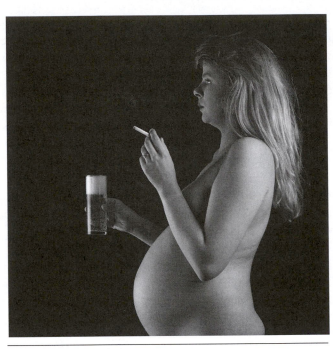

Source: Pearce/Photolink/Getty Images

later in the chapter. Social workers can be invaluable in helping clients to access quality and timely care.

Birth Defects

Approximately 120,000 babies are born with birth defects each year in the United States. Worldwide, approximately 8 million babies are born with birth defects each year. A **birth defect** can be defined as a structural or physiological abnormality present at birth that causes disability or death (March of Dimes, 2009). We will look at a few of the many identifiable birth defects in relation to their causes.

Alcohol and Drugs   Maternal substance use can cause serious birth defects. One of the most common is **fetal alcohol syndrome (FAS)**, a cluster of characteristics that occur in some infants who have been exposed to alcohol prenatally. FAS is one among many disorders categorized under fetal alcohol spectrum disorders. No evidence currently exists to suggest exactly how much alcohol might be considered safe to consume during different stages of pregnancy. It is difficult to develop "safe" guidelines on drinking while pregnant for many reasons; for example, each woman metabolizes alcohol differently; the amount and timing of alcohol consumption can affect the fetus differently, and not every baby exposed to prenatal alcohol exhibits adverse symptoms (Centers for Disease Control and Prevention, 2006). Therefore, physicians and other health care professionals recommend that pregnant women and women thinking about becoming pregnant should not drink alcohol at all.

Characteristics of children born with FAS include a small head for body size; facial characteristics such as widely spaced eyes, flat nose, and thin upper lip; heart defects; defective joints; low IQ; behavioral problems; poor mental capabilities; and a shortened attention span (Barr & Streissguth, 2001; Centers for Disease Control and Prevention, 2006; Jacobsen, Jacobson, Sokol, Martier, & Ager, 1993; Thackray & Tifft, 2001). It is estimated that as many as 40,000 children with symptoms of prenatal alcohol exposure are born each year in the United States. However, this estimate may be low because many children who are affected by prenatal alcohol exposure do not show these outward characteristics, although they experience related problems later in life (Lupton, 2003; Stratton, Howe, & Battaglia, 1996).

Smoking is another hazard to the prenatal environment. Fetal and postnatal problems such as premature birth, low birth weight, respiratory difficulties, high risk of death and sudden infant death syndrome (SIDS), and poor language and cognitive skills have been associated with nicotine use (Fried & Watkinson, 1990; National Institute of Environmental Health, 2008; Schoendorf & Kiely, 1992). Exposure to secondhand smoke in childhood has also been associated with behavioral problems among children (National Institute on Drug Abuse, 2008; Weitzman, Gortmaker, & Sobol, 1992).

Maternal use of cocaine and other illicit drugs can cause severe problems for the fetus. Many babies whose mothers use cocaine or heroin during pregnancy are born addicted and experience long-term problems. For example, babies exposed to cocaine are at risk for low birth weight and impaired motor development and cognitive abilities (Arendt, Angelopouos, Salzaler, & Singer, 1999; Bauer et al., 2005; Chiriboga, Burst, Bateman, & Hauser, 1999; Frank, Augustyn, Knight, Pel, & Zuckerman, 2001). Babies exposed to heroin are at risk for withdrawal symptoms upon birth (for example, tremors, irritability, and disturbed sleep) as well as behavioral and concentration problems (Chiriboga, 2003; Smith et al., 2003; Weinstein, 2000). Effects of prenatal exposure to marijuana are not as clear. There is a lack of research on the topic, although some studies indicate that exposed babies are at risk for low birth weight and poor attention skills (Fried & Smith, 2001; National Institute on Drug Abuse, 2001; Richardson, Ryan, Willford, Day, & Goldschmidt, 2002).

Rh Incompatibility Another hazard to fetal development involves the presence or absence of a blood protein known as the Rh factor. Specifically, when a mother has an Rh negative blood factor—that is, her blood does not contain the protein—and the father is Rh positive, the fetus can also be Rh positive. In these cases, the mother's body may produce antibodies that attack the fetus, which can result in anemia, jaundice, miscarriage, stillbirth, heart defects, or brain damage. Fortunately, blood transfusions and vaccines can prevent problems for the fetus as well as for the mother's future babies (Narang & Jain, 2001).

Environmental Toxins Radiation, pesticides, chemicals, emissions, and other environmental toxins have been associated with birth defects and long-term developmental problems. Prenatal exposure to X-rays, mercury, and other chemicals and pesticides can affect the development of the fetus as well as cause problems such as miscarriage, disfigurement, low birth weight, and slow cognitive processing. Keep in mind that paternal exposure to environmental toxins can affect the genetic makeup of sperm as well, causing chromosomal and other abnormalities that can be passed on to the fetus (Gardella & Hill, 2000; Lanphear, Vorhees, & Bellinger, 2005; Timins, 2001). Some communities are seeing the deleterious effects of environmental toxins on birth patterns. For example, a community of the Aamjiwnaang First Nation in Canada has seen the number of male babies being born decline dramatically since the 1990s. This decline is being blamed on environmental toxins and stress due to economic hardships (Ecojustice, 2008; Global Community Monitor, 2007).

Paternal Age We have explored some of the issues surrounding maternal age with regard to prenatal development. Keep in mind, however, that sperm can also be affected by age, again, increasing the chance for chromosomal damage that can be passed on to the baby (LaRochebrochard & Thonneau, 2002; Schrag & Dixon, 1985). For instance, children of older fathers are at increased risk for problems such as autism, dyslexia, epilepsy, schizophrenia, and lower IQ (Nybo Andersen, Hansen, Andersen, & Smith, 2004; Saha et al., 2009; Vestergaard, Mork, Madsen, & Olsen, 2005).

Maternal Diseases Other factors that can affect fetal development include diseases contracted by the mother. One example is rubella—also known as German measles—which can cause infant death and structural malformations. Similarly, syphilis can damage organs later in fetal development and, if present at birth, can cause problems with the central nervous system and gastrointestinal tract. Herpes, which babies can contract as they move through the birth canal, can cause death or brain damage. Toxoplasmosis, a parasitic disease that the mother can contract through eating raw meat or coming into contact with animal feces, can cause brain damage and premature birth (Westheimer & Lopater, 2004).

Another hazard is HIV, which can be transmitted to the fetus from the mother through the placenta, bodily fluids during birth, and breast milk. Not only do HIV infection and AIDS have ramifications for the baby's quality of life, but mothers who learn of HIV infection during pregnancy may be at risk for developing disorders such as anxiety and depression, which can further threaten the health of the fetus (Kwalombota, 2002).

Genetic Disorders   Various genetic disorders can have severe consequences for the fetus. Chromosomal abnormalities are caused by errors that occur as the egg or sperm cell develops or as cells in a developing embryo divide. Down syndrome is one of the most frequently occurring chromosomal abnormalities that occur in a developing fetus. **Down syndrome** occurs when a fetus has an extra chromosome attached to chromosome pair number 21; hence, Down syndrome is also known as *trisomy 21*. Down syndrome causes a combination of problems, ranging from mild to severe, including mental retardation, identifiable facial characteristics, heart defects, and problems with hearing and eyesight. The average life expectancy of a child with Down syndrome is 55 years, with some people living into their 60s, depending on the severity of the symptoms (Hassold & Patterson, 1998; National Association for Down Syndrome, 2009).

The risks of having a baby with Down syndrome increase with maternal age. Women 25 years old have a 1 in 1,200 chance of having a baby with Down syndrome. These odds increase to about 1 in 100 for women 40 years old. Some evidence suggests that women who have had a Down syndrome baby also have had an abnormality in how their bodies metabolized folic acid, one of the B vitamins (National Down Syndrome Society, 2009; Santos-Reboucas et al., 2009). Other chromosomal abnormalities include trisomy 18, Turner's syndrome, Triple X syndrome, and Klinefelter's syndrome.

Spina bifida, also known as *open spine*, is a defect that affects the backbone and sometimes the spinal cord. It occurs when the neural tube—the embryonic structure that forms into the brain and spinal cord—does not close completely during development. Spina bifida is one of the most common severe birth defects, affecting 1,500 to 2,000 babies in the United States each year. It occurs more frequently among Hispanics and whites of European descent than among African Americans or Asians. Affected babies can exhibit no problems, or they can experience spinal fluid leakage, high risk of infections, bladder and bowel control problems, and paralysis. There is no known cause of spina bifida, although women who have diabetes or seizure disorders seem to be at higher risk. Also, although 95 percent of babies born with spina bifida come from families with no history of the disorder, chances of recurrence of the disorder increase with subsequent births (Menkes & Till, 1995; Spina Bifida Association, 2008).

Many genetic problems can be diagnosed prenatally. Increasingly, pregnant women aged 35 and over are being referred for tests that can detect problems early in pregnancy. For example, ultrasound, amniocentesis, blood testing, and chorionic villus sampling can detect many problems if conducted at certain stages of pregnancy. **Ultrasound** uses sound waves to capture images of the fetus and can offer views of basic anatomy. Although regular ultrasound exams are limited in terms of the types of defects they can detect, more technologically advanced ultrasounds are available that can aid in detecting Down syndrome, spina bifida, and other abnormalities. **Amniocentesis**, a test that uses a small amount of amniotic fluid, and **chorionic villus sampling (CVS)**, an exam that uses tissue samples from the placenta, are both used to determine whether birth defects are present. In addition, blood tests can detect fetal proteins that indicate the likelihood of defects (American College of Obstetricians and Gynecologists, 1996; Centers for Disease Control and Prevention, 1995; Hobbins, 1997; Spencer, Spencer, Power, Dawson, & Nicolaides, 2003).

Many of these tests carry some risks, and ultimately, none can offer results that are 100 percent accurate. For these reasons, many women decide against testing, choosing to avoid the anxiety that it can create. Further, some women may not have insurance coverage for these tests, which can be cost prohibitive.

Increasingly, families are suing hospitals and physicians for "wrongful birth" related to prenatal testing. Specifically, some families seek damages when prenatal tests fail to catch birth defects or when birth control procedures such as tubal ligation fail to prevent pregnancy, claiming that they deserve the right to recoup the life-long medical and other costs that raising an unexpected or special needs child will incur. Some states have barred these types of law suits, but other states allow them. Issues around costs, access, and information gleaned from prenatal testing create interesting ethical dilemmas for social workers and the families they work with. How do social workers help ensure that all families have accurate information about and access to prenatal testing? How do social workers help families decide whether or not to test? How do social workers work with families who find out they will have a child with a disability or a terminal illness? What rights do families have if prenatal testing is inaccurate, particularly if faulty information restricts the options and decisions a family can make about the pregnancy? At what point do we decide a birth defect is severe enough to warrant terminating the pregnancy? Should we blame parents for wanting to terminate such pregnancies? Should we consider the quality of life for the child and the family? And should individuals be responsible for all of the costs related to raising a child with disabilities or should society help support these families?

Ethical dilemmas aside, social workers can provide a great deal of support and information about birth defects and genetic testing to clients, which can be very empowering. They can educate clients on these issues, provide basic information, help clients access health care resources, and counsel clients about their options in cases where defects are an issue. In Josie's case, you can provide her with information about prevention measures that she can take to avoid some of the serious problems just discussed. Particularly because of Josie's age and current situation, your help in terms of education, information, referrals, and emotional support will be crucial.

PREGNANCY, BIRTH, AND THE FAMILY AND IMMEDIATE ENVIRONMENT

As mentioned at the beginning of the chapter, working with individuals requires social workers to assess their clients' problems and strengths from multiple levels.

This rule clearly applies when working with clients like Josie, who present with multilayered yet interconnected issues. This section discusses some aspects of pregnancy that need to be considered in clients' immediate environmental context.

Access to Health Care

Access to affordable and quality health care is an issue for many people in the United States. Though health care, in general, can be considered a macro issue, we discuss it here because of its strong links with income and employment. Health care, of course, is a particularly pertinent topic for pregnant women or women who are planning to become pregnant. Indeed, two of the most fundamental roles for practitioners who work with women and children are advocating for health care and assisting clients in receiving care.

Receiving good care early in pregnancy can prevent many long-term problems that are likely to result in high personal, economic, and social costs later on. However, even with the high level of awareness of the benefits of prenatal and postnatal care, many women still do not receive timely or adequate care. What are the barriers to receiving this care? Three major, interrelated barriers are poverty, lack of health insurance, and spiraling health care costs.

Two big issues for many clients are poverty and lack of health insurance. Many people are unemployed or underemployed; thus, they either cannot afford to purchase health insurance on their own or they do not receive health benefits from their employers. In 2007, 45.7 million people (15.3 percent) in the United States were uninsured (U.S. Census Bureau, 2008). Many of the uninsured do not qualify for government programs such as Medicaid that cover health care costs, including prenatal care. The lack of health insurance and access to affordable and culturally appropriate care disproportionately affects members of minority groups, creating health disparities resulting in higher rates of mortality and untreated chronic illness for these groups (U.S. Department of Health and Human Services, 2004).

A related issue is the high cost of health care. Rising health care costs can be attributed to three developments: (1) technological advances, (2) growing numbers of people without health insurance, and (3) increases in the number of malpractice suits. Regarding the first factor, although high-tech facilities and procedures have their advantages, they are also expensive. For example, the technology used to treat newborns with disabilities in the U.S. costs over $2.5 billion annually (Robbins et al., 2007). Thus, wealthy people or persons with insurance are generally those who have access to that technology—or the costs are passed on through higher prices and higher costs of insurance premiums. Allowing people to remain uninsured also contributes to the problem because uninsured patients often postpone treatment until their health problems become severe. Serious problems are more costly to treat in both the short and long terms, which in turn raises the overall costs of health care. Finally, as the number of malpractice suits increases, doctors' malpractice insurance fees rise, which they pass on to consumers. This last point is related to the ethical dilemma posed earlier with regard to prenatal testing. The more prenatal tests that are conducted, the more expense that is incurred from providing the tests. Increased testing leads to increased law suits due to incorrect results, leading to higher health care costs. But, the increase in law suits promotes more use of prenatal testing to avoid law suits. As this scenario illustrates, increased technology has its advantages, but it also brings with it a whole host of ethical and cost-related dilemmas.

Social workers who intervene with women and children need to be aware of these issues and to stay current on laws and policies that affect clients' access to health care and their eligibility. This responsibility becomes particularly important when clients need services but are not eligible for them because of restrictive policy criteria or rigid service boundaries.

Let us look at some considerations you might take into account while developing an intervention in Josie's case. One way to approach Josie's situation is to explore the programs available that will help Josie with prenatal and postnatal care should she decide to keep and parent her baby. This step will become crucial if Josie's parents decide not to support her, if Josie decides to continue with school rather than work, and if her boyfriend also refuses to participate in the process. Another approach is to rely on community organization or social action approaches to ensure that appropriate services are made available to people like Josie. For example, you may need to examine school policies to ensure that Josie has the support necessary for her to continue with her education should she decide to parent her child. You also need to work with the communities in which Josie lives and interacts to secure support for Josie in her decision-making processes.

The Relationship between the Birth Mother and Her Care Providers

With regard to health care, another consideration for social workers is the support that clients receive from their health care providers. Because so many people in the United States lack health insurance or depend on Medicaid to cover health care costs, finding physicians who accept either Medicaid payments or fees on a sliding scale and who are geographically accessible can be difficult for many pregnant women.

These observations also apply to many women whose private health insurance doesn't allow them to "shop around" for a physician who will be a good fit for their physical and emotional needs. These women frequently must use doctors who do not share their philosophies toward childbirth and child rearing or who do not have the time to spend with them to discuss their problems or anxieties regarding pregnancy and childbirth. As a result, these women sometimes postpone or reduce the number of prenatal visits they make to their doctor.

Control over the Childbirth Environment

Pregnancy and childbirth in the United States tend to be treated as an illness and disability rather than a natural event (Esposito, 1999). Consequently, control over the process tends to be given to the health professionals and not the women who are experiencing pregnancy. For many women, becoming educated about the childbirth process and asserting control over decisions about childbirth are a necessary part of the experience. The degree to which women achieve education and control depends a great deal on their access to literature on childbirth and to facilities with staff who will support their decisions. Women who can afford expensive care generally have much greater access to these choices than women living in or close to poverty.

Over the past few decades, physicians and health care facilities have responded to research that encourages them to allow women to birth in more natural settings in which they can move around and control the types of procedures that are performed during the labor process. Indeed, over this period of time, many women have chosen to give birth at home, bypassing medical facilities altogether. Most communities and health care facilities offer birthing classes that help prepare women and their partners for the processes of labor, breastfeeding, and caring for the newborn. In these classes the woman and her partner compose a birth plan that specifies which procedures she wishes to undergo and which ones she wishes to avoid.

Episiotomies   One example of women's exercising greater control over the birthing process is the decision by many to avoid having an episiotomy. An **episiotomy** is a procedure in which the doctor makes an incision in the perineum (the area of skin between the vaginal opening and the anus) to avoid tearing during childbirth. Although episiotomies were popular throughout much of the 20th century, recent research suggests that they are painful, and that women who undergo this procedure often require longer healing time than women who tear naturally. In fact, research suggests that few women tear anyway, making these procedures largely unnecessary. Critics of the procedure contend that some doctors who perform episiotomies do so to make stitching up the incision easier after birth. Episiotomy rates tend to differ based on country, culture, practices, beliefs, ethnic group, and training philosophies, which means that social workers who advocate for women in health care facilities need to be aware of the history, rationale, benefits, and risks behind the procedure (Carroli & Mignini, 2009; Goldberg, Holtz, Hyslop, & Tolosa, 2002)

C-Sections   There has also been a great deal of debate over the need for **Cesarean sections (C-sections)**, which involve an incision in the abdomen to deliver the baby. Research has suggested that the rate of C-sections in the United States— currently around 28 percent—is much higher than that in other developed countries (National Vital Statistics Reports, 2005). Significantly, the World Health

Organization (2003) suggests that rates over 15 percent indicate inappropriate use of the procedure. Reasons for high C-section rates include a trend toward hospital births and technological advances related to childbirth.

How has technology increased the rate of unnecessary C-sections? Because technology has increased the control that physicians have over the birthing process, women are now more likely to initiate a malpractice suit in the event that problems arise during childbirth. As we already observed, malpractice insurance for doctors is skyrocketing because the overall number of suits is escalating. Moreover, these suits often result in astronomical awards being given to the plaintiffs. Indeed, obstetrics is one of the medical specialties whose malpractice costs are spiraling out of control. Consequently, many doctors are abandoning the specialty and leaving many areas, particularly rural areas, without their services. In some rural areas, women must travel more than 100 miles to find an obstetrician. To avoid being sued, many doctors now take all possible precautions, including performing a C-section at the slightest sign of trouble during the birthing process. Finally, some women prefer C-sections because this procedure enables them to select a date and time of birth that fits into their busy schedules. Regardless of the reason, compared to vaginal births, C-sections tend to be riskier and more expensive, and they require a much longer healing time (AbouZahr & Wardlaw, 2001; Anderson, 2004).

Breastfeeding   In contrast to episiotomies and C-sections, breastfeeding is actually becoming more popular after years of reliance on scientifically developed formula. Only recently have women and physicians acknowledged the benefits of breast-feeding for both mothers and babies. With the rise of the medical model, many companies developed formulas that were touted as superior to breast milk. However, recent research indicates that the components in breast milk cannot be duplicated through formulas, mostly because researchers still cannot identify all of the components that make up breast milk (Gokcay, 2009; Oddy, 2002).

Research further suggests that children who are breastfed from birth are generally healthier than children reared on formula. They suffer from fewer infections over their lifetime, are better able to maintain their weight, handle stress better later in life, and have slightly higher IQs than children given formula. Mothers also benefit from breastfeeding. They return to their pre-pregnancy weights much faster, exhibit lower rates of cervical and breast cancer, and recover from childbirth more quickly than women who do not breastfeed. Specifically, breastfeeding helps the uterus to return to its pre-pregnancy shape, and it helps to stop bleeding after delivering the placenta (Gokcay, 2009; Habicht, Davanzo, & Butz, 1986; Howie et al., 1990; Montgomery, Ehlin, & Sacker, 2006). Social workers can certainly help to educate clients on the benefits of breastfeeding and help support clients who choose to do so. However, it is also important for social workers to support clients when they decide not to breastfeed. Many women, for a variety of reasons, choose to breastfeed for a short time or not at all. Often, these women face criticism from physicians, family members, and other mothers for their decision. Social workers

EXHIBIT 6.2

Breastfeeding carries many benefits for the child and mother

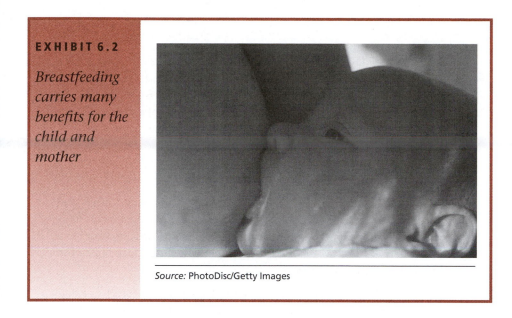

Source: PhotoDisc/Getty Images

can provide a great deal of emotional and other support to these women, helping to ensure the best possible outcomes for them and their babies.

Doulas and Midwives   With the movement toward more natural childbirth and against such traditional practices as C-sections and episiotomies, more women are turning to doulas and midwives to assist in childbirth. **Doulas** are assistants who provide physical, emotional, and informational support to women during the pre- and post-labor process. They specialize in nonmedical skills and do not perform clinical tasks such as exams. Women sometimes rely on doulas for assistance with healing, breastfeeding, and other aspects of caring for the newborn. Generally, doulas are not regulated except within the profession itself, which has various organizations that offer training, oversee certification, and maintain a code of ethics.

In contrast, **certified midwives** are registered nurses who have completed graduate-level programs in midwifery. Midwives offer an alternative to physicians for women who want extra attention and plan on a low-risk, natural childbirth. Increasingly, medical facilities are supporting the services of doulas and midwives, who often work side by side with the physician in the birthing process. Further, many women who opt for home birth use these services as well.

Birthing Classes   In addition to supportive assistance during and after childbirth, increasing numbers of women and their partners are taking advantage of birthing classes. There are several different approaches to birthing, and most communities offer courses that provide training on these different methods. Box 6.3 lists several of the more popular birthing methods and options currently available.

BOX 6.3

Birthing Methods, Options, and Classes

LOCATIONS AND PROCEDURES

- *Hospitals:* Options for hospital births can vary a great deal by facility. Some popular options are labor and recovery rooms, homelike "suites," and birthing centers. Hospitals also vary in the types of methods used for birth. Some offer tubs, Jacuzzis, birthing bars and balls, and rooms that accommodate movement and encourage massage, snacking, and listening to music. All of these settings allow doulas, midwives, and physicians to attend births, and they all provide access to pain relief and other medical procedures if needed. Some hospitals allow rooming-in, which is when the baby stays in the room with the mother for the entire hospital stay.

- *Freestanding birthing centers:* These centers provide an environment that is more homelike than many hospitals. Birthing centers encourage medication-free birthing techniques such as tubs, massage, and relaxation techniques. Births may be attended by doulas or midwives. However, most birthing centers are not equipped to perform C-sections or other medical procedures.

- *Home births:* Most people who choose home births have an assistant such as a doula or midwife. Many physicians will agree to serve as a backup to a home birth should complications arise. Tubs can be rented for use in the home. Many professionals do not recommend home births for women with high-risk pregnancies.

EDUCATION

- *Hospital classes:* Most facilities offer classes taught by doulas, midwives, or other childbirth specialists. These classes vary, but most incorporate information on nutrition, processes of labor, pain management, breastfeeding, and infant care.

- *Bradley method:* Many communities offer classes on natural methods of childbirth. They focus on techniques that do not require medication and that promote the participation of the husband or partner. Relaxation and breathing techniques are used that focus on "tuning into" the body.

- *Lamaze method:* Most communities, and many hospital programs, offer classes in the Lamaze method. This method advocates for natural childbirth techniques and active support by others during the labor process. It teaches relaxation and breathing techniques that train women to control pain by focusing outward to minimize pain.

- *Hypnosis/Hypnobirthing:* Classes explain that pain is not a necessary part of labor. They instruct women in the physiology of childbirth to reduce fear and anxiety and to help women control the process of labor. They also teach relaxation and focus techniques to allow the body to use its own source of pain relief.

Social workers can be strong advocates for women and their partners during pregnancy and childbirth, particularly for women who have trouble accessing care or who face difficult and confusing decisions about their care. Returning to the case of Josie, should Josie decide to carry out her pregnancy, she will need assistance in locating and securing a good physician. Given Josie's age and familial status, she will probably need to secure extra support, most likely from community sources, because her family may not help provide for her needs. A doula or midwife might be useful for her later in her pregnancy. This person can provide knowledge on positive health practices that will increase Josie's chances of experiencing a healthy pregnancy and birth. Moreover, along with the physician and a midwife or other practitioner, you can help Josie identify her strengths and needs to better cope with the many decisions she will have to make. Ultimately, you can help empower Josie to become her own advocate throughout the process and into parenthood. In this case, systems theory is one approach that you can use to organize all of this information and develop interventions that will benefit Josie.

Adoption

One choice that Josie can make is to give her baby up for adoption. Social workers often play a pivotal role in national and international adoption agencies, helping birth mothers and prospective adoptive parents navigate their way through the process of making decisions, filling out paperwork, meeting agency requirements, and working through the emotional aspects of adoption. Further, social workers can help mothers and their partners make decisions about whether to give their child up for adoption. They not only assist both the birth and adoptive parents in adjusting to the adoption, but they also work with the children to ensure that they are adjusting well to their new situation. Social workers also have been key players in securing rights for gay couples to adopt.

One trend that is becoming more common is **open adoption**, a policy that permits the biological parents, in collaboration with the adoptive family, to visit and communicate with their children. Usually, agencies help devise ground rules that guide the number and types of visits, and at times they also help facilitate the initial meetings between the two parties. Although problems with this approach do exist, research indicates that open adoptions tend to have emotional advantages for both the adoptive children and their biological parents (Gross, 1993). Still other research suggests that openness in adoption has little impact on families' adjustment to adoption (Berry, Cavazos Dylla, Barth, & Needell, 1998). However, many adoptive families feel that these contacts offer continuity in their children's lives and help the children adjust to the adoptive situation. Social workers can facilitate these processes while helping clients work through the emotions that open adoptions can generate.

One controversial issue that can confront social workers is interracial adoption. Some people argue that children need to be placed in loving homes, regardless of racial or ethnic background. Indeed, some research (e.g., Hamilton, Cheng, & Powell, 2007) suggests that adoptive parents, regardless of ethnic background, invest more time and financial resources into their adoptive children than do biological parents. This argument suggests that there are not enough families from all racial and ethnic groups to adopt the number of children from these groups who are waiting for homes, and children who are adopted are better off in general than children who are not. Critics of this approach contend that children should be placed only with families who share common ethnic origins, culture, and traditions. They further argue that ethnic groups experience discrimination when trying to adopt children and that Caucasian families receive preference for placement (Glazer, 1993; Samuels, 2009).

Social workers need to be well informed on the debates that occur regarding open and interracial adoptions so they can work effectively with their clients and make educated decisions about how to affect social policies on these issues. For example, if Josie decides to give her baby up for adoption, you will need to understand state and federal laws, agency procedures, and Josie's own feelings on interracial adoption. We will examine adoption in greater detail in Chapter 7.

Workplace Policies

Social workers often play an important role in assisting women with issues concerning employment policies when they are thinking of becoming pregnant, when they are going through pregnancy, after they have given birth, and while they are raising their children. Historically, and maybe even more so today, employment policies have not been supportive of family responsibilities. Many businesses lack maternity policies that clearly identify the rights of mothers, fathers, and other caregivers during pregnancy and afterward. In addition, many employers still do not allow women time or sterile facilities to breastfeed or pump and store breastmilk, nor do they provide quality day care resources. To address these problems, some states have enacted laws to force businesses and public places to allow women to breastfeed without harassment.

Unfortunately, when businesses allow women to take time off for maternity leave, breastfeeding, and other family responsibilities, it is unpaid time. Thus, women often find that they must choose between having and caring for a family and receiving a paycheck. Also, many women lose time and seniority when they take time off to have a child, which affects the amount of money that they earn for Social Security and pensions. Indeed, many women choose to leave their jobs because they want to stay home to raise their children, because they cannot afford day care, or for some other reason.

Regardless of the reasons behind their choice, many women lose income, and this can have short- and long-term effects on their economic well-being. Social workers can advocate for equitable workplace policies as well as broader social policies that will support all mothers and other caregivers regardless of their choice to remain employed or to stay at home. Federal policies concerning families are discussed in the next section.

PREGNANCY, BIRTH, AND THE LARGER SOCIAL ENVIRONMENT

When working with clients, social workers need to be able to negotiate the complex social and economic issues that can affect individual lives. This section examines some of the issues that social workers are likely to encounter in their work with pregnant mothers and their partners, particularly poverty, social policies, and environmental issues.

Effects of Poverty on Pregnancy and Birth

Poverty and its related facets can have devastating effects on new mothers, their babies, and their families. You have already seen how issues of health insurance and health care are related to poverty. In addition, social workers must consider how many other aspects of poverty can affect new families. For example, many families face challenges regarding food, safety, shelter, clothing, and transportation, all of which are affected by income. Also related are issues of substance abuse, domestic violence, and other familial and relational problems that can be aggravated by poverty. For example, one study found that poor women who are victims of domestic violence are less likely than nonabused women to use prenatal care and childbirth classes (Martin et al., 2001).

Poor women also face discrimination that can affect their treatment or medical care during pregnancy. For instance, poor women who use or abuse substances while they are pregnant are more likely to be prosecuted or lose custody of their children than are wealthy women. This treatment may be due to many factors, including lack of legal representation or access to services that can support their attempts at recovery; but it may also be due to stigmas attached to poor, pregnant women who are addicted to substances. Specifically, these women are often viewed as immoral, incompetent, and undeserving of their children or support services. These attitudes, which are often held by health care and other workers, can make it less likely that these women will receive appropriate or equitable care (Carter, 2002).

Maslow's Hierarchy of Needs Model   One way to view poverty and its effects on pregnant women is through the **hierarchy of needs** model developed by psychologist Abraham Maslow (1954). Maslow, who died in 1970, developed his model primarily through his clinical experiences. Maslow viewed humans as active players in their development, and he believed that people are naturally motivated to promote their well-being.

Maslow's theory is based on the ideas that humans have multiple needs and that they will actively work toward meeting their needs to maintain stability in their level of functioning. Exhibit 6.3 displays the needs that Maslow felt are common to all humans. This list is presented in hierarchical order of importance. As you can see,

EXHIBIT 6.3

Maslow's Hierarchy of Needs

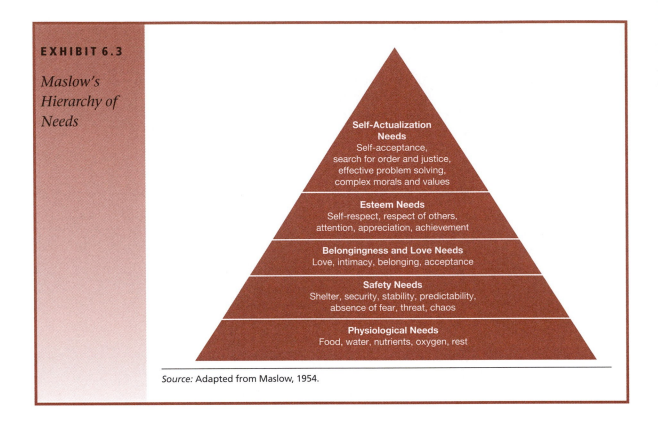

Source: Adapted from Maslow, 1954.

Maslow considered basic physiological needs to be more fundamental than needs of safety, love, and self-esteem. At the top of the hierarchy is **self-actualization**, Maslow's term for the desire of each individual to achieve her or his fullest potential. Theoretically, people need to meet fundamental needs before they can move up in the hierarchy to address higher needs. For example, our need for food is more critical to our survival than our need for love.

However, Maslow conceded that not all individuals satisfy needs in this order. In some cases, people might satisfy needs indirectly by meeting other needs. For example, a person might be able to satisfy the need for belonging and love through satisfying the need for esteem. That is, feelings of esteem, respect, and acceptance may be sufficient for a person to feel love and belonging, which ultimately can lead to feelings of self-actualization.

Although Maslow recognized that people can satisfy their needs in diverse ways, he nevertheless maintained that movement toward self-actualization is universal. According to Maslow, self-actualized people are self-accepting and respectful of others. They seek order and justice; appreciate truth and beauty; can effectively solve problems; are involved in satisfying relationships; show creativity, stability, and variety in emotional response; and have developed complex morals and values.

However, although all people seek self-actualization, many people never achieve it. Rather, they spend their lives simply trying to fulfill lower-priority needs.

Poverty, Pregnancy, and the Hierarchy of Needs   With regard to poverty and expectant mothers, Maslow's hierarchy of needs can be used to better understand the roadblocks that many low-income women have to overcome to achieve self-actualization and satisfy other needs. For instance, many pregnant women who are living in poverty struggle to secure food and shelter for themselves and their families. Most of their energy and motivation is directed toward these activities, leaving them with little energy or motivation to satisfy other needs such as belonging and achievement. In Josie's case, she might be more worried about her physical well-being than her need for love or other higher-order needs. In addition, she might need to focus on her baby's health and on securing adequate nutrition, shelter, and clothing for her baby as well as for herself. Consequently, she will likely postpone any efforts at addressing higher-order needs until she can meet her more basic needs. This kind of conceptualization can help you prioritize her needs and guide interventions that can assist Josie in meeting basic needs so that she can move on to meet more complex needs, with the goal of working toward self-actualization.

To a certain extent, Maslow's theory promotes a positive conceptualization of human behavior. Its view of humans as active and dynamic players in their development can be empowering for clients. Moreover, this theory can provide much-needed structure and direction in work with clients who present with many problems. It offers social workers and clients a way to prioritize problems and interventions, helping to keep both parties from feeling overwhelmed. Further, many of the lower-level needs are more concrete and "easier" for clients to satisfy than, say, working toward feeling a sense of peace and well-being in their life. In other words, locating housing can be a realistic place to begin with clients and can help clients feel in control of their lives more quickly than working on abstract ideas of happiness, which may seem out of reach to clients.

At the same time, moving through a hierarchy with clients can seem rigid and may go against the idea of "starting where the client is," which is a central tenet in social work practice. For example, a homeless, unemployed pregnant woman may want to begin by exploring her fears about being a parent. Or she may insist on talking about her desire to avoid the parenting mistakes that her parents made instead of focusing on good nutrition, prenatal care, and secure housing. Sometimes clients might not be amenable to adhering to the structure imposed by a hierarchical model, so social workers need to be flexible in their applications of such models.

Social Policies Related to Pregnancy and Birth

The United States has been criticized by many citizens and other countries for its lack of attention to issues involving children and families. Some of this criticism is based on the relative lack of social policy that ensures equitable rights and services, including health care, employment leave, and assistance for stay-at-home parents, to various groups such as women, children, and underemployed and unemployed people. Of the numerous social policy considerations relating to children and families, we will consider two critical issues: laws regarding medical leave and policies affecting international family planning.

Medical Leave Laws   The **Family and Medical Leave Act (FMLA)** of 1993 allows employees to take up to 12 weeks of unpaid time off from work within a 12-month period for the following reasons: (1) the birth or adoption of a child, (2) to care for a sick family member, or (3) serious health problems. This policy ensures that workers will not lose their job if they take time off. The FMLA applies only to businesses that employ more than 50 people and to employees who have been employed at the same business for at least 12 months (U.S. Office of Personnel Management, 1993). In 1997, the FMLA was expanded to allow employees unpaid leave up to 24 hours in a 12-month period for school activities, medical purposes, or elderly relatives' health care (U.S. Office of Personnel Management, 1997). In 2009, new military family leave entitlements within FMLA became effective. These additions allow family members to take time away from work to care for military personnel and to attend to matters that arise when military personnel are deployed, such as participating in military-sponsored functions or arranging for child care in the absence of a parent who is on active duty (U.S. Department of Labor, 2009).

Unfortunately, many of the people covered by this law either do not know that it exists or do not know how to use it. Social workers can assist these workers by ensuring that they are treated fairly with regard to this policy. Moreover, although the FMLA is a step in the direction of helping individuals balance work with family life, it does not go far enough with regard to securing wages when workers need time off for family matters. Simply put, many workers cannot afford to take this time without pay. Therefore, social workers must continue to campaign for policies that include compensation for time spent on family responsibilities.

International Family Planning   An important but sometimes controversial issue has emerged in the past few years. **International family planning** refers to support for policies in foreign—and usually less-developed—countries that provide funds for abortions, birth control, reproductive health, and other family services. Depending on the administration in power, the U.S. government tends to shift its philosophy on how international family planning should be conducted and for which activities it will pay. For example, conservative administrations tend to withhold funding from agencies that provide abortion services, regardless of the other services they provide; whereas liberal administrations generally support such agencies. There is ongoing debate about how U.S. policy should be applied to international family planning and what role family planning should play with regard to population control and women's health.

Within the social work discipline, the philosophy toward family planning and women's rights globally tends to be congruent with feminist perspectives. A good example of how family planning might be viewed through a feminist lens comes from a symposium held in 1997 by the International Women's Health Coalition, which consists of political, human rights, and other leaders from around the world. At this symposium, various lectures and discussions focused on women's issues, including health care, economic sufficiency, and human rights. Central to the ideas generated at this symposium is that women's rights, particularly those involving access to health and reproductive care, are not the focus of U.S. foreign policy or funding. Indeed, according to symposium participants, many U.S. policies that support foreign economic trade encourage the abuse of women's rights. As one example, potential female employees in U.S.-run businesses in Mexico are forced to undergo pregnancy tests to ensure that women who are pregnant or who report behaviors that put them at high risk for becoming pregnant are not hired.

The Coalition further charged that the goal behind family planning abroad historically has been to provide women with contraception or sterilization to avoid future pregnancies. According to the Coalition, this mind-set invalidates the varied reasons (for example, high infant mortality rates) why many women, particularly in poor countries, have multiple births. It also places little or no value on women's worth in the family and the economic structure of their community. Instead of providing services that encourage healthy pregnancies and ensure healthy children who can contribute to the community, current policies undermine women's abilities to contribute to the growth and well-being of their communities by focusing exclusively on contraception. This approach ignores the other problems that women face in achieving optimal health, such as poverty, illness, discrimination, and high maternal and infant mortality rates. It also undermines women's self-determination (International Women's Health Coalition, 1997).

Reflecting ideas similar to those espoused by the International Women's Health Coalition, social workers tend to support funding and strategies for family planning that offer a wide range of services and maximize individuals' right to self-determination. Although some social workers may disagree with offering certain services such as abortion, they can still work within a feminist framework that advocates for human rights and lifestyle choices (for example, allowing women to remain at home with the child or securing quality day care that enables women to work full time) without compromising their own values. For example, they can advocate for policies that enhance the safety and effectiveness of contraceptive methods, widen the range of family planning methods available to men and women, and improve the quality of family planning service delivery. They can also work to eliminate violence toward women, including genital mutilation, and retaliation against women who become pregnant outside of wedlock. Abortion services, including counseling to avoid abortions or repeat abortions, are just one aspect of a complex array of services that social workers can provide to help improve the lives of women (World Health Organization, 2003).

Research clearly shows that family planning saves the lives of millions of women and children in developing countries. Planning efforts promote the healthy spacing of births, prevent the spread of sexually transmitted infections like AIDS/HIV, reduce the number of low birth weight babies, allow for longer breast-feeding, prevent unsafe or repeated abortions, and decrease the mortality rates of mothers and babies (Ahmad, 2000; Krisberg, 2003; Smith, Ashford, Gribble, & Clifton, 2009; Women's International Network, 1998). Further, research indicates that women are just as likely to seek abortions in countries where such procedures are illegal as they are in locations where abortions are legal. Unfortunately, women who receive abortions in locations where they are illegal are at higher risk for mortality due to unsafe procedures (Sedgh, Henshaw, Singh, Ahman, & Shah, 2007). Ultimately, healthy women and children contribute to the economic base and overall development of their communities. This is very much in keeping with social work goals.

Environmental Issues Related to Pregnancy and Birth

Many issues discussed in the section on family planning can also be applied to issues of environmental viability and safety. The environment clearly plays a significant role in the health and well-being of pregnant women and their children. Environmentally based problems such as violence, disease, famine, pollution, and over-crowding severely affect millions of children and pregnant women around the world, particularly in less-developed countries.

Social workers have been criticized by other helping professionals and by some within the social work profession for not paying enough attention to global issues that affect human health and well-being. Though social workers cannot be expected to solve the world's environmental problems singlehandedly, they can act locally, nationally, and globally to alleviate these problems. For example, they can advocate for stricter regulation of immigrant workers' exposure to pesticides in the fields in which they work. These pesticides can cause irreparable damage to sperm and egg cells, which in turn can harm the fetus, causing birth defects. Social workers can also lobby for higher wages for these workers and for access to better health care services that provide prenatal and postnatal care for their children.

Social workers who provide services in foreign countries can campaign for improved and safer working conditions in factories. This strategy would include advocating for the rights of workers not to be exposed to harmful chemicals and to receive equitable benefits that allow them to tend to family responsibilities. Social workers can also assist communities in developing sustainable farms and economic structures that enable people to maintain self-sufficiency and support their families. Understanding social action and community organization theories and approaches helps social workers to become effective practitioners and social change agents on this level.

CONCLUSION

Prenatal development is an important concept that social workers need to understand in the course of their work. Though social workers often work collaboratively with other health care professionals, they often have frequent contact with pregnant clients and their partners, which means that they can have great impact on clients' decisions and behaviors regarding prenatal and other issues. Many clients will approach social workers with issues surrounding pregnancy, pregnancy planning, health care, parenting issues, and similar concerns.

While much of the focus of this chapter has been on biological issues affecting the fetus, many of the theories discussed in previous chapters can help guide social workers' assessment and intervention with clients who are pregnant. Regardless of the issues that clients bring to the working relationship (for example, whether or not to abort, adopt out, or keep the baby; how to secure good health care or other services after the baby is born; or how to acquire good parenting skills), various theories, models, and perspectives can be used in conjunction with the information discussed in this chapter to provide effective services to clients. For instance, you can use systems and ecological theories to help ascertain the various factors, besides biological ones, that might impact a pregnant woman and her decisions and overall well-being. You can use Erikson's theory of psychosocial development to better understand the developmental stages of clients and how pregnancy may impact the tasks that clients must complete to successfully move on to subsequent stages. You may find conflict and other sociological theories helpful in considering how social factors help or hinder clients' access to support services. Finally, community organization theories may help you to ensure that services such as abortion, adoption, and pre- and postnatal care are available in all communities.

MAIN POINTS

- The first trimester involves the most complex and crucial development in the fetus; thus, it is considered the most critical with regard to prenatal care and fetal exposure to maternal and environmental toxins. Social workers need to be aware of factors that can cause low birth weight and premature birth and consider interventions that can help prevent them or alleviate their consequences.

- Client self-determination, a core ethical standard in social work, is particularly relevant when working with women who are pregnant or considering becoming pregnant. Social workers must be prepared in advance to deal with personal, value-laden issues surrounding pregnancy, both planned and unplanned.

- Many hazards to fetal development exist, including birth defects; exposure to teratogens, toxins, and other substances; Rh incompatibility; paternal age; maternal diseases; and genetic disorders.

- Poverty, lack of health insurance, and lack of access to quality health care are major problems for many clients. Employers' policies on family leave also have considerable impact on clients.

- Social workers need to attend to the relationship between pregnant clients and their health care providers because it is important to clients' well-being and many clients do not get to choose their health care providers.

- Maslow's hierarchy of needs views people as active agents who strive to meet physiological, safety, belongingness, esteem, and self-actualization needs. Although it is a positive and useful conceptualization, it is not always amenable to "starting where the client is."

- The Family and Medical Leave Act is an attempt to address issues of workers needing to take care of their family responsibilities. International family planning is a controversial policy issue in the United States that tends to reflect federal administrative philosophy about women's and family health issues.

- Environmental issues such as pollution, violence against women, and trade policies present opportunities for advocacy by the social work profession, especially as they relate to women who are pregnant. Parents often face issues on many levels that influence the health of their children and that dictate the nature of care that parents provide to their children.

EXERCISES

Using the Sanchez Family interactive case (go to www.routledgesw.com/cases), review the major issues involving the Sanchez family, particularly those involving Emilia, who is experiencing an unplanned pregnancy. After thoroughly reviewing this information, answer the following questions:

1. What problems, either existing or potential, do you see in the Sanchez family that are related to the topics discussed in this chapter? What strengths can you identify?

2. In what ways might these problems affect individual family members and the family as a whole? (Remember to include aspects related to individual, family, and larger social levels.)
3. As a social worker who intervenes with the family, how would you prioritize these problems and why?
4. What types of interventions might you develop for the individual members and/or the family as a whole?
5. What ethical issues might you face in working with the family?

CHAPTER 7

Development in Infancy and Early Childhood

Sam is a four-year-old Native American boy who has been attending Head Start classes in his community, an urban town located several hundred miles from the reservation where he was born. Sam's parents moved to this town shortly after Sam was born to look for better employment. Sam's teacher asked a social worker from a mental health agency to come and observe Sam because she noticed that his cognitive and social development seemed to lag behind that of the other children. For example, Sam has trouble remembering when to use the bathroom, has not developed a very large vocabulary, and seems overly withdrawn when other children try to engage him in play.

The teacher has discussed her concerns with Sam's parents, who state that they notice nothing unusual in his behavior at home. Sam's mother states that Sam has no problem with toileting at home and is able to express his needs well to his parents. Sam has no siblings, but his mother states that Sam frequently plays with neighborhood children. Sam's parents see no need for concern and are upset that the Head Start teacher would ask a social worker to observe Sam.

DEVELOPMENTAL MILESTONES IN INFANTS AND YOUNG CHILDREN

AS WITH DEVELOPMENT IN THE FETUS, WE SEE RAPID DEVELOPMENT in infants and young children. Many parents are amazed (and sometimes disheartened!) to see how quickly their children develop motor, language, cognitive, and other skills and how rapidly they become assertive individuals who verbalize their needs and wishes. Indeed, development in young childhood takes place so quickly that many parents are taken by surprise at how their children seem to change overnight. These rapid developments can also be a source of stress for parents if they think that their children are not developing "normally" or keeping pace with other children in the same age range.

This chapter explores just some of the developmental milestones that occur in infants and young children up until five or six years of age. Though the pace at which infants and children develop varies greatly, this discussion offers you some basic guidelines to follow that will help you in your work with clients. For social workers in situations like Sam's, understanding basic developmental milestones in infants and young children will help them make an accurate biopsychosocial assessment, which will then help to inform them whether or not some kind of intervention is, indeed, necessary.

Language Acquisition

For most parents, hearing a child's first words can be one of the most exciting events of parenthood. From the day their child is born, most parents spout a near-constant stream of words, sounds, and phrases in hopes that the child will offer a verbal response. After all, language is a crucial aspect of human interactions. It is the way we communicate, whether that communication takes place through written, verbal, or nonverbal form. Even though infants cannot communicate through spoken language, they can communicate in other ways that ensure that their needs will be met until they are able to articulate their needs through spoken words. A comprehensive discussion of language acquisition must address a fundamental question: Are language development and proficiency genetically preprogrammed, or do environmental factors influence these skills? Specifically, are we born with language skills, or is language development solely a product of our environment and learning? We will explore this question in this section.

Right after birth, infants interact by using vocalizations that convey different messages to their caregivers. Generally, these vocalizations develop beginning with basic sounds and progress to more complex verbalizations (Sigelman & Rider, 2005). Table 7.1 lists these vocalizations in order of development and complexity.

Evidence suggests that infants recognize meaningful spoken sounds before they understand words. For instance, infants can distinguish the 150 sounds that make up speech, and by six months of age, they can specialize in the sounds that make up their native language. Moreover, the clearer mothers' articulation is in making those sounds, the more infants can discriminate various sounds (Kuhl, 1993; Liu, Kuhl, & Tsao, 2003).

On average, children speak their first words between 10 and 15 months of age, after which their vocabulary increases at a rapid rate. By about 18 months of age children have a vocabulary of 50 words, and by two years of age their vocabulary has expanded to include around 200 words. Usually, children will begin using words that have meaning to them, such as *dada, mama, doggie, juice, bye-bye,* and so on. Between the ages of 18 and 24 months, children use two-word combinations to express thoughts such as "more juice" and "want ball." Though children do not begin to speak words until around 10 months of age, they show signs of comprehending words at an earlier age, usually around eight months of age (Sigelman &

TABLE 7.1	VOCALIZATION	AGE EXHIBITED	DESCRIPTION
Early Vocalizations in Language Development of the Infant	Crying	Beginning from birth	Can signal fear, anger, pain, and hunger.
	Cooing	Approximately three weeks to two months	Repeated vowel-like sounds such as "ooh" or "aah." Cooing is often associated with contented states.
	Babbling	Approximately four to six months	Repeated consonant and vowel combinations that sound like words but have no outward meaning such as "baba."
	Gestures	Approximately 8 to 12 months	Behaviors that include pointing and showing, such as waving, nodding, and pointing out objects.

Source: Adapted from Hopper & Naremore, 1978; Snow, 1999.

Rider, 2005). By three years of age, most children have a vocabulary of approximately 1,000 words and can speak in full sentences.

Some evidence suggests that there are separate and unique tasks that must be mastered in speech production. For example, Dodd and Carr (2003) examined children between the ages of four and six and found that children perform better at recognizing print forms of letters and words and the sounds that different letters make before they are able to recall or reproduce those letters and sounds or understand the rules of grammar. Moreover, these researchers found that children who came from groups of lower socioeconomic status (SES) had more difficulty in developing all of these tasks than children from higher-income groups. This suggests that the environmental context may influence the rate of speech development. The effects of SES on language development have been articulated in other studies (e.g., Hoff, 2003), which have suggested that children from higher SES families develop larger vocabularies than children from lower-SES families.

Biological vs. Behavioral Perspectives on Language Development Language development is universal, meaning that children across the globe tend to reach various milestones at roughly the same time. For this reason, many psychologists argue that there is a biological basis of language. Indeed, mounting evidence suggests that biological factors do influence speech and speech development. For example, two specific areas of the brain have been identified in speech production and comprehension. Broca's area, associated with speech production, is located in the left frontal lobe, and Wernicke's area, associated with speech comprehension, is located in the left hemisphere. Injuries to these areas can lead to significant impairment in language skills (Brown, 1977). Additionally, Noam Chomsky (1975), a well-known linguist, has argued that humans are prewired to develop language skills at certain times. That is, according to his theory, children are born with a **language acquisition device (LAD),** a built-in mechanism for acquiring language that allows them to make sense of language and eventually master it.

In contrast, B. F. Skinner and other behaviorists posit that children learn language through listening to others in their environment and repeating the sounds, words, and phrases that they hear. Parents and those around them reinforce children for appropriate speech patterns, which in turn helps children learn language. As children grow older, they continue to be corrected when they make mistakes in speech, which helps them to learn correct forms of grammar.

Balancing the Biological and Behavioral Perspectives   A more balanced view of language development can be found somewhere between biologically and behaviorally centered views. Evidence suggests that although the capacity to develop language skills is genetic, children must be exposed to various environmental stimulants, such as interaction with others, to master these skills (Berwick, 2009; Harkness, 1990; Hopper & Naremore, 1978; Snow, 1999). There has been no specific evidence to suggest that language development is strictly based on either genetic or behavioral and environmental influences. Indeed, several studies examining behavioral influences have found that although parents offer praise and reinforcement for their children's vocalizations, they tend to reinforce incorrect verbalizations along with correct ones. However, children are able to correct themselves without appropriate models. Further, many children in societies or conditions where little interaction or reinforcement is given still manage to develop skills comparable to children reared in more interactive contexts (Clark, 2000). These studies suggest that factors other than behavioral influences affect language acquisition skills. However, at the same time, some evidence indicates that children reared in environments in which interaction is limited exhibit smaller vocabularies and less-developed language skills than children who have more exposure to regular discourse (Hart & Risley, 1995; Hoff, 2003). In sum, then, genetic and environmental factors appear to work together to influence language development.

In what ways might information on language development be helpful in Sam's situation? If you were Sam's social worker, you may want to assess the degree to which his limited vocabulary is a product of genetic issues, learning problems, or environmental context—so you could assess this situation from a biopsychosocial or ecological approach. Based on the research, you might want to pay attention to all of these aspects, including cultural factors that could be impacting his use of language. Given his mother's lack of concern for Sam's developmental level, it may be that his performance is "normal" for his culture.

Emotional Development

Emotion, as a concept, is difficult to define because it encompasses so many facets of the human experience. Generally, **emotion** constitutes affect, or a feeling that causes some kind of physiological, behavioral, or cognitive response. Izard (1991) defines emotion as a "feeling that motivates, organizes, and guides perception, thought and action" (p. 14). In infants, you can generally sense what kind of emotion they are experiencing through their use of language (for example, cries or coos, as described in Table 7.1). As children grow older, they can verbalize their emotions, making it clearer how they feel.

You may wonder how emotion develops. Is it present at birth? Research suggests that infants express interest, distress, and disgust from birth. As with language, emotions become increasingly complex as children grow. At about four to six weeks, infants exhibit social smiling; that is, smiling in response to external stimuli. At about three to four months, they will show anger, sadness, and surprise. By five to seven months, children express fear; by six to eight months, shame and shyness; and by two years, guilt and contempt (Izard, 1982).

Stranger and separation anxiety are two common forms of emotion among infants and young children. **Stranger anxiety**, or intense fear of unfamiliar people, tends to develop around six months of age. Infants vary widely in the ways they display this reaction, if they demonstrate it at all. Infants' reactions tend to depend on the stranger and the situation in which infants encounter the stranger. **Separation anxiety** is a fear that many children have of being separated from their caregivers. It can manifest itself as early as eight to nine months of age, but it more typically appears at around 12 to 18 months and then gradually decreases after 18 months. As with stranger anxiety, the intensity and frequency with which children show separation anxiety tend to vary a great deal. Childrens' reactions may depend on the situation as well as personality characteristics such as their temperaments, discussed later in the chapter (Partamian, 2009; Rende, 2000; Scher & Mayseless, 2000).

Another emotional development milestone in infants and young children is **social referencing**, in which children can detect emotional cues in others and respond to them appropriately. This skill helps children make sense of their environments and various situations so that they are better able to react to those around them. Beginning in early infancy, children look to their caregivers for cues. While facial cues are important in social referencing, one study (Vaish & Striano, 2004) suggests that infants react more strongly to caregivers' vocal cues. For example, in dangerous situations, infants tended to react more strongly to caregivers' verbal warnings than to their facial expressions, suggesting that the voice may be a more powerful mode of communication than facial cues alone. As infants get older, they become more adept at reading and responding to these cues (Mumme, Fernald, & Herrera, 1996). As infants develop, they are more capable of using adaptive functions and coping strategies to regulate their emotions. Children between the ages of two and three years old can use language to describe their emotions, and they have a better understanding of the causes and consequences of emotions. Children between the ages of four and five years old begin to understand how events bring about emotions in themselves and others, and they become aware of the importance of controlling emotions (Denham, 1998).

When observing Sam, you might certainly want to pay attention to "normal" emotional developmental milestones such as those relating to separation anxiety and regulation of emotion. However, because emotion is such a complex construct, you might also want to explore how cultural, biological, behavioral, and environmental factors might be affecting Sam's emotional development, which is why assessing his situation from a biopsychosocial perspective might be useful. For example, it would be useful to know what cultural expectations Sam's parents may have with regard to how they express emotions toward Sam or how they expect him to react to them. You might also want to consider the type of attachment that Sam has with his parents, as well as the developmental tasks (for example, from Erikson's or Piaget's point of view) with which Sam is grappling.

These perspectives may help you organize the information that is gathered in observation and assessment. For example, these constructs may help you answer such questions as, "Cognitively, how might Sam be able to control his emotions?" or "Which emotions might be 'normal' for Sam at this particular psychosocial stage?" Moreover, you may want to attend to the strengths that Sam and his family exhibit, using these as a starting point from which to develop an intervention, if one is warranted. For example, perhaps Sam's family encourages emotional expression; this might be viewed as a strength upon which you can build an intervention to help Sam work through emotional issues, if present.

Motor Development

Many motor developments take place during infancy and early childhood. As with other areas of development, these behaviors begin as simple reflex actions and develop into more complex and deliberate movements as the child grows. Motor skill development can be considered in two main categories: gross motor skills and fine motor skills. **Gross motor skills** include those movements that use large muscle activities, such as walking or pushing an object. During the first year, infants develop gross motor skills very rapidly. Some of the major tasks that children master in this first year are controlling their heads, controlling their balance, and stabilizing their arm and leg muscles for walking and manipulating their environments. Preschoolers are more coordinated in their gross motor skills than infants, and by three years of age children can easily perform actions such as jumping, skipping, and running. By ages four and five, children become even more adept at these skills and can become very adventurous in their play. Table 7.2 lists the ages at which infants and young children generally reach some of the major milestones for gross motor skills.

TABLE 7.2	AGE	SKILL
Major Milestones in Gross Motor Development	0–1 month	Infants can stabilize the head and neck.
	2–4 months	Infants can lift their chest and use arms for stabilization.
	2–5 months	Infants can roll over.
	3–6 months	Infants can use their legs to support weight.
	5–8 months	Infants can sit up on their own.
	5–10 months	Infants can stand with some support.
	6–10 months	Infants can use their arms to pull themselves to standing position.
	7–13 months	Infants can walk using supports.
	10–14 months	Infants can stand without support.
	11–14 months	Infants can walk without support.

Source: Adapted from Sigelman & Rider, 2005.

Fine motor skills involve small movements made by small muscle groups such as those found in the fingers and toes. By two months of age, infants can hold objects, albeit only briefly. By four months, they can hold onto objects, and by six months they are able to manipulate objects by banging them against other objects. At eight months infants can lift objects with all fingers, and by one year they can grasp small objects such as handles and cords. (This means, of course, that they can now get into drawers, cupboards, and other places that parents need to secure!) By 18 months children can manipulate objects by pushing and pulling, and by age two children can manipulate even smaller objects such as pages in a book. At age three, most children can manipulate small objects, but they are still clumsy at it. By age four, children become much more coordinated, and their movements are more precise. At age five, children's eye–hand coordination improves significantly, making movements even more precise (Sigelman & Rider, 2005).

The developmental progression of both types of motor skills tends to follow an orderly, predictable pattern. One aspect of this progression is **cephalocaudal development**, which means that development occurs from head to toe; that is, infants learn to control their necks, heads, and arms before they learn to crawl or walk. Another aspect is **proximodistal development,** which refers to the tendency of the trunk area to develop before the extremities do. For example, infants learn to sit up and manipulate their trunks before they are able to use two fingers to grasp an object.

As Sam's social worker, having a basic understanding of these milestones can be useful in determining how well he is progressing in developing his motor skills. Although there are no apparent problems in this area for Sam, with some observation, you may find some problems that could offer insight into other developmental issues, such as toileting and shyness in play. Because the pace and order of motor skill development tend to be universal, with some variability, Sam should be exhibiting certain skills based on his age. However, keep in mind that cultural differences in expectations of certain skills could exist for Sam's family. Further, because Sam seemingly shows no troubles with skills at home, something about the classroom environment could be causing Sam trouble. You could also rely on Piaget's theory of cognitive development to help guide your assessment of various motor skills, keeping in mind the limitations of this theory, as discussed in Chapter 3.

THE INDIVIDUAL IN INFANCY AND EARLY CHILDHOOD

In addition to the physical changes that occur in infants and young children as they develop, social workers need to consider other significant areas in development. Although physical milestones can be conceptualized through medical and similar models, many of the areas discussed next are viewed through psychological, sociological, or person-in-environment theories.

Attachment

Many theorists and practitioners maintain that attachment is a critical facet of infant development. **Attachment**, as discussed here, refers to the bond or relationship between an infant and her or his caregivers, particularly the mother. Though there have been many famous studies on attachment in infancy (for example, J. Bowlby, 1969; Harlow & Zimmerman, 1959; Lorenz, 1965), perhaps the most popular theory of attachment was developed by Mary Ainsworth. Through her research, Ainsworth (1979) described four different types of attachment styles between infants and their mothers, which are listed in Box 7.1.

BOX 7.1

Ainsworth's Styles of Attachment

- *Secure:* The caregiver serves as a safe base from which an infant can explore the outside environment. The infant seems confident in exploring her world but will return to the caregiver if unsure or afraid.

- *Insecure avoidant:* Infants show little interaction with the caregiver but will cry when the caregiver leaves. The infant shows reluctance in interacting with the caregiver when that person returns.

- *Insecure resistant:* The infant may be clingy with the caregiver and refuse to explore but try to push away when being comforted.

- *Insecure disorganized:* Infants appear confused and fearful. They may show fear, anxiety, or resistance around the caregiver.

Source: Adapted from Ainsworth, 1979.

Ainsworth proposed that the quality of attachment in early infancy affects subsequent social behavior and development. However, studies on attachment show mixed results. Some studies suggest that secure attachments lead to better friendships and positive relationships in late childhood and adolescence (for example, McElwain, Booth-LaForce, Lansford, Wu, & Dyer, 2008; Salter, 1940; Schneider, Atkinson, & Tardif, 2001; Zimmerman, 2004); whereas others suggest that the relationship between attachment and the development of later peer relationships may be more complex, with other psychosocial factors also influencing the development of friendships (for example, Coleman, 2002; Polenski, 2002; Thompson, 2000).

Attachment theory can be useful for social workers who work with children and families, particularly those who focus on parenting skills and child–parent relationships. However, social workers should keep in mind that research findings on the consequences of attachment are inconclusive.

Secure Attachments: The Debates   For many researchers and practitioners, positive attachment between infants and their caregivers is viewed as the primary foundation of stable and healthy development in later life. Recall that Erikson espoused this view in his first stage of psychosocial development. Based on Ainsworth's and subsequent research, caregivers (usually defined as mothers) who are consistently responsive to their infants' needs and who serve as a secure base to which infants can turn when needed will provide a secure attachment for their infants. For example, one study (McElwain & Booth-LaForce, 2006) found that mothers' responses to their infants' distress were more important for secure attachments than attention given when infants were content. Other researchers (McElwain et al., 2008; Zimmerman, 2004) argue that these infants, in turn, are more likely than infants and mothers who display other attachment styles to develop secure and healthy relationships with others in the future.

This view on attachment has raised many questions and sparked many debates. To begin with, many people argue that the relationship between the infant and the father (or partner) should be examined as well as that between the infant and mother. Moreover, critics posit that the relationship between caregivers should be examined to determine how this relationship affects attachment between caregivers and the infant. Does a child who has a secure attachment to any caregiver fare just as well as one who has a secure attachment to her or his mother? What effect does a marital or similar relationship have on the quality and type of an infant's attachment to her or his caregivers? Even more volatile is the question of how day care affects an infant's attachment. Some researchers contend that day care, particularly in the early months of an infant's life, negatively affects the attachment between the infant and her or his primary caregiver (for example, Belsky & Braungart, 1991; Brandtjen & Thomas, 2001).

Other studies have challenged this negative assessment of day care. At the heart of these debates are questions about the quality of day care and the quality of attachments that infants have with their caregivers. Some evidence suggests that infants placed in quality day care settings do not show any problems in attachment (for example, R. Bowlby, 2007; Owen, 2002). Moreover, when studying the effects of day care on infant attachment, researchers have difficulty controlling for other variables that might contribute to secure or insecure attachments. For example, stress, poverty, poor relationships, and other problems occurring outside the day care setting may compound other problems that caregivers encounter in responding to their infants' needs.

Insecure Attachments: The Causes   Issues such as stress, poverty, and substance abuse need to be considered when examining relationships between infants and their caregivers. Often, clinicians and others are too quick to blame caregivers, particularly mothers, for insecure attachments between the mothers and their infants. Many caregivers who are experiencing multifaceted problems brought on by unemployment and lack of resources, for example, may be less likely or able to respond to their infants in a secure and loving way than caregivers who have adequate social supports and resources and are not investing all their energy in survival. As an example, one study found that infants exposed to prenatal alcohol were more likely than those not exposed to exhibit insecure attachments with their mothers (O'Connor, Kogan, & Findlay, 2002). However, attachments became more secure if mothers showed support to their infants. Though this study focuses on some of the possible biological mediators that can influence attachment (such as developmental problems caused by alcohol that can interfere with attachment), it also exemplifies the complex nature of attachment and environment. Specifically, mothers who drink during pregnancy may also be dealing with a multitude of problems such as stress and poverty. Determining which variables, and in which combinations, are affecting attachment styles is a difficult task. Consequently, approaching such an assessment using multiple theories and perspectives may help to ensure that you, as a social worker, don't miss important influences on attachment that might need attention.

In Sam's case, although no evidence suggests that his attachment to his caregivers is anything but secure, assessing these relationships might be useful, particularly if you are using a theoretical perspective such as Erikson's or Ainsworth's to assess Sam's level of development. Specifically, the quality of Sam's attachments, in combination with developmental milestones, may tell you a great deal about Sam's developmental level. They might also suggest the kinds of problems that Sam might face in later development if intervention does not take place. If Sam is dealing with issues regarding physical development or establishing trust, for example, and these issues are not addressed, he could experience more serious problems as he moves into the next stage (in Erikson's theory) and is expected to perform at levels that are more physically and emotionally complex.

Temperament

The complex concept of **temperament** can be thought of as the consistent ways in which we respond, behaviorally and emotionally, to our environment. Significantly, temperament is generally thought to be present at birth and is considered to be a fairly stable trait throughout life, although it can be shaped by later experiences. Research suggests that temperament in infancy is associated with heredity; however, this association tends to lessen as infants grow older, further supporting the notion that environmental influences may play a part in temperament (Barry, Kochanska, & Philibert, 2008; Goldsmith, Buss, & Lemery, 1997; Goldsmith, Lemery, Buss, & Campos, 1999; Lemery, Goldsmith, Klinnert, & Mrazek, 1999). Indeed, many developmental researchers spend a great deal of time and effort studying infant temperament and how it impacts and interacts with the infant's environment.

Social scientists have created a variety of ways of classifying temperament. One classification scheme developed by Chess and Thomas (1977), based on their research, conceptualizes three main temperament styles:

- *The easy child:* These children generally display happy, positive moods and adapt easily to their environment.

- *The difficult child:* These children are fussy, cry frequently, and have trouble adapting to changes in the environment.

- *The slow-to-warm-up child:* These children tend to show low levels of activity, emotion, and adaptability and tend to be somewhat negative.

Temperament theories have generated a lot of discussion and controversy. One of the biggest issues is whether the current classifications accurately capture the complete range of temperaments. This issue can be resolved only through further study. In the meantime, using these classifications as guidelines for understanding emotions and their effects on relationships can be useful in practice. For example, social workers can help parents or caregivers better understand their infants' temperament and possible reactions to their environment, which in turn can help parents alter their own reactions to their children when problems occur. Further, parents can better understand how their own temperaments interact with those of their children, which can help to improve interactions and relationships.

Why is temperament considered an important aspect of infant development? Much of the importance has to do with "goodness of fit." This concept relates to how well infants' temperaments fit with their environmental context and what consequences might occur because of this fit (e.g., Daniel, Grzywacz, Leerkes, Tucker, & Han, 2009; Pluess & Belsky, 2009). For example, an easy child exposed to a strange and intimidating situation may react by taking things in their stride and adapting readily to the context, limiting the amount of stress experienced by the infant and those in her environment. Conversely, a difficult child who is exposed to the same

Source: Jack Star/PhotoLink/Getty Images

EXHIBIT 7.1

At birth, babies already display individual temperaments

strange situation may react by crying and fussing and not adapting to the situation. This behavior will create stress not only for the infant but for those around her, as they will probably fail to console her and may blame themselves for her distress.

This interaction between an infant's temperament and the environment becomes an issue for parenting, and many social workers tackle parenting issues in their work with clients. Specifically, social workers need to help parents and care-givers become knowledgeable about and sensitive to the individual temperaments of their children. Social workers can help parents become more flexible and adaptable to the unique characteristics of their children, which may help parents avoid unfairly or prematurely labeling their children in negative ways and responding to them based on these labels. Parents who understand temperament issues of their children are more likely to adapt their own parenting style and their environmental context to better fit the temperament of the child, which may alleviate some of the problems that the parents experience in dealing with their children. Some health care clinics offer computerized assessments of children's temperaments that parents can use to learn more about their children's behavior. These computer programs also offer suggestions about how to use certain parenting skills to adjust to particular temperament styles.

In Sam's case, you might want to assess his temperament style to ascertain whether some of the behaviors labeled as problematic by the teacher might be due to a problematic fit between his temperament and the school environment. It may be that Sam has trouble adjusting to the classroom, which may cause him to withdraw and display other behaviors that might not seem age-appropriate.

Autism

Autism is a developmental disability characterized by impaired social interaction and communication (American Psychiatric Association, 2000; National Institute of Child Health and Human Development, 2008). Autism falls under a larger umbrella of autism spectrum disorders that include Childhood Disintegrative (CDD) and Rhett's Disorders, Asperger Syndrome, and Pervasive Developmental Disorder Not Otherwise Specified (PDD). All of these disorders share characteristics of problematic communication, social interaction, and repetitive or restricted patterns of behaviors, but it is important to remember that individuals diagnosed with these disorders, particularly autism and Asperger Syndrome, often display a set of unique symptoms that range in severity with regard to how disabling the symptoms are for psycho-social functioning (National Institute of Child Health and Human Development, 2008).

The exact prevalence of autism is difficult to ascertain, but estimates are that approximately one in every 100 children in the United States is autistic, with some communities seeing higher rates than others. Over the past several decades, rates of autism have been increasing, but this may be due to improved diagnostic tools as well as the fact that more behaviors and symptoms are now included under the autistic spectrum disorder umbrella (Centers for Disease Control and Prevention, 2008a).

Autism affects children from all ethnic and SES groups. However, boys are three to four more times likely to be diagnosed as autistic than girls, and siblings of those who have the disorder as well as children with other developmental disorders are also more likely to be diagnosed with autism (National Institute of Child Health and Human Development, 2008).

By the age of 18 months, many signs of autism are evident. For example, children may exhibit problems with eye contact, nonverbal communication, age-appropriate play, and responding to directions or to one's name. Some signs are even detectable at earlier ages—for example, infants may not coo or make other verbalizations or they may not point, wave, or grasp objects. However, many parents do not notice symptoms until around two or three years of age, when children have noticeable problems with verbal communication or when they drastically lose skills they had mastered. Increasingly, physicians, educators, and even parents are better equipped to look for early signs of autism as research indicates that early diagnosis and treatment, which can include a whole host of behavioral, educational, and medication therapies, may lead to an improved life-long prognosis, minimizing the symptoms that a child may exhibit (National Autism Association, 2009; National Institute of Child Health and Human Development, 2008).

While the exact cause of autism is unknown, research into the cause is ongoing and ever growing. It is likely that autism is caused by a combination of biopsycho-social factors, and research is probing into these areas. Studies on autism to date have found links to many potential causes including mutated genes, viruses, immuno-logical diseases, and environmental triggers. For example, a consortium of researchers is working on identifying genes associated with autism (Autism Consortium, 2009), and other researchers (Auyeung et al., 2009; Korvatska, Van de Water, Anders, & Gershwin, 2002) have identified increased fetal testosterone levels and immune abnormalities in children with autism. Still others have found links between rates of autism and environmental factors. One study conducted by Waldman, Nicholson, Adilov, and Williams (2008) found that children in areas with high precipitation such as Washington and Oregon had higher rates of autism, suggesting that children in these areas stay indoors more often, leading to increased Vitamin D deficiency and exposure to household chemicals, which might trigger the disorder. To date, studies have found no clear connection between autism and childhood vaccines (National Institute of Child Health and Human Development, 2008), though many physicians and parent groups argue otherwise (Cave & Mitchell, 2001).

Because of increasing rates of autism and some studies that have suggested a link between autism and vaccines (e.g., Wakefield et al., 1998), parents are justifiably anxious about the health and well-being of their children. Social workers can help parents by remaining current on autism research, treatment, and debates over causes. There are many resources available to help parents make informed decisions about health care issues for their children including vaccination and autism diagnosis and treatment, which social workers can use in their work with parents.

Other Considerations in Individual Development

In addition to attachment and temperament, a family's socioeconomic status is a primary aspect of physical development in infants and young children. Though SES could be considered a mezzo issue, we discuss it here because of its effects on individual development. In an extensive literature review, Bradley and Corwyn (2002) discuss the many findings linking SES with developmental problems in infants and young children. With regard to health, their findings from the literature concluded that children from low-SES groups are more likely to die and suffer from injuries, illnesses, infections, low IQ, tooth decay, lead poisoning, sensory delays, cognitive delays, and neurological problems than children from high-SES groups. Many of these findings have been replicated across cultural contexts.

Bradley and Corwyn also found that children from low-SES groups have lower rates of attendance and achievement at school and higher school dropout rates than children from high-SES groups. Low-SES children also exhibit more symptoms of maladaptive social functioning and psychiatric problems than children from high SES groups, though these finding must be interpreted with caution. Specifically, those living in poverty are often diagnosed with mental illness more frequently than wealthier individuals, even when displaying similar symptoms. Also, there is no evidence to suggest a causal relationship between low SES and mental illness, only an association between the two. Often, people with mental illness move into low-SES categories because of loss of family, employment, benefits, and other resources.

All of the consequences of low SES on development can be explained in many different ways. Some of the effects could be due, in part, to genetics, biology, and problems in development, while others can be attributed to a lack of resources, opportunities, and exposure to a nurturing environment. Environmental factors as well as issues around discrimination may disproportionately impact members of minority groups. When working with children and families from low-SES groups, social workers may want to assess potential problems from a person-in-environment framework to capture the many facets that may be contributing to problems in development. For example, although you do not know the specifics of Sam's SES, because he is attending Head Start it is likely that he comes from a low-income family. This factor should be considered in your assessment, as it could be contributing to Sam's problems at school. However, given Sam's seemingly "normal" behavior at home, SES may not be an issue in his case. Be careful not to let research on the effects of SES on behavior bias your assessment and subsequent intervention.

THE FAMILY AND IMMEDIATE ENVIRONMENT IN INFANCY AND EARLY CHILDHOOD

Because infants and young children are so dependent on their caregivers for their well-being, social workers must assess many different aspects of the environment when working with children and families. Many families bring their children to social workers in an attempt to "fix" the children. However, as you learned from systems theory, only rarely is a problem isolated to one individual. More frequently, social workers must assess and intervene with the family and larger systems to help people overcome problems that seem to be stemming from an individual's behavior. This section discusses some of the more common topics that social workers face when working with children and families.

Parenting

Earlier, we examined parenting issues related to children's temperaments, but many other facets of parenting are important for social workers to understand when working with children and families. Many of these are related to parenting styles, feelings of competency, and skills that can be used to improve parenting.

Unfortunately, parenting is not an innate skill; many new and even seasoned parents express anxiety over the daunting task of rearing a child. Part of this anxiety can be traced to the inundation of advice, much of which is contradictory, that is available in the popular media. Many parents become overwhelmed with information and find it difficult to make decisions about their parenting. This is particularly true for parents of children who are disabled or who have other special challenges. Moreover, new research is perpetually being produced, adding to the confusion about what constitutes a "good parent." Most parents would like their children to become caring, responsible adults. But, what are the characteristics of a good parent? Which skills are needed to be successful? How much of a child's healthy development and ultimate success in life can be attributed to nature or to nurture? None of these questions is straightforward or easy to answer. However, there is some basic knowledge that social workers can use in their work with parents.

Through her research, Diana Baumrind (1968, 1971) established different styles of parenting that help describe patterns that parents consistently use in child rearing. These are described in Box 7.2. Some evidence suggests that in Western culture, authoritative parenting is the most effective style with regard to rearing well-adjusted children (Bronstein & Clauson, 1993; Eisenberg, Chang, Ma, & Huang,

---

BOX 7.2

Parenting Styles

- *Authoritarian:* Parent is controlling and insists on conformity; establishes rules and ideas about how child should behave. This style is associated with children who are unhappy, fearful, and anxious and who lack initiative and communication skills.

- *Authoritative:* Parent offers some control, consistent support, and compromise; encourages independence with limits and negotiation. This style is associated with children who are cheerful, motivated, and self-directed and who demonstrate social competence in communication and cooperation.

- *Neglectful:* Parent is uninvolved with the child; offers little structure for or control over the child. This style is associated with children who have low self-esteem and poor self-control and who are immature and socially incompetent.

- *Indulgent:* Parent is highly involved with child; does not offer much structure for or control over the child; makes few demands of the child. This style is associated with children who show poor self-control and a lack of respect for others.

Source: Adapted from Baumrind, 1968, 1971.

2009; Slicker, 1998). Researchers argue that this style helps to teach children skills of compromise, negotiation, and decision making while helping them to value independence. However, this conclusion may not hold true for parents in other cultures. Not all cultures hold the same values with regard to child rearing, and parenting styles vary widely to reflect what characteristics are valued and thus instilled in children. Evidence suggests that what is important and most effective in parenting, maybe even more so than a particular style, is consistency and caring (Luxton, 2008; Whiting & Edwards, 1988).

Another factor that tends to be associated with positive parenting and child-rearing environment is parental self-efficacy. Recall the discussion on Bandura's social learning theory in Chapter 3. A central tenet of his theory is self-efficacy—our expectation that we can successfully perform a task. From their research, Coleman and Karraker (2003) and Jones (2007) suggest that parental feelings of self-efficacy are associated with certain positive child behaviors such as compliance, enthusiasm, persistence, and affection toward the caregiver as well as with positive cognitive performance by the child. It may be that parents who feel efficacious in their parenting also feel empowered to manage their responsibilities and to find intrinsic interest in parenting and their children. Keeping in mind the limitations to this research (for example, no causal relationship has been established between self-efficacy and positive child outcomes), social workers who work with children and families can apply these ideas using Bandura's theory as well as concepts from other frameworks such as the strengths perspective. Identifying parent strengths and building on those will help increase parents' feelings of self-efficacy and empower-ment, which may in turn help promote positive development among their children.

As Sam's social worker, you may want to assess how his parents' parenting styles may be affecting his behavior at school, keeping in mind that cultural variations in patterns and expectations may exist. Perhaps working with any problems that Sam's parents may be experiencing in feeling effective in their parenting skills might improve those skills, which may influence his behavior at school. To begin, you might identify strengths that Sam's parents have in their parenting skills, building on these to increase their feelings of self-efficacy.

Grandparenting

Because people are living longer, they have more opportunities to interact with their grandchildren and great-grandchildren and, in some cases, to take on parenting responsibilities. Today many older adults are caring for their grandchildren because their own children have problems such as unemployment, substance abuse, chronic illness or disability, and issues related to criminal behavior. Even when grandparents do not act as primary caregivers, they can fulfill vital roles in the lives of their grandchildren.

Neugarten and Weinstein (1964) have described different categories of grand-parents that tend to characterize Western society, listed in Box 7.3. Whether or not

- *Fun seeker:* Grandparent acts as a playmate to grandchild; both achieve mutual enjoyment out of the relationship.

- *Distant figure:* Grandparent has only occasional contact with grandchild; grandparent has little involvement in grandchild's life.

- *Surrogate parent:* Grandparent assumes much of the caregiving responsibility for the grandchild.

- *Formal figure:* Grandparent is involved only to provide babysitting services occasionally or to give special treats to the grandchild; all child rearing is left to the parents.

- *Reservoir of family wisdom:* Grandparent takes on the authoritarian role and acts as sage to pass on skills, traditions, stories, and so on.

Source: Adapted from Neugarten & Weinstein, 1964.

BOX 7.3

Grandparenting Styles

they want to, grandparents are increasingly assuming the surrogate parent role. And, because more generations are living simultaneously, grandparents have more opportunity to assume other roles as well, such as the fun seeker. However, geographic boundaries also create situations where grandparents find themselves in the distant figure role. Generally, grandparents can provide stable and loving environments for their grandchildren. Moreover, in cases of parental abuse or neglect, grandparents can provide some consistency in their grandchildren's lives that may improve the children's chances of becoming well-adjusted adults despite an inhospitable environment.

Moreover, many grandparents benefit emotionally and psychologically from interacting with their grandchildren. For example, positive grandparenting may be a useful developmental task for older adults in Erikson's integrity versus despair stage or in continuity and activity theories, which are described in Chapter 12. If older adults can remain active and feel useful to younger generations, they may be more likely to feel a sense of accomplishment. More on grandparenting is presented in Chapter 12.

The case scenario does not say whether Sam has grandparents. If he does, and if the relationship between Sam's immediate family and his grandparents is positive, this relationship could be considered a strength in Sam's case. You could discuss with the family the roles that Sam's grandparents could take in his life to support his development, keeping in mind the cultural expectations of immediate and extended family in child-rearing practices.

EXHIBIT 7.2

Grandparents often play significant roles in their grandchildren's lives

Source: Scott T. Baxter/Getty Images

Siblings

Sibling interaction has been a topic of much research and debate. In the United States, more than 80 percent of children have at least one sibling, and the influences that siblings have on one another are factors to consider in social work. The role that siblings play in one another's lives is probably even more important than that of parents. Siblings take on many roles in the socialization process for one another, including mentor, teacher, playmate, adversary, and supporter; these roles usually last a lifetime (Cicirelli, 1994).

Personality Traits and Birth Order   One area of study that has brought with it a great deal of interest is personality traits and birth order. Some evidence supports the idea that characteristics of first-born children differ from those of later-born children, though much of the difference can be accounted for by the different ways in which parents interact with first-born and later-born children as well as other factors such as the spacing of children and the resources available to the family.

Generally, first-born children tend to have more access to parental time and energy than later-born children, and parents show more engagement in first-born children's lives (Steelman, Powell, Werum, & Carter, 2002). A literature review on birth order conducted by Eckstein (2000) found that first-born children tend to be higher achievers with higher IQs and self-esteem. One study conducted on over 240,000 men and controlling for numerous psychosocial factors found that eldest children scored about 3 percent higher on IQ tests than second children and 4 percent higher than third-born children (Bjerkedal, Kristensen, Skjeret, & Brevik, 2007). In addition, first-born children have greater academic success, mature earlier socially and sexually, are more easily influenced by authority, are more conformist to parents' values and dependent on approval, and are more likely to be leaders, responsible, and self-disciplined than later-born children. Conversely, later-born children tend to be more empathic, popular, and "spoiled" than first-born children.

Some evidence suggests that later-born children are more likely to be the beneficiaries of their parents' economic resources (for example, obtain financial assistance in college) because their parents are older and more financially stable. Their parents are also more likely to have renewed energy to focus on them, particularly if the first-born is older, independent, and lives away from home (Steelman et al., 2002).

Eckstein (2000) concluded from the literature review that children without siblings showed similar characteristics as first-born children. They are more likely to have a high need for achievement, go to college, and be selfish, trusting, and cooperative.

Family Size   Another consideration that social workers should keep in mind when working with children and families is the size of the family. In addition to many other challenges, large families are more likely to live in poverty, and their children are more likely to have lower levels of educational achievement than smaller families. One explanation for this is the **resource dilution model**. This model posits that the resources that families have to give to children are directly related to the size of the family; thus, the larger the family, the fewer the resources available to give to each member (Steelman et al., 2002).

Social workers need to consider how birth order might affect a family and its individual members. Some researchers argue that as a society, North Americans tend to "buy into" birth order differences without thinking about the limitations to the research on birth order issues or how mediating variables might affect birth order differences. People may behave in ways that are expected of children born in a certain order, and social and reproductive policies are often based on stereotypes about birth order (Herrera, Zajonc, Wieczorkowska, & Cichomski, 2003; Steelman et al., 2002). For example, family planning and other services may be more accessible to families with more than one child with the assumption being that families with only one child do not need extra support. Specifically, these services may target families with multiple children to prevent or intervene with problems associated with birth order such as rebelliousness or acting out that might be expected of later-born children. Families with only one child may be viewed as not being at risk for such problems. Social workers can help educate clients and policy-makers about the strengths and limitations surrounding knowledge on birth order to ensure that issues related to it are viewed more realistically.

Since Sam is an only child, you may expect certain behaviors from him based on the resources his parents are able to give him. However, cultural dynamics may make these behaviors more or less pronounced, depending on Sam's parents' expectations of him as an only child. You will need to better understand Sam's parents' beliefs about the role of children to accurately assess how being an only child in this family may affect Sam's behavior. Using multiple perspectives, such as person-in-environment and biopsychosocial perspectives, while bringing in information discussed here may help you to more accurately and comprehensively assess Sam's situation.

Day Care

Given the importance of early caregiving on positive child developmental outcomes, it is not surprising that there is so much debate about the strengths and limitations of day care. Currently, approximately two million children in the United States, many of whom are from low-income families, receive formal care. The use of day care is directly related to the number of single parent households, the number of women in the workforce (particularly women who are receiving welfare), and the recognition of the impact of early educational experiences on child development. However, even with trends toward nonparental care, social policy has not kept pace with the funding or developing of quality day care for children (Shapiro & Applegate, 2002).

Day care facilities in the United States vary greatly in type and quality of care that they provide. Arrangements can range from large centers providing care for large groups of children, to small nonprofit facilities run by religious organizations, to care given in private homes. The cost for these arrangements also varies a great deal; unfortunately, many low-income families cannot afford quality day care.

In an earlier section, we looked at the effects of day care on the attachment of infants. Other studies have examined how day care affects the development of infants and children. Data from a longitudinal study on day care experiences suggests that quality day care in which caregivers are responsive to children shows no adverse effects on child behavior (Owen, 2002). More recent research suggests that aggressive behavior might be an exception to this generalization; that is, the more time children spend in nonparental care, the more likely they are to exhibit disruptive behavior. However, this research also suggests that behavioral problems tend to dissipate after the 6th grade and that children in nonparental care also tend to exhibit higher vocabulary scores than children who don't spend time in nonparental care (Belsky, 2009). Other research supports this idea that the higher the quality of care, the more advanced the children's verbal and cognitive abilities. This research also concludes that children from low-income families are more likely to receive low-quality care (Owen, 2002), which disproportionately affects those from some minority groups.

Other studies have indicated that parental knowledge of day care facilities is lacking. For instance, many parents are not familiar with center policies on hiring, firing, and training, what licensure requirements the center meets (or does not meet), or how their children spend the day (Shpancer et al., 2002). Social workers can be a source of education for parents as they seek day care facilities for their children, and they can help parents, particularly those with low incomes, to advocate for more quality care. Simply by making parents more aware of what constitutes quality care, social workers can help empower parents to secure the best possible care for their children.

Policy-makers need to be educated about the role of day care for families. Using theories and perspectives such as family systems, person-in-environment, or even Erikson's or Piaget's theories, social workers can articulate the influence of day care on the developmental needs of children as well as the short- and long-term ramifications that care has on children, families, and larger society. Those who are making decisions about the structure of day care should be knowledgeable about how care affects children and families on multiple levels, particularly low-income families, who typically do not have access to high-quality day care. In addition to designing interventions on the individual level, social workers may need to rely on community organization theory to guide interventions that will increase the availability of affordable, quality day care.

As Sam's social worker, you may want to find out what child care arrangements his parents used when Sam was younger. It may be that Sam's parents had to rely on low-quality day care, which could have impacted his development when he was an infant. Problems with early development could be affecting his current development and behavior.

Child Abuse and Neglect

Child maltreatment is a widespread problem in the United States. The term maltreatment is a broad one that encompasses both abuse and neglect. Abuse refers to specific and repeated acts of sexual, physical, and emotional mistreatment; whereas neglect refers to an ongoing pattern in which caregivers fail to meet their children's basic needs. According to the U.S. Department of Health and Human Services (2007a), approximately 794,000 children were abused or neglected in 2007. Over half of these (59 percent) were neglect cases, 22 percent of the cases were children younger than 12 months, and about half were Caucasian, while 22 percent were African American and 21 percent were Hispanic. An estimated 1,760 children died due to maltreatment. Close to 80 percent of perpetrators of maltreatment were parents, and women comprised more than half (57 percent) of all perpetrators. Keep in mind that these are likely to be underestimates of the occurrence of maltreatment since these numbers represent reported cases. No estimates exist for how many cases

TABLE 7.3 Common Signs of Child Maltreatment	PHYSICAL ABUSE	SEXUAL ABUSE	EMOTIONAL ABUSE	NEGLECT
	• Frequently occurring cuts, scrapes, or scratches • Multiple fractures • Head injuries • Internal injuries (for example, spleen, kidney) • Burns, especially those that take the shape of common objects (for example, cigarettes) or that occur in unlikely places (for example, bottom, stomach)	• Sexually transmitted diseases • Throat or mouth problems • Pregnancy • Bruising in the genital area • Genital discharge or problems urinating • Low self-esteem • Anger, fear, anxiety, depression • Withdrawal or aggression • Inappropriate sexual behavior	• Low self-esteem • Anxiety, depression • Poor outlook on life • Suicidal behavior • Emotional instability and poor impulse control • Substance abuse and eating disorders • Relationship problems • Violent or criminal behavior • Poor school performance	• Failure to thrive syndrome • Psychosocial dwarfism • Lack of supervision • Poor hygiene • Lack of appropriate health and mental health care • Exposure to hazards • Poor household sanitation

Source: Adapted from Mather & Lager, 2000.

of maltreatment go unreported each year. Table 7.3 lists common signs of child maltreatment.

Consequences of maltreatment extend to the physical, cognitive, emotional, psychological, and behavioral development of children. Some of the effects of abuse and neglect include physical injuries, brain damage, low self-esteem, substance abuse, teen pregnancy, relational problems, low academic achievement, and aggressive and criminal behavior (Child Welfare Information Gateway, 2008; Hildyard & Wolfe, 2002; Kelley, Thornberry, & Smith, 1997). There are also social costs to maltreatment. Each year, the judicial, health care, child welfare, mental health care, and law enforcement systems respond directly to cases of child maltreatment. Moreover, costs are incurred in areas such as special education, teen pregnancy support, domestic violence services, and welfare payments, which are indirectly related to child maltreatment (U.S. Department of Health and Human Services, 2003, 2007b).

The causes of child maltreatment must be viewed from a person-in-environment or ecological perspective because they are multifaceted and complex. In assessing cases of maltreatment, social workers will find issues contributing to maltreatment on many different levels, from the individual and familial levels to the social, economic, and cultural levels. Indeed, research points to the multifaceted nature of maltreatment. For example, research suggests that factors such as poverty, economic and other stressors, poor parenting skills, familial strife, lack of support systems, parental youth and inexperience, and characteristics common among special needs children (for example, disabilities, behavioral problems) increase the likelihood of maltreatment (Baumrind, 1994; Cicchetti & Toth, 2005; Martin & Lindsey, 2003).

Within child welfare services, social workers and other professionals and para-professionals work with children and families in maltreatment cases. Much of this work is reactive; that is, it takes place after maltreatment has occurred. There is certainly much that can be done for families who have entered the system due to maltreatment. However, there are many other roles that social workers can play to prevent maltreatment. Activities on the micro, mezzo, and macro levels are useful in the prevention of potential abuse and neglect problems. These might include making support resources accessible for new parents, particularly teen parents; providing quality and affordable day care, health care, and other professional services; and working toward more flexible legislation that supports and empowers women in the welfare system. Unfortunately in U.S. society, dollars tend to be spent on reactionary services, while preventive services are ultimately cheaper in both economic and human costs.

THE LARGER SOCIAL ENVIRONMENT IN INFANCY AND EARLY CHILDHOOD

In this section, we will take a look at some of the macro issues that affect children and families. Although we touch on just a few topics that you will work with in your practice, they are important to consider, as they have far-reaching implications for the well-being of your clients. These topics include child protection, permanency planning, health care, and educational policy.

Child Protection

The previous section discussed issues related to child maltreatment. Many social workers work with children and families after abuse and neglect has already occurred. Much of this work takes place on a governmental level, where social workers are often involved in child protective services.

Child maltreatment remains a major problem in the United States, despite federal and state attempts to prevent it. Across the country, a complex network of child welfare services has been developed to work with the issue. For the most part, states have much control of these services and have a great deal of power in developing policies and guidelines for child protective services, though federal guidelines and mandates as well as local forces have some influence on policy development at the state level (Webb & Harden, 2003).

Generally, abused or neglected children are referred to a local child protective services (CPS) office. Anyone can report abuse or neglect; however, since 1974, professionals, including social workers, are mandated by federal law to report suspected abuse. The role of CPS is to investigate reports of abuse and neglect and to assess the risks posed for the child. CPS also has the authority to remove the child from the home and make placements in the foster care system. CPS workers work in concert with court and family systems to develop plans that will best meet the needs of the maltreated child and her or his family (Waldfogel, 2001).

Among the many policies that directly or indirectly address maltreatment issues, we will look at a few federal laws that focus on child protection since they impact social work with children and families. One is the Child Abuse Prevention and Treatment Act of 1974. This act was established to provide support to states in developing and delivering child protective services. It also established the mandatory reporting requirements mentioned earlier. This act also makes available some funds for research and pilot programs on maltreatment. Another law is the Adoption and Safe Families Act of 1997, which, among other things, places a higher priority on the safety and well-being of the child than on family preservation (Waldfogel, 2001; Webb & Harden, 2003). This policy represents a shift in focus from previous decades, when family preservation was viewed as paramount, regardless of the family situation.

Many of the policies dealing with child maltreatment are the crux of social workers' work with children and families. These policies dictate the scope and nature of their work, which means that social workers, particularly those in government agencies, must be familiar with policy guidelines and laws. In Sam's case, you do not know if there is any reason to suspect maltreatment, but both the Head Start teacher and you would be responsible for observing Sam and his behavior and reporting any suspicions about potential maltreatment. Social workers use guidelines such as those presented in Table 7.3, presented earlier, to assess whether certain children are at risk for abuse or neglect.

Permanency Planning: Foster Care, Adoption, and Family Support

You have just learned about the role of CPS in removing abused and neglected children from the home and making placements in the foster care system. Because of these roles, CPS workers often work in conjunction with others to develop service objectives for families in the CPS system, which include permanency planning. **Permanency planning**, an idea that came to fruition in 1980 with the Adoption Assistance and Child Welfare Act (discussed shortly), focuses on long-term planning for children and families either to prevent out-of-home placements or to make foster or adoptive placements as quickly as possible. The goal is to achieve stability for the child and her or his family without lengthy delays (Waldfogel, 2001).

Legislation associated with permanency planning includes the Child Welfare Services, Foster Care, and Adoption Assistance Reforms of 1993, which created the Family Preservation and Support Services Program. This law was enacted to provide funding for family preservation and support and prevention services that are delivered concomitantly by CPS and community agencies. In addition, the Multi-ethnic Placement Act of 1994 was developed to address issues of interracial adoptions. This legislation prevents agencies from discriminating against prospective foster or adoptive parents based on ethnic or national origin, although it does require that children's cultural needs be considered in placements.

Another important law is the 1978 Indian Child Welfare Act, which gave tribes the right to intervene in child welfare issues, including the right to assume legal jurisdiction over children and their care. Finally, the Adoption and Safe Families Act of 1997 revisited and revised the Adoption Assistance and Child Welfare Act of 1980, which required CPS to make reasonable efforts to prevent placements and provide service plans to avoid them. The 1997 revisions specified when placement should not be made and pushed for permanency planning, reducing the amount of time for placement from 18 to 12 months (Waldfogel, 2001).

As discussed earlier, social workers need to keep abreast of current legislation that influences work with children and families. These policies have direct consequences for the services that social workers can provide, but they also make statements about the current philosophy on issues such as abuse, neglect, the role of the family, and governmental and social responsibility for family support. Often, social workers find that they either disagree with current federal philosophy on such issues or that the mandates coming from these philosophies are difficult to carry out in practice. Because clients' problems are usually multifaceted, a policy that seems reasonable on paper may be troublesome or even counterproductive to clients' goals in practice. For example, while permanency planning may seem like a noble goal, often social workers and families find that other barriers such as unemployment, mental illness, lack of housing, and other problems can stand in the way of achieving this goal in the time frame mandated by law.

Further, processes that take place during planning can create unintended problems. One study (Haight, Kagle, & Black, 2003) describes how developmental and attachment needs of children can be undermined by proscribed visits by parents when children are in foster care if they are not planned carefully and deliberately, using theoretical and other knowledge to guide the visits. This issue helps to exemplify the need for social workers to have a broad knowledge base of theoretical and developmental information to help inform policy and practice guidelines. Social workers' knowledge of social action and legislative and policy development is also useful, as social workers are often the professionals who shape and interpret these policies and advocate for services for their clients.

Health Care

Throughout the book we have touched on the importance of health care for children. Much of this discussion has centered on problems that poverty and lack of access to care can cause in the short and long terms for the development of children. Access to health care is crucial for healthy prenatal development; however, once a child is born, the importance of access to regular, quality health care does not diminish.

Not surprisingly, lack of access to quality health care tends to be more common among children living in poverty than among children from wealthier families. For example, researchers concluded from an analysis of data collected in the 1997 National Health Interview Survey that low-income children were at substantially higher risk of having their health care needs unmet. Specifically, after reviewing data on almost 3,500 children, the researchers found that low-income, minority children—many of whom lacked health insurance—were 3 to 12 times more likely than higher-income children to be without a consistent health care source, and 2 to 30 times more likely to have unmet health care needs (Newacheck, Hung, Hochstein, & Halfon, 2002). Research continues to demonstrate the problems that low-income, minority children face with regard to access to health care (DeVoe, Graham, Angier, Baez, & Krois, 2008; Huang, Yu, Liu, Young, & Wong, 2009; Scott & Ni, 2004). Indeed, one large study of 1,536 children in 12 metropolitan areas indicated that children, regardless of SES, received appropriate medical care only 47 percent of the time, suggesting that all children are at risk for more long-term health problems due to the lack of proper medical attention when they are younger (Mangione-Smith et al., 2007).

Access to health care alone does not necessarily dictate positive developmental outcomes; many other factors such as income, housing, safety, and education also come into play (Roberts, 2002). Social workers who work with children may be able to mediate some of the problems caused by lack of health care by ensuring that other facets contributing to healthy development are in place while also working to ensure access to quality health care.

One role that social workers perform in their work with children and families is to facilitate access to federal, state, and local programs such as Medicaid and the State Children's Health Insurance Program (SCHIP). Medicaid, created in 1965 under the Social Security Act, is a joint federal and state program that provides medical care to low-income people. Many Medicaid recipients are children. SCHIP is a health insurance program created in 1997, and reauthorized in 2009, also under the Social Security Act. SCHIP expands health care benefits to uninsured children. Social workers can educate low-income families about programs like these as well as help them navigate the systems necessary to gain access to these and similar programs.

As part of a comprehensive assessment of Sam, you would want to make certain that he has access to quality health care. Because so much of Sam's development and behavior depends on good health, this would be a primary element of the intervention. Although there is no indication from the case scenario that Sam has any health problems or that he does not receive regular care, you could discuss with his family the importance of timely preventive and treatment services to ward off any future problems.

Educational Policy: Head Start

Provision of and access to quality education have been long-standing issues for social workers. Because educational opportunities are vital for the short-term and long-term development of children, ensuring that quality programs exist for children from all backgrounds is an important charge of the profession.

One controversial area regarding education has to do with Head Start programs. Initiated in 1964 under the Lyndon Johnson administration as part of his Great Society, Head Start programs were developed to serve low-income children and families. These programs aspired to end the cycle of poverty by providing services that met children's social, nutritional, emotional, educational, and psychological needs.

Currently, more than 900,000 children attend Head Start programs nationwide. Ninety-seven percent of these children are four years old or younger, and approximately 60 percent are from ethnic minority groups (Administration for Children and Families, 2008).

Generally, research indicates that Head Start programs can have some positive effects for low-income children. For example, several studies have suggested that children who attend Head Start show short-term cognitive gains and over time exhibit fewer personal and social problems, including dropping out of school and being unemployed. However, many studies have reported mixed results in Head Start's ability to break the cycle of poverty for families and to help African American children maintain cognitive gains over time (Caputo, 2003).

Head Start: Current Debates Although many social workers, legislators, and families agree that Head Start is beneficial to low-income children, they disagree as to how these programs should be funded, who should have control over their services and curricula, and how beneficial they truly are with regard to preventing future problems for children and allowing them to begin their elementary years on equal footing with other, more advantaged children. The conservative philosophy about entitlement programs that characterized the 1996 welfare reform measures during the Clinton administration, and which continued in the George W. Bush administration, brought the debate over Head Start back to the forefront. Though political tones change from administration to administration, the debate over Head Start and similar programs will likely continue.

One current debate revolves around who should administer the program. Some people argue that states should control the funding and development of programs so that these programs can be integrated with local preschool programs. Advocates of state control also propose that states become more accountable for raising the quality of Head Start curricula and focusing on literacy and math skills. Critics respond that the shift to state control would dismantle the program as it has been established, making its administration and evaluation disparate across states, which may make "proving" that such programs help low-income children even more difficult (Jacobson, 2003).

Educational Policy from an Ecological Perspective   Despite the unclear consequences of Head Start programs on the long-term development and adjustment of low-income children, recent developmental research has underscored the importance of the environmental context in which low-income children are reared and receive academic and other interventions. Specifically, this body of literature posits that the ecological model is an appropriate and effective way in which to view the problems of low-income children and from which to build interventions (Anderson et al., 2002; Berlin, 2001; Evans, 2001). Because Head Start programs approach problems from a framework that closely parallels the ecological model, they may provide a more effective and comprehensive way to develop services to promote optimal development of young, low-income children.

Returning to Sam's case, you might be able to make some useful progress by conceptualizing Sam's situation from the ecological model. For example, many factors influence Sam's development besides biological processes and elements of Sam's immediate environment. Recognizing that many ethnic minorities may not reap long-term benefits from Head Start and that the program may not be addressing cultural needs important to Sam and his family, there may be other ways in which you can help Sam and his family meet those needs. Moreover, you may be able to help the program itself modify some of its practices to better fit the emotional, cognitive, cultural, and social needs of Sam and his family.

One mandate within the *Code of Ethics* (NASW, approved 1996, revised 2008) states that "social workers should monitor and evaluate policies, the implementation of programs, and practice interventions" (p. 25). In keeping with ethical and effective social work practice, remember that you can help the program review its evaluation processes to ensure that reliable data is collected on program effectiveness that will add to the knowledge base on program outcomes. Because results in outcome research on Head Start programs tend to be mixed, social workers can provide a great deal of support in helping programs to design and implement research methods that can add reliable and valid information that will help ensure the viability of these important programs.

CONCLUSION

Infancy and early childhood are a time of rapid growth and development. Some of the hallmark developmental activities that take place during this time include language acquisition and emotional and motor development.

In addition to physical changes, infants and children experience other changes on individual and social levels that affect their long-term development. When problems with development occur, social workers need to be able to comprehensively assess issues on different levels to develop effective interventions that will bring about permanent, positive change. Moreover, because of the great variability that exists in development, including variability in cultural definitions of what "normal" development is, social workers must be aware of their own ethnocentric viewpoints on developmental issues. This awareness will help to ensure that social workers provide ethical and culturally appropriate services that promote optimal development of clients in their own cultural and environmental context.

Given all of the emphasis on "normal" development during infancy and early childhood, social workers also need to consider the strengths that clients and their families and communities possess. When dealing with developmental issues, social workers can easily become entrenched in the medical and similar models to guide assessment and intervention. Thus, using the strengths perspective as well as other perspectives that incorporate environmental factors will help social workers move beyond physical considerations when working with young children and their families.

MAIN POINTS

- Major developmental milestones in infancy and early childhood include language acquisition, emotional development, and fine and gross motor skill development. Understanding the debates over biological versus behavioral sources of language acquisition and how young children progress through these milestones helps social workers to assess and intervene with their clients effectively.

- Attachment theory suggests that the quality of attachment affects the infant's development. Ainsworth developed four infant attachment styles: secure, insecure avoidant, insecure resistant, and insecure disorganized.

- Temperament is the consistent ways in which individuals respond to their environment and is thought to be present at birth. Chess and Thomas identified three main temperament types in infants: the easy child, difficult child, and slow-to-warm-up child.

- Research indicates that children from low-SES groups are more likely to suffer from poor health and long-term developmental outcomes than children from high-SES groups.

- Several parenting and grandparenting styles have been identified that can be used by social workers in their work with children and families. Parenting styles include authoritarian, authoritative, neglectful, and indulgent; grandparents can be fun seekers, distant figures, surrogate parents, formal figures, or reservoirs of family wisdom.

- Sibling interaction and day care are heavily researched and debated topics, and research suggests that birth order does play a role in development of children. Research into day care examines the quality of care—how it differs for different members of U.S. society and how it affects children.

- Social workers often work directly with children who have been abused or neglected. This work entails being familiar with federal and state protective policies and services. Along with protective services, social workers are often involved in permanency planning for children and families who have abuse and neglect issues.

- Lack of access to quality health care is a major problem for many children, and it can have long-term consequences for children's development. Programs like SCHIP and Medicaid are designed to provide health care services for these children.

- Head Start is a federal program geared toward enhancing the social, psychological, and educational needs of low-income children. It is often the subject of debates over funding, administration, and effectiveness.

EXERCISES

1. Using the Sanchez Family interactive case (go to www.routledgesw.com/cases), review the major issues involving the Sanchez family. Pay particular attention to the description of Joey, the grandson. After giving this information thorough review, answer the following questions:
   a. Given Joey's age, what developmental milestones might you expect him to be experiencing?
   b. In what ways might his environment (for example, exposure to cocaine, placement in foster and kinship care, eligibility for services) affect his physical and emotional development (for example, developmental milestones, attachments)?
   c. If you were to work with Joey, what ethical and cultural issues might you want to consider?

d. What strengths might Joey or the family possess that could be used in working with Joey?

2. Go to the Riverton interactive case (at www.routledgesw.com/cases) and review the situations of Mary Stark and her family and Felipe and Maria Gonzales. Then answer the following questions:

a. What issues presented in this chapter might be relevant to Mary's situation and why?

b. Do you think there might be any information presented in Chapter 6 that might be relevant to Mary's case? In what ways?

c. What theoretical perspective might be useful to you in conceptualizing Mary's situation and why?

d. Using the theory you chose in the last question and the information in this and/or the last chapter, how could you proceed with an intervention for Mary and her family?

e. How might the information presented in this chapter be relevant to the problems faced by Felipe and Maria Gonzales? Be specific.

f. How could you use this information to work with Felipe and Maria?

CHAPTER 8

Development in Middle Childhood

Sue is an eight-year-old girl being reared by lesbian parents who underwent artificial insemination to become pregnant. Sue's biological mother is Caucasian, and the sperm donor is of Chinese descent. Sue's other parent is also Caucasian.

Sue's parents have brought her to a social worker because of "behavioral problems." Sue's parents complain that she refuses to do what she is told, has trouble keeping up with her school work, and does not get along with other children her age. In fact, Sue's parents claim that she does not have any close friends and spends a lot of her time playing by herself. Sue shows little interest in age-appropriate activities, and she frequently appears withdrawn and incapable of attending to school or other activities. Sue's parents are concerned that she will fall behind developmentally and will be held back a grade in school if her performance does not improve.

MIDDLE CHILDHOOD IS A TIME OF CONTINUED BIOPSYCHOSOCIAL development and, as such, can be characterized by problems and worries for parents. In the case scenario, we see Sue struggling with issues in many areas, and naturally, her parents are worried that she will be "left behind" in her physical, emotional, and social development. In this chapter, we explore some developmental milestones that occur in middle childhood as well as common issues surrounding education, family, the media, and peer relations that social workers face when working with children in this age range and their families.

DEVELOPMENTAL MILESTONES IN OLDER CHILDREN

Middle childhood, or the age range of 5 or 6 to approximately 11 years old, is a time when growth and development continue at a steady, consistent pace, particularly in the area of physical, cognitive, and motor skills. During this time, children are increasingly exposed to the outside world of their peers, and they become more focused on achievement and self-control.

Physically, middle childhood is characterized by increases in height, weight, muscle mass, and coordination skills. Children's skeletal structure is taking its adult shape as permanent teeth are established and bones become harder. These last changes are important to note because children's dental hygiene and other nutritional habits can have a great impact on their health later in life. During middle childhood, children continue to develop and refine their motor skills such as hitting, running, jumping, climbing, and other activities that require fine motor skills with the fingers and hands. Though children are able to sit still and attend to tasks, they need to be physically active to continue to develop their motor skills (Nuba, Searson, & Sheiman, 1994). Unfortunately, with computers, television, and other electronic media competing for their time and attention, many children do not get the exercise they need to refine their skills, which often leads to childhood obesity and other problems in adolescence and adulthood. From the medical model, middle childhood is a crucial time for physical development in which children need a balance of physical and intellectual stimulation as well as proper nutrition and other positive habits to promote lifelong health.

Cognitively, children continue to develop critical thinking skills and the ability to think with more flexibility and complexity than before. Children show gains in memory, attention, and the ability to think about details of tasks. Long-term memory tends to increase during this time, as does their ability to link new information with existing knowledge. Recall that Piaget posited that we all develop schemas, or frameworks, that help us organize information. According to this idea, children develop schemas as they grow older, which helps them incorporate increasing amounts of information. In turn, acquiring more information helps children to improve their memories and further develop schemas for other things. Along with improving memory, children also become better at critical thinking skills, which means that they are better able to understand things on a deeper level, taking into consideration different points of view to evaluate perspectives and information. This latter point also relates to Piaget's ideas in his cognitive development theory. Children who are in the concrete operational stage can think flexibly, which allows them to compare and contrast information and use abstract skills to consider information (Piaget, 1952).

With regard to emotional and personality development, middle childhood is a time for continued development and increased abilities to define self and emotions. In younger years, children tend to define themselves based on external characteristics such as age and eye and hair color. In middle childhood, children tend to use more internal characteristics to define themselves. For example, children can describe themselves as kind, intelligent, generous, or popular (Harter, 1999).

Emotionally, middle childhood is characterized by an increased ability to understand and express complex emotions such as pride, guilt, and jealousy. Moreover, these emotional states tend to become more integrated into children's sense of self and sense of personal responsibility for causing and controlling different emotions. Children can better understand how emotions are related to various

TABLE 8.1 *Developmental Milestones in Middle Childhood*	**PHYSICAL**	**COGNITIVE**	**PERSONALITY AND EMOTION**
	• Increases in height, weight, muscle mass, and coordination skills. • Skeletal structure is taking its adult shape as permanent teeth are established and bones become harder. • Continued development and refinement of motor skills such as hitting, running, jumping climbing, and other activities that require fine motor skills with the fingers and hands.	• Continued development of critical thinking skills and the ability to think with more flexibility and complexity than before. • Gains in memory, attention, and the ability to think about details of tasks. • Long-term memory tends to increase during this time as does children's ability to link new information with existing knowledge.	• Increased ability to define self through internal and social characteristics. • Increased ability to understand complex emotions. • Improvements in the ability to control and redirect emotions.

events and actions, and they become more adept at concealing certain emotions and finding alternative or more socially acceptable ways of expressing certain emotions (Wintre & Vallance, 1994). Table 8.1 summarizes the developmental milestones for middle childhood.

Let us look at the kinds of developmental issues that might be occurring with Sue. You are not given much information about her physical and cognitive development, but you could collect this information through a biopsychosocial assessment. Sue's parents are complaining about her lack of interest in "age-appropriate" activities; you might want to know what kinds of activities Sue's parents consider age-appropriate. Because children develop at different rates and because parents are often misinformed about what is "normal," it is possible that Sue is not experiencing any problems in this area. Rather, her parents may have expectations for Sue that are not necessarily appropriate. However, they have reported that Sue does not spend much time interacting with peers or engaging in schoolwork, which may be a sign that she is struggling, because children at this age tend to be focused in these areas. In general, you will need to conduct an in-depth and detailed assessment of particular behaviors, which may include a referral to a physician or psychologist for additional testing, to ascertain the level of Sue's development and whether she may be experiencing some developmental problems that need attention.

THE INDIVIDUAL IN MIDDLE CHILDHOOD

Developmental processes that take place in middle childhood can impact individual children and their families in many ways. Some children move through middle childhood smoothly, with no remarkable events that cause concern. Others may have some trouble developmentally that can cause problems in other areas academically, socially, or otherwise. This section focuses on some of the issues on an individual level that may come to the attention of social workers who work with clients in this age range and their families.

Intelligence and Intelligence Testing

In contrast to the traditional ways in which we think about intelligence (for example, intelligence as defined by IQ, which is discussed later in the chapter), Sternberg's **triarchic theory of intelligence** emphasizes people's environmental contexts as well as how they adapt to their environment. This theory focuses on how people think and solve problems (Sternberg, 1977, 1985).

Sternberg's theory has three main components (hence the name "triarchic") that explain a range of ways in which intelligence can be expressed. These components—componential intelligence, experiential intelligence, and contextual intelligence—are described in Box 8.1. As you can see, each component allows for individual differences in the way people approach problems, which deviates from

---

BOX 8.1

Sternberg's Triarchic Theory of Intelligence

- *Componential intelligence:* This is akin to the usual way we think about intelligence. It describes intelligence that is based in the way people process and analyze information. This component focuses on the way people formulate ideas, argue points, and evaluate results. People who are high in componential intelligence perform well on standardized IQ tests.

- *Experiential intelligence:* This component focuses on how people perform tasks. It describes how people bring in new information and incorporate it into what they already know to solve problems. People who are high in experiential intelligence can master knowledge and tasks to perform them as if on automatic pilot, which frees them to learn new things. This is also known as "insightful" intelligence.

- *Contextual intelligence:* This component stresses the practical side of a person's intelligence. It emphasizes a person's ability to adapt to new situations and to successfully navigate in different environments. Another way to describe this component is "street smarts." People who are high in contextual intelligence are good at "working the system" or "jumping through the hoops."

Source: Adapted from Sternberg, 1977, 1985.

the usual ways we think about and assess intelligence. Many professionals view Sternberg's approach to intelligence as a positive way to think about people's strengths, especially people who score below average on standardized intelligence tests. Thus, his theory allows social workers to find unique ways in which their clients can conceptualize and solve problems. This process helps social workers to develop successful interventions.

Obviously, Sternberg's theory is limited in that it describes only one of many factors that can impact human behavior. After all, how useful can a theory be to social workers that describes whether someone is more likely to be good at crunching numbers or "jumping through the hoops" at her or his workplace? Nevertheless, given the debates about the value of standardized intelligence testing (some of which are discussed shortly) as well as debates about relying on those tests to make policy and program decisions, some social workers would argue that a theory such as this one is invaluable in their work with clients. In particular, this theory can help to explain why some people who do not seem to possess high levels of typical intelligence are able to succeed in life, despite barriers that appear insurmountable to others. It also speaks to the need to revisit the ways in which cognitive skills of children and adults are evaluated, given that these evaluations are often used as criteria for access to services and programs.

Unfortunately, the underlying concepts in Sternberg's theory can be difficult to define, measure, and evaluate. How do social workers define "street smarts," for example? How can they prove to policy-makers the value of investing in people who have skills that differ from those included in traditional definitions of intelligence? Given the widespread use of standardized intelligence testing, finding ways to validate and justify the use of alternative forms of intelligence can be daunting. For example, some researchers have supported the notion that people can possess emotional intelligence, which involves characteristics such as empathy, motivation, and self-awareness (Goleman, 2006), but these ideas have yet to take hold in many professional communities.

For some time, the idea that intelligence encompasses a singular characteristic has been debated. Sternberg challenged this idea, as have many other theorists. For example, in addition to Sternberg's ideas on intelligence, Gardner (1983) proposed the theory of **multiple intelligences**, which states that individuals can possess competencies in many areas, including the linguistic, spatial, interpersonal, and natural.

Although there have been several theories that describe other types of intelligence and knowing, traditional definitions of intelligence still play a significant role in society. Indeed, many social institutions use standardized definitions and assessments to categorize people into groups based on their intellectual abilities. These groupings often form the basis for receiving certain services, being placed in certain programs, and being labeled as competent to perform certain tasks. While standardized definitions of intelligence have their uses, a great deal of controversy surrounds the degree to which society relies on these definitions. In fact, there is not one agreed-upon definition of traditional intelligence, so the concept can mean very different things to different people.

Standardized Intelligence Tests   One of the major issues associated with defining intelligence has to do with the way intelligence is assessed or tested, which in turn leads to how policies and programs are delivered to meet the needs of people whose intelligence scores are considered either above or below average. Indeed, because both those giving standardized intelligence tests and those taking them often believe that they are tests of ability or capability in specific areas, this belief can have long-term consequences for those who take the tests. Many people view traditional intelligence as a genetic characteristic that can be represented by a numerical value, which can predetermine a person's limits with regard to her or his capabilities (Nash, 2001). Because these tests measure specific abilities and capabilities, many argue that intelligence testing plays down other strengths that people may have.

Social work with children and their families frequently involves some use of standardized intelligence tests. For example, social workers often use test scores to help develop interventions because many school-based and other programs rely on these scores to determine individual needs. Understanding the structure of intelligence tests, their uses, and their strengths and limitations can help social workers to ensure that these tests are applied as fairly and appropriately as possible and that they do not end up harming clients in the long run.

Common standardized intelligence tests include the Stanford-Binet tests and the Wechsler scales. The Stanford-Binet intelligence test was first developed by French psychologist Alfred Binet in 1905 to identify children with learning problems. Binet developed the concept of mental age, which compares a person's mental development with that of others. Mental age was used by William Stern to devise the **intelligence quotient (IQ)** that we are familiar with today. The IQ score is calculated by dividing a person's mental age by her or his chronological age and then multiplying the quotient by 100. Thus, a person whose mental and chronological ages are the same will have an IQ of 100, which is considered to be an average score on standardized tests. Over time, the Stanford-Binet test has been revised and used with large and diverse samples. The test, which can be administered to persons age two years and older, consists of questions that tap into verbal, quantitative, and abstract/visual reasoning as well as short-term memory.

The Wechsler scales were developed by David Wechsler and include three different scales to test three different age groups: 4 to 6½ years of age, 6 to 16 years of age, and adults 17+. These scales provide an overall IQ score as well as two separate scores on verbal and performance IQ.

Critiques of Standardized Intelligence Tests   Although standardized intelligence tests provide some information on various skills, they have been criticized for being biased against different minority groups and for not assessing different types of intelligence, thus making those who score below average appear to be less capable than those who score above average. Specifically, many critics have argued that standardized tests are Eurocentric, meaning that they test for people's abilities to perform in ways that follow standards of the white majority, which are deemed the only valid standards. Consequently, minority group members are often faced with questions that are foreign to them and do not represent their experiences (Craig & Beishuizen, 2002; Freedle, 2006; Gould, 2008). For example, professionals and researchers considered earlier versions of these standardized tests to be culturally biased against nonwhites living in rural areas and in low-socioeconomic groups. Specifically, correct answers to questions were often those that would likely be given by someone living in a particular cultural environment. So, even though someone not living in the dominant environment might offer a perfectly sound, rational answer to a question, given that person's environment and experience, it would be marked incorrect because it was not the answer thought to be rational by those constructing the test.

Moreover, historically, minority groups have scored lower on these tests than majority groups. However, as minority groups gain in socioeconomic and social status, their scores become more comparable to those in majority groups.

Thus, there seems to be some evidence that intelligence is connected to factors beyond just the biological (Neisser et al., 1996). Because IQ testing and scores have the potential to be biased and because scores can have so many individual and social ramifications, particularly for children, social workers need to be aware of the ethical dilemmas that standardized testing can pose.

In Sue's case, regardless of your perspective on intelligence and the value of testing, you will probably want to refer Sue for IQ testing. Because she is exhibiting so many problems at school, an IQ test is a logical step. It may be that she is having trouble with verbal or comprehension skills, for example, that keep her from understanding what is happening in the classroom. If she is not following along in the classroom, she may respond with behaviors similar to boredom or withdrawal. Similarly, if her skills are more developed than her peers', she may need a more advanced and challenging learning experience. IQ testing may also help to identify any potential learning disabilities that she might have; these are discussed in the next section. Despite the outcome of an IQ test, you will need to keep in mind the debates and potential ethical dilemmas associated with intelligence testing, along with the strengths and limitations of testing, to ensure that factors such as culture, definitions of intelligence, and other issues do not negatively impact Sue's situation.

Learning Disabilities

Often, standardized intelligence tests as well as other assessments are used to determine whether children have various learning disabilities that might necessitate additional services or special accommodations to ensure that these children receive an adequate education. **Learning disabilities** are generally defined as problems among children who demonstrate normal or above normal intelligence and who show no signs of developmental disability, but who struggle in some area of their academic performance. The numbers of children diagnosed with learning disabilities have been increasing. Boys tend to be diagnosed with learning disabilities more frequently than girls; however, it is difficult to determine whether there is a higher occurrence of disabilities among boys than girls. Specifically, boys tend to be referred for help more often than girls because of the behaviors caused by disabilities such as aggression and acting out. Boys do tend to be more biologically susceptible to learning disabilities than girls, however (Hallahan & Kauffman, 2000). Learning disabilities tend to be manifested through problems with listening, speaking, thinking, and concentration skills, which often result in performance problems in academic subjects such as math, reading, spelling, and composition. One of the most common types of learning disability is **dyslexia**, which results in severe reading and spelling impairments (Grigorenko, 2001; Ziegler & Goswami, 2005).

Children diagnosed with learning disabilities usually progress successfully through the public school system, generally with the assistance of special support services. However, there has been much debate about how best to educate children with special needs associated with learning disabilities (Kauffman & Hallahan, 2005). This debate generally centers on whether to keep these children in the classroom with others who do not demonstrate disabilities or to separate them and offer them specialized services tailored to their particular needs. Adding to this debate is the issue that diagnosing learning disabilities can be challenging. Because many other problems can occur along with learning disabilities, social workers and other professionals need to be careful about how assessments are conducted and used with children who might have learning disabilities. Indeed, many psychosocial variables associated with learning problems (such as stress, abuse, poverty, illness) come into play when labeling children with learning disabilities. We will examine services for children with learning disabilities and roles of social workers later in the chapter.

As discussed in the previous section, as Sue's social worker, you might want to assess her for possible learning disabilities that may or may not be related to her intellectual functioning. For example, Sue might be experiencing trouble reading or writing, which could be creating a whole host of problems with regard to her ability to maintain progress in the classroom. Since there is a wide range of potential problems, from the biological and developmental to the social, related to learning that Sue could be experiencing, you need to undertake a thorough assessment to develop appropriate interventions, if necessary.

Attention Deficit Hyperactivity Disorder

One condition often associated with learning disabilities is **attention deficit hyperactivity disorder (ADHD)**. This disorder is characterized by consistent displays of inattention, hyperactivity, and impulsivity. Children with symptoms of ADHD seem easily bored, have trouble focusing on tasks and activities, demonstrate high levels of activity, show an unwillingness or inability to think before acting, and exhibit low levels of impulse control. Symptoms can present themselves in various combinations. For example, some children may exhibit inattention with little hyperactivity, or hyperactivity with an ability to focus their attention (American Psychiatric Association, 2000). A study conducted by Rapport et al. (2009) on 23 preteen boys suggested that the fidgety behavior seen among children with ADHD may actually help them maintain alertness and focus on tasks; so asking kids with ADHD symptoms to "sit still" may actually be detrimental to their learning. These researchers hypothesize that kids with ADHD may be under-aroused—their brains don't produce sufficient amounts of dopamine to keep them alert, so they need to move around to keep their brains and bodies aroused, which is essential for learning to take place.

Diagnoses of ADHD among children have been increasing over the past few decades. A study by the Centers for Disease Control and Prevention (Bloom & Cohen, 2007) suggests that in 2006, 4.5 million children in the United States were diagnosed with the disorder. Moreover, Caucasian males are more frequently diagnosed with ADHD than any other gender or ethnic group. Some professionals speculate that increases in diagnoses are caused, in part, by increased knowledge of the disorder and better recognition of the symptoms. Further, many children diagnosed with ADHD have frequent contact with those who might make the diagnosis, such as primary care physicians. Diagnoses tend to be much lower among children who did not have health insurance, for example. Attention difficulties have become the most common reason why children are referred to mental health specialists, and over half of those children who receive special education are diagnosed with ADHD (Forness & Kavale, 2001; MMWR, 2005; Pastor & Reuben, 2008). For the most part, many children diagnosed with ADHD can benefit from medical and academic interventions.

Social workers who work with children must also remain aware of other variables associated with an ADHD diagnosis and their implications for work with children. For example, given the popularity of the diagnosis, some children who exhibit undesirable or uncontrollable behavior in the classroom may be unfairly labeled with the disorder, regardless of whether their symptoms actually warrant it. Problems in the education system such as lack of funding, support, and overcrowding may contribute to increases in ADHD diagnoses simply because teachers and other staff do not have the resources to accurately identify or deal with problem behavior when it occurs. Moreover, some professionals speculate that otherwise "normal" behavior such as high activity levels may be labeled as maladaptive and abnormal in the context of contemporary settings such as the controlled, formal classroom (Brewis, Meyer, & Schmidt, 2002). Consequently, some children may be misdiagnosed and inappropriately referred to physicians, psychologists, social workers, and special education programs.

Conversely, given the potential ramifications of ADHD on learning and development, accurate identification and assessment of symptoms as well as appropriate intervention are important when working with children. Reflecting on developmental tasks that children undergo during this time, problems associated with ADHD can interfere with successful biopsychosocial development. Social workers can be integral to ensuring optimal development of children who exhibit issues surrounding ADHD. Indeed, medications, while controversial, have shown promising results in managing symptoms of ADHD as have other psychosocial interventions such as parent training and behavior modification (Barkley, 2002; Olfson, Gameroff, Marcus, & Jensen, 2003). Social workers can be instrumental in developing and implementing such interventions in the home and academic settings.

As with learning disabilities, assessing Sue for ADHD could be worthwhile, particularly because the two problems frequently occur together. Although you cannot ascertain from the description how likely it is that Sue has symptoms of the disorder, you should not rule this out as a possibility.

THE FAMILY AND IMMEDIATE ENVIRONMENT IN MIDDLE CHILDHOOD

Of course, much of what happens to a child on an individual level also affects the child's family and vice versa. The previous section focused on individual problems that tend to be individual phenomena; in this section, we move to issues that tend to originate outside of the individual but impact the individual through her or his interaction with the immediate environment.

Peer Groups in Middle Childhood

Although families fulfill an important function with regard to socialization and providing feedback to children about the world and their behavior, the role of peer groups in this process is equally important if not more so. **Peer groups**, which consist of children of roughly the same age, are a part of children's immediate environment that can have lasting effects on their development. Because of their similarity in age and experience, peers can offer one another valuable information about their abilities and their relation to the outside world.

Various theories discussed in earlier chapters touch on the importance of peer relationships in childhood. For example, Bandura refers to modeling and social learning, and Erikson's theory as well as ecological and sociological theories emphasize interaction with the environment as a factor in development. All of these theories highlight the need for children to have peers as reference points as they explore their environments, express their opinions, try on new roles, and test their social, physical, and academic capabilities. Indeed, some theorists argue that it is through peer relationships that children learn to develop intimate, sensitive relationships in which compromise and empathy are a part (Buhrmester & Furman, 1987; Parker, Rubin, Erath, Wojslawowicz, & Buskirk, 2006).

Conversely, peer relationships can have negative effects on childhood development. All children experience negative relationships and problems with friends. However, some children experience constant rejection and negative interactions with their peers, which can have lasting consequences on development. Feelings of rejection, hostility, loneliness, and depression can result from poor interactions with peers, which can impact later relationships with others (Hodges & Card, 2003).

In Sue's case, you may want to explore how she has been getting along with her peers, since she is at an age when peer reactions and acceptance are significant. For instance, Sue's friends may be rejecting her because she has two mothers or because of her ethnic background. Sue's family history is unusual enough that she may be experiencing loneliness and confusion if she is unable to relate to the other children her age and their family backgrounds. From a strengths perspective, you could help Sue focus on the positive aspects of her ethnic background and family situation as well as the ways in which her situation is similar to that of her peers. In doing so, Sue may find new and more positive ways to interact and relate with her peers.

Play

An integral part of the peer interaction of play serves many functions in childhood development. Apart from the obvious goal of having fun, play affords children opportunities to exercise their imagination, interact with others, practice social and other roles, develop cognitive and physical skills, and find natural ways to release tension and frustration. As with peer relationships, many theorists support the functional aspects of play in childhood development.

Much research has been conducted on play and its role in development. One of the first attempts to classify play comes from Mildred Parten (1932). Through her research, she developed categories of play, which are listed in Table 8.2. These classifications help to identify different situations in which children engage in play and what that play might look like. More current research has focused on other types of play and various goals or purposes that play might have in development. One type is play that helps children practice a multitude of skills such as those involved in sensorimotor activities, coordination, symbolism, imagination, social interaction, and self-regulation (Bergin, 1988).

The latter goals of play relate well to various theoretical conceptualizations of childhood development. For example, Piaget focused on issues of sensorimotor and cognitive development. According to the goals of play listed previously, infants engage in play that stimulates visual and motor skills, and as they grow, they become better able to manipulate their environment in play, which stimulates development of coordination and other skills. Older children use their imaginations to manipulate objects in their play, and they have the ability to take the perspectives of others in role playing. Older children also gain the ability to understand rules

CATEGORY OF PLAY	DESCRIPTION	
Unoccupied	Type of play that is uncharacteristic of typical play. Child often appears to be standing around, not doing anything, or engaging in movements or activities that seem to lack a goal or purpose. Child is often watching events happening around him or her.	**TABLE 8.2** *Classifications of Play*
Solitary	Play that involves solitary or independent activities. Child is often unconcerned with what others are doing. Common among children two to three years old.	
Onlooker	Type of play in which child observes the play of others. The child might ask questions or seem interested in others' play but does not participate.	
Parallel	Play that occurs simultaneously but separately from play of other children. Child may play with similar toys or in similar manner as other children. As children age, they are less likely to engage in this type of play.	
Associative	Type of play that involves a great deal of social interaction with other children, but play is still very individualistic. Though children play together, there is no real organization of or attention being paid to the play that is occurring. For example, children may talk together or share toys, but they are focused on their own activities.	
Cooperative	Play that includes social interaction with organized activity and a sense of group identity. Children share a purpose in play and work toward a common goal.	

Source: Adapted from Parten, 1932.

and to organize their play, resulting in games that involve competition and negotiation.

According to Sue's parents, Sue spends a great deal of time by herself and seldom engages in play with peers. You might want to assess Sue's play to better understand what purposes her activities might have in her development and whether her play seems age or developmentally appropriate. For example, Sue may be engaging in frequent unoccupied play, which could appear odd to her parents. Alternatively, Sue may not be engaging in other types of play that include interaction and that build on various motor skills, which may have ramifications for her future development. A detailed assessment of Sue's activities would help you understand potential issues in Sue's play that could impact other areas of her well-being.

EXHIBIT 8.1

Play is an important part of childhood development

Source: Ryan McVay/Getty Images

Parental Discipline

As children grow older, parents find themselves struggling with many new issues surrounding discipline and parenting. Physically, cognitively, and emotionally, children are becoming capable of performing new tasks and taking on new challenges. According to Piaget, they are able to better understand reason and to think concretely about their actions and those of others. Erikson suggests that children at five or six years old and later are working on becoming industrious; they are curious, enthusiastic, and focused on mastering their environment. As mentioned earlier, systems, ecological, social learning, and similar theories emphasize the importance of interaction between the individual and her or his environment on development. Thus, because of multiple changes that are taking place within complex environmental contexts, there are a myriad of parenting challenges that are posed during this particular time in childhood.

Discipline in Middle Childhood   Many discipline issues that present themselves during this time involve school, self-regulation of behavior, responsibilities at home, and balance between time spent in and outside the home. Discipline during this time of childhood may be comparatively easier for parents than it was earlier in the child's development. This is because children's cognitive abilities allow for greater understanding and reasoning about rules and consequences. Discipline at this stage in development may also be easier than it will be during adolescence when teens begin to assert their independence and may resist discipline. Middle childhood, then, is the period when children can understand the reasons behind their parents' actions, although they still do not possess the capabilities to act completely independently. Thus, major tasks in parental discipline at this point include helping children to develop the skills needed to act responsibly and independently while providing structured guidance to support them and ward against dangerous situations that they may not foresee.

Parents and professionals often disagree about the best way to provide parental discipline. Parents are often overwhelmed by the vast amounts of information available on disciplinary techniques, much of which is contradictory. In addition, they frequently worry about the long-term effects of using one method over another, as if their child will be scarred for life should some well-meaning technique be found harmful later. To make matters more complicated, advice about what is "best" for children is constantly changing. Moreover, parenting styles and child temperament (discussed in Chapter 7), among many other factors, influence how discipline actually plays out. It is a wonder that parents feel capable of providing any discipline at all!

The Debate over Physical Punishment   One ongoing debate on discipline revolves around **corporal punishment**—the use of physical punishment, particularly spanking, on children. Spanking as a disciplinary technique has been around since people have been having children. In the United States, spanking as punishment is relatively prevalent; however, attitudes about its use have shifted over time. For example, data indicates that during the 1960s, 94 percent of parents perceived spanking as a legitimate form of discipline. By 1999, that number had declined to 55 percent (Children's Institute International, 1999; Gallup Organization, 1995). Indeed, many U.S. states and other nations have banned its use in public education settings and many states include excessive corporal punishment in their definitions of child maltreatment (Davidson, 1997; Gaten, 2009; Straus, 2008). However, a vast majority—over 90 percent—of parents still report using corporal punishment at least once (Straus, 2001).

Attitudes about spanking specifically and corporal punishment generally are deeply embedded in the fabric of social, cultural, religious, and political life. As such, debates about the utility of spanking are usually heated, and middle ground on disciplinary techniques is difficult to establish. For example, several states have recently passed laws to secure parental rights to spank, which has refueled the debate about where parents should draw the line with regard to discipline. Research has attempted to offer some scientific insight into the pros and cons of spanking, but even these attempts are limited and are often met with much criticism. Among professionals, much disagreement exists about the utility of spanking and other forms of corporal punishment.

In general, the main debates among scholars, parents, and professionals tend to center around whether spanking (or other forms of corporal punishment) promotes violent behavior among children who are spanked and whether spanking helps to reinforce other modes of discipline such as time-outs (Benjet & Kazdin, 2003). Those who support the notion that spanking reinforces violent behavior in children often reflect Bandura's view of social learning. Children model behaviors of others, and they learn that an effective way to get someone to comply with a demand is through physical violence. Conversely, others might argue, again using Bandura's theory, that spanking is an effective disciplinary technique because children who witness another child being spanked for undesirable behavior will be more likely to behave in desirable ways to avoid the same punishment. Still others might argue that cognitively, young children are unable to understand the consequences of misbehavior, so techniques such as explanation and time-outs are unlikely to work to correct behavior until children reach a more mature age. Thus, spanking is a more effective approach, particularly when it is paired with other techniques such as the use of rewards.

Research on spanking dates back several decades, but only a few consistent findings across studies exist. The majority of findings agree that spanking is positively correlated with aggression, misconduct, and similar behaviors among children, even in cultures where it is socially acceptable and normative (Gershoff, 2002; Lansford & Dodge, 2008; Straus, 2008). At the same time, the studies also confirm that spanking does succeed at getting children to comply with parents' demands (Harvard Mental Health Letter, 2002). However, this association cannot establish causation, which tends to be at the heart of the spanking debate. The question remains: Does spanking cause increased aggression in children, or are children spanked more because they show aggressive behavior? Moreover, studies cannot possibly account for the many individual, familial, social, and other contextual variables that might be associated with relationships between spanking and aggressive behavior among children.

Because of the debates and conflicting information on discipline, as Sue's social worker, you might want to explore discipline issues with her parents. Sue's parents could benefit from discussion of the topic, and they might be relieved to know that many parents are confused about conflicting and changing knowledge on the subject. You may be able to provide some guidance to Sue's parents on how to evaluate knowledge and research to make some educated decisions about how to proceed with disciplining Sue.

Separation, Divorce, and Alternative Family Forms

Many parents experiencing separation and divorce worry about how their actions will affect their children (see Box 8.2). To complicate matters, definitions of families

BOX 8.2

*Separation
and Divorce*

Probably one of the biggest concerns parents have involves the effects of separation and divorce on children. Parents often question whether they should remain together for the sake of the children. In general, research indicates that many children who experience divorce do have trouble with adjustment, but the type and extent of this difficulty depend on many factors and vary a great deal from child to child (Sun & Li, 2002, 2009). Some of the major issues facing children who have experienced divorce include academic, attachment, behavioral (for example, acting out, delinquency, promiscuity in teen years), and emotional problems (for example, anxiety, depression), and low self-esteem (Hetherington, 2000; Leon, 2003; Pelkonen, Marttunen, Kaprio, Huurre, & Aro, 2008; Shansky, 2002). Research into the effects of divorce on children has yielded conflicting results. While some research indicates that relatively few children face these types of problems and that the extent of these problems is rather small, other research indicates that the extent of problems associated with divorce is significant (Amato, 2000, 2001; Bing, Nelson, & Wesolowski, 2009; Hetherington, 2000).

What factors seem to place children at risk for experiencing adjustment problems with separation and divorce? Though it is impossible to account for all variables that might impact a child's ability to cope with separation and divorce, research has focused on several factors that seem to make a difference in children's adjustment:

- How children cope with problems, including predivorce stress, is a good predictor of how they will cope with the divorce and its aftermath (Amato, 2000; Eldar-Avidan, Haj-Yahia, & Greenbaum, 2009).

- Children's level of development at the time of the divorce has a lot to do with how well they cope. Children who are able to cognitively process the divorce as well as understand the complex nuances behind the reasons for the divorce will probably fare better than their younger counterparts, who are less likely to grasp why the divorce is occurring (Ängarne-Lindberg & Wadsby, 2009; Zill, Morrison, & Coiro, 1993).

- Children's gender may have some impact on their ability to cope. Earlier research had indicated that boys adjust better to divorce than girls. However, more current research suggests that these differences may be less significant than originally thought. Though girls may still struggle slightly more than their male counterparts, increasing participation by fathers after divorce and varying custody arrangements may be easing the difficulties that female children experience throughout the divorce (Amato, 2000; Ruschena, Prior, Sanson, & Smart, 2005).

Whereas parents cannot control some of these factors, such as a child's temperament and personality, they can control others. For example, parents can (Hetherington, 2003; Moxnes, 2003):

- Maintain open and respectful communication with children.

- Ensure that children (especially young children) understand that they are not to blame for the divorce.

- Maintain a consistent daily routine.

BOX 8.2

continued

- Remain realistic but hopeful about the situation.

- Be supportive of the children.

    Moreover, sometimes when there is a great deal of conflict and strife in the home before divorce takes place, separation and divorce can actually improve children's coping and functioning, especially if a consistent routine and respectful communication and relations can be established and maintained (Waite & Gallagher, 2000).

    Though many more postdivorce custody and living arrangements occur today than in the past, the reality is still that single mothers take on the majority of child care and custody responsibilities. Unfortunately, after divorce, the income of many women decreases dramatically, causing potential problems such as stress, poverty, job instability, increased workload, and frequent moves and disruption in the child's life (Amato, 2000; Wang & Amato, 2000). As you might imagine, factors such as these can make children's adjustment to divorce more difficult as well.

and the ways in which families are forming are changing. Increasing numbers of blended families, gay and lesbian families, and single parent and cohabiting partner household families are driving questions about how family structures affect child development.

Stepfamilies and Blended Families   In addition to single parent families, more and more children in the United States are being reared in stepfamilies and blended families. Given the high rates of divorce in this country, it is common for people to remarry and to combine families. Generally, children are reared in families with a biological parent and a stepparent after remarriage. Often, these families bring together two sets of children from each parent, which results in **blended families**.

    As with divorce, blended families and stepfamilies can bring about difficulties in adjustment for the children. Usually these problems stem from families readjusting to roles, responsibilities, and relocation as well as getting to know one another and what the expectations are for each new family member. Moreover, the newly wed couple often needs time to adjust to marriage and living together, which can create additional stress for the children. When families are blended, the children from each parent also need time to get to know one another and build relationships (Bray & Kelly, 1998; Gonzales, 2009).

Gay and Lesbian Parents   Another hotly debated issue surrounding parenting involves the ability of gay and lesbian individuals to be fit parents. Millions of gays and lesbians are parents, many as a result of prior heterosexual relationships in which biological children were born. Usually in these past relationships, the other partner is heterosexual, as are the judges and others who might become involved in custody battles. Many gays and lesbians face discrimination when entering such battles. For example, at least six states automatically assume that gays and lesbians are unfit to parent, thus requiring gay and lesbian parents to prove that they can be appropriate parents to their children (Kendall, 2003).

Moreover, gays and lesbians face considerable discrimination when attempting to adopt or foster a child. Though the number of children needing such homes is increasing and gay and lesbian individuals could help fill the void of prospective parents, the current system fails to tap into this viable resource because of prejudices. One of these prejudices is that gays and lesbians are unfit to parent, even though empirical evidence suggests that children of gay and lesbian parents are as well adjusted as children reared by heterosexual parents (Anderssen, Amlie, & Ytteroy, 2002; Brooks & Goldberg, 2001; Tasker, 2005). Indeed, based on the benefits for children of having parents who are involved in a loving, stable relationship, the American Academy of Pediatrics supports the adoption of children by gay or lesbian couples (American Academy of Pediatrics, 2002).

However, some professionals have responded negatively to the position of the American Academy of Pediatrics. They state that the high HIV/AIDS rate among homosexual males (and thus the relatively short life span of such individuals); the moral and religious beliefs of many people who do not support exposing children to homosexual lifestyles; and the likelihood that children raised in same-sex couple households will consider a same-sex relationship for themselves in the future (though there is no evidence to support this claim) are reasons to rethink the support for homosexual couples who want to parent (Golombok, 2002; Guttery, Friday, Field, Riggs, & Hagan, 2002). Though some professionals and scholars argue that gay and lesbian individuals should not be allowed to parent based on moral and religious grounds, empirical evidence suggests that children reared in such households show similar levels of development in cognitive, emotional, social, and sexual functioning as children reared in households with heterosexual couples (Anderssen, Amlie, & Ytteroy, 2002; Brooks & Goldberg, 2001; Hagan, 2002; Perrin, 2002; Tasker, 2005).

In addition to focusing on common issues surrounding parenting and normal childhood development, social workers working with gay and lesbian families may also need to focus on attitudes about homosexuality when dealing with adoption, foster care, or other parenting issues. They will also likely be dealing with religious and moral issues embedded in the social institutions that serve these families, as these issues are likely to be concerns of many who run related agencies and who are clients of them. Unfortunately, dealing with these latter issues may take precedence over focusing on positive parenting and development of the child and family, as any ill effects on childhood development may come from prejudicial and discriminatory attitudes from others rather than from actual parenting issues.

Further, advances in technology that allow gay and lesbian individuals to become parents are pushing the limits of courts and legislation, which are also challenging the definition of the traditional family. Social workers will continue to be at the forefront of these challenges and debates, shaping the way in which social attitudes and policies affect parenthood and grappling with ethical dilemmas as issues surrounding technology and morality intersect.

You can see many of these factors coming together in Sue's situation. Not only is she living with lesbian parents, but she was the product of technological advances. Sue is likely to have faced and will continue to face many challenges in the future because of her unique situation, many of which may affect her development and overall well-being. Sue is probably facing much discrimination from her peers, and possibly from her teachers, because of her situation. Unfortunately, Sue's cognitive abilities at this point in her development will not be adequate for her to deal effectively with this discrimination without support. Many of the behavioral problems that Sue is allegedly having may be a result of her attempts to cope with an environment that is less than ideal for her to flourish. You may need to intervene on mezzo and macro levels as well as the micro level to help build resources that will maximize Sue's coping abilities given her developmental level. This means that you may need to focus on the school environment, the teachers' attitudes and behaviors toward Sue and her parents, Sue's interactions with her peers, Sue's parents' actions, and Sue's own self-concept. In addition, you need to assess Sue's strengths as well as those of her family when considering ways in which to intervene. Since it is likely that Sue is experiencing a great deal of negativity in her environment, discussing strengths is an important part of work with Sue.

THE LARGER SOCIAL ENVIRONMENT IN MIDDLE CHILDHOOD

We have looked at many issues on the individual and immediate environmental levels affecting the development of children that social workers must consider when working with children and their families. Additionally, there are other issues on a larger environmental level that impact children and their families. These areas often involve policy and other social issues with which social workers must deal either directly or indirectly when working with clients. This section addresses some of these macro issues and how they relate to the development and well-being of children.

The Mass Media

One continual question that most parents have involves the effects of media on children's development and behavior. With technological advances speeding ahead of our ability to answer ethical and other questions regarding their effects on humans, many parents and professionals often find themselves debating the strengths, limitations, and positive and negative ramifications of such technology on our lives. Indeed, extensive research has been generated on the topic in an attempt to untangle the endless array of psychosocial variables associated with the use of technology and its effects on everyday life. However, rather than provide concrete answers about how media can affect our well-being, much of this research has only generated more questions about the use of technology and media.

Much of the discussion surrounding media and development focuses on violence on television and the use of other media such as video games, the Internet, and exposure to unregulated content. In the United States, according to the last known statistics, children watch an average of 28 hours of television per week, and by the time they reach their 18th birthday, they will have witnessed some 200,000 acts of violence (American Psychiatric Association, 1998). The Kaiser Family Foundation (2005a) reported that children spend an average of just under 6½ hours per day using media (e.g., TV, computers, video games, etc.)—or around 44½ hours per week. In addition, children account for approximately 20 percent of Internet traffic, most spending their time in chat rooms and using instant messaging (NUA Internet Surveys, 2002). Though advances in programming are helping to filter violent or otherwise inappropriate content on the Internet, parents and educators often find themselves frustrated when these programs turn out to be less than perfect in policing the content to which children are exposed online.

The Mass Media and Violence   One fundamental question surrounding media use and exposure is how these activities affect child development. A great deal of research has been conducted on the effects of media violence on children and their behavior. Generally, this body of research has concluded that witnessing violent acts on television and through other media does have adverse effects on child behavior (Funk, Buchman, Jenks, & Bechtoldt, 2002; Huesmann, Moise-Titus, Podolski, & Eron, 2003; Strasburger & Grossman, 2001). For example, media violence has been associated with increased aggressive and antisocial behavior among children as well as increased feelings of fear and insecurity (American Academy of Pediatrics, 2001; Cantor, 2000; Christakis & Zimmerman, 2005; Huesmann et al., 2003). In a famous study by Bandura (1965), children who had watched an adult perform aggressive actions against an inflatable "Bobo" doll and get rewarded for it tended to replicate this violent behavior toward the doll. Many parents and professionals are concerned that violence shown on television and portrayed in video games is set within a context in which the violence is glamorized, and those perpetrating the violence are either rewarded, or at least not punished, leading children to believe that violence is not a serious issue.

Many of the concerns surrounding media violence revolve around the developmental capacities of the children who are exposed to it. Reflecting back on Piaget's work on cognitive development, young children are not able to separate reality from fantasy until various cognitive processes are in place. Preschoolers, for example, still engage in magical thinking, which means that they are likely to take what they view on television at face value. They do not understand that people on television are simply playing roles. Thus, young children do not understand that much of the violence seen on television is for "entertainment value"; rather they may interpret violent behavior as something that is commonplace and acceptable in society.

The Mass Media and Physical Inactivity   A related issue has to do with the amount of time that children spend watching television, playing video games, or surfing the Internet. Recently, attention has been given to the increasing rates of obesity and diabetes among U.S. children. Many professionals attribute these problems, in part, to decreased activity rates among children who are spending more and more time on sedentary activities such as television watching and interacting with other media (Clocksin, Watson, & Ransdell, 2002; Kaiser Family Foundation, 2005a).

As various forms of media become more mainstream in the lives of many children, social workers will be working with educators, parents, and other professionals to help find solutions to the problems that technology may bring for children's development. Mediating the effects of violence to which children are exposed, helping families find a balance between media use and other forms of entertainment that allow for physical activity and peer interaction, and influencing public policies and legislation that help to maximize children's development are all issues with which social workers will continue to grapple.

In Sue's situation, you may want to assess the amount of exposure that Sue has to television and other media, which could impact her development. You could also discuss with Sue's parents their values about media use as well as what the research has to say about the positive and negative effects of various forms of media on childhood development.

EXHIBIT 8.2

Media use can have a negative impact on development in childhood

Source: Escobar Studios

The Educational Context

Increasingly, academic issues and the learning environment have been centers of debate in the United States. With shrinking budgets, growing classrooms, and questions about the best curricula to use for optimal learning and how to meet the needs of a diverse student body, knowing how to proceed with choosing schools and understanding the issues can be perplexing for parents and professionals.

Social workers often deal with these issues on a daily basis, particularly if they are working directly with children and their families. In addition to working with children and their parents, social workers often work with teachers and schools as well as with school board officials, legislators, and communities to help educate others on the issues affecting education, which usually directly affect the policies and funding that go into the education system.

Special Education and the Least Restrictive Environment   Until recently, children with physical and mental disabilities were unable to access fair and equitable education in the public school system. In the 1960s and 1970s federal and state movements were undertaken to provide educational and other resources to children with disabilities and special needs. These movements culminated in the 1975 Education for All Handicapped Children Act (Public Law 94–142), which mandated that all children with disabilities have access to free and appropriate education. In 1990, the name of this law was changed to the **Individuals with Disabilities Education Act (IDEA)**. Some of the main provisions of IDEA are that eligibility criteria for services be clearly defined and that evaluations for these criteria be readily accessible to children who need them. IDEA also ensures that children who meet criteria can receive individualized education plans, which offer students specialized services targeted to their specific needs.

IDEA further mandates that students with disabilities be offered educational services in the **least restrictive environment (LRE)**, which means that the setting in which education for students with disabilities takes place is as similar and equal to that of other students as possible. This last effort is to ensure that students with disabilities do not end up in facilities that are less equipped or somehow inferior to those offered to students without disabilities (Crockett & Kauffman, 1999; Kauffman & Hallahan, 2005).

Further, the current philosophy on educating children with disabilities is that they should spend time in regular classrooms interacting with children who do not have disabilities; this process has been referred to as **mainstreaming**, or inclusion. For mainstreaming to be implemented successfully, teachers must receive special-ized training to meet the needs of children with disabilities, and social workers must provide support services for teachers, children, and their families. Often, teachers, schools, and social workers complain that funding is inadequate to truly provide for the needs mandated by IDEA. Moreover, some professionals argue that regardless of the efforts made to provide appropriate services to children with special needs—

whether through mainstreaming or separate classrooms—recipients of these services often experience discrimination because of educational policies and services that lack clear goals and fiscal, cultural, and other support (Davis & Watson, 2001). Social workers are often the professionals who interpret policies on special education, develop programs to meet policy mandates, evaluate students for eligibility for special programs, and support families whose children need such services. Therefore, they need to be familiar with the issues and problems surrounding education for children with disabilities to ensure that programs and policies are as equitable and effective as possible.

School Vouchers   Other controversial issues with which social workers are often involved include experimental and changing methods of providing educational services to children and families. In recent decades, novel programs have been developed in an attempt to solve problems faced by existing but failing public educational systems. Poor student achievement, shaky funding, and low academic standards are just a few of the issues that many experts argue are plaguing the public school system. In response to these issues, there has been an increase in the number of charter schools, school voucher programs, and student busing initiatives that allow students to attend schools of their choice.

Although many parents, educators, professionals, and researchers agree that the public school system is in dire need of reform, there is less agreement about how to proceed with that reform and whether or not novel approaches to education are warranted or more effective than those already in place. For example, **school vouchers**, or certificates that can be used to pay for schools of parents' choosing, have been touted as a solution to poorly performing schools by allowing students to take their allotted education tax dollars to a school of their choice. Specifically, vouchers are given to parents in lieu of tax dollars that are spent on public education. Instead of using tax dollars to educate their children in public schools, parents can use vouchers to have their children educated at schools of the parents' choosing. Consequently, poorly performing schools will lose students and money, forcing the schools to improve their standards or risk closure.

Critics of school vouchers argue that the money allotted is not sufficient to provide students, particularly poor students, with a real choice. Specifically, most vouchers provide each student with between $1,000 and $4,000 to pay for education. Most private schools cost more than this, and many students cannot find public schools that perform better and that are worth the transfer. Consequently, many students who take advantage of voucher programs transfer to private religious schools, which, critics argue, should not be funded by public tax dollars.

Research conducted on the effectiveness of voucher programs to increase student learning and academic performance has been largely inconclusive. Most research has not found a significant difference in academic performance between students using voucher programs and those not using the programs. Findings are also inconclusive with regard to whether voucher programs benefit minority students, who largely attend inadequately funded and poor performing schools (Viadero, 2003).

Along with educators and other professionals, social workers grapple with the debates about education provision on the policy and service-delivery levels. Social workers help shape opinions and debates on education through research, program evaluation, and service development and provision. Further, in the confusion that can easily ensue in debates over education, social workers must ensure that ethical standards are upheld in the provision of educational services and that clients are not lost in the debates. Generally, social workers are responsible for ensuring that all clients have access to quality and equitable education.

Although there is no indication that Sue needs any special education services, as her social worker, you could advocate for these should the situation warrant it. You could also educate Sue's parents about their rights to services in the education system if Sue were to present with any kind of disability or special need.

CONCLUSION

Middle childhood is a time of continued physical, emotional, and cognitive growth, particularly as children are increasingly exposed to others in their environment. Interactions with peers, teachers, technology, and other aspects of the outside world have an impact on the development of children. Healthy and steady development in middle childhood relies on physical, mental, and emotional stimulation and positive relationships with others. Theories of development such as those posited by Piaget and Erikson can help social workers to conceptualize development of their young clients in this time of life.

Social workers can be of great benefit to families who have children in the age range of middle childhood. Often, problems regarding development, parenting, family issues, school performance, and relationships with peers bring families to social workers for help. Understanding the ways in which individual and social factors can influence children and their families is crucial to providing effective assessment and intervention that will enhance clients' individual, familial, and social functioning. Further, social workers need to understand debates surrounding issues such as intelligence testing and education so that they can advocate for and support the needs of clients in the most ethical and appropriate way possible.

MAIN POINTS

- Motor, emotional, cognitive, and physical development continues to progress during middle childhood, the ages of 5 or 6 to approximately 11.
- Sternberg's triarchic theory of intelligence describes three main modes of intellectual functioning: componential, experiential, and contextual.

Though professionals acknowledge the benefits of recognizing concepts such as multiple intelligence, standardized intelligence tests and traditional definitions of intelligence still predominate in policy and service delivery, particularly relating to learning disabilities.

- There are debates over diagnosis of learning disabilities, including dyslexia and ADHD, as well as how best to educate children with special needs associated with learning disabilities.

- Peer relationships have a profound impact on children's motor, social, emotional, and cognitive development. Types of play children engage in as well as parental discipline are two additional factors in the immediate environment that impact development.

- Research results on the effects of divorce and remarriage on children and their development show that some children experience problems in development and behavior, while others seemingly show no adverse effects. A combination of factors such as children's temperament, their level of development, their gender, and whether parents maintain open communication and support their children during the divorce contribute to how well children cope.

- Although much controversy remains, research indicates that children reared by gay or lesbian parents do just as well developmentally as children reared by heterosexual parents.

- Evidence suggests that exposure to violence on television and through other media is associated with aggressive behavior in children as well as with decreased time spent engaging in physical and social activity.

- Though there is consensus that the current public education system needs reform, many alternatives to education such as voucher and busing programs have mixed results with regard to their effectiveness in providing quality and equitable education. Laws enacted in the 1970s and updated in the 1990s have contributed to mainstreaming children with disabilities and special needs.

EXERCISES

1. Using the Sanchez Family interactive case (go to www.routledgesw.com/cases), review the major issues involving the Sanchez family. After giving this information thorough review, answer the following questions:
   a. Given the various issues discussed in this chapter, which ones might be of concern for the Sanchez family and why? Describe, in some detail, how individual members might be affected by these issues and how they might impact the family as a system.

b. How might these issues be impacted by cultural factors? Offer a thorough exploration of the cultural context in which the family lives and how you, as a social worker, would take into consideration this context as you pinpoint issues.

c. Based on problems that you identify for this family and your ideas about how to work with these problems and the family, what ethical dilemmas, if any, could potentially emerge for this family?

d. Briefly describe what type of interventions you would recommend for this family based on your assessment of problems. Justify your plans.

e. What theories might you want to use to guide your interventions and why?

2. Review the Riverton interactive case (go to www.routledgesw.com/cases), paying particular attention to issues surrounding Felipe and Maria Gonzales, their family, and the school in the community. Based on the information in this chapter, answer the following questions:

a. How might the information in this chapter be useful in your work with the Gonzales family and the community's school, if at all?

b. Could any of the information presented in this and the preceding chapters be used with the family or community to prevent future problems? In what ways?

c. What strengths do you see with the family and the community's school that could be used to help solve problems?

CHAPTER 9

Development in Adolescence

Alicia is a 14-year-old Caucasian teen who has been living part time with her single mother and part time at a friend's home. Alicia has been having trouble getting along with her mother and has threatened several times to run away from home. She has been doing poorly in school and spends a great deal of her time roaming the streets and hanging out with kids who are homeless. Alicia's troubles began about one year ago when her mother discovered that Alicia was purposely vomiting immediately after eating dinner. When Alicia's mother confronted Alicia, she became angry and withdrew from her mother, turning more and more to her "street friends."

Alicia has come to your attention as a social worker at a community center with a program for homeless teens where Alicia spends some of her time. You are concerned about Alicia's weight loss, depressed mood, low self-esteem, and seemingly slow developmental progress for her age. Though you don't have proof, you are also concerned that Alicia has been engaging in sexual intercourse with some of her male friends; Alicia refuses to discuss sex, contraception, or sexually transmitted infections, telling you that she would never get pregnant or get an infection. You have tried to get Alicia to come to the center with her mother for counseling, but Alicia doesn't see the need for it.

A CHALLENGING TIME FOR THOSE EXPERIENCING IT AS WELL AS for their families, **adolescence** typically begins around ages 10 to 12 and lasts until ages 18 to 22. Because of the many biopsychosocial changes that take place during this time, problems can emerge for individuals and their families. Further, because adolescents are developing their identity and independence while still legally dependent on their parents and guardians, social workers can face many legal, ethical, and practical challenges when working with teen clients. In the sections to follow, we will explore some of the most prevalent issues that affect clients during this period of the life span.

DEVELOPMENTAL MILESTONES IN THE TEEN YEARS

The teen years are characterized by continued physical growth and significant changes that signal the onset of sexual maturity and development into adulthood. This section discusses some of these processes and their effects on teens.

Physical Development

With regard to physical development, a hallmark of adolescence is puberty and the hormonal changes associated with it. **Puberty** is characterized by rapid physical and sexual growth, and it is often accompanied by hormonal, emotional, and other changes. The hypothalamus and pituitary glands in the brain and the sex glands, or gonads (testes in males and ovaries in females), are the main structures involved in hormonal changes during adolescence. Androgen in males and estrogen in females are the main sex hormones that are involved in genital, sexual, and other physical development.

One basic component of puberty is the development of **primary sex characteristics**, or those aspects of development directly related to reproduction. For girls, this includes the development of the uterus, ovaries, and vagina. For boys, it is the development of the prostate gland and growth of the penis. Puberty also brings with it the development of **secondary sex characteristics**, or those aspects related to gender but not directly related to reproduction. Secondary characteristics include changes such as hair growth, breast development, and voice and skin changes.

With regard to puberty, studies have indicated a **secular trend**, or pattern, toward earlier onset of development in industrialized countries. Over the course of the 19th and 20th centuries, for example, the average age of menarche in the United States decreased from 15 years of age to 12½ years of age. Though this trend is likely due to improved sanitation, nutrition, and related factors, it has slowed down somewhat over the past few decades (Martorell, Mendoza, & Castillo, 1988).

A central question surrounding hormonal and other changes during adolescence is whether these changes cause dramatic changes in behavior. For example, many parents and professionals wonder to what extent increases in testosterone cause aggressive behavior in males. Similarly, some people ask to what extent increases in estrogen in females contribute to increases in depressive symptoms. Recent research indicates that there is no clear cause-and-effect relationship between hormones and behavior. However, evidence suggests that the two are associated. For example, a growing body of literature indicates that increases in androgens are related to increases in aggression among boys (Dorn et al., 2009; Pasterski et al., 2007; Van Goozen, Matthys, Cohen-Kettenis, Thisjssen, & Van Engeland, 1998).

Keep in mind, though, that other physical, emotional, cognitive, and environmental factors play a role in determining behavior. In girls, for example, factors such as stress, peers, heredity, and timing of puberty along with hormonal changes can impact the development of depressive symptoms (Angold, Costello, & Worthman, 1998; Brooks-Gunn & Warren, 1989; Neiss, Stevenson, Legrand, Iacono, & Sedikides, 2009). So, in addition to viewing puberty from the medical model, social workers need to assess issues using other models such as the ecological or systems perspective since a complex array of factors can influence behavior.

Cognitive Development

Though a great deal of important cognitive development has occurred by adolescence, the teen years are a time when cognitive skills become more complex and sophisticated. To examine the cognitive milestones achieved during adolescence, we can revisit Piaget's theory. Recall that Piaget posited that adolescents enter the formal operations stage with regard to cognitive development. This means that teens are able to think more abstractly than younger children. Adolescents move away from concrete thinking to think hypothetically about situations. They use reason and logic and take the perspective of others when considering situations.

With formal operations also comes the ability for **meta-thought**, or the ability to think about thinking. This also means that adolescents are able to think about abstract ideas such as ideals, qualities, and characteristics that describe people and their personalities as well as concepts related to right and wrong (Piaget, 1972; Piaget & Inhelder, 1969). Because of these increased reasoning abilities, adolescents become capable of grappling with complex issues such as morality and spirituality. Achieving higher stages of moral thinking, as posited by theories of moral development (discussed in the next section), requires the capability to think abstractly and logically.

Although Piaget's theory of cognitive development offers helpful ideas about cognitive development and abilities in adolescence, keep in mind that this theory has limitations. For example, there tends to be great variability in the achievement of complex cognitive skills; that is, not all people achieve certain skills at the same time. Moreover, some adults never exhibit the cognitive skills described in the formal operations stage. This is particularly true of individuals in non-Western cultures. Skills pertaining to logic and abstract thinking may not be deemed valuable by people in different cultures, so they are not encouraged or labeled as higher-order skills.

Personality and emotional development continue into adolescence, and identity reaches a more adultlike state by this point. Although identity development is really a lifetime process, by adolescence many of the physical, cognitive, and emotional changes that occur in childhood have stabilized to a point where adolescents can begin to think of themselves in mature terms. Many adolescents have established identities that will endure into adulthood, although these identities likely will be modified somewhat throughout adulthood and into old age. Adolescence is a time when many decisions must be made, such as whom to date, whether to experiment with drugs and alcohol, and whether to have intercourse. Adolescents also begin to

PHYSICAL	COGNITIVE	PERSONALITY AND EMOTION	TABLE 9.1
• Onset of puberty and the hormonal changes associated with it. • Development of primary and secondary sex characteristics.	• Cognitive skills become more complex and sophisticated. • Thinking becomes more abstract, and teens can think hypothetically about situations. • Teens can use reason and logic and take the perspective of others when considering situations.	• Identity development continues with the integration of physical, cognitive, and emotional components to form a more mature identity. • Movement toward autonomy.	*Developmental Milestones in Adolescence*

think about their values and beliefs in many areas (politically, religiously, and socially) and how to live their lives based on these values and beliefs. All of these questions and considerations help adolescents to firmly establish their identities, which is the foundation for their adult experiences (Habermas & Bluck, 2000). Table 9.1 summarizes the developmental milestones in adolescence.

How might this knowledge help you as the social worker in the scenario with Alicia? When considering her development, you would most likely view it from the medical model. The medical model does provide valuable information regarding "normal" physical development, hormonal changes, and issues associated with these changes. For instance, you may want to assess whether Alicia is developing at a rate that is similar to her same-age peers. The fact that Alicia's development seems "slow" may be of some concern, particularly because she has been vomiting and losing weight. These problems, though they may not be caused by physical factors, may exacerbate problems with her physical growth in the long run. For example, she may not get the adequate nutrition she needs to continue to grow.

In looking at physical aspects of growth, it may be more useful to assess Alicia's situation from a biopsychosocial perspective, bringing in aspects of other theories such as ecological theory and Piaget's theory of cognitive development. These theories will help you assess many other areas in Alicia's life beyond the physical that may impact her physical development. For instance, you may want to examine how family and peer dynamics are affecting Alicia's eating patterns, and you may want to ascertain how Alicia's environment at home or school impacts her eating patterns. Specifically, does Alicia's mother have enough money to afford nutritious foods? Has her family established nutritious eating patterns? Does Alicia have access to low-cost lunch programs at school if cost is an issue? Because Alicia spends a great deal of time in the "street," where is she getting her meals?

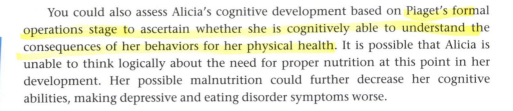

You could also assess Alicia's cognitive development based on Piaget's formal operations stage to ascertain whether she is cognitively able to understand the consequences of her behaviors for her physical health. It is possible that Alicia is unable to think logically about the need for proper nutrition at this point in her development. Her possible malnutrition could further decrease her cognitive abilities, making depressive and eating disorder symptoms worse.

Theories of Moral Development

Another way to conceptualize developmental and other issues that might be relevant in adolescence is through theories of moral development. You can use these theories to conceptualize moral development at other stages in the life span as well. The theories focus on how people come to espouse certain values and beliefs about what is right, wrong, good, and bad.

Kohlberg's Theory of Moral Development   One of the best-known theorists on moral development is Lawrence Kohlberg, who developed his ideas through studying children. His theory defines moral development as a process that occurs in six stages categorized in three levels, and progresses from simple rewards and punishment to behavior based on moral principles concerned with the common good (Kohlberg, 1976). Box 9.1 describes these levels and stages.

According to Kohlberg's theory, people develop their moral thinking at different rates. Ideally, this development takes place during childhood; however, not everyone will develop to the third, or final, level. Rather, people may remain in different stages depending on their experiences and cognitive development.

This last idea is also a point of criticism. Some critics argue that Kohlberg's theory places too much emphasis on cognition. That is, the theory describes what people *think* is right, but that does not necessarily translate into what people actually *do*. Moreover, we can understand what people are thinking only if they can verbalize their reasoning. Unfortunately, not everyone can do this in the same way. Consequently, some people might seem as though they are not as morally "advanced" as others because they cannot verbalize their thinking. A final criticism is that Kohlberg's theory is biased in that it may not apply to women or people of other cultures. Specifically, Kohlberg's theory is based in individualistic thinking, which may not apply to people who are more concerned with the perspectives of others and who take those perspectives into consideration when making decisions (Kohlberg, 1978). However, this theory does offer social workers a broad way to think about the moral development of their clients and how this development might affect clients' behaviors and responses to problems.

Gilligan's Theory of Moral Development   In response to some of the criticisms of Kohlberg's theory, particularly its focus on men's development, Carol Gilligan devised her own theory of moral development. Gilligan's theory emphasizes the

BOX 9.1

*Kohlberg's
Theory of
Moral
Development*

LEVEL 1: PRECONVENTIONAL REASONING (CONVENTIONAL ROLE CONFORMITY)

At this level, people have not internalized moral values. Rather, moral thinking is ruled by rewards and punishments.

Stage 1: Punishment and obedience orientation. People make decisions about what is good and bad to avoid punishment.

Stage 2: Naïve instrumental hedonism. People obey rules to get rewarded.

LEVEL 2: CONVENTIONAL REASONING (ROLE CONFORMITY)

At this level, people value the opinions of others. Behavior is guided by external social expectations.

Stage 3: Good boy/girl mentality. People behave in ways that please others.

Stage 4: Authority-maintaining morality. People strongly believe in law and order. Social order is paramount and people will defer to higher authority to guide behavior.

LEVEL 3: POSTCONVENTIONAL REASONING (SELF-ACCEPTED MORAL PRINCIPLES)

At this level, people have internalized moral values. Morality extends beyond laws and self-interest.

Stage 5: Morality of contract, of individual rights, and of democratically accepted law. People view laws and social order as necessary; however, laws need to be questioned in light of the common good.

Stage 6: Morality of individual principles and conscience. People's behavior is based on internal principles of what is right and wrong. People make decisions based on what is right for the common good, regardless of whether or not decisions go against law or higher authority.

Source: Adapted from Kohlberg, 1969, 1976, 1981.

individual's development of an ability to focus on care, inclusion, and attention to others (Gilligan, 1982; Gilligan & Attanucci, 1988). Box 9.2 displays the levels of this theory.

Gilligan's theory provides some balance to Kohlberg's by demonstrating how people may place more importance on cooperation and inclusiveness than on independence and self-interest. By addressing the ways in which women tend to be socialized, it better accounts for how women achieve the highest level of moral reasoning. From Kohlberg's perspective, women may be viewed as morally inferior to men. Although both theories have their strengths and limitations (Gilligan's theory could claim the same strengths and limitations as Kohlberg's theory), they both offer intriguing frameworks from which to conceptualize moral thinking and development.

BOX 9.2

Gilligan's Theory of Moral Development

LEVEL 1: ORIENTATION TO PERSONAL SURVIVAL

This level describes women's orientation to self-interest and survival. Consideration of others is not important.

Transition 1: Transition from personal selfishness to responsibility. Women begin to take the considerations of others into account in moral reasoning. Self is still important, but women realize that the well-being of others is also important.

LEVEL 2: GOODNESS AS SELF-SACRIFICE

Women see morality as sacrificing their own needs for the sake of others. Women become dependent on the perspectives of others, to the point that they may sacrifice their own needs and feelings.

Transition 2: From goodness to reality. Women are able to balance the needs of others with their own. They consider what is best for others as well as themselves and make decisions that will benefit both.

LEVEL 3: THE MORALITY OF NONVIOLENT RESPONSIBILITY

At this level, women think about the consequences of their moral decisions. Opinions of others are not as important as the integrity of their decisions and the impact those decisions will have on everyone's well-being.

Source: Adapted from Gilligan, 1982.

In Alicia's case, you could identify which stage of moral development Alicia seems to have reached to better determine how she might be viewing her situation. For example, based on the information given in the scenario, Alicia might be only at level 1 in Gilligan's theory. Alicia seems to be focused on survival and her own needs. However, it could also be that this kind of focus is "normal" for an adolescent Alicia's age. Regardless, you could use this conceptualization as a base from which to proceed with an intervention for Alicia. If Alicia is primarily concerned with her own needs at this point, an intervention that uses her concern for others probably will not be effective. Further, interventions that use family members and peers as supports might not be immediately effective since Alicia will probably not be concerned with what they think; but this kind of approach could help Alicia move into transition 1 of Gilligan's theory. Specifically, through working with family and peers, Alicia may begin to understand how others feel, which may lead her to take responsibility for her actions and her situation.

As mentioned earlier, many of the physical changes that occur during adolescence as well as the behavioral and emotional changes associated with them tend to be influenced by the immediate and larger social environment. In the sections that follow, we will explore some of the issues associated with growth and development in the teen years.

THE INDIVIDUAL IN ADOLESCENCE

Though physical changes during puberty can be dramatic, many other changes and issues that teens experience during this time can wreak havoc for them. Often, it is these issues that bring adolescents and their families to seek the help of social workers. Here, we will look at some of the micro-level problems that may present themselves during this time in life.

Early and Late Maturation

The timing and progress of physical development can have far-reaching emotional and other effects on teens. Since there is so much variability in the rate of development among teens as well as in the end result of that development (for example, differing body types), many professionals are interested in how developmental processes impact the emotional well-being and long-term adjustment of teens.

Generally, research has indicated that both early and late maturation patterns can have positive and negative effects for teens. For boys, early maturation often means increased physical ability, which can bring respect and admiration from their peers. Evidence from one longitudinal study suggests that early maturing boys are better adjusted and more confident than late maturing boys. Conversely, late maturing boys may be perceived as less physically desirable due to their small size. Thus, late maturing boys may engage in more attention-seeking behaviors that are viewed by others as immature and inappropriate (M. C. Jones, 1965; Jones & Bayley, 1950). However, some evidence suggests that early maturing boys may feel more pressure than late maturing boys, since others may expect the former to behave responsibly and to act as positive role models for other boys (Papalia, Olds, & Feldman, 2001).

For girls, the effects of early versus late maturation may be less clear. In a recent longitudinal study, researchers found that for girls, those who matured early showed some problems in school, but they were more popular with boys and showed more independence than late maturing girls (Simmons & Blyth, 1987). More recent evidence suggests that early maturation among girls may place them at higher risk for anxiety, depression, substance use, early sexual exploration, dysfunctional responses to stress, and problems in school than their late maturing counterparts (Reardon, Leen-Feldner, & Hayward, 2009; Sarigiani & Petersen, 2000; Sontag, Graber, Brooks-Gunn, & Warren, 2008; Stattin & Magnusson, 1990).

Keep in mind that the research discussed here offers only a general idea of how maturation patterns can affect individuals. There is much variability among individuals, and responses to timing can also be affected by many other psychosocial factors such as peers, family, culture, personality, and cognitive and emotional development. In Alicia's case, you may choose to assess her physical development to ascertain whether she may be at risk for some of the problems associated with early development among girls. For example, Alicia's possible sexual activity may be due to early development. However, you would also want to keep in mind that many other factors are probably influencing her sexual behaviors; so any intervention that targeted sexual issues would need to incorporate a comprehensive assessment of factors contributing to her behavior.

Self-Esteem

Different aspects of physical, cognitive, emotional, and social development can have profound short- and long-term effects on how adolescents view and evaluate themselves. Similarly, their evaluation can influence how they view the world, which can affect further development and well-being. The overall evaluation of the self is what we call **self-esteem**.

As we saw in the previous section, the timing of physical development and the onset of puberty often influence self-esteem. Other factors such as peer and family relationships and social norms and expectations can also shape the ways in which adolescents view and evaluate themselves. Indeed, research has pointed to certain psychosocial aspects that can put adolescents at risk for poor self-esteem and possible related mental health issues later in life (Polce-Lynch, Myers, Kliewer, & Kilmartin, 2001).

Some research indicates that self-esteem is fairly stable, at least over short periods of time (Tesser, 2000). Other research suggests that self-esteem tends to fluctuate throughout adolescence; it is not a static characteristic that persists over time (Baldwin & Hoffmann, 2002). Perhaps one reason why it is difficult to fully understand how patterns of self-esteem unfold during adolescence is because so many variables can influence it, particularly during this time of life. Moreover, aspects such as resilience, personality, coping skills, and environmental factors can serve as protective or risk factors in the process of developing self-esteem. For instance, research indicates that self-esteem is influenced by family relationships and various life events (Baldwin & Hoffmann, 2002). Strong, positive family relationships and successful, rewarding life events help to strengthen self-esteem, while negative relationships and experiences can erode it. However, much depends on when certain life events occur and how they are perceived by those experiencing them.

Research findings tend to be mixed with regard to gender differences in levels of self-esteem throughout adolescence. Some studies have found boys to have higher self-esteem than girls, particularly in later adolescence, while others have not found this pattern (for example, Kling, Hyde, Showers, & Buswell, 1999; Polce-Lynch et al., 2001). The relationship between gender and self-esteem seems to be influenced by certain psychosocial factors such as body image, emotional expression, and media messages that dictate social norms on appearance. For example, gender differences seem to be influenced by the media, which glorify thinness and pre-adolescent-like bodies for girls. As girls grow older, their bodies deviate from this norm, which can have a negative effect on self-esteem for some girls. For boys, self-esteem seems to increase as they get older because they "fill out" and better fit the image of the "macho" male (Baldwin & Hoffmann, 2002; Polce-Lynch et al., 2001; Tiggemann, 2001). Interestingly, some research has indicated that high levels of masculinity tend to be associated with high self-esteem and few mental health problems, specifically depression, for both boys and girls (Barrett & White, 2002). It could be that masculine traits are validated by social norms; those who possess and exhibit them are validated by society, thus strengthening self-esteem.

In Alicia's situation, you would certainly benefit from assessing her self-esteem at this point. Because Alicia's problems (possible eating disorder, early maturation, and familial support issues) could be related to low self-esteem, building an intervention around her self-concept might be a useful approach. Moreover, as a girl, she could be at higher risk for low self-esteem than if she were a boy: Media messages, issues at home, and relationships with her peers could put her at risk for poor self-image and subsequent depression later on.

According to Erikson, Alicia would be in the stage of identity versus identity confusion. If you adhere to this theory, you would focus on ways in which Alicia's self-esteem are influencing her developing identity and vice versa. You might consider how cultural and social messages are affecting her sense of identity and how familial and peer relationships could be strengthened to buffer her from environmental pressures that may negatively impact her self-esteem. The interactionist perspective would also be useful in conceptualizing Alicia's situation, as her point of view and the ways she interprets the messages that surround her in her environment will significantly affect her development. A feminist model would also be useful in this scenario, since society tends to set norms that are different for boys and girls. Socialization can affect self-esteem and mental health, but positive interactions with family, peers, and social institutions may help to mediate these affects (for example, education in all-girl schools has been shown to promote positive self-esteem) (Polce-Lynch et al., 2001).

Eating Disorders

In the United States and other Western countries, eating disorders have become a major problem among teens and young adults. Though obesity, binge eating, and other issues surrounding eating patterns fall under the rubric of eating disorders, this section will focus on anorexia and bulimia nervosa, since these tend to be primary concerns for many clients who seek the help of social workers. We will examine the factors that contribute to these disorders and consider how these disorders can affect social work.

Anorexia Nervosa   A disorder characterized by behaviors that lead to extreme thinness, **anorexia nervosa** tends to develop in the early and middle teen years. Though boys also develop the disorder, it is much more common among girls, who are about 10 times more likely to suffer from the disorder (Fairburn & Harrison, 2003; Garner & Desai, 2001). The disorder generally affects white, middle- and upper-class girls who come from highly educated and achieving families (Striegel-Moore, Silberstein, & Rodin, 1993). Although anorexia is clearly associated with environmental pressures, some studies indicate a genetic link to the disorder as well. The prevalence of anorexia among teens in the United States is approximately 0.7 percent (Fairburn & Harrison, 2003), and its incidence appears to have increased since the 1970s, particularly among girls between ages 15 and 24 (Hoek, 2006).

Typically, anorexia begins after dieting and experiencing some kind of stressor. Dieting turns into a severe restriction of food intake, excessive exercise, and sometimes vomiting or intake of laxatives. Often, individuals demonstrate symptoms of anxiety, depression, flat affect, and obsessive-compulsive behaviors. Anorexia contributes to many physical problems, including dry skin, stunted growth, reduced bone density, loss of menstruation, fine downy hair on the body and face, heightened sensitivity to cold, cardiac problems, and ultimately, death. People with anorexia are generally unable to see the destructive nature of their behaviors and are reinforced by weight loss and by comments made by others about their appearance. If properly treated, many of these problems are reversible. The most effective treatment methods appear to be antidepressant medications and family-based and psychodynamic therapies (Fairburn & Harrison, 2003).

Bulimia Nervosa   Although similar in some ways to anorexia, **bulimia nervosa** is characterized by a consistent eating binge and purge pattern, which occurs through exercise, vomiting, or laxative use. Bulimia usually develops in late adolescence or early adulthood and can persist through later adulthood. Bulimia often begins in similar ways as anorexia, but it is more prevalent—it afflicts approximately 1 percent to 2 percent of teens in the United States—and is found across social classes (Fairburn & Harrison, 2003).

Like people with anorexia, people with bulimia are obsessed with thinness and suffer from a distorted body image. However, unlike people with anorexia, those with bulimia generally are of average weight, are ashamed of their behaviors, and have some insight into the disordered nature of their habits (Fairburn & Harrison, 2003).

Because many people with bulimia go to great lengths to hide their behaviors and tend to maintain average or above-average weight, bulimia can be more difficult to detect than anorexia. People suffering from bulimia exhibit similar psychological problems as those with anorexia, such as depression and obsessive-compulsive behaviors as well as substance abuse (Zaider, Johnson, & Cockell, 2002). Physically, bulimia can cause dehydration, dizziness, cardiac problems, electrolyte imbalances, and erosion of tooth enamel, among other problems. As with anorexia, the most effective treatments for bulimia appear to be antidepressant, cognitive-behavioral, and family-based therapies (Fairburn & Harrison, 2003).

EXHIBIT 9.1

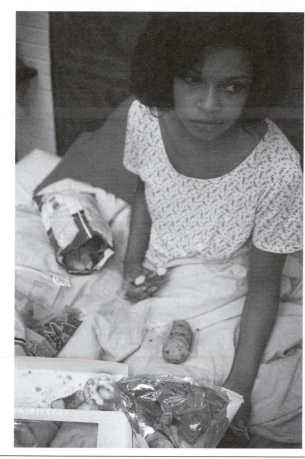

EXHIBIT 9.1

Bulimia is a serious eating disorder that can cause many physical and other problems for people who suffer from it

Source: Jack Star/PhotoLink/Getty Images

As mentioned previously, the media have been shown to be a powerful influence on body image, and body image tends to impact self-esteem, particularly for young women. A body of research indicates that women tend to evaluate their bodies negatively more often and place more emphasis on their looks than do men (Muth & Cash, 1997; Tiggemann, 2001). However, other studies have found that men attend to their bodies as much as women, which may account for the increasing numbers of men suffering from eating disorders (Striegel et al., 2009; Wilcox, 1997). Media images that promote thin bodies have been found to be important predictors for a person's drive toward thinness, distorted body image, and eating problems (Vartanian, Giant, & Passino, 2001). All of these factors as well as others such as stress, genetics, and family and peer dynamics seem to contribute

TABLE 9.2	DISORDER	DESCRIPTION
Diagnostic Criteria for Anorexia and Bulimia Nervosa	Anorexia nervosa	Refusal to maintain body weight that is appropriate for age and height. Intense fear of gaining weight. Disturbance in perceived body image. Loss of menstruation for at least three consecutive months.
	Bulimia nervosa	Recurrent binge-eating episodes (must occur in discrete time periods and person must feel loss of control over eating). Behaviors to avoid weight gain such as use of laxatives, excessive exercise, or vomiting. Behaviors must occur at least twice a week for at least three months. Disturbance in perceived body image. Disturbance does not occur with an episode of anorexia.

Source: Adapted from American Psychiatric Association, 2000.

to the development of eating disorders (Pauls & Daniels, 2000). Table 9.2 lists the diagnostic criteria for anorexia and bulimia nervosa.

From the information presented on Alicia, she appears to have several symptoms that are consistent with an eating disorder. Poor growth and development, depression, weight loss, family problems, and, of course, vomiting are all areas that you will want to assess. Because there are many physical and psychological problems associated with an eating disorder that could be making Alicia's current situation worse, you will want to focus on these particular issues. Though you could view the cause of her potential eating disorder from many different theories and perspectives, this is probably not as important as seeking treatments that have been shown to be effective through research. For example, rather than conceptualizing Alicia's eating problems through a biopsychosocial perspective, you might want to begin with a cognitive or behavioral intervention, since their effectiveness has been empirically supported.

Sexuality and Sexual Identity Development

During puberty, many physical changes take place that cause teens to think about and struggle with the person they are becoming. This can be a particularly tumultuous time for teens who are questioning their sexuality or who identify with being homosexual. Sexual identity, in general, refers to a person's sexual orientation as well as an array of beliefs, attitudes, and behaviors related to sexuality (Buzwell & Rosenthal, 1996). Sexual orientation refers to the gender with which a person prefers to have sex (men, women, or both) (Westheimer & Lopater, 2004). Forming a sexual identity also includes experiencing and managing sexual feelings and incorporating this identity into an overarching self-concept as a member of a larger societal context.

The development of a sexual identity is a complex process that is affected by many biopsychosocial factors. Because of the great diversity of individual experience, researchers find it difficult not only to articulate precisely what sexual identity is but also to study how identity develops in ways that are "normal" and that apply to the experiences of most people.

For many people, the first sexual intercourse experience is associated with sexual maturity. They often see this as a "coming of age" event. Many adolescents decide to have sex because they feel they are in love, they want to be loved, they want to feel attractive, or they want to please their partners. Others do it to rebel against authority or because they are giving in to peer pressure (Westheimer & Lopater, 2004). Regardless of the reasons, one of the issues surrounding sexual intercourse among teens is the age and circumstance under which they have sex. As we will see later in this chapter, teen pregnancy and sexually transmitted infections (STIs) are serious issues that must be considered when working with sexually active teens. In addition, teens who are having sex at very young ages are at risk for other biopsychosocial problems such as low academic achievement and familial conflict.

In 2000, the Centers for Disease Control and Prevention found that approximately half of all adolescents between the ages of 14 and 18 have had sexual intercourse. This average tended to vary by ethnic group: Slightly less than half of Caucasian (46 percent) and Hispanic (47 percent) teens reported having had intercourse during this time frame and slightly more than half (67 percent) of African American teens reported having had intercourse (Centers for Disease Control and Prevention, 2000a). Data analysis from the Youth Risk Behavior Survey (1991–1997) and other studies conducted in the 1990s indicate that the percentage of high school students who have ever had sex decreased, while condom use increased (Centers for Disease Control and Prevention, 1998; Lindberg, Boggs, Porter, & Williams, 2000). Although research cannot provide precise information about the sexual behaviors of teens, it is useful in understanding patterns of behaviors that can have lasting and profound effects on the health and well-being of teens.

Sexual Development in Heterosexual Teens   For teens who identify as heterosexual, dealing with the tasks of sexual development can be challenging. Because of the complex nature of this process, the biopsychosocial lens helps to conceptualize sexual development within teens' environment. Various theories can be used to describe "normal" sexual development, all of which have something to offer in terms of the ways in which teens go through sexual developmental milestones and the many cognitive, emotional, and social factors that influence development. For example, the medical model offers a great deal of information about how hormones influence physical development and sexual preferences. Research is uncovering biological bases to hetero- and homosexuality through studies that involve genetics, hormones, and the brain (for example, studies on siblings, birth order, fingerprints, handedness). (See Westheimer & Lopater, 2004, for a comprehensive discussion.)

On a more cognitive level, you can use Erikson's stage of identity versus identity confusion to conceptualize how teens go through developing and articulating their sexual orientation. Similarly, Freud's theory can explain how teens may have become fixated in previous stages, which may influence their sexuality as they age. Feminist theory can help you to better understand how sex and gender roles, and even the idea of heterosexuality, are socially constructed and how these concepts might influence sexual identity. However, though these theories can contribute to understanding sexuality and identity development, they are also limited with regard to explaining all aspects of sexuality and the complexities involved in its development.

Sexual Development in Gay, Lesbian, and Bisexual Teens   Many theories on which social workers rely do not address the variations that can occur in sexual development. Many theories and perspectives view variations as abnormal or as deviations from "normal" behavior ("normal" usually being defined from the Western cultural perspective). Negative connotations are generally attached to sexual deviations, which are viewed as problems that need intervention. Only recently have so-called deviations from sexual development norms, such as homosexuality, transgenderism, masturbation, and certain sexual fantasies and sex play, been viewed as issues and behaviors that are not necessarily problematic. For example, it was in the 1970s that the American Psychiatric Association and the American Psychological Association took the stance that homosexuality was not a disorder (O'Donohue & Caselles, 1993).

In response to limitations to existing theoretical explanations of normal sexual development and behavior, various models of sexual development for gay, lesbian, and bisexual teens have been presented (Appleby & Anastas, 1998; Johnson & Johnson, 2000). One of these models identifies adaptive tasks (from the perspective of Western cultures) that are required of homosexual teens. These tasks, described in Box 9.3, may include some of those experienced by heterosexual teens, but many are in addition to the expected tasks associated with development.

Models such as these help to guide social workers in their work with gay, lesbian, bisexual, transgendered, and questioning teens as they grapple with their sexuality and other psychosocial issues associated with it. Social workers can provide a great deal of information and support to teens on all levels, including exploring teens' personal feelings and beliefs, helping teens explore how to involve family and friends in their work, and how to negotiate larger social issues such as heterosexism and negative attitudes toward homosexuality.

With regard to homosexuality, there are several ethical issues that may arise for social workers and their clients. Although in general, helping professionals do not view homosexuality as a disorder, many problems associated with it (such as

BOX 9.3

Adaptive Tasks for Homosexual Adolescents

Sexual development for homosexual teens requires some of the tasks experienced by heterosexual teens, but many are in addition to the expected tasks associated with development.

Expanding one's self-concept within the context of gender, family, and cultural group: Many homosexual teens must come to terms with the discrepancies between how they think, feel, and behave and a world that assumes people are heterosexual. Teens must learn to develop positive feelings about themselves in an environment that rewards heterosexuality.

Changing one's relationships and establishing independence: Adolescence is normally a time when people begin to question the values and beliefs of their parents. Many families hold heterosexist beliefs and may even openly condemn homosexuality as immoral. Homosexual teens must confront these beliefs and attempt to define themselves within the context of their relationships and social environment.

Building social supports: Though peer groups can be helpful to teens in exploring identity, many homosexual teens may have trouble finding appropriate social supports in which to do this. Heterosexual peers may not be accepting of homosexuality and may aggravate homosexual teens' attempts to establish an identity and place within a social structure.

Exploring career, vocational, and educational goals: Adolescence is a time to work on self-efficacy through achievement and success in academics, setting the stage for pursuing higher education and career-related goals. Homosexual teens must confront institutional discrimination and find ways to move toward their goals while fighting social barriers that may impede their success.

Establishing intimate relationships: Dating, flirting, holding hands, falling in love, and other activities that occur during adolescence that help teens prepare for adult relationships are difficult for homosexual teens to do, at least in public. Homosexual teens must find other ways to "practice" relationship skills; often this is done through passing as heterosexual or lying about one's identity, which hinders the development of honest, trusting intimate relationships.

Source: Adapted from Appleby & Anastas, 1998.

depression, isolation, violence, discrimination, relationship problems) are seen as problematic. These problems, among others, have prompted actions such as opening separate high schools for gay, lesbian, and bisexual teens in some communities. Although many teens enjoy the separation—they argue that in a separate facility they are free to learn rather than spending energy on fighting harassment—critics contend that this policy only perpetuates discrimination, since one way to combat fear of homosexuality is through exposure to gay, lesbian, bisexual, and transgendered individuals. Social workers must play a central role in thinking through these issues, educating those making such decisions about ethical and social considerations involved in their actions, and devising ways to eradicate the discrimination that propels people to take such actions in the first place.

Another issue that raises ethical questions for social workers has to do with views on homosexuality. Even within the helping professions, some practitioners believe that homosexuality is immoral. Ethically, practitioners have a responsibility to explore their own beliefs on the issue to better understand how these might interfere with their work with clients. This is particularly important since social workers are expected to support client self-determination (NASW, approved 1996, revised 2008). Social workers especially need to be cognizant of how their own prejudiced beliefs about sexuality might harm gay, lesbian, and bisexual clients.

Practitioners also need to be aware of questionable interventions that are offered to "change" client's orientation (often known as *conversion therapy*) from homosexual to heterosexual. Even if practitioners do not agree with a client's sexual orientation, suggesting interventions that are not empirically supported or that could be harmful to clients is unethical. For example, there is no research that supports the effectiveness of conversion therapy; indeed, most professionals agree that this type of intervention only perpetuates prejudice and ignorance about homosexuality (Behavioral Health Treatment, 1997; Cianciotto & Cahill, 2006; Shidlo & Schroeder, 2002). Given the amount of research that supports the bio-logical and other underpinnings of homosexuality, simply changing an individual's orientation through therapy should be viewed with much skepticism. According to the *Code of Ethics* (NASW, approved 1996, revised 2008), practitioners have a responsibility to examine research on these and other interventions in order to make sound judgments on which seem effective and which do not before suggesting such interventions to clients.

Conversely, social workers may work with clients who, because of religious beliefs or other reasons, wish to attempt to change their orientation or at least to live as a heterosexual while acknowledging homosexual feelings. Again, social workers need to understand how their own values in this area might affect their work with clients. And, having sound, empirically based information to share with clients so that they can make educated decisions about their problems is an important step in working with clients.

Given Alicia's age and presenting problems, you may want to assess her sexual identity development. This may be helpful in better understanding how Alicia may or may not be dealing with developmental tasks and how her sexual activity may be impacting her physical, emotional, and psychological development. Peer pressure or loneliness, for example, may be driving Alicia to have sexual experiences before she is ready. These premature experiences could have further ramifications for her development as she ages. For instance, she could contract a sexually transmitted infection, as discussed in the next section.

STIs, HIV, and AIDS

Social workers need to understand sexually transmitted infections, or STIs, especially if they work with adolescents. Teens are having their first sexual experiences at young ages, and these actions will impact their health and well-being. It is usually when teens experience negative consequences of sexual behavior (for example, contracting an STI or becoming pregnant) that social workers are asked to intervene. Table 9.3 lists common STIs as well as brief descriptions and treatments for each.

If Alicia, in the case scenario, is having sexual intercourse, you need to ascertain how much she knows about STIs and the things that she can do to protect herself.

INFECTION	DESCRIPTION	TREATMENT	TABLE 9.3
Chlamydia	Caused by a bacteria. Most common STI in the United States. Often goes unrecognized and untreated in men and women. Can cause infertility in women and eye disease, prematurity, and pneumonia in infants. Can make contraction of HIV easier.	Antibiotics	*Common Sexually Transmitted Infections*
Genital herpes	Caused by a virus. One of the most common STIs in the United States. Often goes unrecognized and can be fatal to a fetus. Can make contraction of HIV easier.	No cure; outbreaks can be controlled by antiviral medication.	
Gonorrhea	Caused by a bacteria. Can cause pelvic inflammatory disease, infertility, and tubal pregnancy in women. Can make contraction of HIV easier.	Penicillin or other antibiotics.	
Hepatitis B	Caused by a virus. May go away without treatment. Can cause chronic liver disease, liver cancer, and death. Can be passed to a fetus.	Vaccination or antiviral or other medications.	
Syphilis	Caused by a bacteria. Progression takes place in stages, which if left untreated can cause cardiovascular and neurological problems and blindness. Can be transmitted to a fetus.	Penicillin	
HIV/AIDS	Caused by a virus. Destroys the body's immune system, which leads to a host of illnesses leading to death. Can be passed to a fetus.	No cure; "cocktails" consisting of various drugs can slow the progression of HIV to AIDS.	

Source: Adapted from Centers for Disease Control and Prevention, 2000b.

From a biopsychosocial standpoint, Alicia may be biologically and physically ready for sex, especially if she is an early developer, but she may not be cognitively or emotionally prepared for it and the ramifications it may bring. According to Piaget, Alicia will be in the formal operations stage in which she should be able to reason and use logic. If, for some reason, she has not moved to or mastered this stage, she may not be able to cognitively understand the possible consequences of her actions. Or, from an ecological or systems perspective, you may consider that Alicia is experiencing a great deal of peer pressure, lack of familial support, and lack of educational and other services to help her learn about STIs and ways to protect herself if she is sexually active. All of these models, as well as many others, can provide useful ways in which to think about, assess, and work with Alicia's situation.

BOX 9.4

STIs: Occurrence and Costs

Every year, approximately three million cases of STIs among teens are reported (Institute of Medicine, 1997). Because teens are more likely than people in other age groups to have multiple sex partners and engage in unprotected sex, they are more likely to contract an STI (Centers for Disease Control and Prevention, 2000b). Further, psychosocial factors such as developmental (for example, emotional, cognitive) immaturity, peer pressure, perceived invulnerability, and other issues may make some teens more likely to engage in risky behaviors leading to the contraction of STIs.

Among teens, gonorrhea and chlamydia are the most commonly occurring STIs. Though these STIs are curable, many teens who have contracted them do not seek treatment because they are not aware that they have a disease. This failure to seek treatment can lead to severe and irreversible problems later in life such as pelvic inflammatory disease (PID) (Centers for Disease Control and Prevention, 2007a, 2007b). Herpes, an incurable STI, has been estimated to infect at least 45 million people ages 12+ (Centers for Disease Control and Prevention, 2007c).

The Centers for Disease Control and Prevention (2007a, 2007d, 2007e) estimate that rates of chlamydia and syphilis are rising, and after declines in rates of gonorrhea, they also are now on the rise. Although rates of herpes increased in the early 1990s, the percentage of Americans with herpes is declining as are rates for hepatitis B (Centers for Disease Control and Prevention, 2007c, 2007d). In the United States since the beginning of the epidemic, over 40,000 young people (aged 13 to 24) have been diagnosed with HIV/AIDS, indicating that many of these people were likely infected in their teen or earlier years. African Americans represent 55 percent of all HIV infections in this age group (Centers for Disease Control and Prevention, 2008b). Currently, approximately half of all new cases of HIV infection occur in people 25 years of age and younger (Morris, Ulmer, & Chimnani, 2003). In various countries outside of the United States, HIV/AIDS is a much more serious problem. In Africa, for example, AIDS has reached epidemic proportions, particularly among young people (World Health Organization, 2000). Indeed, in the next 25 years, AIDS is projected to be one of the top three causes of death worldwide (Mathers & Loncar, 2006).

Estimates on the financial burden caused by STIs among young people in the year 2000 suggest that STIs cost the United States more than $6.5 billion in direct costs that year alone (Chesson, Blandford, Gift, Tao, & Irwin, 2004). Since teens are at high risk for contracting STIs and are the group most likely to have their STIs go untreated, many will undoubtedly have costly complications throughout their lives. Thus, in focusing on this issue when working with teens, social workers will not only be cost effective but also save teens a great deal of physical and emotional grief over the course of their lifetimes.

BOX 9.4

continued

Substance Abuse

Unfortunately, the United States is the leader in adolescent drug use compared to other industrialized nations, with alcohol being the most commonly used substance (Johnston, O'Malley, & Bachman, 2001). The popularity of alcohol and other drugs tends to ebb and flow over time depending on factors such as the economy and availability of various drugs; so social workers who may be concerned with such issues need to keep up to date on drug use trends in their local communities.

Teen drug use, including the use of nicotine, declined during the 1980s but increased during the 1990s. This trend hit its peak in the mid-1990s, after which the rates declined slightly until 2001 and have remained steady ever since. Some of the common drugs used by teens in the 1990s included LSD and other hallucinogenics, inhalants, marijuana, and amphetamines. With the more recent dance parties and raves that many teens frequent, there has been an increase in the use of club drugs such as ecstasy, a methamphetamine, and Rohypnol, the so-called date rape drug. The latter drug is so named because it causes amnesia in users (Johnston, O'Malley, & Bachman, 2001; Moolchan & Mermelstein, 2002).

Alcohol and other substance use and abuse can cause myriad short- and long-term problems for adolescents and their families. For example, teens who abuse drugs exhibit higher rates of violence, accidents, early sexual intercourse, unintended pregnancies, and STIs than teens who do not have substance abuse problems (Bryan & Stallings, 2002). They are also at risk for disrupted development and low academic achievement, which can impact their long-term health and chances for financial and other success in adulthood (McCluskey, Krohn, Lizotte, & Rodriguez, 2002).

Factors Associated with Substance Abuse   Extensive research has been conducted on the factors associated with substance abuse among teens. Results of this research indicate that aspects such as stressful life events (such as illness and divorce) and conflicted relationships with peers and parents tend to be consistent predictors for substance abuse among teens. Specifically, poor social supports from peers and parents, lack of quality relationships, and frequent conflict and arguments in relationships tend to place teens at risk for substance abuse. Conversely, close, supportive relationships with parents tend to buffer teens from substance abuse. This may be why alcohol use among teens tends to increase during high school years; this is a time, developmentally, when teens are attempting to assert their independence, which may cause conflict with their parents. When teens enter their 20s, these conflicts tend to decrease, as does alcohol use (Aseltine & Gore, 2000). So, while the cause-and-effect relationship between substance use and relationships may not be clear-cut, the two do seem to be associated.

Of course, many other mediating factors impact the association between relationships and substance use; so social workers need to explore other situational and personality factors that might influence substance abuse among their teen clients. For example, exposure to familial alcohol abuse in childhood also tends to be significantly associated with teenage substance abuse, particularly among males. Thus, there may be a genetic or behavioral component to later substance abuse (Ritter, Stewart, Bernet, Coe, & Brown, 2002). That is, a tendency to abuse or become dependent on alcohol may be inherited, or teens may model their using behaviors after watching these behaviors carried out by their parents or caregivers.

Smoking and nicotine addiction are another significant issue for teens. Many of the addictions that adults have are established in the teen years. Moreover, the health problems that result from these addictions do not manifest themselves until much later in life. Social workers often see clients who present with significant health and addiction problems as adults. Thus, social workers who work with teens can play a significant role in preventing these addictions from developing in the first place.

Research with Teens: An Ethical Dilemma   According to the *Code of Ethics* (NASW, approved 1996, revised 2008), social workers have an ethical responsibility to conduct research that will advance knowledge in the field and promote effective practice. Having current and accurate information on issues such as teen substance use as well as other issues such as sexuality, teen pregnancy, and sex education is crucial if social workers are to develop appropriate and effective interventions.

However, social workers and other professionals are often faced with dilemmas when conducting research that uses children or teens as participants. Although many sources of research grants such as the National Institutes of Health (NIH) now require that children and teens be included in research, there are many barriers that must be overcome in doing so. For example, parents or legal guardians are required to give consent for minors to participate in research projects. Researching touchy subjects such as drug use or sexual behaviors (some of which include illegal behaviors) may lead to inaccurate or biased results because of this consent issue. That is, participants who need consent from guardians to participate may not truthfully disclose the nature of their behaviors because they are afraid that their parents might have access to this information. Participants may also fear that they will be turned over to authorities if they disclose that they are participating in any illegal activity.

Some parents may also volunteer their children for participation in a study even though, because of developmental limitations, their children may not fully understand the nature of the study or be able to weigh its risks and benefits (Moolchan & Mermelstein, 2002). So, some researchers question if this situation can lead to true informed consent. Even though social workers need to conduct research on these issues to gain knowledge, they run into problems of whether or not they are producing valid and reliable knowledge and whether or not they are protecting the dignity and worth of the participants of this research. More than ever, it is crucial that social workers take an active role in dealing with and providing solutions for these dilemmas.

As the social worker in this chapter's opening scenario, you may be concerned about Alicia's possible substance use or abuse. The fact that she is having relationship problems—particularly with her mother—problems coping, and other acting out behaviors such as vomiting after meals, running away, and possible sexual involvement, means she is at risk for abusing drugs or alcohol. You may choose to conduct an in-depth assessment to determine which factors are present that increase her risk for substance abuse and develop an intervention that will target these areas. Since substance abuse could lead to many other serious and long-term problems for Alicia, this may be an area worth pursuing if you work with Alicia.

Suicide

Suicide among adolescents has been an increasing problem over the past several decades. Suicide is the third leading cause of death for young people aged 10 to 24, with approximately 4,500 deaths in this age range each year. Boys are more likely to die from suicide than girls, with 83 percent of deaths being boys. Further, Native American and Hispanic youth are more likely to die from suicide than young people from other ethnic groups (Centers for Disease Control and Prevention, 2008c). Because of the complex relationship of biopsychosocial factors that contribute to suicidal thoughts and attempts, understanding which factors, by themselves or in combination, contribute to the problem is difficult. However, research on adolescent suicide has pointed to some consistent factors that seem to play a part in suicide.

To begin with, many studies have found that stressful life events such as academic problems, unintended pregnancy, and strained relationships with peers, friends, parents, boyfriends, and girlfriends contribute to a high risk for suicide (National Center for Health Statistics, 2000). Substance abuse also tends to be strongly associated with suicide attempts among adolescents (Bolognini et al., 2002).

A study by Perkins and Hartless (2002) used this ecological model to conceptualize and examine variables that may put teens at risk for suicide. Analyzing responses from almost 15,000 adolescents, these researchers identified several factors associated with suicide risk for teens, including feelings of hopelessness, alcohol and drug use, physical and sexual abuse, lack of family supports, and previous suicidal thoughts and attempts. Results indicated that female teens had significantly more suicidal thoughts and attempts than males. Also, white male and female adolescents had more suicidal thoughts than African American male and female adolescents.

Suicide is a particularly important issue among homosexual youths. Gay, lesbian, bisexual, and transgendered adolescents are at even higher risk for suicide than heterosexual youths. Moreover, many teens may be questioning their sexuality or be victims of discrimination, violence, or family rejection because of their sexuality, which may leave them vulnerable to additional stressors that increase their risk for suicide (Almeida, Johnson, Corliss, Molnar, & Azrael, 2009; Plöderl & Fartacek, 2009; Ryan, Huebner, Diaz, & Sanchez, 2009). One study found that a higher percentage of gay (28 percent) and lesbian (21 percent) students reported suicide attempts than heterosexual male (4 percent) and female (15 percent) students (Remafedi, French, Story, Resnick, & Blum, 1998). Other research found that approximately 15 percent of gay and lesbian teens said they had attempted suicide compared to only 7 percent of heterosexual teens (Russell & Joyner, 2001). Another study examining suicide patterns among almost 3,000 young gay men suggested that a significant percentage (21 percent) had made a suicide plan. Further, younger gay men were found to be at higher risk for planning and attempting suicide than older gay men, particularly those exposed to a hostile environment, defined as antigay harassment, parental abuse, and similar behaviors (Paul et al., 2002).

In an earlier section, we looked at sexual identity development as it relates to gay, lesbian, and bisexual adolescents. Many of the adaptive tasks discussed there (see Box 9.3) can lead to problems such as depression, substance abuse, and feelings of isolation (Sullivan & Wodarski, 2002). These are factors that contribute to a higher suicide rate for sexual minority youth. Social workers need to be aware of these pressures so they can provide the added support that these young people often require.

Many of the behaviors that Alicia is exhibiting, particularly weight loss, depressed mood, low self-esteem, and problems with her mother, could indicate that she is at risk for suicide. You would need to do a more thorough assessment to determine whether or not this may be a problem that needs intervention. A useful tool for assessing the possibility of suicide is the SAD PERSONS scale (Patterson, Dohn, Bird, & Patterson, 1983). The acronym makes it easy to remember, and the components to be assessed are empirically based predictors for suicide, as shown in Box 9.5. The social worker gives one point to each component that is present for a client; the higher the score, the higher the risk for suicide for that particular client (Patterson et al., 1983). For example, for a male client, the social worker would add one point. If the client is 20 years old, the social worker would add another point. In Alicia's case, you would need to gain some additional information to use this assessment, but it would give you a fairly quick idea of whether or not suicide might be an issue for her.

BOX 9.5

SAD PERSONS: Suicide Assessment

*S*ex (Males are more likely to complete suicide.)
*A*ge (Younger than 25 and older than 45 are more likely to complete suicide.)
*D*epression

*P*revious attempt
*E*thanol abuse
*R*ational thinking loss
*S*ocial support loss
*O*rganized plan
*N*o spouse
*S*ickness

Source: Adapted from Patterson, Dohn, Bird, & Patterson, 1983.

THE FAMILY AND IMMEDIATE ENVIRONMENT IN ADOLESCENCE

Many of the issues discussed so far can have a profound impact on the adolescent's immediate environment. Families, peers, and other close social systems are areas that social workers must consider when they are working with adolescents. Because teens, developmentally, tend to be working toward independence but are still somewhat dependent on their families for emotional, financial, and other support, this is a time when paying attention to the connections between the individual and the environmental realms is especially relevant for social workers.

Peer Groups in Adolescence

Just as in middle childhood, peer groups play a major role in the lives of adolescents. Most parents, professionals, and theorists (for example, Freud, Erikson, Bandura, interactionists) recognize this reality. In fact, peer pressure is one of the main concerns for parents of teenagers. Peers can exert a great deal of influence over an adolescent's behaviors, both in positive and negative ways. Thus, social workers need to understand the dynamics of peer relationships during adolescence and ways in which they can help their adolescent clients avoid and deal with negative consequences of these relationships.

The extent to which one teen influences the behavior of another teen can depend on many factors such as personality, coping skills, and other support systems. For example, a teenager may not be easily pressured into trying drugs if she has close, positive, and supportive relationships with her parents. Conversely, a teen who lacks positive parental relationships may benefit from modeling positive behaviors of close friends. An important consideration for social workers, then, is that peer pressure and peer relationships are not necessarily straightforward, making a thorough assessment of the situation necessary.

One helpful way to conceptualize peer relationships is through attachment theory. Some research suggests that the quality of attachments with parents influences attachments with peers during adolescence and later in life. For instance, secure and supportive attachments with parents help to model secure attachments with peers. This may also make teens more resilient to negative peer pressure.

Conversely, teens who have insecure attachments with their parents may be more vulnerable to negative peer pressure because they place more importance on peer relationships, feeling more pressure to conform to group norms and to please friends. For example, one recent study found that adolescents who lacked parental support but who had close relationships with peers showed higher levels of emotional problems (Helsen, Vollebergh, & Meeus, 2000). This may be because in addition to negative relationships with their parents, these teens had not learned from their parents the basics of stable, positive relationships. Thus, relationships with friends took on great importance, and when these relationships ran into problems, the teens had no skills to mend them or other support systems to help them. Thus, they may have been more likely to engage in negative behaviors just to please their friends rather than risk losing those relationships.

From an attachment point of view, Alicia may be vulnerable to negative peer pressure because of her strained relationship with her mother. In fact, her "street friends" might be her only source of support. You may want to assess Alicia's support systems to understand the extent to which she is or may be influenced by her peers.

Teen Pregnancy

You can view teen pregnancy as an individual issue, but we discuss it in this section because of its far-reaching effects on families and other social systems. Although the outcome of every teen pregnancy is not unfavorable, it frequently leads to a variety of individual, familial, and social problems in which social workers intervene.

Among industrialized nations, the United States has one of the highest teen pregnancy rates (Centers for Disease Control and Prevention, 2001). Though rates of teen pregnancy had been declining from 1991 to 2005 among teens between the ages of 15 and 19, rates have increased significantly since (Centers for Disease Control and Prevention, 2009). One study found that teen pregnancy rates (as well as abortion and STI rates) in the U.S. were higher (22 percent) than in Great Britain (15 percent), Canada (11 percent), France (6 percent), and Sweden (4 percent) (Darroch, Singh, & Frost, 2001); the United States still remains the leader in teen pregnancy, abortion, and STI rates (Centers for Disease Control and Prevention, 2009). Rates for Latinas in the United States continue to be high and of some concern (Centers for Disease Control and Prevention, 2001, 2009; Child Trends, 2001; Maynard, 1996).

As discussed in Chapter 6, many health problems are associated with teen pregnancy, particularly for the baby. However, many other problems can arise with teen pregnancy. For instance, girls who become pregnant in their teen years are more likely to come from impoverished environments, drop out of high school, and spend much of their lifetime as single parents dependent on public assistance than teens who delay childbirth until adulthood. Moreover, children born to teens are more likely than children born to older parents to be incarcerated, to drop out of school or have low academic achievement, and to become teen parents themselves. Preventing teen pregnancy and childbearing in the United States could save around $9 billion per year (Centers for Disease Control and Prevention, 2009). Others estimate the total costs of teen pregnancy to be between $35 billion and $50 billion per year (Women's International Network News, 1997). Moreover, this total does not account for the psychological, social, and other costs of teen pregnancy that cannot be quantified.

Many of the theories and perspectives discussed in this book can help explain why teens become pregnant, but a combination of theories aids in understanding this issue more effectively. For example, Piaget's theory may posit that teens do not have the cognitive capacity to understand the consequences of unprotected sex or the reality of parenting a child. However, some research suggests that this is not exactly true. One study suggests that rather than viewing themselves as "invincible," which is a popular social conception of teens, many adolescents display "unrealistic optimism." This means that many teens view themselves to be at low risk for certain problems such as STIs or teen pregnancy, so they are unlikely to take extra precautions to prevent them (Whaley, 2000).

This line of thinking has been supported by other studies indicating that some teens seem overly optimistic about their financial situation, level of support from partners, and ability to continue with higher education; so they choose to become pregnant at an early age, often overestimating their capabilities to parent and underestimating their level of support to pursue their goals. Some teens may also have a strong need for stability and control and may view becoming pregnant as the only way to accomplish this (Montgomery, 2001).

Regardless of the approach taken in conceptualizing teen pregnancy, social workers clearly need to be involved in providing services that either delay pregnancy among adolescents or that support teens who become young parents. Much of the focus of current programs is on the pregnancy itself, ignoring the many other psychosocial factors associated with pregnancy and parenting that ultimately influence the health and well-being of parents and their children. Programs in this area will be discussed in "Sex Education," later in this chapter.

Given the chances of poor outcomes for teen parents, Alicia's possible sexual activity is cause for concern. You will want to ascertain what kind of knowledge Alicia has about sexual intercourse and contraception as well as what her perceptions are about pregnancy and parenting. Since Alicia appears to be lacking support and stability, she may view becoming pregnant as the only way to gain a sense of control in her life. If Alicia needs a sense of self-efficacy, it may be particularly important for you to focus on Alicia's strengths in other areas of her life to help her build self-esteem and a sense of control that will allow her to make informed decisions about sex and parenting.

THE LARGER SOCIAL ENVIRONMENT IN ADOLESCENCE

Just as many physical changes take place during adolescence, many larger social issues affect the well-being of adolescents. This section explores some global issues that social workers are likely to face when working with adolescent clients.

Runaway and Homeless Teens

The problem of runaway and homeless teenagers has become increasingly serious over the past several decades. Although the exact number of homeless teens is impossible to pinpoint, estimates are that over 1.6 million youth are homeless, with the majority of them being between the ages of 15 and 17 and approximately 6 percent of homeless youth being gay, lesbian, bisexual, or transgender (Molino, 2007; National Coalition for the Homeless, 2008).

Adolescents who run away and who are homeless often come from chaotic and traumatic family circumstances. Problems at home include physical and sexual abuse, parental alcohol abuse and violence, and behavioral problems on the part of the teen, including drug abuse and discipline problems. Still other teens leave home or foster care situations because they lack self-esteem and strong attachments with caregivers (Kools, 1997; National Coalition for the Homeless, 2008).

Runaway and homeless teens face many challenges. Their situation places them at risk for many of the problems discussed in this chapter such as STIs, pregnancy, violence, substance abuse, and dropping out of school (Whitebeck & Hoyt, 1999). In turn, these problems can lead to a whole host of developmental and social problems such as disease, mental illness, and relationship and employment difficulties.

Many of the shelters and other programs available to runaway and homeless youths provide only short-term services, such as beds, meals, clothes, counseling, and family mediation. Depending on their age, some older teens deciding not to return home can petition to become independent from their parents. Younger teens will likely enter the state foster system. Unfortunately, many of the programs and options available to runaway and homeless teens, because of their time limits, lack of funding, and overworked staff, do not address the underlying causes of homelessness, such as low self-esteem and lack of trust and self-efficacy, which may only make the problem worse (Williams, Lindsey, Kurtz, & Jarvis, 2001).

A study of five runaway teens who were considered to be resilient to many of the problems surrounding homelessness found that for a couple of the teens, establishing secure, trusting attachments with shelter and program workers was particularly helpful in increasing self-esteem, self-efficacy, and ultimately, resiliency (Williams et al., 2001). Unfortunately, as we have seen, the short-term nature of many programs does not facilitate the building of such attachments. Although this study used a small sample, it still provides social workers with useful information that helps in conceptualizing problems related to teen runaways and barriers to solving these problems.

Looking at Alicia's case, she seems to lack secure attachments with adults; she spends most of her time with her peers on the streets. Nevertheless, the connections she has established with you and the community center, however tenuous they may be, may provide some needed support to build trust and self-efficacy if she can maintain these connections over the long term.

Many theories and perspectives offer ways to work with Alicia, but they also depend on time for interventions to be effective. Although building attachments and self-efficacy takes time, you can bring in the strengths perspective to facilitate the building of Alicia's self-efficacy. Specifically, you can use Alicia's strengths as immediate examples of the positive aspects in her life, helping to build a sense of self-efficacy. Because many programs are time limited, you may also choose to employ a community organization or some other model to help change the service system for this population. Specifically, it would be useful to change the structure of these programs so they can provide more long-term, attachment-oriented services.

Deviance, Crime, and Violence

Violence and delinquency among adolescents are other problems of concern for teens, families, and social workers (see Box 9.6). Unfortunately, social workers usually come into contact with teens who have problems with these issues after a crime or act of violence has occurred.

What causes violent and delinquent behavior? What propels teens to commit crimes, and what can be done to prevent this criminal behavior? Extensive research has been conducted on these issues. The results indicate that different factors on the micro, mezzo, and macro levels predict violence and delinquency in adolescence (Kosterman et al., 2001; Walker, 1998):

The rate of violence among teens is increasing. In 2005, the National Center for Health Statistics (2008b) estimated that approximately 6.5 percent of high school students had carried a weapon to school, almost 8 percent had been threatened or injured by a weapon, and almost 14 percent had been in a physical fight at school. One study of more than 800 adolescents found that 55 percent had engaged in violent behavior at some point during their adolescent years (Kosterman, Graham, Hawkins, Catalano, & Herrenkohl, 2001). Approximately 16 percent of these teens continued this violent behavior until their early 20s.

BOX 9.6

Teens and Violence

- *Factors in violence on the micro level:* being male; substance use; low educational achievement; low impulse control; feelings of powerlessness; childhood aggression, hyperactivity, and withdrawal.

- *Factors in violence on the mezzo level:* family conflict, lack of familial support and discipline, negative peer pressure.

- *Factors in violence on the macro level:* poverty, living in high-crime urban neighborhoods, exposure to violence through the media and social environment.

Of course, many of these factors are interrelated. For example, poverty conditions can create problems for parents in providing adequate supervision of their children or in offering support, and many poor urban communities have high crime rates, exposing children to violence. For example, parents living in poverty may be working several jobs or may be experiencing extreme stress, making it difficult to engage or spend adequate time with children. Moreover, these communities often lack adequate schools, which can contribute to poor academic performance among students. Thus, interventions geared toward preventing or stopping delinquent behaviors need to focus on the interactive dynamics of the many psychosocial factors involved. For instance, social workers can help to work toward establishing sufficient funding for better schools and can help to support parents in their child-rearing efforts, particularly those parents who are living in poverty. Social workers can also help to promote self-efficacy and hopefulness in children and teens who are exposed to chaotic, violent, and poverty-stricken environments.

Social workers can use several theories to help guide their interventions in this area. For example, in Alicia's case, symbolic interaction or social learning theory may be applicable in understanding how to prevent potential delinquent behavior. Alicia's negative interactions with her mother as well as her interactions with friends on the street may be shaping her view on which behaviors are acceptable and useful to meet her needs. Specifically, her friends may engage in some delinquent behaviors, such as stealing, to survive. In Alicia's interactions with these people, she may learn to justify certain delinquent behaviors.

This view intersects with aspects of social learning theory as well. Alicia may see people get rewarded, or at least go without punishment, for various delinquent behaviors. She may also learn how to engage in crimes without getting caught and receive praise from her friends when she is successful, which further reinforces her delinquency. Using these theories, you could expose Alicia to other individuals (such as yourself or other peers who do not engage in delinquent behaviors) who can show Alicia that some people value nondelinquent behaviors and can model other, more appropriate ways for her to meet her needs.

Sex Education

Earlier in this chapter, we explored sexuality and sexual identity development. With regard to these issues, there are many debates in the United States concerning how to deal with sexual issues and how to provide services for teens (if services are provided at all). Here, we will look at some of these debates and service issues that affect teens, families, and the social workers who work with them.

Many programs and policies have been developed to curb teenage pregnancy. Many of these programs adopt a unilateral approach, focusing on specific aspects of sex education such as abstinence or promoting responsible sexual behavior. In addition, many of the programs that address teen pregnancy are geared toward girls. However, few programs offer comprehensive education that addresses the realities of sexual behavior among teens and that provides information on the choices available to teens should they become sexually active.

The Debate over Sex Education   Part of the problem behind a lack of appropriate and effective programming has to do with ongoing debates about whether sex education should be provided in schools and if it is provided, what kinds of information should be presented. Some people argue that sex education is best provided by parents, and schools should not offer such programming. Other people maintain that programs should provide abstinence-only education. Still others feel that more comprehensive programming that provides information on abstinence as well as contraceptive options, life choices, and health care should be available in schools.

Conservative views on teen pregnancy and sex education in general tend to take the position that teens should wait until marriage to have sex; therefore, information on contraception choices and abortion should not be made available to them. Moreover, this viewpoint tends to support the notion that if information on sex is given in schools, it will pique teens' curiosity about sex, spurring more teens to have sex. A more liberal viewpoint insists that a lack of information on sex only puts teens at risk for pregnancy and STIs. Many teens will choose to have sex with or without information; so they should be armed with information intended to keep them as safe as possible.

A Critique of Sex Education   Currently, many schools provide education that leans toward an abstinence perspective on sex. However, research on sex education has indicated that abstinence-only programs are not effective at reducing teen pregnancy rates or problems with STIs. Further, many professionals argue that abstinence-only programs fail those teens who are sexually active or who choose early parenthood (Rothenberg & Weissman, 2002; Women's International Network News, 1997). For example, one study of close to 3,500 teens found that those who made a "virginity pledge" to abstain from intercourse until marriage were just as likely as nonpledgers to have intercourse outside of marriage within five years of taking the pledge (81 percent of teens weren't virgins five years after taking the pledge). There were no differences between teens who made the pledge and those who didn't with regard to age at first intercourse, average number of sexual partners, types of sexual behaviors in which teens engaged, or having sexual partners with STIs. Further, teens who made the pledge were less likely than nonpledgers to protect themselves against STIs, leaving them at higher risk for disease and pregnancy (Rosenbaum, 2009). Indeed, based on research indicating that comprehensive sex education is more effective at reducing the rates of teen pregnancy and STIs, many of the George W. Bush administration's funding and other priorities favoring abstinence-only programs were reversed after he left office (Tanne, 2009).

Conversely, comprehensive education programs have been criticized for being too limited and shortsighted. Specifically, some experts posit that teens get inadequate information about sex from their parents and siblings, and many teens are made to feel guilty about using contraception. So, even if teens have access to contraceptives through school or other programs, they may be unlikely to use them because of the stigma placed on them through family and school-based programs (Westheimer & Lopater, 2004). Even if accurate information is available at home or at school, teens are likely to turn to peers first for information. This can be risky because information from peer sources tends to be unreliable and even incorrect; it tends to be replete with myths, stereotypes, and misinformation about sex and contraception (Guthrie & Bates, 2003). Thus, comprehensive education programs need to consider these issues when developing and providing sex education curricula.

Effective sex education is probably best viewed from an ecological or systems approach. Research on sex education programming indicates that comprehensive programs, even with their limitations, are the most effective in reducing rates of teen pregnancy and STIs. In general, reducing teen pregnancy relies on providing information on life options, access to contraceptive choices, sex education and family planning, community involvement and support, and abstinence for young teens (Omar, Fowler, & McClanahan, 2008; Potera, 2008; Zabin, Hirsch, Smith, & Hardy, 1986).

Short-term programs are inadequate because they do not deal with the multifaceted nature of teen sex and pregnancy. Rather, evidence suggests that programs need to be built around a comprehensive model that incorporates myriad components including but not limited to parenting, job training, employment opportunities, academic support, health and mental health care, parental and familial support, developmentally and culturally appropriate sex and contraceptive education (including abstinence), and recreation (for example, sports, drama, and art activities) to promote self-esteem and appropriate emotional outlets. Supportive services for teens and their families also need to be provided after teens become parents.

Further, these programs need to use multidisciplinary staff (for example, social workers, health educators, nurses, physicians, educators, and community and business organizations). Programs need to be long term in order for staff and teens to develop trusting relationships and to engage teens in activities. Many studies have indicated that when teens and staff have sufficient time to build relationships, teens are more likely to participate fully in program activities. These studies also stress the importance of respecting teens' attitudes, beliefs, and decisions about sex and parenting, which helps to facilitate relationship building and engagement by teens (Morris, Ulmer, & Chimnani, 2003; Philliber, Kaye, Herrling, & West, 2002; Rothenberg & Weissman, 2002). This latter point is also in keeping with NASW's (approved 1996, revised 2008) *Code of Ethics* relating to the value of respecting clients' self-determination. That is, even if social workers disagree with the opinions of clients and the choices that they make, social workers have an obligation to ensure that clients have access to information and to support clients based on informed decisions.

Heterosexism and Homophobia

As with other isms, such as ageism and sexism, heterosexism is a problem that is embedded in our social fabric. **Heterosexism** is the prejudice or discrimination in favor of those who are heterosexual (and against those who are homosexual). This type of prejudice and discrimination exists on various levels in society, some being more visible and overt than others.

Individual prejudice and discrimination against people who are homosexual can be hurtful and damaging (certainly, it can be deadly), but institutional hetero-sexism is often the most problematic. Social and other policies that keep homo-sexual individuals from marrying, being employed, advancing in work, adopting children, and securing housing, among many other things, affect people in all facets of their lives. Moreover, this type of heterosexism is the most covert and difficult to change.

Homophobia can be described as a type of prejudice that involves a fear of or anger, disgust, or discomfort with homosexuals and homosexuality. Studies indicate that people who are homophobic are generally men, often think that they do not know anyone who is homosexual, have a social network of people who are also homophobic, demonstrate rigidity in gender roles, and have a lower educational level than people who are not homophobic (Reinisch, 1990).

Many of the "causes" of prejudice discussed in Chapter 5 can help to explain how some people might develop homophobic characteristics. However, a com-bination of theories such as social interactionism and behaviorism also offers reasonable explanations for how some people come to hold prejudicial attitudes toward sexual minorities. For example, homophobia may be described as a process whereby people are reared with prejudicial beliefs about homosexuality. These beliefs keep people from (knowingly) having positive interactions with gays and lesbians, which gives them fewer opportunities to question and analyze the beliefs on which they were reared (or to change their schema for homosexuality). Further, prejudicial beliefs help to ensure that people will attend to the negative aspects of homosexuality that reinforce the prejudices that they hold. Thus, by the time people are in their teen years, heterosexist beliefs and homophobia are well established.

Other scholars have espoused a more feminist-oriented explanation of homophobia that is based on social constructionism. This view posits that although homophobia is often exhibited through acts of hatred and violence, homophobic behaviors are, in fact, based on fear. It argues that society values traditional, socially constructed masculine traits, which are reinforced at a very young age. Boys who conform to these traits and who disdain nonmasculine traits are positively reinforced. Because society offers little flexibility for men in the way of gender roles, those who deviate from masculine norms or who might not "measure up" to these norms feel inferior. Thus, men are fearful of any thought, feeling, or situation that may call into question their masculinity (as defined by society). When this occurs, they use violence (even though it is fear driven) to defend their masculinity because violence is a socially recognized masculine trait. Thus, violent behavior proves their masculinity and conformance to social norms (Herek, 2001). This view explains why some men may be afraid of being "seduced" or "hit on" by a gay man; this would be the ultimate threat to their masculinity. Using violence against someone who is gay not only reinforces masculinity but also helps to alleviate the fear of being viewed as effeminate (which is not socially acceptable for men).

Interventions toward eradicating homophobia are often based on these types of theories. Social workers can use interventions that maximize positive interactions with sexual minorities to help challenge myths, stereotypes, and prejudicial beliefs about gays and lesbians. Further, as discussed earlier in the chapter, social workers need to be aware of how their own beliefs and values about homosexuality might affect their work with clients. For example, one study that examined prejudice against homosexuality among helping professionals found that social workers who had frequent contact with gay and lesbian clients had lower levels of homophobia than those with less frequent contact. However, social workers who held deep religious beliefs against homosexuality had higher levels of homophobia than social workers who did not have these beliefs (Berkman & Zinberg, 1997).

These conclusions do not suggest that working in a helping profession and having beliefs against homosexuality are incompatible. However, they do indicate that social workers and other professionals must be aware of their own personal values that might bias their work or harm their clients. They also raise myriad ethical questions for practitioners such as those raised earlier in the chapter. Consider again, for example, how a social worker who believes that homosexuality is immoral would work with a teen client who thinks she is a lesbian and wants to discuss this in a session. On a broader level, how would social workers' personal beliefs affect their handling of issues such as communities that advocate separate high schools for gay, lesbian, and bisexual students?

CONCLUSION

Adolescence is a time of rapid development and many biopsychosocial changes. Many social workers see teens and their families in their practice because of the issues that can arise during this time. For many teens, this is a time in life when self-exploration, identity development, and increasing independence are priorities. These activities are vital to development and can lead to positive experiences, but they can also bring with them problems and issues that need to be addressed to assure optimal health and well-being later in life.

Social work with adolescents often consists of a balance between promoting and supporting growth, development, and independence while acknowledging the interdependence between individual, familial, and societal factors. Many forces are helping to shape the emerging identity of teens, and sometimes these forces create tension and problems for individuals. Social workers play a valuable role in helping teens to work through these issues to help them become healthy, well-adjusted, and successful adults.

MAIN POINTS

- One of the hallmarks of adolescent development is puberty and the hormonal changes associated with it. Patterns in development can impact well-being depending on the timing of maturation and the gender of the individual.

- Kohlberg's stage theory consists of three levels—preconventional, conventional, and postconventional—that describe a person's moral development. Gilligan's stage-based theory of moral development, which focuses on caring, also has three levels: orientation to personal survival, goodness as self-sacrifice, and the morality of nonviolent responsibility.

- Self-esteem can be influenced by a number of factors from an individual's immediate and larger social environments such as timing of the onset of puberty, family relationships, and the media.

- Developing a sexual identity includes experiencing and managing sexual feelings and incorporating this identity into an overarching self-concept as a member of a larger societal context. Teens of all sexual orientations grapple with the tasks of sexual development, but gay, lesbian, and bisexual teens have additional tasks related to discrimination and heterosexism.

- Eating disorders, sexually transmitted infections, substance abuse, and suicide are major problems for adolescents in the United States, and they have many short- and long-term consequences for adolescents' overall health and well-being. Social workers need to educate themselves, and even advance the knowledge, about these issues and understand the interrelated factors that put youth at risk.

- Peer pressure can have both positive and negative effects on teens. The extent to which one teen influences the behavior of another can depend on many factors such as personality, coping skills, and the presence of other support systems, particularly parents.

- The United States has one of the highest teen pregnancy rates among industrialized nations. Although its outcomes are not always unfavorable, teen pregnancy generally leads to a variety of individual, familial, and social problems.

- Runaway and homeless teens and teen violence are major problems in the United States. Many programs that deal with these issues offer only short-term solutions, which do not address the complex psychosocial issues that cause or intensify the problems.

- There are many debates in the United States about how to deal with sexual issues and how to provide services for teens. Generally, these debates center on whether to provide sex education in the schools and, if education is provided, what should be included in the curriculum.

- Heterosexism and homophobia exist at both the individual and institutional levels, and they greatly affect the well-being of gay and lesbian people. Social workers can use interventions that maximize positive interactions with sexual minorities, but they need to be aware of how their own beliefs and values might affect this work.

EXERCISES

1. Using the Sanchez Family interactive case (go to www.routledgesw.com/cases), review the major issues involving the Sanchez family; pay particular attention to Carmen's situation. After giving this information thorough review, answer the following questions:
   a. In Carmen's case, are there any developmental issues that might need attention? Explain.
   b. Do any of these issues put Carmen at risk for problems as she moves into adulthood?
   c. Regarding your answers to the first two questions, what interventions might you develop for Carmen to help her avoid potential problems as she matures?
   d. Is there evidence that older family members might now be struggling with issues that relate to developmental issues in adolescence? What might these be?

2. Using the Riverton interactive case (go to www.routledgesw.com/cases), review the issues faced by the individuals and the community as a whole and answer the following questions:

   a. How could information in this chapter, if any, be used to intervene with problems faced by individuals or the community as a whole?

   b. In what ways could this information be useful to help prevent future problems?

   c. Are there ways in which the theory of moral development could be applied to any particular situation to help you conceptualize or work with problems?

CHAPTER 10

Development in
Early Adulthood

Gudrun is a 25-year-old German American woman who has been admitted into the psychiatric unit of a local hospital. She was brought to the hospital emergency room by the police for "harassing" customers at a downtown business: She accused them of following her and attempting to control her thoughts, so she yelled at them as they walked by.

The social worker in the unit discovered that Gudrun lives alone in a small apartment and is employed part time as a salesclerk. Gudrun's parents, who came to the United States from Germany 20 years ago, live near her apartment. However, Gudrun states that her parents frequently have violent fights, so she doesn't like to spend much time with them. Gudrun has a boyfriend, but she says that he recently told her that he wanted to break off the relationship. Over the past year, Gudrun has been disciplined twice by her employer for excessive absenteeism. During the interview with the social worker, Gudrun admitted that recently she has been hearing voices, and she believes that the government and her employer have been monitoring her movements through her television set.

EARLY ADULTHOOD, GENERALLY REFERRED TO AS THE TIME period between late adolescence and the early 40s, is a time when a majority of individuals experience continued and enhanced growth in many areas such as the sexual, cognitive, emotional, and interpersonal realms. Many young adults are testing out their newfound independence by going to college, securing a job that can support them financially, and moving out on their own. In this chapter, we will explore some issues that tend to highlight this particular time in life and the ways in which social workers can help young adults who face problems.

DEVELOPMENTAL MILESTONES IN YOUNG ADULTS

With the conclusion of puberty, physical development tends to stabilize, and many individuals enjoy peak physical performance during young adulthood. Moreover, many young adults enjoy optimal physical health and find themselves relatively free of pain, disease, and illness. However, young adulthood is also a time when the negative consequences of lifestyle factors such as stress, smoking, overeating, substance abuse, lack of exercise, and poor sleep habits can begin to accumulate, causing illness and disease later in life.

Many of the processes of cognitive development that occur earlier in life begin to stabilize during young adulthood. According to Piaget (1972), most people reach the formal operations stage in their early teens, when they become capable of qualitative thought, using logic and reason to guide their thinking. Specifically, then, teenagers have the cognitive abilities to "think like" adults. However, other theorists and researchers posit that cognitively, young adults are slightly different from their younger counterparts. Specifically, young adults may be more sophisticated in the ways that they proceed through formal operational thought than they were in their teen years. Some researchers further argue that young adults become more reflective and realistic as they gain experience, and they become more adept at applying knowledge to real-world situations, although the development of these skills is very individualistic, meaning that not all people develop these skills fully or at the same time—there is evidence to suggest that the development of these advanced skills is not necessarily predictable or universal as Piaget asserted (for example, Keating, 1990; Kuhn, 2008; Schaie & Willis, 2000).

In addition, young adults continue to develop intellectually and interpersonally while learning to master their emotions and deal with independence. Young adulthood is a time when most individuals in Western societies become autonomous, self-sufficient, and responsible for their actions, while also learning how to balance interdependence with independence in intimate relationships. It is also a time when individuals continue to develop their self-identity and form their own opinions, values, and beliefs about the world. Although these concepts have been partially shaped over time by their peers, families, and other outside forces, young adults learn not to be easily swayed by the opinions of others (Chickering & Reisser, 1993). Table 10.1 summarizes the highlights of development in early adulthood.

Social workers can play an instrumental role in the lives of young adults who are experiencing problems with development. For example, according to Erikson, young adulthood is a time when individuals work toward closeness in their relationships. Young adults learn to sacrifice in their relationships with others without losing a sense of their identity. Some young adults may find that they are unable to relate to others in an intimate way, or they may experience difficulties in maintaining a stable sense of self when they are involved in close relationships. Social workers might assist clients who experience these types of problems by working with them to build self-identity, healthy boundaries, and relationship skills.

As Gudrun's social worker, you can assist her with relationship issues after her symptoms have been stabilized. Because of her mental health issues, Gudrun will likely need extra support in working on relationships with friends, co-workers, family members, and others with whom she has contact. The social worker can also

TABLE 10.1	PHYSICAL	COGNITIVE	PERSONALITY AND EMOTION
Developmental Milestones in Early Adulthood	• Stabilization of physical growth. • Optimal physical performance, with declines beginning in the latter part of early adulthood. • Bad health habits are established.	• Thought becomes more reflective, sophisticated. • Capable of using reason and logic in thinking processes. • Begin to connect new information to past experiences to enhance learning.	• Stabilization of emotional growth; master emotions. • Development of interpersonal, intimate relationships. • In Western culture, establishment of independence. • Established self-identity.

assess Gudrun's physical, cognitive, and emotional functioning to help minimize any symptoms of mental illness and ensure that symptoms do not seriously impact her health and well-being in these areas.

THE INDIVIDUAL IN EARLY ADULTHOOD

Though physical development has slowed down somewhat by early adulthood, many changes still take place in other areas that, although generally positive, can create problems for some young adults. The next several sections discuss just a few of the issues that young adults may bring to social workers.

Mental Illness

Though mental illness and problems associated with poor mental health can arise at any point in the life span, we discuss this issue in this chapter because many individuals with serious mental illnesses tend to exhibit initial symptoms in early adulthood. Further, symptoms of mental illness can begin to cause problems with functioning as young adults attempt to establish independence.

Schizophrenia: Possible Causes   Schizophrenia is an example of a mental illness whose symptoms tend to exhibit themselves in late adolescence or early adulthood. Symptoms include some or all of the following: delusions, hallucinations, flat affect, and disorganized and meaningless speech and behavior (American Psychiatric Association, 2000). The exact cause of schizophrenia is unknown; however, there is a great deal of evidence, particularly through twin studies, to suggest that genetic and biological factors contribute to the disorder (Andreasen, 2001; Maier et al., 2000). For example, research shows that more men than women have the disorder, which may indicate that estrogen serves as a protective factor against the disease (Faraone, Brown, Glatt, & Ming, 2002).

Studies also indicate that a combination of genetic predisposition and environmental stressors tends to place people at risk for developing schizophrenia. For example, some studies indicate that for people who possess a genetic predisposition to schizophrenia, problems such as familial patterns of hostility, criticism, negativity, and dysfunctional communication make the symptoms and course of the disorder more severe (Bateson, 1978; Boye, Bentsen, & Malt, 2002; Schiffman et al., 2001, 2002). Other studies point to the role of reinforcement and cognitive process in the development of symptoms among people with a genetic predisposition to the disorder. For example, researchers argue that some people with schizophrenia have not been positively reinforced for attending to "normal" social cues. Thus, these people attend to irrelevant cues in their environment, which results in seemingly odd behavior. Moreover, these researchers argue that people who experience abnormal cognitive processes resulting from biological problems attempt to "make sense" of these processes, which ultimately results in illogical thinking patterns and odd behavior (Garety, 1991; Murphy, 2007).

People with schizophrenia are more likely to have experienced a premature birth, low birth weight, and other fetal and birth complications than people who do not have the disorder. Some researchers suspect that these conditions may play a part in activating genes associated with schizophrenia. Similarly, people with schizophrenia tend to be born in the late winter and early spring months, leading some experts to speculate that viruses common in these months interact with a genetic predisposition to the disorder, creating conditions that lead to the development of symptoms (Faraone et al., 2002).

Mental Illness and Social Work Strategies   The research on schizophrenia underscores the importance of social workers' use of a variety of theories and models when working with clients. In this case, an understanding of the medical model and other biopsychosocial approaches is useful when working with clients who have serious and persistent mental illnesses such as schizophrenia. Further, since interventions with many of these disorders call for a combination of methods such as drug therapy and case management to help optimize clients' biopsychosocial and economic well-being, social workers need a comprehensive knowledge base to work effectively with these clients.

Social workers can also concentrate on prevention efforts that are geared toward children of parents who have been diagnosed with certain mental illnesses. For example, early warning signs of schizophrenia include social impairments, poor motor skills, and attention deficits. If a thorough assessment indicates that children are at risk for developing a mental illness, social workers can assist in eliminating some of the environmental risk factors such as stress and poor coping and communication skills that can leave children more vulnerable to developing the disorder later in life (Faraone et al., 2002).

Because many young adults are entering the workforce, establishing intimate relationships, and attempting to become financially and physically independent from their parents, problems with mental health are likely to interfere with a successful transition into adulthood. Thus, problems in the workplace or with relationships that are caused by mental illness are likely to come to the attention of social workers. Moreover, any unresolved problems with mental health that individuals experienced in childhood will likely become more severe in young adulthood as individuals experience changing roles and new stressors caused by changing life experiences.

Chapter 7 discussed issues surrounding child abuse and neglect. One reason why social workers need to attend to abuse and neglect issues in families with young children is because of the ramifications that these problems can have for victims in young adulthood. For example, abuse and neglect are correlated with mental health problems (Bifulco et al., 2002) as well as with a variety of social and relational problems in adulthood (Malinosky-Rummell & Hansen, 1993).

In addition, many young adults who experience their parents' divorce, separation, or marital problems tend to demonstrate lower psychological well-being than young adults whose parents did not have severe marital problems. Some children from homes with severe marital problems tend to have ongoing relationship troubles with their parents. It may be that divorce and stress caused by marital conflict are just some of the issues with which these children must contend, even as they grow older. In other words, marital conflict is often accompanied by other problems, such as relationship strain, that can affect children's well-being as they move into adulthood (Amato & Sobolewski, 2001).

These issues are explained well through the lenses of systems and ecological theories. For example, when the homeostasis of the family system is disrupted through conflict, children must adjust in order to adjust to the new circumstances. Sometimes, this adjustment is negative and has long-lasting effects on the children's future relationships with peers, family members, and significant others. Other factors that are often part of marital strife, such as economic and legal issues, can also adversely affect children. Social workers can help families find resolutions to marital troubles that will not undermine their children's development or that at least will minimize the amount of emotional, psychological, and physical harm generated by that conflict.

Conversely, social workers can assess these issues from a strengths perspective. From this perspective, individuals are seen as resourceful and resilient beings who have many skills and abilities that transcend their problems. Thus, in the case of mental illness, it is also important for social workers to examine the unique strengths and resources that clients bring and that can help them to work through problems caused by symptoms of mental illness. Focusing on client strengths can help social workers and clients with symptoms of mental illness draw on existing supports that will enhance clients' well-being.

Given Gudrun's symptoms, it is likely that she is dealing with a mental illness. And given her age, it is also likely that this is the first time she has experienced such symptoms. The description indicates that Gudrun has been able to maintain housing, employment, and relationships; so if she has experienced symptoms before, they were probably mild. Further, her ability to function in the past will be a strength that you can use when working with her; she clearly has many strengths and resources upon which to draw. You will want to conduct a thorough biopsychosocial and strengths assessment to ascertain the resources available to Gudrun as well as the issues that might intensify her mental illness in the future. With the appropriate medications and case management, Gudrun may be able to continue to live and function independently.

Disability

Like mental illness, disability can occur at any age. Again, we discuss disability here because of its implications for the well-being of young adults. Young adults with a disability may find working toward independence and self-sufficiency difficult, depending on the type of disability, the psychosocial circumstances surrounding it, and the resources available in the community.

With more than 90 percent of individuals with disabilities surviving into adulthood, there are many challenges on individual, familial, and social levels with regard to ensuring health and well-being. The majority of people with disabilities rely on Medicaid for health insurance, partly because many of them are unemployed and thus cannot secure private health insurance. Children with disabilities are often covered under their parents' insurance; however, when they reach young adulthood, they are often dropped from those policies, leaving them uninsured. Those covered by the State Children's Health Insurance Program (SCHIP) are also dropped at age 18. Depending on the disability, many young adults have difficulty securing private insurance because of preexisting condition clauses, limits to coverage, and expenses (White, 2002).

Because many disabilities need medical attention and intervention, social workers and other helping professionals frequently use the medical model to help guide assessment and intervention when working with people with disabilities. However, they also need to consider other factors on the micro, mezzo, and macro levels that influence the health and functioning of people with disabilities. For example, coping skills and personal resources as well as community resources and policies can play an important role in determining the quality of life for people with disabilities.

Gudrun, depending on her symptoms and how well she responds to intervention, may find herself disabled due to mental illness. Though she may be eligible for various governmental programs to help support herself financially and to cover her health care costs, she will likely need help in navigating through the paperwork and bureaucracy to secure these resources. She will also need assistance with maintaining these resources, as some programs require proof of continuing eligibility. Through case management, you will be able to ensure that Gudrun has access to programs that will help her to maintain a maximum level of independence and well-being.

Spirituality

In recent years, social workers have devoted greater attention to their clients' spiritual development. Within social work, spirituality tends to be seen as one aspect within the biopsychosocial view of an individual. One prominent researcher (Canda, 2008) in social work and spirituality refers to spirituality as, "the human search for a sense of meaning, purpose, and morally fulfilling relations with oneself, other people, the universe, and the ground of being, however that's understood . . ." (p. 27). Further, "spirituality . . . involves centrally important life-orienting beliefs, values, and practices that may be expressed in religious and/or nonreligious ways" (p. 27).

With this growing interest in spirituality has come an increasing body of literature examining how spirituality develops and how people use spirituality to enhance their well-being. Of course, opinions vary concerning the importance of religion and spirituality throughout the life span. This is particularly true of studies conducted with young adults, who are experiencing many changes that can influence their definition and perception of spirituality as well as their level of religious activity.

Some researchers have found that individuals who actively participated in religious activities during their younger years tend to spend less time in these activities in young adulthood. However, these individuals tend to increase their participation later in life, particularly if they were very active in youth and other programs offered by their religious institution. Further, when these young adults return to participating in their church, synagogue, mosque, or temple, they generally adopt the religious affiliation of their childhood (O'Connor, Hoge, & Alexander, 2002).

Conversely, other researchers have found that while religious beliefs tend to decline over time, religious participation tends to increase as individuals enter young adulthood and beyond. Their work indicates that religious participation seems to be related to traditional roles expected in adulthood such as marriage and having children. That is, some young adults perceive religious participation as an expected role that accompanies starting a family. Further, older adults may find social support in religious gatherings (Bengtson, Horlacher, Putney, & Silverstein, 2008; Stolzenberg, Blair-Loy, & Waite, 1995).

Spirituality and faith, though tied to religion for some young adults, can be totally different constructs from religion for others. For instance, some people may consider themselves to be very spiritual even though they do not participate in religious activities or identify with specific religious institutions. Others may perceive themselves to be spiritual because they participate in religious activities.

EXHIBIT 10.1

Spiritual development is an important consideration in social work practice

Source: M. Freeman/PhotoLink/Getty Images

Because these concepts have different meanings for different individuals, they can be difficult to define, study, and apply to client situations. Moreover, various theories attempt to explain faith and beliefs, and in doing so, they can offer disparate views on how people engage in religious activities throughout the life span. Thus, social workers may find it difficult to interpret research on the subject or to make sense of clients' particular faith issues.

For example, from the perspective of social learning theory, you might view religiosity and spirituality as learned; that is, they are socialized into us as we model the beliefs and behaviors of people who are close to us. Thus, if our parents attend church regularly, we will be exposed to this activity and will likely carry on the activity as we grow older. Though we may question our parents' activity as well as their beliefs as we move into adolescence, we are likely to carry with us into young adulthood the same tendencies and beliefs as our parents.

Alternatively, from the perspective of Erikson's theory, you might view faith and religious participation as dependent on the particular developmental tasks and crises with which people must grapple in certain life stages. For example, some young adults in the intimacy versus isolation stage may turn to religious institutions to find closeness to other like-minded people. They may use faith to help them establish intimacy with themselves and others. Conversely, some young adults may abandon their religious beliefs and practices because they cause conflict for their intimate relationships. Still other theories specifically seek to explain faith and spirituality development. One of these theories is Fowler's theory of faith development.

Fowler's Theory of Faith Development   One theory of spirituality, which was developed by James Fowler, a developmental psychologist, describes stages that people go through in finding spirituality. Fowler suggests that faith does not necessarily relate to organized religion or even God, but rather to ways in which people find meaning and connection with others. Fowler's theory posits that people begin developing their faith early in life and can continue doing so into old age (Fowler, 1981, 1996). Table 10.2 describes the stages in this theory.

TABLE 10.2 Fowler's Theory of Faith Development	STAGE	DESCRIPTION
	Stage 1: Primal or Undifferentiated Faith (Birth to 2 years)	All infants begin life determining whether the world is safe and their needs are met. Children begin to use language to articulate their relationships with others.
	Stage 2: Intuitive-Projective Faith (2 to 6 years)	Children take in information from their environments. They are unable to rationally think through what is spiritual, but they subscribe to what they are told.
	Stage 3: Mythic-Literal Faith (6 to 12 years)	Children relate to stories and symbolism and use these elements to represent their faith. They still cannot think critically about facets of beliefs.
	Stage 4: Synthetic-Conventional Faith (12+ years)	People are exposed to information through their interactions with others. They find meaning in symbols and traditions, but they still adhere to conventional ways of thinking about faith.
	Stage 5: Individuative-Reflective Faith (Early adulthood+)	People think critically about the meaning of faith and what their personal beliefs are. People are able to compare their beliefs with those they were taught.
	Stage 6: Conjunctive Faith (Midlife+)	People accept that conflicts exist between their beliefs and those of conventional religions. Spirituality takes on deeper meaning.
	Stage 7: Universalizing Faith (Midlife+)	People integrate conflicts in beliefs and work toward ensuring the well-being of humankind. They recognize injustice and find meaning in self-sacrifice for the greater good.

Source: Adapted from Fowler, 1981.

DEVELOPMENT IN EARLY ADULTHOOD

As you can see in the table, this theory posits that people move through consistent developmental stages to achieve a point at which they experience a universalizing faith in which they are concerned with the well-being of all humankind. Although this theory suggests that, in general, people develop faith in a fairly straightforward, consistent manner as they age, Fowler argues that only a small percentage of people actually reach Stage 6 or Stage 7. Moreover, people may vary with regard to the ages at which they reach certain stages and the extent to which they achieve developmental tasks in various stages.

According to Fowler (1981), young adults should be in Stage 5, in which they begin to think critically about their own personal beliefs, comparing them to those with which they were socialized. Assuming that many young adults reach this stage, Fowler's theory can help explain why many individuals are more tolerant of different religious beliefs in young adulthood than they were in younger years and why many young adults begin to develop their own definitions of spirituality. It also helps explain why young adults, as a group, may be at their lowest point of spirituality compared to their older years. One recent longitudinal study found that spirituality tended to increase as individuals got older; it was at its lowest point in early adulthood and increased beginning in the 30s, reaching a peak at older adulthood (Wink & Dillon, 2002). Perhaps adolescence and early adulthood are periods of questioning faith, spirituality, and religious beliefs in the context of increasing experience and exposure to others (Paloutzian, 2000).

As with many other theories of human development, social workers can benefit from having a broad understanding of certain aspects of their clients' development and personalities. Issues of faith can arise in work with clients, so having a model from which to work is helpful. However, keep in mind that theories of faith development are difficult to form and articulate, and like so many other theories, they may not capture the rich cultural and spiritual context in which clients live.

Incorporating Spirituality into Social Work Practice   Because of the influences that spirituality and church attendance can have on people's worldviews as well as the social and other support networks that religious affiliations provide, social workers need to incorporate elements of spirituality and religious participation in their assessments and interventions when working with clients. Often, clients' religious beliefs and views on spirituality provide insights into the ways in which clients view problems and solutions, and they can be sources of strength in helping clients to overcome obstacles.

In Gudrun's case, you will want to find out if she has any religious affiliations in the community. A church or other organization may be able to provide needed support as she works to maintain her independence. Further, depending on her views, Gudrun's spirituality may be a strength that you can use in your work with her. You could also explore Gudrun's moral and spiritual development if she agrees that it might be useful. In terms of morality, you may not need to know which stage Gudrun has reached, but discussing with Gudrun her overall worldview and perspective on life might be helpful. Gudrun seems to be at a crisis point in her life, so exploring issues of faith may be useful to her in making sense of her situation. You might want to explore Gudrun's beliefs and her views on faith and whether her views are consistent with those espoused by her religious leaders. In doing so, you may be able to help Gudrun come to terms with how her symptoms are impacting her life.

THE FAMILY AND IMMEDIATE ENVIRONMENT IN EARLY ADULTHOOD

Young adulthood tends to be a time when many individuals begin to redefine their relationships with others. Many young adults find themselves exploring their roles and relationships in the family, with peers, in the workplace, and in intimate relationships. This section includes a discussion on a few issues that may impact the well-being of young adults on this level.

Domestic Violence

Since young adulthood is a time when many people experience their first intimate relationships, it is also a time when domestic violence can become a serious problem for some couples. Because many young adults live on their own, problems that can occur in their relationships may be more difficult to identify, making intervention more difficult. Further, independence in young adulthood may exacerbate the problem of domestic violence since the abuser may work to keep the partner isolated from friends and family.

Statistics from the National Violence Against Women survey suggest that almost six million acts of physical violence are committed against women in the United States each year, almost 80 percent of which are perpetrated by husbands, partners, boyfriends, or ex-husbands (Tjaden & Thoennes, 1998). Further, according to the National Crime Victimization Survey, approximately 30 percent of murdered women are killed by their male partners (Bachman & Saltzman, 1995). Indeed, seven in ten female sexual assault victims stated that the perpetrator was known to them and females are more likely than males to be victimized by someone they know (Bureau of Justice Statistics, 2009).

The effects of domestic violence on children are well documented (for example, Heugten & Wilson, 2008; Humphreys, Lowe, & Williams, 2009; Perloff & Buckner, 1996; Shepard, 1992) and are similar to those found for abused children (see the discussion in Chapter 7). Children who witness domestic violence are at risk for developing into young adults who either perpetrate violence against their partners or become targets for abuse (Evans, Davies, & DiLillo, 2008; Tutty & Wagar, 1994). In young and later adulthood, victims of domestic violence can be exposed to myriad problems that include mental illness, physical injury, loss of employment, post-traumatic stress, and of course, death.

Theories of Domestic Violence Social learning and family systems theories are just two of the perspectives that maintain that violence is cyclical and can be passed on from generation to generation. For example, some research suggests that factors such as child abuse, poor family cohesion, familial substance abuse, witnessing domestic violence, and exposure to violence in the media are associated with domestic violence problems in adulthood (Bevan & Higgins, 2002). Children who are abused and exposed to violence and substance abuse are more likely to carry out these behaviors as adults.

Some feminist theories posit that patriarchal society, which gives power to men, perpetuates the problem of violence against women and children. Specifically, the problem of domestic violence is rooted in society because it condones the power of men and the subjugation and second-class status of women. Domestic violence can also be viewed from ecological theory, which would include the aforementioned factors in explaining domestic violence as well as other factors such as a genetic disposition to violent behavior and other problems such as poverty, unemployment, and shifting gender roles.

For social workers, poverty and welfare reform are particularly salient issues connected to domestic violence. The 1996 welfare reforms have far-reaching implications for all those in need of welfare resources, but they also have impacts on victims of domestic violence who rely on public assistance, particularly those who have left their abusers. For instance, the 60-month lifetime limit that was included in the reform package hurts many victims of domestic violence. Since they cannot control when and for how long the abuse will occur, and since it often takes many years to successfully end abusive relationships, lifetime program limits make valuable resources inaccessible to many women who rely on them to gain and maintain their independence. Moreover, the mandatory work requirements included in the reform can also harm victims of domestic violence. Abusers often isolate their victims from employment in order to control them; thus, many women may be unable to work or do not have the skills and experience necessary to find and keep stable, well-paying employment (Chanley & Alozie, 2001).

Going further, child support and paternity identification requirements included in the reform can actually increase the likelihood of violence against women, particularly for women who are still living with their abusers or who are hiding from them. Women who need medical attention due to abuse are harmed by limits to medical benefits that were imposed in the reform, and immigrant women are cut off from benefits altogether. And because states control programs, benefits and eligibility requirements can vary drastically from state to state. Thus, women may find it difficult to relocate if they need to move away from their abusers. Of course, states have the option to consider domestic violence circumstances when designing programs, but the treatment of this issue is by no means consistent, and there is no guarantee that requirements will be flexible for victims (Chanley & Alozie, 2001).

Domestic Violence and Social Work Though social workers frequently deal with policies and interventions surrounding domestic violence, the profession has been accused of not responding to the issue in a way that benefits persons who are victims of domestic violence. Some critics have accused social workers of not giving domestic violence priority and for allowing harmful policies, such as welfare reform, to be developed and implemented. Because so many social workers work in agencies that serve children and families, many critics argue that they should be on the front lines, fighting for policies and programs that will support persons who are victims of domestic violence. Instead, social workers are often seen as bureaucrats who per-petuate the problem by blaming victims, not using comprehensive theories to guide assessment and intervention, and hindering the development and implementation of programs that allow these individuals to gain independence (Danis, 2003). In fact, many social workers have been involved in developing policies and programs that advocate for persons who are victims of domestic violence. For example, many social workers have trained law enforcement officers in dealing with domestic violence situations and have worked to make the court system more accessible to and effective in ways that support efforts by these individuals to move out of abusive relationships.

Many of the issues discussed here are evident in Gudrun's case. The description indicates that Gudrun has witnessed domestic violence with her parents. This situation may have put her at risk for being abused in her relationships, which may be part of the reason for her problems with her boyfriend. You may choose to assess this situation, as Gudrun could be at risk for being abused by significant others, which will impact her future relationships and her overall well-being.

Alternative Relationships and Living Arrangements

Since the 1950s, young adults increasingly have been choosing to remain single. Instead of marrying, many young people are either remaining in their parents' homes, living by themselves, or living with friends or significant others. Not only is the median age for first marriages increasing, but so are the numbers of people who have never married. According the U.S. Census Bureau (2003), between the years 1950 and 2000 the percentage of men and women aged 15 to 24 who chose to delay marriage increased from 77 percent to 88 percent and 56 percent to 82 percent, respectively. The U.S Census Bureau (2006) reported that in 2005, less than half (49.7 percent) of all households were made up of married couples.

Currently, cohabitation before marriage is a common arrangement between couples. Trends in delaying marriage are likely due to increasing numbers of women participating in the labor force, leaving them economically able to delay marriage or to choose other relationship and living options. Still, many women who are single express a desire to marry in the future, and because of the pay gap between men and women as well as other factors, marriage often improves the economic status of women. Specifically, although the economic status of both men and women increases after marriage if both partners are working, women still have more to gain financially from marriage than do men (Clarkberg, 1999).

One study of over 500 undergraduate students captured this attitude about marriage and family (O'Laughlin, 2001). Results indicated that 80 percent of respondents had a desire to have a family of their own, although those who expressed ambivalence seemed to have realistic worries about the difficulties of balancing family with work, school, and other responsibilities. Realistic expectations about starting a family also increased as age increased: Those aged 18 to 30 held more unrealistic ideas about marriage and family than those aged 30 and older. For example, younger people thought it would be relatively easy to balance work with family and to support a family financially. In this study, men seemed to have more unrealistic expectations about parenting than women, which may reflect the reality that parenting often impacts women more negatively in all realms of life than it does men. This conclusion also reflects findings in some studies that marital satisfaction after having a child tends to decrease for women. These issues may be behind the reasons why so many women are currently waiting longer before they marry and have children.

Increased acceptance of gay and lesbian couples may be another reason why some young people are remaining single and cohabiting. That is, many gay and lesbian people may be choosing to remain true to their sexual identity by dating and entering into committed relationships with same-sex partners rather than succumbing to pressure to marry opposite-sex partners. Though gay and lesbian couples still face many legal and social obstacles in maintaining committed relationships, they may also enjoy stronger relationships than heterosexual couples. Some research indicates that gay and lesbian couples may possess stronger problem-solving skills and have more favorable opinions about their partners than heterosexual couples. Gay and lesbian couples may also be more autonomous and open-minded than their heterosexual counterparts. However, gay and lesbian couples tend to report fewer social supports than heterosexual couples, which may reflect societal opinions about homosexuality. The exception to this is that lesbian women do report more support from their friends and higher relationship satisfaction than either gay men or heterosexual couples, which may be indicative of the way in which females tend to be socialized (Kurdek, 2001).

As relationship and living arrangement patterns change in Western society, social workers must stay abreast of the social implications that these changes can have for individuals and communities. These changes bring new challenges to realms such as economics, communication, family dynamics, and family and gender roles. Social workers can benefit from applying models such as systems and ecological theories when conceptualizing and intervening with the issues that some couples face. Other models, such as attachment theory and psychodynamic theories, can be useful when working with young adults dealing with relationship issues.

For example, research suggests that separation-individuation from parents, particularly for men, is a factor in healthy marriages. In Western society, independence is an important construct and is seen as paramount for well-being. Men, especially, are expected to be independent from their parents, so separation marks the movement into young adulthood and proves that they are ready for an intimate relationship and marriage (Haws & Mallinckrodt, 1998). Social workers can work with young adults who may have problems separating from parents or who may be struggling, on an individual or social level, with changing roles, social support, starting a family, definitions of relationships, expectations for intimacy, and living with significant others.

Gudrun, because of her problems with mental health and family dynamics, will likely need extra support in developing and maintaining relationships. She has shown the ability to form relationships in the past, which is a strength; however, other problems related to her mental health and family relationships may pose problems for future relationships. You can apply systems or ecological theories in Gudrun's case to help guide assessment and intervention and to ensure that various factors affecting her well-being are considered to maximize the effectiveness of an intervention in this area.

THE LARGER SOCIAL ENVIRONMENT IN EARLY ADULTHOOD

As young adults move out into the world to assert themselves and find their place in the larger community, they are increasingly likely to encounter various issues on the macro level that will impact their lives. Politics, the economy, workplace policies, and educational issues are just a few of the factors with which young adults may find themselves grappling. We look next at some of the areas that may impact the lives of young adults on this level.

Sexism

Chapter 5 discussed facets involved in racism, prejudice, and oppression. Sexism is similar to these issues in definition and in the ways in which it tends to occur and affect individuals and society. Like other isms, **sexism** involves stereotyping and generalizing about women and men and treating them in particular ways based on these stereotypes. Most often, social workers deal with sexism when it has negative impacts on their clients or some aspect of society. As men and women move into young adulthood, they are likely to become increasingly aware of sexism and its effects since they will be expanding their contacts with areas of society, such as employment and education, where it is likely to be found. Though people may

experience sexism in younger years, young adulthood is when they begin to articulate the ramifications that sexism has for their lives and for society in general.

Sexism is a particularly important issue for social workers because it endangers
the well-being of women. Though it does have negative consequences for men (for
example, men are expected to be nonemotional, which can have ramifications
for their health), sexism tends to be a more pervasive problem for women, and
women tend to have more negative stereotypes attributed to them than men.
Further, as feminists would argue, women have less power than men. This disparity
makes stereotypes more damaging and more effective at keeping women from
gaining power and equality. Sexism, particularly institutional sexism and the discrimination that results, can create and maintain a cycle of poverty, which can
contribute to many problems, including mental illness, reduced life expectancy, and
poor physical health (Belle & Doucet, 2003). To help prevent some of the damage
created by sexism, social workers who work with young women need to educate
them about issues surrounding sexism and to pinpoint ways in which it can be
prevented in young adulthood to help ward off problems in middle and older
adulthood.

Sexism in the Workforce   One area in which sexism continues to be a problem is in
the workforce. Currently, women's pay is close to 79 percent of men's pay, even
when factors such as education, seniority, and type of job are held constant. In 2009,
the median income for men was $832.00 per week while for women it was $649.00.
Wage discrepancies between the sexes can be seen in almost all professions. For
example, male computer analysts make approximately 26 percent more than their
female counterparts. Male lawyers earn 44 percent more than female lawyers, and
male accountants earn 39 percent more than female accountants (U.S. Bureau of
Labor Statistics, 2009). Moreover, professions that are dominated by women are paid
less than those dominated by men (Fogg, 2003).

To illustrate this situation, Table 10.3 displays the percentages of women in
various fields, along with the average salary of persons employed in each. As you can
see, there is a clear inverse relationship between the percentage of female employees
and the average salary. This is particularly troublesome for women in young adulthood because they begin their careers at a disadvantage that will follow them
throughout the remainder of their work years and into retirement. When these
young women reach old age, they will have less money on which to rely for living,
medical, and other expenses. While the experience and career advancement that
age can bring do help many workers to earn more, older women tend to be at a
bigger disadvantage than younger women and men of all ages because of family
obligations. Specifically, women who have started families often have less time to
spend at work, and they are less mobile geographically when opportunities for
promotion arise (Hacker, 2003). Further, evidence suggests that, all other things
being equal, women who are mothers (or who are thought to be mothers) are discriminated against in hiring decisions—a phenomenon known as the "motherhood

TABLE 10.3

Relationship between Dominance of Women in a Profession and the Profession's Average Salary

PROFESSION	PERCENTAGE OF WOMEN IN PROFESSION	AVERAGE SALARY*
Engineering	11	$ 73,736
Architecture	23	$ 58,656
Chief Executives	24	$ 98,956
Physicians & Surgeons	32	$ 90,012
Law	38	$ 91,052
Cashiers	74	$ 18,720
Elementary Education	81	$ 46,280
Librarians	82	$ 45,656
Child Care Workers	94	$ 20,592

Source: Adapted from Hacker, 2003; U.S. Bureau of Labor Statistics, 2002.

* Salaries represent an average wage within a profession. Salaries may be higher or lower, depending on specialty and geographic location.

penalty." One study compared the work experiences of two groups of women. Both groups had identical sets of top-notch resumes and work histories, but one set of resumes included experience with a parent–teacher organization, which could suggest that the women were mothers. The study showed that the women who were perceived to be "moms" were viewed as less competent and committed to work; judged more harshly for lateness; and were offered $11,000 less in starting salary than the "non-moms" (Correll, Benard, & Paik, 2007). Issues such as these mean that not only will women's wages be less than men's over the course of their work lives, but the amount received in Social Security and other pensions will be less because they earned less and contributed fewer tax and other dollars to these sources. They will also have earned less money to invest in savings and other sources that could generate interest and wealth on which they could rely in older age.

While women are making advances into male-dominated professions and more males are moving into predominantly female-dominated professions, the wage gap persists. For example, women still make up 90 percent of the nursing profession where the average salary is $52,572. Men now make up the other 10 percent of the nursing workforce, but their average pay is $60,736. More women are becoming truck drivers, but their median weekly income is $542.00 compared to $709.00 for men (U.S. Bureau of Labor Statistics, 2009).

Many people argue that unequal pay is rooted in institutional sexism; that is, opportunities for high-paying jobs and positions of power still elude women. And because few women are in these positions, policy and other changes cannot be initiated that will open more opportunities for women. Many critics posit that laws and policies do not go far enough to guard against discrimination. For example, the **Civil Rights Act of 1964** required desegregation of public facilities, prohibited discrimination in hiring practices for institutions receiving federal dollars, and established the Equal Employment Opportunity Commission. Laws related to this Act passed afterwards, such as the Equal Employment Opportunity Act of 1972, and others, have not addressed the wage gap between men and women nor do they address inequities that this gap creates for women across the life span.

To alleviate gender-based wage disparities, many feminist advocates have fought for **comparable worth** legislation, in which compensation is based on the calculated value of the work rather than on the sex of the worker. For instance, comparable worth specifies that uncompensated work such as preparing meals, rearing children, and attending to housework should be paid just like comparable jobs that are compensated (for example, taxi services, food preparation, and child care services). However, efforts to pass such legislation have failed, primarily because of opposition by business and prevailing values in society that place emphasis on work outside of the home (Gibelman, 2003).

Sources and Theories of Sexism   Feminists argue that sexism persists in U.S. society because many women, particularly young women, generally lack power and public leadership positions in most venues. Women continue to be perceived as less competent than men, particularly where leadership is concerned, so women are viewed as less worthy and legitimate to hold such positions than men. Further, when women do hold positions of power, those positions tend to be devalued. Or if it is impossible to deny the importance of the position, a woman's success in that position is seen as luck or caused by outside forces, such as the help of colleagues or special treatment. Finally, if it is impossible to deny the competence of the woman in the position, then she tends to be hated for her ability and for violating gender stereotypes and norms. These women tend to be labeled "bitches," "selfish," and "bitter." Interestingly, this phenomenon tends to transcend cultural boundaries (Carli & Eagly, 2001).

Many feminists argue that the media tend to perpetuate sexism and negative stereotypes about women. They accuse fashion magazines, most of which are targeted to young women, of supporting the notion that women can be successful as long as they maintain traditional gender expectations. For example, ads that target professional women show them as being competent but still being dressed in feminine clothing and maintaining their "soft" side. Presumably, this makes women less threatening and ensures that they conform to expected gender norms. Some argue that the negative images of women that are portrayed in the media only aggravate the situation; these images reinforce ideas about the roles, norms, and abilities of women (Fouts & Burggraf, 2000).We will consider the role of the media in greater detail in the next section, "Sexual Harassment."

Gender norms and stereotypes also affect the way women are evaluated in their jobs, which is yet another way in which women are kept from positions of power, where changes can be made. Some scholars argue that being a woman and competent in the workplace may actually hinder women and keep them from advancing in their occupations. Skillful management is often described in masculine terms;

thus, many administrators and other workers presume that women do not have the inherent skills needed to practice skillful management. Even when a woman's work is identical to that of a man's, hers is viewed as inferior. For example, if women work in teams, they are less likely to get credit for good work; whereas men in the same teams will have success credited to their own abilities.

Another way of looking at women's success is to attribute it to affirmative action, which to some people means that standards of good work have been lowered (Heilman, 2001). Young women are especially susceptible to these stereotypes and prejudices because of their age. They could not possibly be skilled because they are too young and naïve. They are more likely than men to have their ideas and skills disregarded and their success attributed to luck. Moreover, any advancements they make in their careers are likely to be attributed to their looks, sexuality, or reliance on a male colleague.

Even the social work profession is guilty of perpetuating sexism. A content analysis conducted on the *Journal of Social Work Education* found sexist language and a general lack of attention to gender issues in its publications (Grise-Owens, 2002). The author of this study posits that it is exactly this type of inattention to gender issues that helps to maintain institutional sexism.

Theories of racism, prejudice, and oppression discussed in Chapter 5 can help to understand the causes and effects of sexism. Processes that take place through history and socialization, for example, can explain how sexism is perpetuated as well as why it can be so difficult to eradicate. Feminist theory also provides a lens through which to view sexism, as you have seen throughout this section. From this perspective, sexism is maintained through structures of patriarchy and power that invalidate women's attempts to gain power and maintain gendered norms and stereotypes that undermine the value of women's work.

According to the *Code of Ethics* (NASW, approved 1996, revised 2008), social workers have an ethical responsibility to challenge discrimination and social injustices, such as those caused by sexism. Because of these charges, social workers need to take the lead in advocating for laws and policies that work toward ending sexism. Social workers can educate lawmakers and policy-makers about the sources and effects of sexism as well as ways in which to design laws and policies to help end it. Further, the ways in which social workers conduct practice and scholarship must be a model for others. Ensuring that sexism does not take place in agencies, classrooms, and research is one avenue through which social workers can help to eradicate sexism.

Though Gudrun's case scenario does not give any information regarding issues of sexism, she could have problems related to sexism as she attempts to establish and maintain employment. Potential employers may have stereotypical expectations about Gudrun's capabilities based on her gender, which may decrease her chances of getting fair treatment in her job. Specifically, an employer could assume that because she is a woman, she is not capable of performing well at her job or that she does not possess the skills needed to advance in the workplace. If Gudrun's mental health issues or lack of job skills in a particular area keep her from performing as needed, her performance problems may be blamed on her gender, which may impede her ability to get the help she needs to improve her performance. Thus, she may be at a disadvantage with regard to ensuring that proper supports are in place as she attempts to secure employment. You can assist Gudrun in this area by helping her advocate for herself to secure needed resources and to ensure that her employers are aware and supportive of her needs and situation.

Sexual Harassment

As discussed in the previous section, sexism is still pervasive in U.S. society, and one way it is played out is through sexual harassment in the workplace and other venues. Young adults entering the workforce may experience or recognize harassment for the first time; they may also become aware of how the media and other social forces reinforce sexist attitudes that lead to harassment.

Sexual Harassment and Popular Culture   Many feminists argue that society continues to condone sexual harassment and that this support of sexist attitudes is reflected in popular culture. For instance, the media tend to reinforce sexist attitudes through advertisements and situation comedies that make light of degrading comments and circumstances. In essence, the media trivialize the devaluing of women. Feminists posit that popular culture is actually representing an underlying hostility toward women, especially as women make advances in gaining equal rights (Montemurro, 2003).

One study that analyzed sexual harassment content in television programming found that harassment was present in 84 percent of the programs studied. Generally, these programs presented sexual content in a joking manner and trivialized potentially degrading and serious situations (Grauerholz & King, 1997). For example, office humor that objectifies women is still prevalent on many sitcoms. The authors of this study concluded that these programs perpetuated the notion that sexual harassment was not a serious issue; rather, it is actually something to joke about.

Another study by DeSouza and Fansler (2003) found widely reported incidents of sexual harassment on college campuses. Results indicated that approximately 33 percent of the 158 college students sampled had sexually harassed a professor. Over half of the 209 professors sampled reported having been harassed by students. Interestingly, men and women reported similar rates of harassment, but women reported more negative psychological ramifications of that harassment than did men. Given the high rate of sexual harassment perpetrated by college students in this study, it seems that many young adults may not fully understand what sexual harassment is or the effects that it can have on others. By targeting young adults, social workers can help to educate them on the subject to prevent this problem from occurring in other venues as these young adults move into the workforce and other situations where they can perpetuate harassment.

Strategies to Prevent Sexual Harassment Various federal policies and laws make it unlawful for employers to discriminate against individuals based on sex, and harassment is included as a form of discrimination. However, these policies and laws are troublesome because concepts such as discrimination and harassment are difficult to define. Although most people would agree that acts such as rape are not tolerable, disagreement abounds about whether behaviors such as joking, touching, compliments, and other "friendly" comments and gestures are appropriate or whether they constitute harassment. Although definitions can be formed through lawsuits and court cases, some social workers agree that prevention is a better approach to warding off harassment than responding only after harassment has occurred. Modeling respect, leadership, and good communication as well as providing education and a safe work environment can help prevent harassment (American Academy of Pediatrics, 2000). Social workers are in positions in which they can provide such modeling and leadership and help to shape definitions and boundaries of harassing behavior.

Another reason why prevention can be more effective than reacting to complaints is that persons who are victims of harassment are often afraid to come forward when they have suffered harassment. They are often blamed for the harassment when they come forth, or they are not believed when they make a complaint, especially if they wait before making a complaint. These individuals' motives may be questioned, particularly if they are young women. Some people may wonder what the woman has to gain from bringing attention to a situation of harassment (for example, money or promotion), or they may accuse her of being too sensitive or of being a troublemaker (Balogh, Kite, Pickel, Canel, & Schroeder, 2003). Young women are especially vulnerable to these types of reactions because they may be viewed as having "asked for" the harassment through dress or behavior.

Both the conflict and the feminist perspectives are useful in conceptualizing harassment and reasons why it occurs. For instance, these perspectives might view harassment as a strategy to perpetuate men's power. Harassment can intimidate victims, and, as noted, many victims hesitate to report the behavior. Thus, the perpetrator of the harassment remains in power through using the behavior to keep the victim in a vulnerable position. If the person being harassed is a woman and she complains, she is likely to be viewed as a troublemaker, which will likely hurt her chances for advancement and keep her from positions of power from which she can challenge the behavior of others.

Social learning theory also provides a lens through which to view sexual harassment. Jokes, comments, and harassing behaviors portrayed by the media and other people in a child's environment are ways in which a child learns what is valued by society. Children who are exposed to sexual harassment, and who see that this behavior is often positively reinforced, learn that this type of behavior is acceptable. Once these children reach young adulthood, they are in positions where their learned behaviors of harassment can be acted out in ways that can harm others. For example, young adults may harass their co-workers or their college professors, as mentioned in the earlier study.

Depending on the particular perspective from which social workers conceptualize sexual harassment, they can do much to help prevent and intervene with problems surrounding it. As mentioned previously, social workers can provide education and a safe environment for open communication when problems arise. From the conflict and feminist perspectives, social workers can strive to alter the power structure in various institutions to help change the environment. Women need to be in positions of power to assist in developing policies and laws that will combat sexual harassment. From the social learning perspective, social workers can act as models for clients and others to demonstrate appropriate ways to interact and treat others.

Civil Rights Laws and Affirmative Action

As young adults move into employment, education, and other realms, discrimination may become a salient issue. For some young adults, discrimination may prevent them from attending their preferred college or from receiving a job promotion. For other young adults, they may be in decision-making positions where they can discriminate against others. In this section, we look at some of the laws and policies in place to help avoid discriminatory actions.

Civil rights laws of the 1960s were developed and enacted to help ensure that everyone was assured the basic rights stated in the U.S. Constitution. **Affirmative action** efforts stem from civil rights laws and require that employers and other institutions actively recruit women and other minority group members (Gibelman, 2000).

The Affirmative Action Debate   Affirmative action is one area that brings out many strong opinions. Most people in the United States believe in equality, but only for the "worthy." This line of thinking supports the notion that affirmative action serves only to promote the well-being of those who are not qualified or willing to work, which makes them "unworthy." Others think that inequality is a result of years of injustice and discrimination, and while laws can help to ensure some level of equality, individuals are responsible for changing society. Many feel that policies like affirmative action make matters worse by disempowering the minority groups they are intended to help and even leading to **reverse discrimination**—a condition in which whites are discriminated against in favor of less qualified or deserving minorities. This line of thinking posits that giving special privileges to minority groups through policies like affirmative action only makes those in the majority hostile toward minority group members and does not allow minority group members to "make it on their own" or to demonstrate their inherent worth and capability (Gibelman, 2000).

Generally, many differing opinions on affirmative action fuel heated debates on whether to preserve, reform, or dismantle the policy. On one end of the continuum is liberal individualism, which posits that individuals are responsible for their behavior, so they do not need any special protections from the government to ensure that their rights are protected or that they will not become victims of discrimination. This point of view takes the stance that problems stem from the individual, not necessarily from systematic errors rooted in society. Thus, those who take this stance would not view institutional sexism or racism as problems; rather, they likely would view these problems as a result of individual behavior. Therefore, affirmative action policies go too far because they actively seek to recruit people from minority groups, seemingly regardless of their capabilities and at the expense of individuals who might be more qualified (Pierce, 2003). From this viewpoint comes the argument that affirmative action is simply a form of reverse discrimination.

Conversely, some people argue that because of institutionalized discrimination, we need more minority representation in positions of power to "equal out the playing field." This viewpoint takes the stance that people from minority groups are not necessarily less qualified than whites, but that minority individuals often have difficulty getting good positions because they lack the power and connections that whites have. Thus, affirmative action policies ensure that people from minority groups can compete for good jobs by taking power and connections out of the hiring process. Further, this point of view posits that society benefits from minority representation in business, education, and other settings because it ensures diversity and exposes others to different cultures and worldviews.

This debate is frequently played out in various private and public venues. For example, the U.S. Supreme Court upheld the University of Michigan Law School's admission policy, which uses race as an admission variable (Lancet, 2003). Indeed, much of the data available on the issue suggests that reverse discrimination has not occurred; that is, there is no evidence to suggest that any one group is at a disadvantage because of affirmative action policies (Kinsley, 1995). Rather, there is evidence that discrimination remains a problem in many businesses and social institutions, and methods to eradicate it, such as affirmative action, are still needed. For example, one study found that white men had an advantage over black men and women in areas such as job training, and over black women in education (Caputo, 2002).

Theoretical Bases of Affirmative Action   Many of the arguments to dismantle affirmative action can be explained by theories of discrimination discussed in Chapter 5. Explanations that include history, frustration-aggression, and competition and exploitation all provide reasons why some people may be hostile toward affirmative action policies. For example, when a member of a minority group is hired for a job instead of a white applicant, it is easy for the white person to complain that affirmative action was the reason why the minority applicant got the job. Thus, the minority person becomes the scapegoat for the frustration that the white person feels for not being hired. Blaming affirmative action may be preferable to the person's acknowledging that she or he was not as qualified as the person who got the job, or perhaps to blaming the economy for not supporting enough jobs to employ everyone.

Social justice theories also offer frameworks from which to view policies like affirmative action. Distributive justice, as discussed in Chapter 5, is concerned with ensuring that everyone in society has equal rights and resources—everyone is deserving. From this perspective, then, affirmative action could be considered an appropriate response to institutional discrimination. On the other hand, this perspective could also be used to argue that affirmative action is not fair because it gives special consideration to some members in society. A libertarian perspective on justice would support the idea of dismantling affirmative action, because this approach posits that government should have a very limited role in the lives of individuals. Thus, from this perspective, affirmative action gives too much power to the government to dictate how businesses and other institutions operate. The utilitarian approach would help to explain the usefulness of affirmative action by arguing that it supports the good of society, even at the expense of a few who may suffer because of preferential treatment of others.

Affirmative Action and Social Work   As with other issues and problems, social workers need to be leaders in the debates over and applications of affirmative action. Historically, the social work profession has not been active in the debates over whether affirmative action works as intended or whether it should remain as a policy. Social work has much to contribute with regard to research and education on discrimination and the strengths and limitations to interventions, such as affirmative action, to eradicate it. Thus, social workers need to remain informed about the debates for and against affirmative action and play an active role in any reformations of the policy that may take place, particularly since fighting dis- crimination is a basic tenet of the *Code of Ethics* and this policy can have dramatic effects on clients. Social workers can be especially effective by applying social planning and policy development theory and knowledge to guide reform and by addressing institutional racism (Gibelman, 2000).

In Gudrun's situation, because of potential sexism, she could benefit from pol- icies like affirmative action. Because she is a member of a minority group, she could take advantage of affirmative action policies as she looks for work. Any barriers that she may face due to her gender would be related to discrimination in general, and you could rely on specific policies such as affirmative action to help advocate for Gudrun's rights.

Higher Education

After graduating from high school, many young adults struggle with the decision of whether to go to college or to work. Some young adults cannot afford to go to college, while others are not aware of their choices because of, among other things, poor guidance in high school from counselors or parents. This is particularly true for schools in low-income areas that have few resources. Students are often not well informed about their options, and they have fewer opportunities to prepare for college admission exams like the SATs than students from wealthier school districts (Hollenshead & Miller, 2001). Moreover, these students often have few role models who encourage or expect them to continue with their education. For students who are the first generation to pursue higher education, the process of getting to college and actually graduating can be difficult.

Further, young adults who come from low-income households often have many disadvantages before they ever graduate from high school. They usually receive a less than adequate high school education, which makes them less competitive in the college admission process. They often do not have the life experiences, such as travel and volunteer experiences, that can make their applications look positive. In addition, they frequently lack the financial or social support to pursue higher education, and they often do not understand how to research schools to choose one that will meet their needs and goals. Compounding these problems, parents in low-income situations tend to be less optimistic about their children's chances of succeeding in college because they either did not go to college themselves or they were not successful because they faced their own barriers. Consequently, these parents are not likely to encourage their children to pursue higher education (Crosnoe, Mistry, & Elder, 2002).

Social learning theory is useful in explaining this phenomenon. If parents have low self-efficacy because of their lack of experience with higher education, they are unlikely to act as positive role models for their children. These young adults are also not likely to be socialized around individuals who have attended college, and they are unlikely to be reared in an environment that values higher education.

The issue of self-efficacy can be an important one for women who are pursuing higher education. Historically, women have been underrepresented in colleges and universities. However, that trend has changed significantly. Indeed, some people argue that men are now at risk for becoming underrepresented among college graduates, at least at the bachelor's level. Currently, women are outperforming men in high school and are entering colleges and universities in larger numbers than men (Conlin, 2003).

Others argue that although women are more likely to enroll in college than men, men's overall enrollment patterns have increased over the years, particularly among men in high-income brackets. Moreover, men still outnumber women in earning professional degrees and PhDs, especially in male-dominated fields such as engineering and physical sciences. Men also outnumber women in faculty and educational administrative positions in colleges and universities, particularly in more prestigious institutions (Hollenshead & Miller, 2001). These patterns have economic and other ramifications on the power and status of women, as discussed earlier in the chapter.

Social workers can be of great support to those students who may want to go to college but who face multiple barriers in achieving their goals. Social workers can also assist young adults who are in college but are struggling with academic or other problems. For example, as Gudrun's social worker, you may want to suggest that she pursue a college degree to help increase her employment skills. If she is dealing with a mental illness, she may fare better enrolling in school to develop skills that will help her obtain and maintain steady employment.

CONCLUSION

Young adulthood is a time of great change. Many individuals undergo changing roles, achieve independence, and embark on new experiences. Although there are no definitive events in Western culture that mark the movement from adolescence to young adulthood, many observers would consider actions such as establishing intimate relationships, going off to college, taking a job, and moving away from home sure signs that the individual has reached this stage in life. For many individuals, young adulthood and the changes associated with it are exciting; however, these changes can also cause stress, confusion, and ambivalence. And because many individuals experience increasing responsibility during this time of life, their problems are more likely to interfere with their functioning and well-being than when they were younger. Often, these problems bring young adults to the attention of social workers.

Social workers may work with young adults in many capacities to assist in increasing independence, self-assurance, decision-making capacities, and functioning as responsible adults. Whether it is in an educational, mental health, workplace, or other setting, social workers can help not only in solving problems that may occur for some young adults, but also in preventing problems that may develop as they move into middle and later adulthood.

MAIN POINTS

- Physical and cognitive growth begins to stabilize during young adulthood, while continued development occurs emotionally, intellectually, and interpersonally.

- Mental illness and disability can arise at any time in the life span, with symptoms affecting well-being and functioning. Social workers frequently use the medical model to guide assessment and intervention in these cases, but they can also draw on systems and ecological theories and consider factors on the micro, mezzo, and macro levels.

- Spirituality and religious participation, for some young adults, are a source of stability, while for others, these aspects of their lives become less important. Fowler's theory of faith development consists of seven stages that describe how people develop faith and meaning in their lives.

- Increasingly, young adults are choosing lifestyles that include cohabiting, delaying marriage, and remaining single. However, for some individuals, living with a partner, regardless of the arrangements, also brings with it issues of domestic violence. Social workers can use the lenses of social learning, family systems, and feminist theories to help understand domestic violence and intervene effectively with clients.

- Young adults—especially women—are likely to face sexism and sexual harassment as they enter the workforce, begin college, and take on other new roles. Women do not receive equal pay for equal work, and they are frequently discriminated against on the job; these are issues with which social workers must contend.

- Some think that affirmative action does nothing but create reverse discrimination, while others think that it is needed to help eradicate institutional discrimination. Social workers need to be informed about these debates and play an active role in policy-making.

- Choosing whether or not to attend college can be a struggle for some young adults; still others do not have the opportunity to pursue a college education because of financial and other constraints. Social workers can use social learning theory to understand clients' situations and help them overcome barriers to achieving their goals—whether they involve getting into the college of their choice or succeeding in school.

EXERCISES

1. Using the Sanchez Family interactive case (go to www.routledgesw.com/cases), review the major issues involving the Sanchez family, focusing on Vicki and Gloria. After giving this information thorough review, answer the following questions:
   a. Given our discussion in this chapter, what issues might be pertinent in working with Vicki and Gloria? Are there other issues not discussed in this chapter that might be relevant in working with these two family members?

b. Imagine that you are a social worker assigned to work with Vicki and her symptoms of autism. Using the case study on the Sanchez family, conduct an assessment for Vicki using ecological theory to guide it. What issues on different levels might impact Vicki and her functioning? What interventions might be warranted based on this assessment?

c. Using the guidelines stated above, conduct an assessment with Gloria and her domestic violence situation. Articulate what your intervention(s) would look like based on your assessment.

d. What strengths and limitations can you see in using ecological theory in your work with these family members? Are there any ethical dilemmas that you might need to work through?

2. Review the Riverton interactive case (go to www.routledgesw.com/cases), paying particular attention to Mary Stark and John Washington. Then answer the following questions:

a. What issues discussed in this chapter might apply to the individual situations of Mary and John?

b. Keeping in mind the issues you picked above, what theoretical perspective(s) might you choose to work with Mary and John?

c. In what ways might the issues presented in this chapter apply to the community as a whole?

CHAPTER 11

Development in Middle Adulthood

Carmen is a 48-year-old married Caucasian woman with two children who are both in their early 20s and live near Carmen and her husband. This is Carmen's second marriage, and it has lasted 10 years. Carmen's first husband, the father of her children, has had no contact with her or her children since the children were very young.

Carmen and her husband own a small business and spend long hours working to keep it successful. Since her children were very young, they have exhibited numerous behavioral problems, and recently her oldest son was arrested for assault. Carmen admits that the hours she puts into the business as well as her children's problems cause her a great deal of stress. She is moody, has frequent migraine headaches, and spends most of her free time drinking or sleeping. Carmen has smoked most of her life and doesn't exercise. She tends to have a negative outlook on life and has few friends or positive relationships with family members. Recently, Carmen consulted a social worker to help her manage stress, and she is complaining of moodiness and restless sleep.

MIDDLE ADULTHOOD CAN BE A VERY ENJOYABLE, SATISFYING time for many people. By the time they enter their 40s, many people have successfully moved through the challenges of early adulthood and have achieved various educational, vocational, and interpersonal goals. Through their 60s, most people maintain a relatively stable period of productiveness.

Nevertheless, for others, middle adulthood can be a time of great stress resulting from problems such as illness, divorce, and employment difficulties. In the following sections we will look at some of the issues relevant to middle adulthood and ways in which social workers might assist people in improving their quality of life.

DEVELOPMENTAL MILESTONES IN MIDDLE AGE

Middle adulthood, in general, can be a time when people enjoy all of the hard work their bodies have put into physical development through puberty and young adulthood. Although middle age is a time when physical aspects such as energy, eyesight, hearing, and metabolism begin to decline, many people usually do not notice a marked difference from when they were younger. Many physical issues that may arise during middle age can be treated, and even prevented, so this becomes a time when people need to get regular checkups and pay attention to their lifestyles. We will consider some of the physical problems associated with middle age in a later section. For an overview of the developmental milestones in middle age, see Table 11.1.

Physical and Cognitive Developments in Middle Adulthood

Probably one of the most troublesome changes that occurs with middle age, at least in U.S. culture, involves the person's physical appearance. Though for many people these changes are gradual, for others, depending on their lifestyles and genetic makeup, the changes can be rapid and dramatic. For example, many men and women begin to see small wrinkles appear on their faces, they may get more and more gray hairs, and their hair may begin to thin. Many men lose their hair and get a "tire" around their middle, while women may gain weight around their hips and be troubled by sagging breasts. Because of these changes, some people in middle age opt for plastic surgery to retain their youthful appearances.

Most women (and many men) in the United States would agree that there is a double standard with regard to aging. Specifically, women argue that they are

PHYSICAL	COGNITIVE	TABLE 11.1
• Some declines in metabolism, energy level, eyesight, hearing, muscle tone.	• Some declines in memory, reaction time if not cognitively active.	*Developmental Milestones in Middle Adulthood*
• Increase in appearance of wrinkles, gray hair, thinning hair.	• Increases in cognitive performance can occur because new information is linked with past experiences.	
• Increased weight gain.	• Increased problem-solving skills.	
• Increased prevalence of chronic illnesses such as cancer, diabetes, and heart disease.	• Increased creativity.	
• Women undergo menopause, and men may experience a male climacteric.		
• Problems in sexual functioning may occur.		

treated more negatively than men when it comes to the consequences of aging. For example, men's graying hair and wrinkles are considered "distinguished," while the same processes in women put them "over the hill." Older men are viewed as more attractive and desirable than older women, a perception that can affect women in many realms, including the workplace. Hollywood and the media are especially guilty of perpetuating these attitudes. Consider, for example, how many aging actors such as Jack Nicholson and Sean Connery are paired with young women in movies and real life. In contrast, seeing older women in major roles in the movies is unusual, let alone seeing them romantically paired with younger or even older men. In reality, some older women do have younger men as partners, but this arrangement is not as common as seeing older men with younger women.

In contrast to their physical appearance, cognitive capacities of most healthy, intellectually active middle-aged adults do not show much decline. When people do not use their intellectual skills or when they have biological problems that cause cognitive decline, they can develop problems such as memory loss and slowed thinking processes (Papalia, Olds, & Feldman, 2003). Otherwise, middle-aged people can match—and often exceed—the cognitive abilities of younger people.

For example, people who engage in mental activity through work, continued education, or reading show increases in mental capacities such as vocabulary. Moreover, people in middle age tend to be at their best creatively, and they are better at integrating new knowledge with what they already know because of their rich experiences. Put simply, people in middle adulthood have lived longer than younger adults, so they have more experiences from which to draw. Because of this experience, middle-aged adults tend to be better problem solvers than young adults. People in middle age also tend to be better at reflecting on information and judging it for its value and worth both personally and practically (Papalia et al., 2003).

Obviously, many of the physical changes described earlier can be explained through the medical model. Biological explanations abound that attempt to describe processes that slow us down as we age. Certainly, having a working knowledge of the physical problems that can develop as a person ages is useful in working with clients.

Other theories, such as Erikson's theory on psychosocial development and various sociological and feminist theories, can help social workers make sense of the psychological and social ramifications of physical aging. For example, according to Erikson, middle adulthood is a time when people are investing in their work, families, and community. This idea fits well when you consider that many middle-aged adults are performing well creatively and intellectually; they have much to contribute to different realms of their lives. However, if people have stopped learning or have a physical problem that keeps them from engaging in work or relationships, they may feel stagnant or be less productive than they would like. Using this theory, social workers can help middle-aged clients to identify ways in which they may not feel fulfilled and can then concentrate their efforts on helping clients move toward productive, more meaningful lives.

Similarly, feminist and various sociological theories may help social workers understand how problems such as the double standard in aging occur and how they may impact the lives of middle-aged women and men. For example, feminists and conflict theorists might argue that patriarchal society perpetuates this type of discrimination because men have power over media and other sources that put out messages about what is attractive and desirable. Social workers relying on these perspectives to inform their work with clients would need to find ways to empower clients and change the social structure that invalidates processes of aging.

Levinson's Theory of Adult Development

Although Erikson and others offer insights into challenges that take place across the life span, including middle age, psychologist Daniel Levinson offers a more detailed approach to development, with emphasis on middle and late adulthood. Levinson proposed a theory of adult development that is built around the idea of **life structures**, or patterns of behavior that in combination with the environment, are shaping forces in people's lives at any given time. Life structures consist of events, people, culture, religion, and other aspects of life that people find important. As people move through life, these life structures may shift and adjust as people gain new experiences and reevaluate what is important to them (Levinson, 1978). Box 11.1 displays the stages in Levinson's theory.

Within each stage, people must master various developmental tasks. For instance, as people move into the entry life structure for adulthood, they must deal with the tasks of establishing an adult identity. They face decisions about work, education, relationships, and independence. By the time they reach the transition into their early 30s, these decisions should be made and serve as the foundation for

---

EARLY ADULT TRANSITION (17 TO 22 YEARS)

Entry life structure for early adulthood (22 to 28 years)

Age 30 transition (28 to 33 years)

Culminating life structure for early adulthood (33 to 40 years)

MIDDLE ADULT TRANSITION (40 TO 45 YEARS)

Entry life structure for middle adulthood (45 to 50 years)

Age 50 transition (50 to 55 years)

Culminating life structure for middle adulthood (55 to 60 years)

LATE ADULT TRANSITION (60 TO 65 YEARS)

Era of late adulthood (60+)

Source: Adapted from Levinson, 1978.

BOX 11.1

Levinson's Theory of Adult Development

an adult identity. The culminating life structure for early adulthood is a time when people determine their goals for adulthood. This could include whether to start a family and what type of a career to pursue. By the middle adult transition, people have established themselves in their families and careers (or they have achieved some success with whatever goals they set in their 30s). During this transition, people question what lies ahead for them in middle adulthood.

The life structures and transitions that take place during the 40s and 50s consist of questioning what it means to grow old, assessing whether choices made previously are satisfying, and making changes that will lead to greater satisfaction. These changes might include divorcing, remarrying, changing careers, or even starting a new family. The late adult transition and era of late adulthood are times when people reflect on their lives and settle into old age and all that it entails based on personal and societal expectations.

One major criticism of Levinson's theory is that its tenets were developed to describe the life course of men. Levinson developed this theory by observing 40 men in prestigious occupations. Thus, some critics contend that his theory cannot be generalized to women or to other culturally and economically diverse populations. However, Levinson has recently developed a similar theory for women (Levinson & Levinson, 1996), and other behavioral scientists have developed theories that address limitations to Levinson's theory.

Turning to Carmen's situation, while her moodiness may have physical causes that you can assess, you may also want to explore how aging has affected Carmen psychologically. Perhaps some of the characteristics described in the opening scenario—for example, moodiness and a negative outlook on life—may be associated to some degree with various changes brought on by aging. Understanding the powerful interplay between aging and women's status in society is helpful in working with female clients, and it might be worth your time to assess Carmen's attitudes and feelings about aging-related physical changes and how they might impact her continued development.

You could apply Levinson's theory to Carmen's case by assessing which stage she is in and which tasks she should be mastering. Based on her age, she should be in the entry life structure for middle adulthood. Therefore, she may be reflecting on her life and the choices she has made thus far regarding her career, education, and family. If she believes that she has made some poor choices or has not achieved the goals she set in young adulthood, she may be feeling regret or despair. In turn, these feelings could be manifesting themselves through symptoms of stress, depression, fatigue, and heavy drinking. You could help Carmen by exploring the areas of her life with which she feels disappointment or regret and helping her to contemplate what she would like to do differently in future stages to achieve greater satisfaction as she ages.

THE INDIVIDUAL IN MIDDLE ADULTHOOD

As just discussed, physical changes in middle adulthood are not necessarily as bad as U.S. society makes them out to be. Although there are some declines in certain areas and people tend to begin to show outward signs of aging, the rate and extent to which people show signs of aging vary a great deal from person to person. Further, not everyone responds to these changes in the same way, and not everyone perceives these changes as negative.

This section deals with specific issues on an individual level that tend to occur in middle age: menopause, the male climacteric, the midlife crisis, and chronic illness and disease. As with the physical changes discussed earlier, these issues do not affect all middle-aged adults. Nevertheless, social workers need to have basic knowledge of these areas and understand how they create problems for some people.

Menopause

For many women, menopause can be a time of much transition. Some women say that they welcome the changes that menopause brings, while others view menopause as a negative sign that they are aging. These disparate views underscore the fact that no two women react or adjust to menopause in quite the same way.

Menopause is the cessation of a woman's menstrual cycle, and the timing of its onset as well as its course vary greatly among women. The average age of onset of menopause is approximately age 51, but it can begin in one's early 30s or as late as the 60s. The average course of menopause is approximately two to five years, during which time women's bodies go through many physiological changes (North American Menopause Society, 2006).

Menopause begins when a woman's periods start to become irregular. Patterns of irregularity include skipped periods, decreased blood flow, and the cessation of periods. During this time, the ovaries stop secreting eggs, levels of estrogen and progesterone drop, the fallopian tubes become shorter and smaller, the uterus becomes smaller and harder, and the vagina becomes shorter and less elastic. Women may also experience decreased lubrication of the vagina, making intercourse uncomfortable or painful. Other symptoms that some women experience include headaches, insomnia, hot flashes, thinning hair, weight gain, skin changes, and growth of hair in unwanted places, including increased facial hair (North American Menopause Society, 2006).

Hormone replacement therapy (HRT) is one option for women to help ease the symptoms of menopause and prevent problems that can be brought on by menopause. This therapy helps to increase declining levels of reproductive hormones in a woman's body. Seen from the medical model, HRT is a way to replace the hormones that women lose through the process of menopause and to alleviate some of its symptoms and negative effects—including bone loss, hot flashes, and sleep problems—that women may experience (North American Menopause Society,

2006; Sommer, 2001). However, recent evidence suggests that HRT may actually increase the risk of stroke, breast cancer, and heart disease for some women, particulary with long-term use. Indeed, recent declines in breast cancer in the U.S. have been linked to decreases in women's use of HRT, which began after research made the link between breast cancer and HRT (Ravdin et al., 2007). The National Institutes of Health and other health experts recommend that women who are considering HRT talk with their health providers to determine whether the benefits of HRT outweigh the risks in their particular situations (North American Menopause Society, 2006; Stephens, Budge, & Carryer, 2002).

Reactions to Menopause: The Psychological Dimension   Psychological reactions to menopause vary significantly among women, depending on their personalities, coping skills, support systems, and general attitudes about life and aging. Some women welcome the changes that occur with menopause: They value their new-found freedom from the hassle and expense of regular periods, and they no longer have to worry about becoming pregnant. Conversely, other women experience anxiety, depression, and lowered self-esteem because they identify menopause with a loss of fertility and attractiveness. Research indicates that women who are well adjusted emotionally before menopause tend to be well adjusted during and after menopause. Specifically, these women are unlikely to experience any negative psychological reactions to menopause (Strong, DeVault, Sayad, & Yarber, 2002).

One study using data from 1,572 women indicated that women tend to place as much importance on the sociocultural aspects of menopause as they do on its health implications (Ballard, Kuh, & Wadsworth, 2001). Specifically, many respondents discussed menopause and its effects in relation to their family and work relationships. With increasing life expectancies and volatile economic circumstances, many women find that they want or need to work longer to care for aging parents and children who are young adults and still living at home. Thus, many women viewed menopause as a developmental milestone, which indicated to them that many possibilities in family and work life lay ahead. In other words, menopause may be a time when a woman is able to reevaluate her life choices and to perceive these choices as new opportunities rather than negative life events. Moreover, because more women have attained higher educational levels than in the past, they have more career and other options to consider as they make a transition into a new chapter of their lives (Ballard et al., 2001).

Reactions to Menopause: The Cultural Dimension   Reactions to menopause also have a cultural component. For example, U.S. culture, which values youth, might view menopause negatively, identifying it with aging, the loss of vitality and attractiveness, and the end of the reproductive years. From this perspective, the symptoms are something that need to be "cured." However, other cultures perceive menopause as a natural progression of lifelong development or even as a rite of passage. Cultures that value the elderly, for example, define menopause as a hallmark or milestone in the life course (Starck, 1993).

In one study on rural African American women's perceptions of menopause, religion and internal strength were important constructs associated with dealing with symptoms. These women turned to prayer and other religious supports to increase their sense of self-efficacy during the onset of menopause, and they were unlikely to use physicians or therapies such as HRT. Indeed, these women were much more likely than white women to view menopause as a natural course of life. These women viewed symptoms as something to be mastered much as they mastered other events and circumstances in their lives such as poverty and oppression (Nixon, Mansfield, Kittell, & Faulkner, 2001).

In line with feminist and similar theories, some theorists speculate that Western culture views menopause negatively because we have "medicalized" or "pathologized" it. That is, we define menopause as a set of symptoms that can be cured or at least reduced. In addition, because we consider reproduction to be a primary function of women, we interpret menopause to mean that women's bodies are ceasing to perform their biological "duties." Thus, much of the psychological stress that many women feel as they go through menopause might arise from the negative messages they receive about their changing roles. Conversely, other experts argue that at least some of the psychological stress that women encounter during this time can be attributed to biological changes in the body rather than to social pressures (Chornesky, 1998). In sum, then, keep in mind that regardless of a person's views on the implications of menopause for a woman's psychological and emotional health, a combination of social, cultural, emotional, biological, cognitive, and psychological processes influence the outcome of menopause for women.

Carmen's Case Revisited   Given Carmen's age and the headaches and moodiness she has described, it would be worthwhile to assess whether Carmen is going through menopause. It could be that she is experiencing some physical changes that may be affecting her mood and other aspects of her well-being. You may want to spend some time talking with Carmen about her perceptions of menopause and whether she is noticing any other symptoms that might indicate that she is undergoing this process. If Carmen is concerned about experiencing menopause or feels that she would benefit from treatment, you would be able to explore Carmen's options with her and refer her to the appropriate resources. Further, because Carmen is a smoker and leads a sedentary lifestyle, she may be at risk for osteoporosis (discussed in Chapter 12) or other diseases associated with menopause. You will want to discuss with Carmen some of the health implications related to her age and lifestyle habits.

The Male Climacteric

Evidence suggests that males also experience a climacteric, or a change in life, that often corresponds with female menopause. Indeed, this change has been referred to as the "male menopause" or "andropause," though no evidence exists to suggest that it is equivalent to the physiological changes that women experience (Sommer, 2001). Thus, the term male climacteric is used to describe the male experience.

The **male climacteric** refers to the period between ages 35 and 60 when many men reevaluate their careers, familial relationships, and other major life decisions. Some men experience physical symptoms of anxiety and depression while going through this assessment process. Moreover, many men experience physical symptoms of aging such as hair loss, weight gain, diminished energy, decreased muscle strength, decreased hormone production, a slowed sexual response cycle, and sexual dysfunction, which may aggravate these feelings of anxiety and depression (Matsumoto, 2002; Vermeulen, 1994; Vermeulen & Kaufman, 1995; Wespes & Schulman, 2002). Other men, however, do not experience a need to reevaluate their situations, nor do they experience any symptoms of distress. Evidence suggests that some men may benefit from testosterone replacement therapy to alleviate symptoms associated with andropause, though as in hormone replacement therapy for women, there are side effects that need to be evaluated. Indeed, many of the long-term implications of testosterone replacement therapy are unknown (Asthana et al., 2004; Isidori, 2008; Matsumoto, 2002; Wespes & Schulman, 2002).

One way to approach the male climacteric is through Levinson's theory of adult development discussed earlier. Recall that according to Levinson (1978), men in their 40s and 50s are in their middle adult transition. During this time, men go through many changes, including reevaluating their choices in careers and relationships and taking advantage of new opportunities to help them find fulfillment. Levinson argues that although this process may be stressful for some men, reevaluation is a natural part of reaching certain milestones in a person's life that can lead to greater satisfaction and fulfillment.

Midlife Crisis

The various processes associated with the male climacteric, especially the psychological processes, also have been referred to as the *midlife crisis*. Popular opinion supports the notion that middle adulthood is a time when many people, particularly men, undergo a crisis in which they reevaluate their lives and often take drastic measures to recapture their youth. Stereotypical behaviors associated with midlife crises include buying an expensive sports car, divorcing and then finding a younger girlfriend or wife (or husband or boyfriend), engaging in risky behaviors such as skydiving, and undergoing plastic surgery.

There is some question about whether the phenomenon of a midlife crisis actually exists. It may be that many people, particularly men, do experience a great deal of anxiety about growing older, which can set into motion various behaviors that appear to be attempts at recapturing or hanging onto youth. As people reevaluate their lives—their careers, relationships, and other life choices—they may experience panic or distress about not achieving their goals as well as dissatisfaction about their current progress. Consequently, some people may develop feelings of depression or other negative responses to their life review. Further, because U.S. culture tends to place great value on youth, any loss of vitality or attractiveness may be enough to cause psychological distress in some people.

In addition, given some of the physical changes that occur in middle adulthood, some people might develop psychological symptoms in response to physiological changes. It is also possible that psychological symptoms of anxiety and depression could have physiological bases in and of themselves. For instance, menopause brings with it hormonal changes that can bring about symptoms such as hot flashes that could be mistaken by some as psychologically oriented anxiety. In other words, psychological distress that occurs in midlife could be a natural reaction to, or consequence of, physiological changes that also occur during this time.

However, at the same time, some people move through middle age without experiencing any psychological distress, regardless of the physiological or other changes that happen to them. Therefore, the notion that there is, indeed, a well-defined, specific crisis that occurs during this time is difficult to support. It is more likely that reactions to aging that can look like crises are individualistic in nature, varying in degree and frequency from person to person, depending on many factors such as coping skills, personality structures, and attitudes about life and aging.

These diverging viewpoints on midlife crises are based on various research studies and theoretical perspectives. Levinson (1978), for example, would describe various points in midlife as crises that people must experience at different phases in life to complete tasks, put closure on past events, and move on to the next phase. According to this perspective, the behaviors associated with the midlife crisis might actually reflect the "normal tasks" of adult development rather than responses to the aging process.

Conversely, other research suggests that most people do not experience crises at specific points in middle adulthood. Rather, most participants in this body of research express increased feelings of stability, security, autonomy, confidence, and competence in midlife compared to their younger years. These studies support the notion that factors such as maturity and emotional stability as well as a sense of responsibility remain relatively stable from young adulthood into later life (Brim, 1999; Keyes & Ryff, 1999; McCrae & Costa, 1990; Röcke & Lachman, 2008).

Some of Carmen's complaints, such as moodiness, drinking, headaches, and a general negative outlook on life, could be attributed to problems of adjustment to midlife changes. Of course, other issues—quite possibly a combination of factors—could be contributing to her symptoms. You need to conduct a thorough assessment of Carmen and her symptoms to better understand which forces may be influencing her well-being. Because numerous issues on the individual, familial, and social levels could be stressors for Carmen, you can help her to examine each one separately and determine which ones merit further attention.

Chronic Illness and Disease

The longer we live, the longer we are exposed to internal and external agents that can cause damage and, ultimately, disease. As discussed earlier, some of this damage is caused by genetic factors, and some of it can be caused by time, lifestyle, and other factors such as poverty, discrimination, and exposure to environmental toxins. While some factors associated with poor health are difficult to control and change, many diseases can be avoided or tempered by lifestyle habits and changes. For example, many common diseases that develop in middle age are related to inactivity or obesity. Many people decrease their level of activity as they age, which can result in weight gain that can contribute to other diseases such as diabetes and hypertension. In addition, poor diet, smoking, and overexposure to the sun or chemicals can lead to various forms of cancer. Further, various health problems and medications taken for different illnesses, such as blood pressure medication, can cause other problems such as sexual dysfunction (Westheimer & Lopater, 2004).

Some of the more common diseases that occur in middle adulthood include diabetes, arthritis, hypertension, and heart disease. Table 11.2 compares the prevalence rates for diabetes between different ethnic groups in the U.S. in 2007. As the table indicates, diabetes rates are highest for Native American/Alaska Native groups followed by certain Hispanic populations. This higher rate is likely caused by a combination of biological and social factors (American Heart Association, 2001; Mitchell, Kammerer, Reinhart, & Stern, 1994; Ramirez, 1996). Approximately 11 percent of people between the ages of 40 and 59 have diabetes, both diagnosed and undiagnosed. In 2007, there were 819,000 new cases diagnosed among people in the 40 to 59 age range, the most for any age group (National Diabetes Information Clearinghouse, 2008). Diabetes rates for both men and women also increase as age increases. This trend also occurs with other common diseases such as heart disease and hypertension. For example, the risk of developing heart disease after age 40 is almost 50 percent for men and 32 percent for women and it accounts for more than 50 percent of all heart problems for people under age 75. After suffering a heart attack, the chances of further illness and death for people aged 40 to 69 are 8 percent for White men, 12 percent for White women, 14 percent for Black men, and 11 percent for Black women. With regard to hypertension, prevalence rates for men go from 13.4 percent between ages 20 and 34 to 64.1 percent after age 75. For women, rates go from 6.2 percent to 76.4 for the same age categories (American Heart Association, 2009).

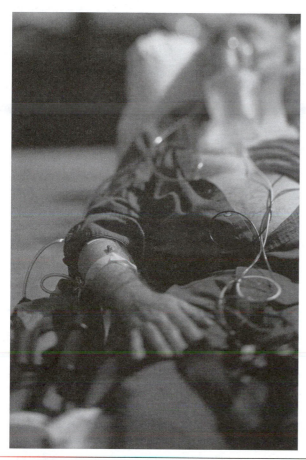

Source: Keith Brofsky/Getty Images

Health Disparities   In Chapters 6 and 7, we touched on problems associated with a lack of access to health care and being uninsured or underinsured and the effects on health, particularly for people in ethnic minority groups. Health disparities for ethnic minority groups in the United States are well documented and are reflected in many of the statistics on chronic illness and disease just presented. Health disparities are also reflected in the fact that African Americans have an infant mortality rate that is more than double that of Caucasians and African American males have a life expectancy of 69.5 years compared to 75.7 years for Caucasian men (National Center for Health Statistics, 2008a).

The exact reasons why those in ethnic minority groups experience poorer health outcomes than their White counterparts are difficult to poinpoint. However,

TABLE 11.2	ETHNIC GROUP	PERCENTAGE WITH DIABETES
Prevalence Rates of Diagnosed and Undiagnosed Diabetes among People of Different Ethnic Groups, Age 20+ in the U.S., 2007	Non-Hispanic Whites	6.6
	Native Americans/Alaskan Natives	16.5
	Asian American	7.5
	Non-Hispanic Blacks	11.8
	Cuban Americans	8.2
	Mexican Americans	11.9
	Puerto Ricans	12.6

Source: Adapted from the National Diabetes Information Clearinghouse, 2008.

many of the issues we've discussed thus far such as poverty; discrimination; environmental issues; lack of education, employment, and other opportunities; and barriers to health care and other resources that promote good health all likely contribute to health disparities. For example, people in ethnic minority groups are more likely to live in poverty without access to recreational opportunities, high-paying jobs, safe neighborhoods, quality health clinics, and stores that sell fresh, quality food. Because of violence, poverty, discrimination, and other related socioeconomic factors, they are more likely to suffer from stress that, in and of itself, can lead to disease, but that can also lead to poor health habits such as smoking, substance abuse, and overeating, which can lead to disease (Kaiser Family Foundation, 2005b; U.S. Department of Health and Human Services, 2004).

Habits that Carmen reports, such as smoking and inactivity, will likely cause health problems later in life, if they have not done so already. You will want to stress the need for a comprehensive physical exam to determine whether Carmen's symptoms are physiologically based. Even if Carmen isn't currently suffering from any physical disorders, you should still assess Carmen's need for education about her risks for developing various diseases and strategies for preventing these diseases from occurring later in life.

THE FAMILY AND IMMEDIATE ENVIRONMENT IN MIDDLE ADULTHOOD

Although some physical changes are inevitable in the aging process, there are still other areas in which people are just hitting their stride. With increased experiences come more opportunities for change, growth, and continued development in many facets of life, which, while often experienced as positive, can create problems. Often, middle adulthood brings with it the need for people to adjust, rely on coping skills, and reevaluate their goals and priorities. In this section, we look at issues surrounding middle adulthood that involve family, relationships, and changing social and other roles.

Marriage and Love

By the time people reach middle adulthood, they have likely experienced at least one significant love relationship. Some of these relationships will have resulted in marriage, cohabitation, civil unions, or divorce. Many of these relationships may have produced children, others not. Still other middle-aged adults may have chosen to remain single.

Though there are many ways in which people form meaningful relationships, marriage still tends to be a popular choice for most people, particularly for people in middle age. Indeed, many married middle-aged people express a great deal of satisfaction with their spousal relationship, particularly when there is a great deal of communication and shared activities in the marriage (Orbuch, House, Mero, & Webster, 1996; Schmitt, Kliegal, & Shapiro, 2007; Ward, 1993). Which factors help to predict successful and long-lasting marital relationships? Research indicates that one key factor is the nature of the couple's relationship when it began. For instance, couples who start out with a lack of trust, love, and liking for one another showed high rates of separation and problems later in their marriages. Further, married individuals who were struggling with psychological problems or other distress when the relationships began also showed high rates of marital discord later as well as overall dissatisfaction with life (Kurdek, 2002).

Conversely, some couples who start out with a great deal of conflict and distress are able to overcome their problems and establish more stable, loving relationships by midlife. This may be because many of the stressors that were straining the relationship early on decreased over time, leaving the couple with more time and energy to focus on the relationship. Specifically, some middle-aged couples may find themselves more financially stable and freer to pursue other things as their children move out, leaving couples with fewer responsibilities. Some couples are able to direct their energies toward working on the relationship and spending more time together (Brim, 1999). Although a rocky start to a marriage may contribute to the separation and divorce of many couples, some couples will overcome these problems and enjoy long-lasting, fulfilling marriages. Social workers may be able to help struggling couples work on trust, conflict, and related issues that put a strain on marriage and lead to its demise.

In relation to the time that couples spend together, one study examined the effects of leisure time on couples' relationship satisfaction. Contrary to other research, this study did not find a strong link between companionship and marital satisfaction. Rather, findings suggested that marital satisfaction was associated with particular patterns of leisure time that couples spend together. Specifically, husbands in this study did not enjoy participating in activities without their wives if the activity was something that both partners enjoyed. For example, if both partners enjoyed traveling, husbands were unhappy if they traveled alone. Wives in this study were dissatisfied when their husbands were off pursuing their own interests or when, as a couple, they participated in activities in which only the husbands were interested. Presumably, the former situation took time away from activities that the couple could enjoy together, and the latter meant that women had to make sacrifices so that they could spend time with their husbands.

These findings have important implications for social workers who work with couples. Specifically, social workers may need to attend to the affective quality of leisure time and not assume that the important thing for couples' well-being in the relationship is that they simply spend time together (Crawford, Houts, Huston, & George, 2002).

Reasons for Marriage   Another stance on marital satisfaction and why some couples stay together while others do not revolves around the reasons couples commit in the first place. One theory posits that many people, particularly in U.S. culture, adhere to the notion of romantic love: We just need to find that one, right person for us, and we will live happily ever after. Many critics argue that this notion alone has caused half of all marriages in the United States to end in divorce (Kornblum & Julian, 2001). That is, because so many people only look for romantic love and expect it to last, they become disappointed in their partners when the romance dies down.

Whether or not this argument is valid, the idea that romantic love, in and of itself, is a reasonable basis for long-term relationships is questionable. Particularly as people live longer and longer, the notion of "until death do you part" can mean many years of hard work that may or may not result in a lasting relationship. The length of time that people may spend together now that our life spans have increased is such that couples will almost assuredly change and potentially grow apart. This is particularly true if a couple marries at a young age. Further, the cultural emphasis on individualism may make it more difficult for some people to sacrifice certain things, such as careers, for a relationship and may cause problems for couples if they remain together. In sum, then, even though plenty of couples succeed in managing very long-term relationships, social workers still see many who do not, and the reasons why relationships ultimately dissolve are numerous.

Sternberg's Theory of Love   Many researchers have been interested in the construct of love, and this interest has led to various studies and theories on types of love and which types are likely to lead to successful relationships. One theoretical approach to love, developed by Robert Sternberg (1988), describes different types and combinations of love. Exhibit 11.2 illustrates the components of Sternberg's theory.

According to Sternberg, passionate love, or infatuation, is the "head over heels" kind of love in which an individual is preoccupied with thoughts of the other person. People feel a strong attraction to, and tend to idealize, each other. Intimate love, or liking, is the type of love that results in feeling close to each other. Couples have a sense of rapport, a sense of "we," and they respect and look out for each other. Couples who experience intimate love enjoy spending time together. Commitment, or empty love, has no elements of closeness. Rather, couples have a steady, enduring, and predictable relationship in which partners trust and are devoted to each other, but they do not necessarily share some of the deeper, intimate feelings associated with passionate love. Empty love might best describe **empty shell marriages**, in which couples stay together for various reasons that are based on practicality rather than intimate feelings. For example, some couples stay together to keep up outward appearances or for financial reasons.

Sternberg's theory also describes the types of love that can result when different elements of the theory are combined. These also are highlighted in Exhibit 11.2. For example, romantic love, a combination of intimate and passionate love, describes people who are drawn to each other with feelings of closeness and intense attraction. Romantic love often begins as infatuation. In contrast, couples who experience companionate love, a combination of intimate and commitment love, feel close to each other and are committed, but the relationship lacks an element of passion. Most romantic relationships eventually become companionate love when passion fades. Not surprisingly, then, companionate love is common in long-term marriages.

Fatuous love is a combination of passionate and commitment love. This is the "silly" love in which people become quickly and intensely involved and might even rush into marriage or move in together right away. Consummate love is a combination of all three components. It is an ideal love, but it is difficult to achieve and maintain. Conversely, non-love is void of all three components. This would describe our casual relationships and our interactions with others.

Although Sternberg's theory in and of itself cannot predict which couples will stay together and which ones will separate, it does offer valuable insights into the qualities that are present or absent in specific types of relationships. These insights can help social workers understand people's expectations about love and intimate relationships as well as their motives for continuing some relationships and not others.

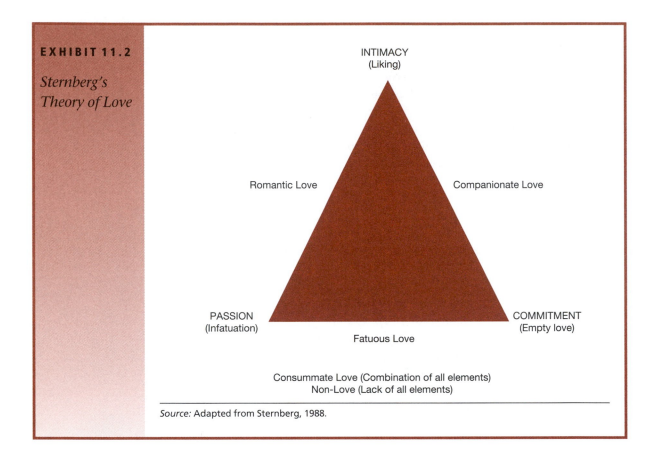

EXHIBIT 11.2

Sternberg's Theory of Love

INTIMACY
(Liking)

Romantic Love

Companionate Love

PASSION
(Infatuation)

Fatuous Love

COMMITMENT
(Empty love)

Consummate Love (Combination of all elements)
Non-Love (Lack of all elements)

Source: Adapted from Sternberg, 1988.

Divorce

Couples separate or divorce for many reasons, including issues surrounding feelings of love, liking, respect, and commitment. Indeed, evidence suggests that couples who divorce tend to feel distant from each other and do not feel much love toward or interest in each other (Gottman & Levenson, 2000).

There are also diverse opinions about the effects of divorce on the couple. In fact, research indicates that the effects can be positive or negative, depending on the people involved and the circumstances surrounding the divorce. For example, a divorce that takes place during middle adulthood may be less intense than a divorce that occurs in younger years. This difference may occur because couples have more time, money, maturity, and resources to deal with the divorce than young adults. In addition, they are less likely to have to worry about the effects of the breakup on young children, which can be very stressful (Corley & Woods, 1991; Tucker, Kressin, Spiro, & Ruscio, 1998; Wrosch & Heckhausen, 1999).

Nevertheless, divorce in middle age can present difficulties. For instance, some couples who have been together for a long time may find themselves socially, emotionally, and financially tied to the relationship. In addition, some couples may have trouble dividing possessions, property, and finances. Moreover, divorce can cause problems at work as well as with relationships with friends and family members, particularly if the couple is experiencing great emotional difficulty and brings negativity into other realms of their lives (Papalia, Olds, & Feldman, 2003).

Divorce can have other deleterious effects as well. In general, divorced people have shorter life spans than married people, and divorced men exhibit higher suicide rates than married men. Significantly, women generally are the ones who suffer financially after a divorce (Papalia et al., 2003). Regardless of the consequences, divorce today does not carry the stigma that it once did, and women have more financial and other choices that allow them to leave relationships that are unfulfilling or abusive. Especially when there is considerable conflict in a marriage, divorce may be a good choice for all involved, and it can lead to more satisfying lives and greater well-being.

Remarriage and Other Familial Patterns

With regard to relationship patterns, many people, by the time they reach middle age, have been married, divorced, and remarried. Indeed, after a divorce, people typically remarry within four years (Cherlin & Furstenberg, 1994). Increasingly, remarriage is a viable option for people, particularly as they age. Though remarriage is often a positive experience, it can present many challenges. Remarriage at any age can mean a great deal of adjustment for the couple. This is particularly true if one or both of the individuals have children from a previous marriage and they are bringing them into the new family. Depending on the ages of the children, this process can generate a variety of considerations and problems that the couple must overcome. In general, most newly formed families must contend with figuring out new roles, rules, expectations, adjustments, and relationships. New family members may be accustomed to the way life used to be before remarriage occurred, and they need time to adjust to the dynamics of the new family and to develop feelings for one another.

Adult Children and the Empty Nest Syndrome Another widely publicized issue regarding families is the **empty nest syndrome**, which refers to the supposedly negative effects that parents experience when their last child leaves the home. Some experts have blamed the empty nest syndrome for decreased marital satisfaction. They cite research that suggests that if parents have based their marital satisfaction in parenting, they may experience problems when their children leave home. At that point couples need to find other interests and sources of fulfillment to remain satisfied in their marriage. However, other evidence suggests that the marital satisfaction of many couples actually increases when their children leave home. These couples can now enjoy time together and invest resources into the marital relationship that were once devoted to child rearing. Couples may find that they are more emotionally available to each other and can spend more time together pursuing mutual interests (Crowley, Hayslip, & Hobdy, 2003; Kausler, Kausler, & Krupsaw, 2007; Ward & Spitze, 2004). Because of these contradictory findings, social workers need to explore the individual perceptions of clients whose children are leaving home. Some clients may be distressed by "losing" their children and the role of caregiver, while others may be excited about the prospect of freedom and independence from their caregiving responsibilities.

Parents who look forward to their children leaving home may be dismayed by adult children who do not leave home when expected. Increasingly, children are leaving home at older ages, and some children who have left return to live with their parents. Circumstances such as divorce, unemployment, and returning to school lead some adult children to live with their parents rather than independently (Kausler et al., 2007). Obviously, some parents may not be prepared for their adult children to live with them, particularly after the children have been living on their own. Often, these arrangements require that family members readjust to their new living arrangements. Problems with roles, rules, communication, and relationships can develop among family members.

Other Familial Patterns   Some people may find themselves a part of the **sandwich generation**. This occurs when parents find themselves caring for their children as well as their parents (Uhlenberg, 1996). Middle-aged people may be particularly susceptible to this situation, as their parents are likely to be of an age when chronic illness and disability require extra care. This situation can be extremely stressful for people who find themselves spending a great deal of time, money, and energy caring for their families. Without appropriate resources and social support, these caregivers may find themselves at risk for various physical and mental health problems.

Social workers may also encounter couples who cannot have children or decide not to parent. Although much depends on the circumstances, there is little evidence to suggest that couples suffer psychologically if they do not have children. Generally, it appears that if women who do not have children hold negative attitudes about their situation, they are at higher risk for psychological problems such as loneliness and depression than women who do not hold negative attitudes. These same patterns do not necessarily hold true for men. Rather, socialization processes regarding gender roles may place more pressure on women to bear children; so if they are unable to or decide not to and feel unhappy about it, they may struggle emotionally later on. Being a parent does not necessarily guarantee psychological well-being either. Evidence suggests that parents who have poor relationships with their children are at risk for psychological problems such as depression (Koropeckyj-Cox, 2002).

Social Work with Families   Social workers who are working with couples and families have a lot to think about with regard to family systems and relationships. Because various issues such as living and relationship arrangements as well as situations regarding children and other family members can be problematic for some families, social workers need to be skilled at assessing and working with these issues for each family and determining how they affect particular family members.

Systems theory can be useful in helping social workers organize a great deal of information about families and conduct a comprehensive assessment on the issues that may affect them. Social workers can rely on concepts such as roles, rules, boundaries, and homeostasis to help a family better understand how these concepts play out in their particular situation. For example, if a couple has remarried and brought children into the new family from previous marriages, these concepts can be particularly helpful in assisting family members to better understand how they are interacting with one another and where problems may occur. The social worker may point out to individual family members that homeostasis for the new family system needs to be developed and maintained; each member has been used to a certain way of functioning in the old system that was probably comfortable for her or him. In this new family system, members will need to find their places and define their relationships to allow the new family to function smoothly. In working toward this goal, the social worker can help new family members identify their roles and boundaries within the system, establish relationships with one another, and articulate new family rules.

Other developmental models could also be useful for clients who may be dealing with issues surrounding not having children or having adult children who move back home, for example. Because these issues potentially can cause psychological problems for some individuals, using developmental models such as Erikson's or Levinson's can help social workers conceptualize the developmental tasks that might be important for clients and how certain issues may pose problems for their developmental progress. For instance, middle-aged people who do not have children, for whatever reason, may struggle with feeling stagnant, according to Erikson. If they have not had a "traditional" family in which to invest and their careers or other areas of their lives have not allowed them to feel productive, they may need to work through these feelings to successfully move through this particular stage.

Carmen's Case Revisited   You may want to assess Carmen's family situation to see if specific areas may be contributing to her complaints. Trouble with her children may be placing stress on her relationships with both her children and her husband. If her relationship with her children deteriorates, it may put her at risk for additional stress and even psychological problems later on.

You could also help Carmen explore her relationship with her husband. To help improve their marriage or to help maintain its quality if it is already strong, the couple might need to find leisure activities that they both enjoy and allow them to spend time together. You may find valuable information by exploring the beginning of Carmen's marriage to ascertain the nature of her and her husband's feelings toward each other when they first married. If there was a lack of trust or positive feelings, Carmen and her husband could be headed for marital conflict. Conversely, if Carmen states that she has a strong marriage, you could help her maintain it and take advantage of this strength as she works on other issues.

Retirement

Retirement, as it is perceived by most people, is a relatively new phenomenon in the United States. Specifically, until recently, most people did not conceive of leaving the workforce at a designated time in life to pursue recreation or other interests. A popular view of retirement is that it is a single event that occurs after a lifetime of education and work. However, this view is not completely accurate. Sociologists and other researchers have discovered many definitions and patterns of retirement. For example, the number of older, male part-time workers has increased over the past several decades (Elder & Pavalko, 1993). And by the year 2004, more than 50 percent of men in their early 60s were still working and over 30 percent of men in their late 60s were working. Women's participation in the workforce has increased since the 1960s, particularly for women in their 50s. Though some people, particularly men, drop out of the workforce in their 50s because of health and other reasons, the majority of people remain working until later life (Quadagno, 2008). Further, older people, both men and women, from different ethnic groups experience varied patterns of employment and retirement, which are affected by lifelong socio-economic issues including discrimination. For example, African Americans face high unemployment rates early on in life, which have ramifications for later employment and financial security, including their ability to retire. Particularly in midlife, African American men face health disparities, which often lead to high rates of disability, affecting their ability to work. Lifelong physical and psychosocial stressors caused by poverty, discrimination, and employment in stressful, blue-collar jobs that lack supportive health care and other benefits also contribute to disabilities that can affect these men's ability to accumulate wealth and participate in the work-force later on in life. This same pattern holds true for men and women in other ethnic minority groups (Brown & Warner, 2008; U.S. Department of Labor, 2007).

Actual retirement patterns for both men and women vary a great deal. For instance, many middle-aged adults decide to begin new careers after retiring from old ones. They may decide to return to school, volunteer, or take a job in a different field. Some people may decide to partially retire by reducing the number of hours they work or by finding new jobs that require fewer hours (Moen & Wethington, 1999). With regard to this last pattern, many people take **bridge jobs**, or jobs that fill the gap between full-time employment and full retirement; this trend has been steadily increasing over the past several decades (Cahill, Giandrea, & Quinn, 2006; Quinn & Kozy, 1996). Many people have to continue working because they cannot afford to retire. These particular patterns can be positive. Recall the discussion earlier in the chapter that people who remain cognitively active as they age are less likely to experience an intellectual decline. Continued activity in work and related activities may help people to stay cognitively healthy as they move into older adulthood. For example, research indicates that engaging in volunteer activities, which many people do before and after retirement, has many social and health-related benefits. Volunteerism is associated with lower rates of mortality, depression, and heart disease and higher rates of life satisfaction and functional mobility (Grimm, Spring, & Dietz, 2007). Regardless of the retirement pattern taken, U.S. workers spend, on average, approximately 10 percent to 15 percent of their lives in retirement. With life expectancy rates rising, older adults can potentially spend, on average, 18 to 20 years in retirement if they retire at age 65 (Atchley & Barusch, 2004).

Women's employment patterns tend to be more varied than men's throughout the life course. For instance, some women begin careers and then put them on hold to rear children, reentering the workforce after their children have grown. Other women work part time or full time while taking care of their family, while still others choose not to have families and devote themselves to full-time work. The employment choices that women make throughout adulthood can have profound economic and other impacts on their retirement plans and later life. We consider the issues related to women's work and retirement in greater detail in Chapter 12.

Though the retirement age has increased in the United States and will probably continue to increase in the face of Social Security solvency issues, many people still opt for early retirement. Many businesses and other sectors offer people incentives to retire early to open up jobs to younger workers who can be paid less than their older counterparts (though this practice is illegal). This practice may also be implemented during poor economic times when unemployment is high (Quadagno, 2008).

Planning for Retirement   Another consideration regarding retirement has to do with how people plan for it. Some people begin financial and other planning early in adulthood, while others find that retirement sneaks up on them before they have thought about their financial, career, or life goals. Particularly when people are working in low-wage jobs that only allow them to live paycheck to paycheck, it can be difficult to save money or imagine a day when they can retire.

Some research has examined the patterns of retirement planning among different groups of people in U.S. society. For example, one study found that same-sex and opposite-sex couples had similar retirement plans with regard to age of retirement, beginning the planning process, and anticipating health and housing needs. However, married couples reported higher rates of actual planning than gay, lesbian, and cohabiting nonmarried heterosexual couples. Of all the groups, lesbian couples reported the lowest level of financial readiness for retirement. During retirement, only the married couples reported plans to spend time volunteering, which has been associated with high levels of well-being in old age. In general, then, gay, lesbian, and nonmarried heterosexual couples may be on a road toward lower levels of financial and psychological well-being in older age than married couples, given their trends of a lack of planning and goal-setting for post-retirement activities (Mock, 2001).

Theoretical Perspectives on Retirement   Adjustment to retirement is a rather complex issue, and positive or negative adjustment depends on many constructs, including individual personalities, situations, and attitudes. Though these complexities must be kept in mind, research suggests that factors such as financial stability, good physical health, a positive social and living environment, and voluntary retirement are associated with positive adjustment to retirement (Lowis, Edwards, & Burton, 2009; Quick & Moen, 1998; Reitzes, Mutran, & Pope, 1991).

Some research on retirement adjustment seems to be supported by continuity theory, which is discussed in detail in Chapter 12. For the purposes of discussion here, continuity theory (Atchley, 1989) posits that as we age, we maintain continuity in our roles, personality, relationships, and activities. This consistency helps us adjust to the aging process. So, during retirement, the more we can maintain the sense of satisfaction and well-being that we might have had during our working years, the better we will adjust to our new circumstances.

Retirement can also be viewed through disengagement and activity theories, also discussed in Chapter 12. That is, retirement can be viewed as a natural process of older people "removing" themselves from the workforce to make way for younger people, or it can be viewed as a transition in which people invest their energies into something other than work. If people do not want to disengage from employment or do not have other meaningful activities in which they can engage, they will likely experience problems upon retirement, according to these last two theories.

Regardless of the theoretical lens through which social workers view retirement, they need to consider the potential impacts that retirement can have on clients. Social workers can attend to the consequences that retirement might have on their clients' economic and psychosocial well-being to prevent problems that might occur when clients face this time in life.

Retirement and Carmen's Case   Although retirement issues may not be a priority for Carmen now, you may still want to explore Carmen's feelings about it. She may have thought about retirement, which may be part of why she has been experiencing some of the troubling symptoms. By asking about it, you can either rule out the association between Carmen's current problems and retirement-related issues or pursue it, if Carmen does want to explore this issue. If it is not an issue now, you can pursue it later on in the working relationship.

THE LARGER SOCIAL ENVIRONMENT IN MIDDLE ADULTHOOD: AGEISM

Biological, psychological, emotional, social, and vocational issues can cause problems for people as they reach middle age. **Ageism**, which involves negative attitudes toward aging and older people based on beliefs that older people cannot function as well as younger people, has the potential to cut across all of these realms. Specifically, ageist beliefs assert that middle-aged and elderly people are not sexual, intelligent, or capable (Atchley & Barusch, 2004). Ageism, and the prejudiced attitudes and beliefs about older people that underlie it, often lead to discrimination or treating people differently, usually in negative ways, because of their age. Though it can affect people at any age, ageism probably becomes more noticeable to many people during middle adulthood than in early adulthood because of the various changes that are occurring, which may leave some people more vulnerable to discrimination.

One area in which ageism tends to be prevalent is the workplace. Stereotypes of older workers often perpetuate ageism in the workplace. For example, misconceptions that older workers cannot learn new tasks, are incapable of producing good work, and are resistant to change are just a few that exist among employers as well as the general public. In fact, research on older workers indicates that older people tend to be better and more effective workers than younger people. In general, research suggests that compared to younger workers, older workers take fewer sick days, are more punctual and reliable, are less likely to be injured on the job, are more loyal to their employers, are less likely to leave a job, express higher job satisfaction, and exhibit better attitudes toward work (Atchley & Barusch, 2004; U.S. Department of Labor, 2008).

In an effort to guard against discrimination in the workplace, Congress passed the **Age Discrimination in Employment Act** in 1967. This law prohibits employers from firing or reducing the wages or positions of people based on age (specifically between 40 and 65 years of age) before they reach a mandatory retirement age. Note, however, that in 1978 the federal government raised the mandatory retirement age from 65 to 70 in both private business and the federal government, which extended the protection against discrimination. Then, in 1986, Congress banned mandatory retirement except in certain industries, including law enforcement and aviation, where the age of the worker might put others at risk (Quadagno, 2008). Because there are no federal mandatory retirement requirements, except in certain industries, age discrimination may be more of an issue for workers as they reach ages that are beyond the norms for retirement. Specifically, people who wish to work into their 70s, 80s, and even 90s may be at high risk for discrimination.

Another way in which ageism occurs is through patronizing and infantilizing people as they get older. Though people who are in late adulthood are more likely to be treated this way, people in middle adulthood can encounter these attitudes as well. For example, younger people often assume that middle-aged adults are not sexual, cannot perform certain tasks, or should be given special treatment because they are perceived to be less physically capable than younger adults.

Unfortunately, Western culture tends to perpetuate ageist myths and stereotypes. Though this happens in many ways, one of the most visible forms of ageism is transmitted through the media, as mentioned previously. Until recently, middle-aged and elderly adults were not frequently cast in television shows, and when they were, their characters were portrayed negatively. More recently, television shows have included middle-aged and older adults as major characters who are confident and competent (Bell, 1992). However, there is still a dearth of serious roles for middle-aged and older adults, particularly for women over the age of 40 (Media Report to Women, 1999, 2001, 2009) and the media still tend to portray older adults negatively, reinforcing harmful stereotypes of older adults and aging. For example, one cross-cultural comparison study of older adults' portrayal in magazines in the U.S. and India found that older women in both countries were underrepresented while younger women were overrepresented (Raman, Harwood, Weis, Anderson, & Miller, 2008). Another study found that by the time children enter elementary school, many have already developed negative stereotypes of older adults through their exposure to media representations of older people, particularly through Disney films and other children's programming (Robinson & Anderson, 2006; Robinson, Callister, Magoffin, & Moore, 2007).

Even with an increasing visibility of older actors on television and in movies, advertisements still tend to portray middle-aged and older people in a negative light. Although a small percentage of advertisements on major network channels now show people over the age of 50, most of the characters are male, and they generally sell food, health, or hygiene-related products or products only associated with stereotypically age-related concerns such as erectile dysfunction (Atkins, Jenkins, & Perkins, 1990–1991; Raman et al., 2008).

Attitudes about aging have been slowly changing, but many myths and stereotypes still exist about middle-aged and older adults. With the aging of the baby boom generation, some of these attitudes will continue to change. However, given the cultural emphasis on youth, young, middle-aged, and elderly people may find themselves succumbing to various ageist attitudes. Further, some theories and perspectives that describe aging can perpetuate ageist attitudes. For example, disengagement theory, discussed in Chapter 12, may serve to reinforce beliefs that people lose their usefulness as they age. That is, people who view aging from this lens may expect aging individuals to naturally step aside from their roles, thereby devaluing their worth and value in society and perpetuating ideas that older adults are not capable of being productive members of society.

As with other isms that exist in society, social workers can be effective agents of change with regard to ageism. On a social scale, social workers can help to eradicate myths and stereotypes of aging through education and modeling behaviors that support the uniqueness and worth of the aging process. This education can also be conducted on an individual level: Social workers can help clients who may be struggling with the aging process to better understand how their own ageist attitudes may be thwarting their well-being as they move into and through middle adulthood and into older age.

Though it is not evident in the case study, Carmen is likely experiencing ageism in her life. Social forces, attitudes of her friends and family, and even her own perceptions of aging may all have a negative influence on the way Carmen views herself and her worth. As part of a biopsychosocial assessment, you can explore how ageism may be impacting Carmen. Any intervention that is conducted with Carmen can incorporate aspects of societal and personal beliefs about aging to reconstruct them into more positive perspectives that will support her healthy aging process.

CONCLUSION

Middle adulthood can be a time for continued growth and development in many ways, including emotionally, spiritually, socially, and vocationally. Although physical decline does occur and some people may notice themselves slowing down in some ways, most changes are not significant enough to cause serious problems for many people.

For many people, middle adulthood is a time to enjoy the fruits of their labor in many areas. With the insecurities, struggles, and hard work of young adulthood behind them, many middle-aged adults find themselves freer to be themselves and enjoy their successes. However, some people find changes in middle adulthood to be troublesome. Adjusting to aging, experiencing illness, changing careers, ending relationships, and beginning new ones can create stress or other psychological and emotional problems.

One role that social workers can fill is to help people who have trouble coping with issues that may present themselves in middle age. Assessing areas that might be troublesome for people during this time, or that might create barriers to well-being in older age, is an important goal for social workers working with middle-aged adults.

MAIN POINTS

- For many, physical aspects such as energy, eyesight, hearing, and metabolism begin to decline in adulthood, but most people usually do not notice a marked difference from when they were younger, especially with cognitive abilities. In U.S. culture with its emphasis on youth, many people are most troubled by changes in physical appearance that can lead to such things as wrinkles, gray hair, and weight gain.

- Levinson proposed a theory of adult development for men, consisting of three transitions, that focuses on life structures, or patterns of behavior that shape experiences. The life structures and transitions that take place during the 40s and 50s consist of questioning what it means to grow old, assessing whether choices made previously are satisfying, and making changes that will lead to greater satisfaction.

- The experience of menopause, or the cessation of a woman's menstrual cycle, varies greatly from woman to woman and from culture to culture. Some women welcome the changes, and others experience anxiety; some cultures regard the process as natural, and others—especially Western culture—regard it as a loss of vitality and attractiveness.

- Many men experience a male climacteric in midlife during which they may reevaluate their careers, familial relationships, and other life decisions they have made. This climacteric (sometimes referred to as a midlife crisis) includes physical changes that many men experience such as hair loss, weight gain, and a decrease in sexual vitality.

- Middle adulthood is a time when genetics and unhealthy lifestyle habits such as smoking and poor diet can catch up to individuals, causing chronic illnesses such as cancer, diabetes, and heart disease.

- During middle adulthood, many people may be dealing with issues related to marriage, divorce, and remarriage that can affect their well-being. Research on why marriages succeed and fail, and theories such as Sternberg's theory of love, can help social workers understand people's expectations about intimate relationships as well as their motives for continuing some relationships and not others.

- Changing relationships can mean changing familial patterns, such as blended families, the empty nest syndrome, and the sandwich generation.

- Retirement patterns for both men and women vary greatly; many people begin second or even third careers in middle age and continue working into old age. Planning for and adjusting to retirement are two areas in which social workers can be helpful to clients.

- Ageism, or discriminating against people because of their age, may begin to be noticeable to people in middle age as they face ageist attitudes in the workplace and society. Although some changes are taking place, social workers need to be at the forefront of eradicating myths and stereotypes of aging.

EXERCISES

1. Using the Sanchez Family interactive case (go to www.routledgesw.com/cases), review the major issues involving the family, particularly for Hector and Celia Sanchez. After giving this information thorough review, answer the following questions:

   a. Developmentally, what issues might Hector be facing at this time in his life? How might these issues impact his current work and family situation and his well-being in older adulthood?

   b. How might ageist and racist attitudes and other social forces affect his well-being emotionally, psychologically, interpersonally, spiritually, socially, and economically?

   c. Using the previous two sets of questions, provide an analysis for Celia.

   d. What issues might affect Hector's and Celia's marital satisfaction?

   e. Which theory or theories do you think would be helpful to employ in working with Hector and Celia? Why? What would be some limitations to using the theory/theories you chose?

2. Review the Carla Washburn interactive case (go to www.routledgesw.com/cases), and review the information presented on Levinson's Theory of Adult Development, including Box 11.1. Then answer the following questions:

   a. Based on the information you have on Carla now, what hunches could you make on her early and middle adult development based on Levinson's theory?

   b. What issues from her earlier development might be creating problems for her now, in later adulthood?

   c. What other issues presented in this chapter might be or have been issues for Carla, impacting the problems she's experiencing now?

CHAPTER 12

Development in Late Adulthood

Judy is an 80-year-old woman who has been living at Sunset Homes, a residential care facility, for the past three years. She has problems dressing, bathing, and managing her medications, and she needs assistance with grocery shopping and making it to her doctor's appointments. With only a modest income from Social Security, Judy relies on Medicaid to fund her care at Sunset Homes.

Recently, budget cuts in social services have necessitated decreases in Medicaid funding to elders living in these types of facilities. The state has mandated that all elders not meeting a specified level of physical care be evicted from their facilities. Judy does not currently meet the new criteria for funding and has received a notice from the state saying that she has two weeks to vacate the facility. Judy has a daughter who lives in another state, but her daughter is unable to provide the care Judy needs. Judy cannot afford to pay the monthly rates of the facility on her income, and there are no other facilities in the city that provide housing for low-income elders who need assistance. Judy can appeal the state's decision, but she will need help from a social worker who understands Medicaid policy, state bureaucracy, and ways to advocate for older people like Judy with special care needs.

UNFORTUNATELY, JUDY'S SITUATION IS NOT UNUSUAL. Worldwide, the population is growing older, and all societies will face special challenges in caring for their elders. As health care improves and new technologies become available, individuals, families, and communities will face a plethora of issues surrounding needs and services for the elderly. Because of these challenges, there is an increasing need for social workers who are trained in gerontology and who can negotiate the complex individual, relational, and societal needs facing older populations.

In this chapter, we explore some of the issues surrounding senescence, or the process of aging. In most cases we will examine these issues from the perspective of the medical model because they tend to be biological in nature. However, many factors relating to processes of physical and cognitive aging have implications for adjustment to growing older and the level of functioning that the older individual maintains. Thus, other theories of development can be useful in helping to understand how biological changes can affect an individual's reactions to the aging process. Also keep in mind that although these changes commonly tend to be associated with aging, not everyone goes through these changes at the same rate, just as some expected changes do not necessarily happen to all people or to the same degree.

DEVELOPMENTAL MILESTONES IN OLDER ADULTS

The aging process can be measured in many different ways. In U.S. culture, we tend to rely on **chronological age**, or a person's age in years, to determine whether a person is old. This measure is often used to determine a person's eligibility for certain programs such as Medicare or a senior citizen's discount at restaurants. However, this particular measure tends to be somewhat arbitrary. Certainly it can help to guide service provision, but it does not tell you much about how old the person feels subjectively or how well the person is functioning physically or psychologically. A related way to discuss aging is to place people into subcategories based on their chronological age. Specifically, the **young-old** generally includes people from 65 to 74, the **middle-old** includes those from 75 to 84, and the **oldest-old** includes those 85 or older.

An alternative to the chronological age measure is **functional age**, which focuses on how well people perform their usual roles in their daily lives. For example, a 50-year-old person who has severe arthritis and is not very mobile without assistance would have an older functional age than a 75-year-old person who runs two marathons a year and needs no assistance with daily tasks. To measure the level of functioning, social workers generally assess the types of activities that older people are able to complete on their own. These activities fall into two general categories. **Activities of daily living (ADLs)** include tasks related to personal care such as eating, walking, dressing, bathing, toileting, and getting in and out of bed. **Instrumental activities in daily living (IADLs)** include tasks related to independent living such as performing housework, shopping, preparing meals, managing money, and using a telephone (Centers for Medicare and Medicaid Services, 2002). Social workers often use these assessments to reliably measure the level of functioning a person is able to manage in daily life. These measures are also used by various social service agencies to determine eligibility for certain services, such as Medicaid.

Physical Changes in Late Adulthood

When we think of aging, we often think of developing wrinkles and gray hair and slowing down physically. Though some of these changes do occur, the amount of

TABLE 12.1	PHYSICAL	COGNITIVE
Developmental Milestones in Later Adulthood	• Declines in bone and muscle mass. • Increased prevalence of diseases such as arthritis and osteoporosis. • Increased appearance of wrinkles, gray hair, loose skin, age spots. • Loss of teeth and dental problems. • Increased vision and hearing problems. • Declines in central nervous system functioning affecting reaction time, coordination.	• Increased prevalence of dementias. • Some declines in memory and functioning if not cognitively active.

change that individuals go through varies a great deal and reflects the interaction of genetics, lifestyle, and societal expectations. Table 12.1 summarizes the physical milestones that characterize later adulthood.

Probably one of the most obvious changes that we go through as we age is bodily changes. Though individuals vary greatly, certain bodily changes are relatively consistent. One of these changes has to do with bone density.

Osteoporosis Our skeletal system develops throughout our 20s and reaches its peak mass during our 30s. As we age past our 30s, bone is broken down faster than our bodies can reproduce it, leaving us with bone loss. When optimal bone mass is not achieved in adolescence or when bone loss in older age is severe, it can lead to osteoporosis, which leaves the bones weak and vulnerable to fractures. In older age, hip and spine breaks are particularly worrisome because they often require surgery, hospitalization, and rehabilitation. Fractures of the spine can result in chronic back pain and loss of height. Though both men and women can develop osteoporosis, women tend to be at higher risk for the disease. This higher risk occurs for two reasons: (1) Women tend to have smaller and lighter bones than men, and (2) after menopause, women's ovaries stop producing estrogen, which appears to protect against bone loss (National Institutes of Health, 2001; Nguyen et al., 1994).

Older Caucasian and Asian women appear to be at higher risk for osteoporosis than African American or Hispanic/Latino women. Approximately 20 percent of Caucasian and Asian women aged 50+ are estimated to have osteoporosis and another 52 percent are estimated to be at risk for osteoporosis because of low bone mass. This is compared to 5 percent of older African American women and 10 percent of older Hispanic women who are estimated to have the disease, though the risk for Hispanic women is increasing rapidly when compared to other ethnic groups. Although older men have a lower risk of developing the disease, it is estimated that osteoporosis affects approximately 7 percent of Asian men, 4 percent of African American men, and 3 percent of Hispanic men. Though the factors contributing to ethnic differences in osteoporosis are unclear, research indicates that, in general, higher peak bone mass and diets rich in calcium may mediate the development of the disease for women in some ethnic groups. Other risk factors for the disease include smoking, a family history of osteoporosis, and a history of bone fractures. Alcohol abuse and excessive caffeine intake may increase the risk for osteoporosis (National Institutes of Health, 2001, 2009; National Osteoporosis Foundation, 2008).

Osteoporosis can have profound personal, financial, and social consequences. Hip fractures often lead to permanent disabilities, which can create fear, anxiety, and depression in people who are at risk. In the United States, the financial costs for treatment of fractures were estimated at $19 billion in 2005 because of hospitalization, community-based care services, and lost wages and productivity; it is predicted that these costs will rise to $25.3 billion by the year 2025 (National Osteoporosis Foundation, 2008).

Much can be done to prevent and treat osteoporosis, including exercise, a balanced diet, and hormone replacement therapy (HRT). However, as you saw in Chapter 11, HRT for postmenopausal women is controversial because of its potential negative side effects. So, although evidence suggests that HRT can be effective for the prevention and management of osteoporosis for high-risk women, particularly for women younger than 60, it may put some older women at higher risk for breast cancer, myocardial infarction (heart attacks), and other diseases (Rymer, Wilson, & Ballard, 2003; Studd, 2009).

Loss of Muscle Mass   Another concern as people age is loss of muscle mass. Typically, people experience a gradual loss of muscle strength in their 30s, but these changes often are not noticeable until their 50s. However, much of the muscle strength that people lose results from inactivity rather than a normal decline in functioning or loss of tissue. Indeed, older individuals who practice regular strength training can actually slow down the losses that often occur with age as well as regain or increase their muscle strength (Campbell & Leidy, 2007; Fielding, 1995).

Arthritis   Another problem that is typically associated with old age is arthritis. In a broad sense, **arthritis** refers to inflammation or degeneration within the joints. These changes can make movement in the affected joints very painful. Although arthritis can occur in younger people, it occurs more frequently in older people.

Two common types of arthritis are osteoarthritis and rheumatoid arthritis. **Osteoarthritis**, which affects approximately 30 million people in the United States, causes the cartilage that covers the joints to deteriorate over time. This deterioration is caused when enzymes break down cartilage during normal use of the joints. In younger people, this cartilage is usually replaced; however, as we age, our bodies are not as efficient in replacing cartilage, resulting in gradual exposure of the joint (Lawrence et al., 2008; Spence, 1999).

Though **rheumatoid arthritis** frequently occurs among older people, it too is also seen in younger people. Symptoms generally appear before age 50, and they gradually become worse as a person ages. Rheumatoid arthritis tends to attack smaller bones such as those in the hands, feet, and wrists, and it is more common among women than men. Rheumatoid arthritis begins by causing inflammation of membranes that surround the joints, which can cause scarring of the surrounding tissue. This scarring can cause severe pain and disability. Several theories exist about the causes of rheumatoid arthritis. One theory suggests that some people have a genetic predisposition to the disease, while another theory suggests that the disease is caused by an autoimmune response in the body, where tissues around the joints are attacked. Yet another theory posits that the disease is caused by a bacterial or viral infection (Hewagama & Richardson, 2009; Spence, 1999).

Changes in Appearance   As discussed in Chapter 11, other notable changes with aging have to do with appearance. Nothing seems as daunting in U.S. culture as the physical changes associated with aging. Indeed, you only need to pay attention to television commercials to get a feel for the latest products that promise to fight wrinkles, whiten teeth, get rid of gray hair, and soften rough spots in the skin. Of course, cosmetic surgery and related procedures are also options to fight the signs of aging. Specifically, botox treatments, chemical peels, and face-lifts are increasingly popular choices for people who want to turn back the hands of time.

Although many changes associated with age cannot be completely prevented, some can be minimized by changes in lifestyle behaviors. For instance, with time and use, skin loses elasticity, leading to wrinkles and sags. However, wrinkles are also caused by excessive exposure to the sun, smoking, dehydration, poor diet, and lack of exercise. Therefore, modifying these behaviors could diminish the extent or severity of wrinkling. Similarly, some people experience age spots, or discolored skin on the face or hands. This spotting is caused by an accumulation of pigment in the skin, which, like wrinkled skin, can be made worse by excessive sun exposure. Although age spots are harmless, they can be a source of embarrassment for some people.

Graying hair is caused by cells that lose their pigment-producing function, resulting in a loss of color in the hair. This graying process occurs at varying ages. Some people discover their first gray hair at age 25; others do not notice any gray hairs until their 70s. One study suggests that stress damages our DNA, depleting the pigment-making cells within our hair follicles, turning our hair gray (Inomata et al., 2009). Many men and women also experience thinning hair or hair loss. Moreover, hair growth may occur more frequently in unwanted places such as the ears, nostrils, and for women, above the lip. Finally, as discussed in Chapter 11, weight gain is also a common complaint among aging individuals (Digiovanna, 1994).

Loss of teeth can be an appearance issue, but it can also lead to more serious problems. As we age, our gums naturally recede, and the development of gum disease leading to tooth loss becomes an increasing problem (Digiovanna, 1994). Many people keep their teeth throughout their entire life, but others must rely on dentures. Dentures can be cost prohibitive for many older people, and if they do not fit correctly or comfortably, they can be very painful. Denture pain can lead to malnutrition in some older people because eating becomes too much of a burden (Semba et al., 2006; Takahashi, Okhravi, Lim, & Kasten, 2004).

Hearing-Related Problems   Hearing tends to reach its peak in the 20s and then decline as people age. Normal hearing loss that occurs from declines associated with aging, called **presbycusis**, can produce numerous types of problems. For example, some people lose sensitivity to sound and require increased volume; some lose the ability to hear high-pitched sounds; some hear sounds that are distorted, particularly when people talk fast or slur their words; and some experience chronic tinnitus, or ringing in the ears (Spence, 1999). Environmental factors can accelerate the loss of hearing. Attending loud rock concerts, listening to music with the volume turned up high, and being exposed to loud noises in the street such as car horns and jackhammers can all cause cumulative damage to hearing and add to troubles that people may experience with older age (Digiovanna, 1994).

Hearing loss is more common among men than women, probably due in part to the types of work in which men engage, such as construction. Hearing loss often leaves the hearing-impaired person feeling isolated because she or he has trouble engaging in conversations and social activities. In addition, people may interpret a person's difficulties in hearing as a lack of interest in interactions, causing them to disengage from the hearing-impaired person (Takahashi, Okhravi, Lim, & Kasten, 2004).

Vision-Related Problems   Like hearing, vision tends to decline with age, usually beginning in young adulthood. By the time most people reach 60, they need glasses or contact lenses. Different parts of the eye, such as the lens, retina, and optic nerve, deteriorate over time, causing various problems. For example, with age the vitreous humor, or fluid behind the lens, becomes more opaque and the lens loses elasticity, creating the need for additional light or more time to adjust to distance changes to see objects accurately. Depth perception can also deteriorate, increasing the risks for tripping or falling. **Presbyopia**, or the inability to focus on nearby objects, can cause problems for people trying to read the fine print on medication bottles or the dials on the stove. Because of these conditions, many older people cannot drive at night or they have difficulty negotiating road signs or traffic signals. These conditions can also lead to problems such as taking the wrong medications in the wrong doses or leaving the stove burners on (Digiovanna, 1994).

Disorders such as glaucoma and cataracts are not necessarily a normal part of aging, but with time many people develop problems that can lead to these disorders. **Glaucoma** is a disorder that results from a buildup of fluid and pressure in the eye, which damages the eye and can result in blindness. Unfortunately, many people do not experience symptoms, but routine eye exams can detect the disease before it progresses. **Cataracts** are caused by clouding of the lens, which decreases the amount of light that can pass through. Though cataracts can severely limit sight, they can now be eliminated through laser treatments. **Macular degeneration** is age related and causes a loss of detail in vision. Because the brain can compensate for partially missing data in the images we see, many people are not diagnosed with the disorder until it is advanced. It is estimated that one in four people between the ages of 64 and 74 and one in three people age 75+ are affected by macular degeneration. Lifestyle factors such as a high-fat diet and smoking as well as genetics have been linked to the disease (Macular Degeneration Foundation, 2002).

Changing various aspects within the environment can help older individuals with vision problems negotiate their homes and other environments. For example, changing the color and size of the typeface on signs and altering the lighting in rooms can greatly enhance an older person's ability to see objects. Often, older adults must make adjustments in their lives to accommodate for failing eyesight, such as purchasing phones with larger numbers and driving only in the day and only on routes with which they are familiar (Stevens-Ratchford & Krause, 2004).

Reaction Time and Coordination   As people age, their central nervous system tends to slow down. This can cause reaction time to slow down as well. It may take people longer to attend to all the cues in their environment and to react to those cues. Sensorimotor coordination can also become less efficient in old age. The use of certain medications can intensify this decline in coordination.

This issue becomes particularly important for older people who want to keep driving. For many elders, driving is a necessary part of maintaining independence, which is why the issue of driving for the elderly can be a touchy subject. Indeed, some communities have tried to pass legislation that requires drivers older than a certain age to take a yearly driving exam. Although older drivers can pose certain risks, some researchers argue that older drivers can compensate sufficiently to drive safely and maintain their independence—indeed, some studies suggest that older drivers are safer than younger drivers because they avoid risky and dangerous driving situations (Langford, Bohensky, Koppel, & Newstead, 2008; Loughran, Seabury, & Zakaras, 2007; McKnight, 2000). One study summarized the top frustrations for 148 older adults about not being able to drive: these included loss of spontaneity, loss of independence, loss of social connections and social activities, and difficulties with emotions associated with not driving such as frustration and being a "nonperson," because so much of U.S. identity is associated with driving (Rosenblum & Corn, 2002).

Social Workers and the Physical Changes of Late Adulthood   With regard to physical changes associated with aging, social workers can do much to support clients who experience negative effects as they age, or to promote optimal well-being for aging clients. For example, social workers can educate clients about prevention and management of diseases like arthritis, osteoporosis, and macular degeneration. They can also assist clients in becoming more active in order to mediate the effects of muscle loss, which may help to prevent more serious problems later on. Social workers can also encourage clients to modify their environment to maximize safety and functionality as well as help clients to access resources that will allow them to maintain independence as long as possible.

Judy is displaying some of the typical changes that take place as people age. In Judy's case, her chronological age is 80, so that would place her in the middle-old group. However, because she has some problems with functioning, her functional age may be viewed as slightly older, depending on how you view the normal functionality of 80-year-old people in general. With regard to functioning, Judy needs some assistance with ADLs and IADLs. You will need to be familiar with physical issues that affect the elderly as well as how various agencies measure ability to best help Judy secure the services she needs.

Psychological Changes

Unfortunately, popular stereotypes associate growing older with senility, forgetfulness, loneliness, and visions of the disagreeable little old lady or little old man. Fortunately, as with most stereotypes, these ideas are highly oversimplified and often inaccurate. However, some psychological changes (which can include cognitive changes such as dementia) can occur that pose special challenges for aging individuals and their support systems. They, too, are summarized in Table 12.1.

Dementia in Late Adulthood   Perhaps one of the main concerns that most people have, beyond changes in appearance, is cognitive changes. Usually when people think about aging and cognition, they think about dementia and Alzheimer's disease. As with physical changes, cognitive changes vary a great deal among individuals, and many people do not suffer any of the symptoms of dementia or memory loss that tend to be associated with growing older. Indeed, dementia in and of itself should not be considered a part of the "normal" aging process. Rather, dementias occur as part of specific disease processes, which may or may not occur as people age. **Dementias** are defined as mental disorders caused by deterioration of the brain, and many forms of dementia can occur in both young and old age.

Alzheimer's disease causes the type of dementia that occurs most frequently and seems to strike the most fear in people (American Psychiatric Association, 2000). The disease causes a generally slow and gradual cognitive decline through the accumulation of twisted protein fragments inside nerve cells, called *tangles*, and the abnormal buildup of dead nerve cells and protein, called *plaques*.

One of the first signs of Alzheimer's disease is a permanent loss of short-term memory. People with the disease may forget a name or an address or how to perform a simple task. Although many people, both young and old, forget these things from time to time, people who are not afflicted with the disease will usually remember them eventually. Unfortunately, people with Alzheimer's disease will not. Other signs of the disease include confusion, disorientation, loss of language skills, and difficulty learning. As the disease progresses, memory loss worsens, and personality changes can emerge. For example, some people may become more aggressive or withdrawn, or they might develop problems with delusions or hallucinations. Eventually, people with the disease lose their long-term memory, and they die from related complications such as pneumonia and infections or from the loss of brain function (Alzheimer's Association, 2002).

Most cases of Alzheimer's disease are found among people age 65+, with the occurrence increasing with age. Early onset Alzheimer's disease is not as prevalent. This form of the disease occurs in people younger than 65, with a few cases developing before age 50 (American Psychiatric Association, 2000). It is estimated that as many as 13 percent of people age 65+ and 50 percent of people age 85+ suffer from Alzheimer's disease (Alzheimer's Association, 2002, 2009).

Although Alzheimer's disease can be diagnosed with some accuracy through evaluation of symptoms and health assessments, the only way to confirm a diagnosis is through an autopsy after death. Currently, there is no cure for the disease, but several medications are available that show promise in slowing its course.

Caregiving for people with Alzheimer's disease is a serious issue. Many social service policies and programs have been developed in the past several decades to address this issue. Services such as respite care, adult day care, in-home care, and skilled nursing facilities have assumed the responsibility to research and develop effective ways to care for people with Alzheimer's disease. We will explore issues of caregiving more thoroughly later in the chapter.

Despite the widespread occurrence of dementias, many people do not lose significant cognitive functioning as they age, and they find great satisfaction in lifelong activity and learning. People may decide to change careers in their 60s or to earn a second or third degree in their 70s. Memory and learning do not necessarily decline because of age. Indeed, many researchers posit that the "use it or lose it" adage is true: The more we use our memories, stimulate our thinking, and expose ourselves to new learning, the more we can maintain the mental capacities we enjoyed in younger years. Although people may experience some slowing in cognitive processes as they age, research indicates that many barriers that older people may face in learning are caused by environmental factors or poor instruction rather than deficits in memory or learning capacity. For example, as discussed earlier, some of the eyesight and hearing changes that take place as people age can be a barrier to learning; however, if modifications are made, many older adults learn just as well as younger adults. Moreover, if new material can be linked with existing experiences of the learner, learning can be just as effective for older adults as it is for younger adults (Dunlosky et al., 2007; Moore & Piland, 1994).

Personality and Aging   With regard to personality and aging, many studies have examined how various personality traits play out over time. This research has addressed such issues as whether personality traits remain stable over time, why some people seem to have a "good attitude" about aging while others are negative about the experience, and why some people are better able than others to cope with loss and change.

There appear to be two major arguments about how personality affects aging. One holds that personality traits tend to remain stable over time. Thus, a person who is easygoing and copes well with change when younger is likely to be easygoing and to cope well as she or he ages. Conversely, a person who is highly strung and has difficulty adjusting to changes in younger age is likely to exhibit the same traits in older age. According to this line of thinking, you can tell a lot about how a person will cope in older age based on her or his responses to events in younger age (Bleidorn, Kandler, Riemann, Angleitner, & Spinath, 2009; Ruth & Coleman, 1996; Tickle, Heatherton, & Wittenberg, 2001).

A second argument posits that personality is partially inherited and that the traits that we express serve, to some degree, as insurance of survival into old age. These traits serve certain purposes at different points of our lives to maximize our adaptation and ensure that our needs are met at different developmental stages. Thus, we will express various traits more actively at different points in our lives, depending on the needs that these traits are fulfilling. This idea is summarized in a cross-cultural study conducted by McCrae and his colleagues (1999), which explored age differences in personality in five different countries (Germany, Italy, Portugal, Croatia, and South Korea). Results from this study suggest that personality traits appear to be universal and present themselves more vigorously at different points in the life span. Respondents in this study showed consistent personality traits based on age across cultures, regardless of different political, cultural, or historical contexts. Respondents younger than 30 tended to show characteristics of extroversion, adventurousness, and less concern for conscientiousness than respondents older than 30. As respondents aged, they tended to show characteristics of increased trust, self-control, self-consciousness, and dutifulness. Older respondents also tended to show lesser degrees of hostility, activity, anxiety, depression, and assertiveness than younger respondents. The authors posit that traits seen in younger respondents may serve them well with regard to tasks appropriate to that developmental stage, such as finding a mate or a job. Conversely, traits seen in older respondents may be advantageous with regard to familial and community responsibilities.

Depression and Suicide in Late Adulthood   Another major concern related to growing older is depression. Although depression can be partially related to personality characteristics such as the ability to cope with change, some situational factors can also influence the chances of an older person's developing this condition. The prevalence of depression among older populations is difficult to determine, mostly because of the different ways in which depression is defined. For example, estimates in the literature range from 2.5 percent to 45 percent, with an average of 20 percent, which is much higher than estimates for younger populations, which range from 0.7 percent to 2.7 percent (McCullough, 1991). However, more conservative estimates suggest that rates of major depression among the elderly range from 1 percent to 5 percent, but this does not include older adults who suffer from symptoms of depression that fall short from meeting the full diagnostic criteria of major depression (Alexopoulos, 2000; Hybels & Blazer, 2003).

Do higher rates of depression among the elderly mean that depression is a by-product of the aging process? Not necessarily. There is no evidence to suggest that depression is a normal part of aging. However, other factors such as illness, disability, discrimination, change in roles, and loss of financial, social, and other supports are often an inevitable part of living a long life. It is much more likely that a combination of socioeconomic factors and a person's ability to cope and adapt to changing circumstances plays a role in the development of depression (George, 1993). This is particularly true for older women, who live longer than men and are more likely than men to be living in poverty.

Several studies have suggested that physical illness may play a significant role in an older person's risk of developing depression (Barusch, Rogers, & Abu-Bader, 1999; Hybels & Blazer, 2003; Rogers, 1999). Indeed, some estimates suggest that depression and physical illness coexist in as many as 45 percent of older adults (Gerety & Farnett, 1995). Though these statistics do not prove that poor health directly causes depression, they suggest that a serious illness, whether physical or mental, may seriously compromise an older adult's ability to cope with the challenges of growing older, thus making the person more vulnerable to developing an additional illness. For example, an older person who is suffering from an illness that causes a disability may be more vulnerable to developing depression if she or he must rely on family members for care, or if she or he experiences financial problems because of the costs of care. Conversely, an older person who is suffering from depression may be at higher risk for developing a physical illness because of poor eating habits, lack of activity and interest in daily activities, and neglect of self-care in general.

One of the biggest concerns about depression among the elderly is a tendency toward suicide. Often when we think about suicide, we think of younger adults. However, suicide is a leading cause of death among elderly people. Suicide risk increases with age, particularly among Caucasian elderly men age 85+, who have the highest rates of suicide in almost all the industrialized nations (Boyd, 2007; National Institute of Mental Health, 2009; Pearson & Conwell, 1995). Elderly people are also more likely than younger people to complete suicide. This is because elderly individuals tend to plan their deaths and give fewer indications of their suicidal thoughts or previous attempts than do younger people (Conwell et al., 1998). Further, suicide rates among older adults may be underestimated. Some elderly people may deliberately stop taking medications, overdose on medications, become

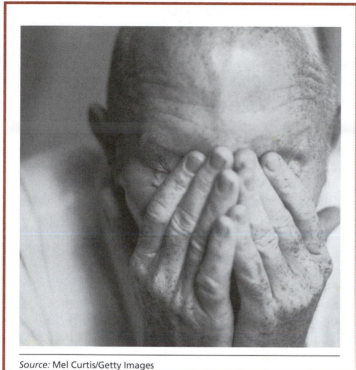

Source: Mel Curtis/Getty Images

EXHIBIT 12.1

Depression in later life is a major concern for many older individuals and their families

self-neglectful, or have accidents that cause death but that are deemed "natural causes" (Osgood, 1991).

Social Workers and the Psychological Changes of Late Adulthood   Social workers are an important part of the service network for people with dementia and other health and mental health problems. Social workers play crucial roles with regard to developing effective interventions and programs for people with dementia as well as support services for caregivers. Social workers also work with older clients who may be having trouble coping with changes associated with aging, and they help older clients maximize their functioning and well-being. Many social workers are involved in researching biopsychosocial issues that affect the health and well-being of older adults, helping to improve the services that are provided to clients.

Given the research that suggests a link between depression and poor physical health, as Judy's social worker, you may want to focus on her mental health in assessment and intervention. Because Judy is coping with issues of functioning, she may be at risk for developing depression or other mental health problems, especially if she is unable to maintain supportive and other services to help with her care.

THE INDIVIDUAL IN LATE ADULTHOOD

In the following sections, we examine some of the issues on an individual level that can affect development in older age. Many of these issues are inextricably linked with areas of development on interpersonal and social levels and must be considered as such when working with older adults.

Psychosocial Theories of Aging

The medical model helps to organize information on disease processes that may occur in later life, but other theories can help social workers to explain various psychosocial issues that may impact the well-being of older adults. Although the list of theories is too exhaustive to discuss all of them here, we will take a look at three popular ones that are used in the literature and in work with older adults: disengagement theory, activity theory, and continuity theory.

Disengagement Theory　The first theory proposed to describe social processes of aging was **disengagement theory** (Cumming & Henry, 1961; Henry, 1963). Disengagement theorists argue that to expect older people to be fully active in societal roles is unrealistic. Rather, they posit that people naturally disengage from formal roles and responsibilities as they age. For example, it is normal for people to retire. At the same time, the larger society pulls away from older people because they are viewed as disruptive to the system. This disengagement, then, is a mutual "agreement" between an aging person and society. The process is viewed as positive, because both the older person and society view this disengagement as necessary for the well-being of both parties.

Obviously, disengagement theory can be viewed as very negative and pessimistic. Particularly in a time when technology is enabling people to live longer, this theory may seem outdated. Some critics argue that disengagement theory is simply a reflection of society's views on older people: Ours is a youth-oriented culture that tends to devalue the experiences of elderly people. Despite this criticism, proponents of disengagement theory point out that it is the first theory that attended to the interaction between the older person and society. Some proponents also argue that disengagement theory is more realistic than other activity-focused theories of aging; specifically, some theories suggest that we should all remain active as we age. This latter view may be overly optimistic.

Activity Theory　A second popular theory is **activity theory**, which states that it is not necessarily normal or natural for people to "drop out" of life as they age (Havighurst, Neugarten, & Tobin, 1968). Rather, the needs and wishes of people as they age are similar to those at any point of life. If people do disengage from their roles, it is usually because of factors outside of their control such as economics, discrimination, and poor health.

EXHIBIT 12.2

Many individuals maintain active lives as they age

Source: Ryan McVay/Getty Images

Activity theory takes a much more positive view on aging than disengagement theory does. It places some emphasis on societal responsibility in changing roles as people age. That is, it holds societal expectations of aging responsible for the reason why people are "forced" out of roles as they age. However, some people feel that this view places pressure on people to remain active as they age: If older adults are not happy, productive seniors, then there is something wrong with them. However, activity theorists maintain that some people prefer to disengage in their later years.

Continuity Theory   One last theory, **continuity theory**, is based on activity theory, but it uses a life span perspective to describe processes of aging (Atchley, 1989). Continuity theory emphasizes the role of personality in determining the outcomes of older age. As people age, they establish life structures, or patterns of being that result from interacting with others and the world, that connect them with their past experiences. These structures not only offer people a foundation on which they continue to develop, but also determine how people will cope and function in the future. People maintain continuity in roles, personality, relationships, and activities, which helps them to adjust (or not) to aging.

As with the other theories on aging, continuity theory does not account for profound changes that can occur as people age. For example, chronic illness and disability can seriously alter an older person's activities and attitude about life. It may be unreasonable to expect people to maintain continuity when such changes occur. Nevertheless, continuity theory may describe what actually happens to many people as they age, particularly if they are lucky enough to escape a serious illness or other events that compromise their well-being. Even if such events do occur, some people cope and adjust in such a way that continuity is not radically disturbed.

Aging Well   Another perspective that helps to explain dynamics of aging, particularly those that relate to individual variation in aging, is aging well or successfully. Various theories exist that explain how some people remain relatively free from disease and maintain optimal cognitive, physical, and social functioning as they age. People who age "successfully" are engaged in life, are emotionally and instrumentally supportive of others, and are proactive with regard to their health, finances, environment, and interpersonal relationships. Indeed, some research suggests that older adults report greater happiness than younger adults, reinforcing the notion of successful aging or aging well (Sorrell, 2009). Conversely, people who age "unsuccessfully" do not possess these qualities and thus show the physical and psychosocial declines that many people associate with aging (Kahana & Kahana, 1996, 2003; Kahana, Kahana, & Kercher, 2003; Rowe & Kahn, 1987, 1997).

Judy's Case Revisited   How might Judy's situation be viewed from these theories and perspectives? This probably depends on your views as the social worker. For example, if you adopt the perspective of disengagement theory, you might view Judy's situation as normal. That is, you might interpret the problems that Judy is having with physical and housing issues as a natural part of aging and the disengagement process. In contrast, if you use activity theory, you might characterize Judy's current state of functioning and her housing problems as "abnormal." Though Judy does have some physical problems, activity theory would dictate that she maintain her normal roles and activities as she ages, as much as her health permits. Judy's problems with housing would be viewed as dysfunctional societal responses to the care of elderly individuals. That is, society is not supporting older adults and their abilities to participate in society by not supporting adequate housing and care. You would thus intervene to improve this care.

Finally, if you were to look at Judy's situation through continuity theory, you would want to know how Judy functioned in the past to help her function as she ages. You might explore characteristics of her roles, personality, relationships, and so on to help her connect with her past and plan for her future. You would also advocate for appropriate housing and care for Judy so that she can maintain her current level of functioning and remain as independent as possible.

Spirituality and Aging

As mentioned in Chapter 10, there is a strong movement in social work to incorporate spirituality into the overall understanding of the human development process. For some researchers who study aging, there has been a call to pay more attention to how spirituality affects the aging process (Kimble, 2001; Nelson-Becker & Canda, 2008; Watkins, 2009). Some researchers argue that in a society that places much emphasis on individuality and independence, many older adults may be faced with increased spiritual isolation and loneliness. This condition may be particularly relevant because many older adults live alone. Consequently, it is important to understand how spirituality can impact the lives of older adults (MacKinlay, 2001; Yoon & Lee, 2007).

Many older adults participate in organized religion, and those who have an affiliation with a particular institution report more subjective feelings of religiosity and spirituality than those who do not identify with a religious institution. Much of the research conducted on religion, spirituality, and aging has focused on the general meaning of religious belief and specific faiths (Atchley & Barusch, 2004). However, little research explores the role of faith and spirituality, in general, on overall life satisfaction of the elderly, especially with regard to issues of loss and disability related to age (Koenig, 1995). Nonetheless, research that explores this area suggests that spirituality may enhance emotional and psychological well-being in the face of loss (Wink, Dillon, & Prettyman, 2007)

Membership in a formal religious organization can have many benefits. Many churches offer programs and services that can support older adults who live in the community. This is particularly true for African American groups. Religious organizations appear to be the foundations for many African American communities (Billingsley & Morrison-Rodriguez, 2007; Chatters & Taylor, 1994). Indeed, regular attendance of religious services can keep elders active in their communities, offer resources for recreation and socialization, and provide additional caregiving support to elders and their families. However, more research needs to be conducted on the effects of regular church attendance for older adults.

Models of faith and spiritual development can be useful in guiding your understanding of the impacts of spirituality on older adults. Recall Fowler's stages of faith development discussed in Chapter 10 (Fowler, 1981). According to Fowler, older adults are in the last stage of faith development, universalizing faith. During this time, older adults resolve conflicts in their beliefs and work toward ensuring the well-being of humankind. Using this theory, social workers can help older clients to explore the meaning of their faith and come to terms with unresolved conflicts that may still be creating barriers to achieving a sense of peace and life satisfaction. In doing so, many older adults may find a sense of purpose in helping others and contributing to the well-being of their communities, which may in turn help them achieve an individual sense of health, well-being, and spirituality that will support their overall development in older adulthood.

In working with Judy, you may want to explore her sense of faith and spirituality. It may be that, if cultivated, these aspects can be a source of strength for Judy as she works through some of her physical and other problems. Moreover, if Judy is affiliated with a specific religious organization, you could help to ensure that she has access to the resources that it might provide.

Sexuality in Late Adulthood

One stereotype of aging is that older adults lose their sexuality and thus no longer enjoy sexual intimacy. This stereotype could not be further from the truth. It may be entrenched in U.S. society because sexuality of older adults tends to be invisible in the media and elsewhere and because people tend to define aging as a lonely stage in life that is filled with disability and illness. In addition, people tend to view older adults as unattractive and past their need for romance and intimate companionship.

Although sexual functioning does decrease somewhat with age, many people find effective ways to compensate for such decreases. For example, products like KY Jelly can be used to supplement vaginal lubrication in older women, and Viagra and penile implants can assist with erectile dysfunctions in men. Some older people do report a decrease in the frequency of sex, but a majority of older people maintain an active sex life and report an increase in their interest in, quality of, and satisfaction with sex as they age, according to recent research (Lindau et al., 2007; Westheimer & Lopater, 2004). According to Segraves and Segraves (1995), sexual changes that occur as people age are closely associated with other psychosocial changes that occur with aging. Specifically, sexual functioning in older age has much to do with health status, the availability of a partner, and the relationship with a partner. Moreover, sexuality tends to be varied among older adults and is inextricably linked with biopsychosocial and cultural factors.

Social workers need to be leaders in correcting myths and stereotypes about sexuality in old age and educating clients and others about the importance of continued sexual intimacy as they age. Because sexual intimacy can be a source of great pleasure and satisfaction in relationships, social workers need to pay attention to this area in assessing and intervening with older adults.

Gay, Lesbian, Bisexual, and Transgendered Older Adults

In regard to aging and sexuality, gay, lesbian, bisexual, and transgendered (GLBT) older adults face a double stereotype: They are gay *and* old. Fortunately, however, many older GLBT adults lead happy and satisfying lives, sexually and otherwise. GLBT couples who are in long-term, committed relationships can offer the same type of support and companionship as heterosexual couples. These relationships provide intimacy, caregiving, and social and financial support. Of course, older GLBT adults face similar obstacles that younger GLBT people face, such as discrimination, social disapproval, familial strife, and laws prohibiting marriage. These laws can cause additional problems with regard to benefits, housing, property, parenting, and guardianship rights. Some older couples may find that their family members disapprove of their relationship and refuse to acknowledge it. This can pose emotional and other problems for older adults, especially if they find themselves reliant in any way on family members for caregiving. Further, older GLBT people may face homophobia and discrimination in care facilities, forcing them back in the closet. In the United States and in other countries, some care facilities are catering to GLBT elders or at least providing services geared toward supporting people in this population (Gulli, 2009).

There are also considerations with regard to how GLBT people perceive their own aging and how their aging plays out in their communities. For example, results from one study that examined perceptions of aging among 183 gay and lesbian respondents found that young and old gay men felt that gay society viewed aging very negatively, whereas a significantly smaller percentage of lesbian women thought that lesbian society viewed aging negatively. Gay men also perceived aging as occurring at significantly younger years than lesbian women, which has implications for gay men's attitudes about being "dateable" and their abilities toward securing partners, especially partners who can serve as caregivers in old age. Gay men did not necessarily define their own aging in very negative terms, but they still perceived the gay community as ageist. Conversely, lesbian women held more positive attitudes about aging and their prospects for intimate relationships as they aged. These relationships, in combination with access to more formal social supports organized by older lesbian women, make it more likely that lesbian women will have more support in old age than gay men (Schope, 2005).

Social workers need to be aware of the various issues that can create potential problems for older GLBT clients. On an individual level, social workers can help older GLBT clients work through personal beliefs and attitudes about aging that might inhibit personal growth as well as help clients deal with the effects of ageism in their community. On a societal and interpersonal level, social workers can be of great assistance in helping clients to work on meaningful relationships that will provide support and fulfillment in older years as well as overcome barriers created by institutional ageism, heterosexism, and discrimination that can put older GLBT clients at risk for poor psychosocial health and well-being.

Grief and Loss

Throughout the discussion so far, many issues have surfaced that could create the potential for grief reactions. Loss of health, abilities, supports, relationships, friendships, and various roles leave people vulnerable to developing grief reactions. As you have seen, people react very differently to various situations depending on many factors such as their personalities, coping skills, and personal resources. However, with the passage of time, everyone will inevitably face losses in one form or another. Social workers who work with older adults need to understand models of grief and loss and consider the various losses that older people can experience as well as the various ways in which they respond to loss. Because older adults often experience losses in various biopsychosocial areas (for example, physically, financially, socially), social workers need to be aware of the complexity of the relationship between physical factors and other psychosocial and environmental factors that can affect well-being.

One approach to conceptualizing grief reactions in clients is through Elisabeth Kübler-Ross's theory of death and dying (1969). This theory can assist social workers in better understanding the processes of grief and how processes may affect clients' reactions to and coping with various losses.

Kübler-Ross, a psychiatrist, conducted extensive interviews with hundreds of dying patients. Through talking with patients about their feelings, thoughts, and experiences, Kübler-Ross developed a model of the stages of dying that were typical among those she interviewed. Although the model is built around those who are experiencing the death process, it can be applied to people who have experienced a major loss such as divorce or unemployment.

Box 12.1 describes the stages in Kübler-Ross's model. She found that many people went through stages in a predictable manner, though the exact process varies from person to person. For example, some people may get "stuck" in a stage, unable to move on to the next. Others may skip a stage or two altogether. Still others may find themselves moving backward into a previous stage, even though it seemed they had done the work necessary in that stage. So, while there may be some predictable pattern to the way some people deal with death and dying, there are circumstances where people do not deal with death in such a predictable manner. Note also that not all people will make it successfully to the final stage; that is, some people may never be able to accept their impending death or their loss (Kübler-Ross, 1969, 1971).

The Kübler-Ross model provides a straightforward approach to reactions to death and dying, and the stages are fairly easy to apply in cases where clients are dealing with loss. Also, in a "death-denying" culture such as the United States, the ideas behind this model are useful to help understand, tolerate, and work with the variety of reactions that can occur with loss. However, the Kübler-Ross model may not account for cultural or spiritual variations that different people bring to their experience. There is the danger that if clients do not adhere to these particular stages, for whatever reason, they may be viewed as deviant or somehow disordered for not dealing with their loss in the expected way.

In Judy's case, she has already experienced various losses through disability and moving into a care facility. She faces the prospect of more loss through receiving notice that she will need to vacate Sunset Homes. These potential losses could affect her physical health if issues surrounding these losses are not addressed. For example, extensive loss could lead to depression, which could compromise her physical health. Though you have limited knowledge of Judy's personality and how Judy has reacted to loss in the past, you can learn more about Judy's coping skills. The fact

BOX 12.1

Kübler-Ross Model of Death and Dying

STAGE ONE: DENIAL

This is the initial stage in which people first learn the news that they or someone they know is dying. Denial can be useful in that it helps to protect the person against the shock of receiving such news. People in the denial stage might respond with, "No, not me," or, "There must be a mistake," or, "Why my child?"

STAGE TWO: ANGER

Once a person has worked through denial, a typical reaction to surface is anger. People often respond with anger as a way to work through their intense feelings. People may lash out at their care providers, family members, or even God. Some anger-based responses might include, "Why me?" or "Why would God do this?" or "What did I do to deserve this?"

STAGE THREE: BARGAINING

Once the anger has dissipated, people may try to bargain with health care professionals or God to restore their health. Typical responses include, "If I could just get healthy again, I'll go to church"; or, "If you'll just give me more time, I'll . . ."; or, "I promise I'll do better if you'll just let me live." Kübler-Ross found that even people who didn't believe in God would often engage in bargaining with a higher power.

STAGE FOUR: DEPRESSION

Once people realize that bargaining isn't working, they frequently become depressed. Sometimes the depression is active: People actively grieve their losses or potential losses. Sometimes depression is passive: People become silent and turn inward.

STAGE FIVE: ACCEPTANCE

This stage occurs after people have worked through the preceding stages and have attained a sense of peace with the realization that they (or a loved one) will die. If people reach this stage, they are often able to resolve unfinished business and bring closure to their relationships and lives.

Source: Kübler-Ross, 1971.

that she seems settled in a care facility speaks well to her ability to adjust to change. Moreover, you can assess Judy's strengths to ensure available resources are used to help her deal with the situation.

Though Judy is not faced with imminent death, you could also make use of Kübler-Ross's theory. According to this theory, the goal in working with Judy is to help her to accept her physical losses and limitations and to come to terms with the changes that she will inevitably experience in the future. To help Judy reach the acceptance stage, you may want to explore her thoughts and feelings about her physical changes. How Judy deals with these losses will depend on many factors, including her personality, coping skills, cultural background, and personal philosophy on life. These are areas that you could explore to evaluate in which stage Judy is currently situated as well as how she can be helped to progress into the final stage.

THE FAMILY AND IMMEDIATE ENVIRONMENT IN LATE ADULTHOOD

So far, we have explored issues that pertain to the individual. In this section, we will look at ways in which older adults are influenced by their immediate environment. While considering issues that can occur at this level, keep in mind how physical factors can influence the dynamics of familial and other functioning.

Families can be a rich source of physical, emotional, financial, and psychological support as people age. Family dynamics are continually changing as people age: New family members are added and lost, roles and relationships change, and events occur to change the way people view themselves in the context of their families. Moreover, as society advances in technology and changes in values, culture, and attitudes, families face new challenges, which in turn affect family dynamics and roles for family members. For aging individuals, these changes can be positive and negative, making it crucial for social workers to understand family issues that can affect the well-being of older adults.

Grandparenting Issues in Late Adulthood

Traditionally, grandparenting is viewed as an important role in U.S. society. The general perception of grandparents is as older, supportive, secondary caregivers to grandchildren. Grandparents usually leave the primary rearing and disciplining responsibilities to the parents. These patterns would reflect the fun seeker, distant figure, and formal figure styles of grandparenting discussed in Chapter 7.

However, with changing economic and social times, more families are finding it necessary to have two breadwinners, leaving them with child care needs. Many families have difficulties affording good day care or after-school programs for their children. With increasing alternative family situations such as single-parent households, families need to be creative and resourceful with regard to finding ways to rear their children. Additionally, issues such as AIDS/HIV, criminal activity, drug abuse, and other problems are leaving families without their primary caregivers. Finally, many people would agree that child rearing today is more challenging and complex than it has ever been.

Because of these situations, more primary caregivers are turning to **kinship care**, which is care given to children by relatives when parents are unable to do so. Often, grandparents help ease the burdens of child care through kinship care (Davitt, 2006). Indeed, increasing numbers of grandparents are assuming the primary caregiver or surrogate parent role for children. According to the 2000 census, 4.5 million children are living in a grandparent-headed household; 2.5 million of those do not have a parent present. Around 63 percent of these grandparents are women. This number has increased by 30 percent since 1990 (U.S. Census Bureau, 2001). Most grandparents raising grandchildren are in the 55 to 64 age range; however, approximately 25 percent of primary caregiving grandparents are age 65+. Further, it appears that grandparents from all ethnic groups are taking responsibility for their grandchildren, with Caucasians comprising almost half (47 percent) of all grandparent caregivers. Unfortunately, grandparents who are primary caregivers are more likely than noncaregivers to be living in poverty—approximately 19 percent are considered poor (American Association of Retired Persons, 2003; U.S. Census Bureau, 2001). In part, this reality could be due to the economic strain children can put on these grandparents, who are likely to be female and living on a fixed income.

Grandparents face many legal issues when taking on primary-care responsibilities for their grandchildren. Some of these issues include legal guardianship and financial and other supports (Kruk, 1994). For example, many grandparents may be eligible for support through Temporary Assistance for Needy Families (TANF), which is the program commonly thought of as "welfare." However, if the grandparent is the one receiving the grant, she or he is required to meet the work requirements mandated by the program. Grandparents can apply for a grant for their grandchildren, but these grants are limited in the amount of money awarded and the amount of time for which the grandparent can receive aid.

Some grandparents may also face challenges because they do not have legal custody of their grandchildren. In addition to the emotional issues that can surface when grandparents assume responsibility for their grandchildren, if grandparents do not have legal custody of the grandchildren, they often do not have any power over finances, and their authority and child-rearing efforts can be undermined when adult children reenter the picture. Many grandparents find that they are emotionally and physically overwhelmed by the complex challenges they face trying to balance relationships between their adult children and their grandchildren. In some cases, grandparents are also grieving for their own children's situations when these children are overcome by drug, criminal, or health problems (Burnette, 1998).

Social workers can assist clients who are providing care for their grandchildren to secure social services or other resources that might help clients in their caregiving. Social workers may also need to help older clients cope with the challenges that often come with caregiving. For example, though parenting a grandchild can bring joy and satisfaction, it can also strain finances and relationships. It may also bring a wide range of feelings such as fear, anger, sadness, and resentment. And, though a caregiving relationship between a grandparent and grandchild might be positive for those involved, it may still take time for all those in the relationship to adjust. Social workers can help facilitate this adjustment and help clients to establish positive relationships.

Older Adults and Their Caregivers

Increasingly, adult children and other family members are becoming the caregivers of their parents and older relatives. Caregiving arrangements vary widely from family to family; but regardless of the situation, caregiving can take a large physical, financial, emotional, and psychological toll on adult children and other family members.

The majority of care for older adults is given by a spouse or an adult child, both of whom are usually female. Of adult children who are caring for elderly parents, approximately 75 percent to 90 percent are daughters who, on average, are married and working full time, making around $35,000 a year (Family Caregiver Alliance, 2003; Mellor, 2000). Adult children caring for their aging parents as well as their own children has led to the phenomenon of the sandwich generation, discussed in Chapter 11. Many of these caregivers find themselves pulling double duty as they struggle to care for an aging parent while raising their children and tending to other familial and work responsibilities.

Effects of Caregiving on Caregivers   A great deal of research has focused on the effects that caregiving can have on caregivers. Much of this research has pointed to feelings of fear, grief, anger, guilt, worry, sadness, fatigue, and isolation in the caregiver, which can lead to more severe health and mental health problems if the caregiver is not able to address the stress of caregiving. These feelings can be even more pronounced among caregivers who are not employed outside of the home or who do not have a good support system on which to rely (Scharlach, 1994). There are also financial consequences; caregivers, who are mostly women, are more likely than noncaregivers to earn low wages, have jobs that offer few benefits, and experience many interruptions in steady employment—all of which have long-term ramifications and contribute to the poverty of women (Family Caregiver Alliance, 2003). Indeed, caregivers spend, on average, about 10 percent of their income on caregiving expenses—many end up taking out loans, spending savings, and foregoing their own health care to help cover caregiving costs (National Alliance for Caregiving, 2007). Conversely, caregiving can bring many benefits to the caregiver and the family. Specifically, it has been shown to have the following positive effects (Plowfield, Raymond, & Blevins, 2000):

- Enables family members to express love and commitment to other members.
- Provides financial and emotional stability to the older adult and the family members.
- Strengthens the bonds among family members.
- Brings a sense of satisfaction and accomplishment to the caregiver.

Various services have been developed to help support caregivers and to provide respite for them—particularly those who are providing care for a victim of Alzheimer's disease—so that they can take care of themselves and address their other responsibilities. Services provided by professionals or financed by the government are referred to as **formal caregiving**. Caregiving that occurs within a person's environment, such as that given by family, friends, and church members, is considered **informal caregiving** (Pickens, 1998). Many formal caregiving services are described in "The Larger Social Environment in Late Adulthood," later in the chapter.

One way of viewing caregiving is through **exchange theory**, which examines the extent to which participants in a particular relationship are satisfied. Specifically, the more that people feel overbenefited (they are getting more from a partnership than they are giving) or underbenefited (they are getting less from a partnership than they are giving) in a relationship, the more dissatisfied they will be (Berkowitz & Walster, 1976; Dowd, 1975, 1980). In a caregiving relationship, an older person who needs care may feel overbenefited because she or he is physically, cognitively, or emotionally unable to contribute to the relationship. The caregiver may feel underbenefited because she or he constantly gives care but receives little in return. This dynamic may leave both parties feeling angry, resentful, and unhappy with the relationship. In working with caregiving situations, social workers can help clients to explore their feelings about the amount of effort and commitment they are contributing to a caregiving relationship and help clients to resolve negative feelings that may result from unequal contributions in the relationship.

Caregiving and Social Work   In many ways, social workers have assumed leadership in the area of caregiving and service provision for older adults and their caregivers. Because of the potential negative consequences that caregiving can have on older adults and their families, social workers need to focus on caregiving issues such as health, mental health, access to resources, and other concerns in their work with older adults and their families. This will become increasingly important as the older population grows in number; more and more people will be living in the community, relying on family members for some form of care.

Judy's care needs provide a good example of how caregiving issues can create problems for older adults. Judy's daughter seems like a natural choice to provide care for Judy, but it appears that there are barriers keeping her daughter from being more involved in Judy's life. In addition, the level of care that Judy needs might be too advanced for her daughter to assume sole responsibility. However, there could be some roles that Judy's daughter could play to improve Judy's situation or at least to improve familial interactions. As the social worker, you may want to learn more about Judy's family dynamics to better understand how these relations are affecting Judy's physical and psychosocial health and whether any intervention could take place.

Elder Abuse and Neglect

One of the unfortunate side effects of caregiver stress can be elder abuse and neglect. Although certainly not the only source of elder abuse and neglect, family members account for much of the mistreatment of older adults. Box 12.2 gives some statistics on maltreatment of older adults.

Exchange theory, discussed in the previous section, can help to explain how elder abuse and neglect occur. If caregivers feel that they are overextended with regard to the amount of time and energy that they are putting into caregiving, they can experience feelings of anger and resentment, which in turn can lead to abuse or neglect. Similarly, family systems theory can be used to help understand how family dynamics in a caregiving situation may lead to problems. Issues such as shifting homeostasis, changing roles and boundaries, and the need for adaptation can all pose problems for people struggling to adjust to a relationship in which caregiving and dependence are permanent defining characteristics.

BOX 12.2

Maltreatment of Older Adults

Neglect, abandonment, physical abuse, sexual abuse, financial exploitation, and emotional or psychological abuse are all forms of maltreatment of older adults. Because many cases of abuse and neglect are not reported to authorities, only estimates exist on how many elders are abused or neglected each year. The National Elder Abuse Incidence Study (Administration on Aging, 1998) estimated that approximately 550,000 people aged 60+ were abused or neglected in 1996, with only 21 percent of these cases being reported to authorities. Of the reported cases, neglect was the most frequently reported problem (49 percent), followed by emotional abuse (35 percent), financial abuse (30 percent), and physical abuse (26 percent). Abandonment, sexual abuse, and other forms of abuse were also reported, and some people may have suffered multiple incidences of abuse and neglect. These statistics reflect a more recent study of over 3,000 older adults which found that approximately 13 percent of elderly individuals experienced some kind of abuse, and few report abuse by family members to authorities (Laumann, Leitsch, & Waite, 2008).

Most victims of abuse and neglect were age 80+, with the exception of abandonment, whose victims tended to be younger than 80. The majority (58 percent) of victims were women, and most (80 percent) were Caucasian. Most victims of abuse and neglect, about 75 percent, are frail and dependent on a caregiver. Men tended to commit most acts of abuse, while women were responsible for the majority of neglect. Overall, 66 percent of perpetrators of abuse and neglect were in the age range of 40 to 59 years old, and 77 percent were Caucasian. Finally, a large proportion (47 percent) of the perpetrators of abuse and neglect were adult children of the victims. The second most frequent perpetrator of abuse and neglect was a spouse (19 percent). When the adult child was financially dependent on the victim, the risk of abuse and neglect increased (Administration on Aging, 1998).

Given the stress that caregiving can bring, as well as changes in the structures and responsibilities of contemporary families, social workers need to be cognizant of the potential for abuse and neglect of elderly individuals. When working with an older adult, social workers must include the caregiver and other familial support systems in the assessment. Assessment of the family situation can offer insights into potential risks for problems, which can be addressed as part of the work with the older adult. Because caregivers provide such crucial services to older adults, social workers need to ensure that caregivers are getting the supports and services that they need to continue to be effective care providers as well as healthy, happy individuals. Moreover, the caregiver's overall health is important to that of the person receiving care.

THE LARGER SOCIAL ENVIRONMENT IN LATE ADULTHOOD

This section discusses broader issues that affect people as they age. Many of these issues have to do with policies and services that impact individuals and that influence the choices people make and the ways in which people live.

Long-Term and Alternative Care

An emerging issue in elder care has to do with long-term care alternatives. Because people are living longer, many individuals and families find themselves dealing with issues of living arrangements and caregiving at some point in their lives. The phrase "long-term care" often invokes images of nursing homes and other institutionalized care. However, it is really much more than that. **Long-term care (LTC)** involves any set of services provided to people who need sustained help with ADLs and IADLs (NASW, 1987).

This broad definition of long-term care implies that care can be classified along a continuum. This continuum is helpful in describing the levels of care that people might need at different points in their lives as well as the array of services that might be provided within each level. Exhibit 12.3 displays a typical continuum of care and the services provided within each level.

The services provided along the continuum can be provided either in the home or in an institutional setting, and they are usually provided by skilled employees from various social service agencies that are funded by a variety of sources. Some services are offered to all seniors, while others are targeted specifically to low-income seniors. Often, agencies will employ social workers or other professionals to provide care management services to ensure that services are appropriate for the level of care needed and that services are not duplicated. Especially when services are tied to eligibility criteria, care managers are needed to assess the level of functioning and economic status of individuals receiving services to ensure that regulations are being followed. Generally, the goal of long-term care is to keep elders independent and

EXHIBIT 12.3

The Continuum of Care

LEVEL OF FUNCTIONING

EXAMPLES OF SERVICES

Independent
Senior centers:
Meals
Recreation/
 Socialization
Support groups:
Caregivers'
 responsibility
Respite
Volunteer activities

Somewhat Independent
Chore services:
Lawn and yard work
Snow removal
Minor home repair
Preventive health
 services:
Screening
Education
Legal services
Information and referral

Increasingly Frail
Friendly visitor
Protective payee
Home health
Telephone
 reassurance
Transportation
Home delivered
 meals
Homemaker services

More Dependent
Alternative
 programs:
Specific in-home
 services
Ombudsman
Adult day care
Adult foster care
Adult protective
 services
Escort
 transportation
Personal care

Highly Dependent
Ombudsman
Skilled nursing care

living in their communities for as long as possible. Often, long-term care options are less costly and preferable to seniors who receive them than alternatives such as residential or skilled nursing care.

Managed Care and LTC Insurance   With health care costs soaring, in combination with older adults who are living longer and experiencing long bouts of chronic illness, long-term care options can be especially cost effective if they prevent more serious problems such as disability and institutionalization. Managed care has also influenced the availability and types of services seniors can receive. Because of increased health care costs, one goal of managed care companies has been to cap spending on health care services. Capping of costs and services has been of primary concern for many senior advocates who fear that older adults will be harmed by this type of system, mostly because of the amount of services that older adults need. For example, managed care programs can dictate the number of days a person may be hospitalized based on the reasons for hospitalization (Atchley & Barusch, 2004). Unfortunately, because decisions are based on a cost-effective timetable, many older adults who suffer from multiple health problems and whose recovery is longer than that for younger adults are discharged before they have fully recuperated. This premature discharge may place them at risk for developing other illnesses or becoming dependent on other caregivers for assistance while they recover.

Long-term care insurance is a relatively new proposed solution to financing care. Several private insurance companies now offer LTC policies that people can purchase to pay for care in older age. These policies are really meant to be purchased in younger years when they are much more affordable than when purchased in older years. However, because these policies are new, few people have heard of them. Even if they have, people are reluctant to buy a policy that will serve them only when they are older, particularly when many families are struggling to afford health and other insurance that will cover their current needs. Though these policies vary a great deal, they are mostly designed to pay for medical and other costs that occur when people need an ongoing high level of care such as that offered in skilled nursing facilities.

Because Medicare and many private insurance policies are limited in the coverage they offer for LTC services, many people find themselves spending all of their assets to pay for care. Once that happens, they become eligible for Medicaid, which will cover many LTC costs. However, many people do not want to use all of their savings and other resources for care, which makes LTC insurance a viable option for many seniors if they can afford it. Later sections discuss some of these issues in more detail.

Housing Options   An issue related to long-term care is housing for the elderly. Over the past few decades, various innovative housing options have become available for older adults who find themselves at different levels of functioning at different points of their lives. Housing options run the continuum from totally independent living to skilled nursing facilities (also known as nursing homes or transitional care units), where people can recover after being discharged from the hospital. These facilities offer intensive medical care for people who need extensive services and equipment, and they tend to be the most expensive option of care.

Between these ends of the continuum, there are retirement or residential living options, where older adults can have their own apartments within a larger community of older adults. Generally, these communities offer services such as on-call health professionals, organized activities and recreation, transportation, and congregate meals. Assisted living facilities offer a bridge between living at home or in a retirement complex and living in a skilled nursing facility. These facilities generally offer private living quarters with more advanced services such as on-site medical and personal care.

Other living options include congregate housing in which people who need minimal support live in one community of individual apartments or shared housing. Life care communities, or **continuing care retirement communities (CCRCs)**, offer housing and services across the continuum. An older adult can initially move into an independent apartment and subsequently move to accommodations that offer higher levels of care as the need arises.

The benefits to this type of arrangement are that people can remain in the same facility regardless of their needs, which minimizes the disruption of moving. Thus, as residents develop friendships and become part of a community, they can maintain these aspects of their lives even as their care needs change. This arrangement is particularly helpful for couples who might each be at different levels of functioning and need different types of facilities. Couples can remain on the same grounds, which can greatly enhance the quality of life for both partners. Be aware that gay and lesbian couples may not be permitted to share housing in many traditional facilities; however, housing communities for gay and lesbian adults are being developed nationwide to address this issue. Finally, boarding and group homes are available for fully independent older adults. Residents usually share chores such as house and yard work, meals, shopping, and running errands.

Judy's Case Revisited   Sunset Homes is a type of CCRC, and because Judy needs a fairly high level of care, she resides in a unit that provides some skilled care. However, this arrangement is quite expensive, so she has to rely on Medicaid to fund it. Because Medicaid eligibility requirements are becoming stricter in Judy's state, as her social worker, you will have to find ways to continue funding her care.

One approach would be to have Judy's ADLs and IADLs reassessed. Because Judy has been living in Sunset Homes for three years, her activity levels may not have been assessed in a while and her care needs may have increased. A new assessment may more accurately reflect her current abilities, which could meet the new Medicaid criteria. Another approach you could take is to appeal Medicaid's decision to cut funding for Judy. You could advocate on Judy's behalf to try to restore funding, even if Judy's needs do not meet new eligibility standards. Finally, you could help Judy find housing elsewhere—possibly with her daughter—and contract with other agencies for in-home care. However, given Judy's situation, it is likely that Judy needs a variety of services and that her daughter would need extra support to prevent the problems that caregiving can create.

Poverty and Older Adults

Contrary to commonly held stereotypes of older adults being wealthy misers, many older adults, particularly women and seniors from ethnic minority groups, live on fixed incomes that barely provide basic necessities. Box 12.3 gives a statistical snapshot of poverty among older people in the United States.

Poverty can be a transitory problem for many younger adults, but it can be a permanent aspect of life for many older adults, particularly elderly minority group members (Hillier & Barrow, 2006; Quadagno, 2008). Widowhood, disability, retirement, unemployment, chronic illness, medication costs, age discrimination, and increased costs of living can all contribute to poverty among older adults. Moreover, women and ethnic minorities are more likely than Caucasian men to experience these problems throughout their lives, leaving them more vulnerable to poverty than men. For example, many women and ethnic minorities earn less than Caucasian men over their lifetime, which means that they will have contributed less to financial supports such as Social Security and pensions. Thus, payments they might receive from these sources are less than Caucasian men receive.

Indeed, the term **triple jeopardy** has been used extensively in the literature to describe "female ethnic-minority elderly." Members of this particular group face discrimination in three ways—being a woman, elderly, and a member of an ethnic minority group—putting them even more at risk for poverty than other older adults.

Living in poverty for older adults can lead to other problems such as stress, prolonged illness and disability, reduced access to health care, and poor living conditions. Poverty, then, becomes inextricably linked with other issues we have

---

Using a poverty threshold of $12,550 per year for people age 65+, the U.S. Census Bureau estimates that in 2007, 9.7 percent of people age 65+ lived in poverty. When medical out-of-pocket expenses were deducted from the total income of people age 65+, the poverty rate jumped to 16.1 percent. The poverty rate for some ethnic minorities was higher than the average. For example, the poverty rate for African Americans age 65+ was 23.2 percent; for Hispanics it was 17.1 percent; and for Asian/Pacific Islanders it was 11.2 percent. For Caucasians, the poverty rate was 7.4 percent. Poverty rates also differed by gender: The average poverty rates in 2007 were 6.6 percent for men and 12.0 percent for women.

BOX 12.3

Poverty among Older People in the United States

Source: DeNavas-Walt, Proctor, & Smith, 2008; National Women's Law Center, 2008.

discussed, potentially decreasing the life satisfaction and well-being of many older adults. Judy's case is a good example of how poverty can cause added stress in the lives of elderly people, especially when poverty is tied to health and other problems.

Policies Linked to Services for Older Adults

Many social service and other policies have been developed and enacted over the centuries to address the needs of the elderly population. Some of the largest and most successful pieces of legislation ever enacted in the United States have been those for the elderly.

Social Security Many people use the term Social Security to describe the payments that older and disabled U.S. citizens receive. In reality, Social Security is a little more complicated. The Social Security Act, passed in 1935, provides Old-Age, Survivors, and Disability Insurance (OASDI). OASDI provides cash payments to retired workers and survivors of insured workers. The Social Security Act represents the first intergenerational contract to provide financial support to older adults. In order for it to pass, younger generations had to agree to pay taxes to support the current cohort of older adults, with the promise that the younger workers in turn would be supported once they turned 65. In 1956, the Act was amended to provide payments to disabled workers and their families, known as Disability Insurance (NASW, 1987).

Social Security provides benefits to workers as an entitlement without any means tests or income tests. In other words, people are entitled to Social Security if they are able to work. Spouses of workers and their children younger than age 18 are also entitled to the worker's benefit should that worker die. Workers who suffer long-term (12 months or more) health or mental health disabilities are also entitled to Social Security. Benefits are calculated through a complex formula that includes the total earnings of workers and the amount of time worked. As discussed previously, women and ethnic minorities tend to receive lower benefits than Caucasian men because they tend to earn lower wages. Further, their work is often interrupted due to childbirth, child care, and adult care. In addition, women and ethnic minorities tend to be overrepresented in part-time and seasonal work, which means that they are often the first to be laid off in times of recession.

Older Americans Act Congress passed the **Older Americans Act (OAA) of 1965** during Lyndon Johnson's administration. The OAA is a comprehensive piece of legislation that seeks to improve the well-being of older adults. It was passed during a time when concern over the poor and disenfranchised was fueling a sense of social responsibility to provide services for those who could not provide for themselves. The OAA consists of several "titles" that articulate the overall charge of the legislation (Administration on Aging, 2006). Box 12.4 lists the titles and describes the basic functions of each.

BOX 12.4

*The Older
Americans Act
(OAA)*

TITLE I: DECLARATION OF OBJECTIVES AND DEFINITIONS

Objectives include aspects such as achievement of an adequate income in retirement, achievement of good health and mental health, access to affordable housing and services, opportunities for employment, benefits from continued research, and protection from abuse and neglect.

TITLE II: ADMINISTRATION ON AGING (AOA)

The AoA, housed in the Department of Health and Human Services, is charged with administering the OAA. It serves to administer funds and grants to social service agencies for the elderly, provide consultation and guidance to states, and manage resources allocated by the legislation. Title II articulates the responsibilities on which to base policies and services for older adults to ensure their well-being.

TITLE III: GRANTS FOR STATE AND COMMUNITY PROGRAMS ON AGING

This is the largest title under the OAA. This title articulates the responsibilities of the states and their respective State Units on Aging (SUA) and Area Agencies on Aging (AAA). SUAs are responsible for dividing states into service areas governed by AAA, which are entities that administer and manage local social service agencies. This title has several parts that describe particular services and programs that must be administered. These include access services such as transportation and case management, in-home services, legal services, supportive services, senior centers, congregate and home delivered meals, disease prevention and health promotion services, and a national family caregiver support program.

TITLE IV: ACTIVITIES FOR HEALTH, INDEPENDENCE AND LONGEVITY

This title administers competitive grants to social service agencies and other organizations and institutions to carry out research and to develop programs.

TITLE V: COMMUNITY SERVICE SENIOR OPPORTUNITIES ACT

This title is charged with promoting part-time employment opportunities for unemployed, low-income older adults.

TITLE VI: GRANTS FOR NATIVE AMERICANS

This title provides advocacy for older Indians, Alaskan Natives, and Native Hawaiians. This includes culturally competent supportive and nutrition services. In 2002, a Native American caregiver support program was added to this title.

TITLE VII: VULNERABLE ELDER RIGHTS PROTECTION

This title establishes protective programs such as the ombudsman program; prevention of elder abuse, neglect, and exploitation; and legal assistance.

Source: Administration on Aging, 2006.

The OAA has established a broad network of administrative bodies that assist in disseminating funding and services from the federal to local levels. The **Administration on Aging (AoA)** is a federal body that oversees the administration of the OAA through State Units on Aging (SUA), which are responsible for organizing states into smaller service areas based on populations of older adults. **Area Agencies on Aging (AAA)** are the entities in charge of each service area in each state, and they administer funds to local service agencies in various communities in each service area. It is these local service agencies that actually provide services to older adults in their respective communities. Many services described earlier under "Long-Term and Alternative Care" are funded through the OAA and are provided by local agencies that contract with their AAAs to respond to the needs of older adults. Exhibit 12.4 offers a visual overview of this administrative structure.

Many programs and services found in state and local governments are authorized through the OAA. Programs such as Adult Protective Services and mental health and health services are often provided through state, city, or county governments, or they are contracted out to local agencies through governmental agencies. For example, **ombudsman programs**, which offer advocacy for older adults who are residing in skilled nursing facilities, generally are offered through governmental

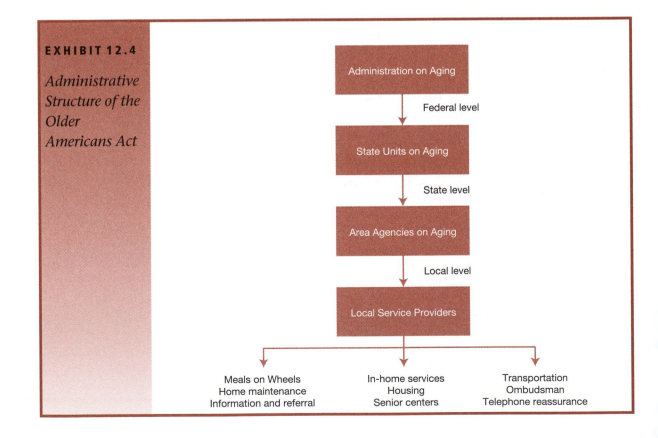

EXHIBIT 12.4

Administrative Structure of the Older Americans Act

Administration on Aging

Federal level

State Units on Aging

State level

Area Agencies on Aging

Local level

Local Service Providers

Meals on Wheels
Home maintenance
Information and referral

In-home services
Housing
Senior centers

Transportation
Ombudsman
Telephone reassurance

organizations. Ombudsmen ensure that the rights of residents are being respected, and they intervene on behalf of residents if a skilled nursing facility is suspected of violating those rights.

Medicare   A federal program enacted in 1965 under the Social Security Act, Medicare has two parts. **Medicare Part A** is hospital insurance to cover hospital stays, and **Medicare Part B** is supplemental insurance that older adults must purchase to pay for some costs not covered by Part A. Older adults age 65+ who are eligible for Social Security are eligible for Medicare Part A. Also eligible are disabled workers, disabled widows and widowers age 50+, workers who have disabled adult children (age 18+) who became disabled before age 22, and workers and family members who need kidney dialysis or transplant (Centers for Medicare and Medicaid Services, 2000).

Part A insurance provides limited coverage for costs incurred through hospitalization, skilled nursing facility care, and home health and hospice care. Coverage under Part A tends to be limited to basic services and has time limits on any one hospital or skilled nursing facility stay as well as lifetime limits on total care that people can receive. Further, insured older adults must pay deductibles, depending on the amount of time hospitalized.

Because this coverage is limited, older adults are encouraged to purchase Part B or supplemental insurance. Part B insurance is designed to cover costs of services not offered through Part A, such as outpatient office visits, laboratory tests, and medical equipment. Although Part B can be useful in curbing health care costs, it too is limited as to which services it will cover. Moreover, premiums and deductibles may be cost prohibitive for low-income seniors. For example, the premium for Part B in 2009 was over $96 a month, which does not include the costs of deductibles for other services that older adults must pay (Centers for Medicare and Medicaid Services, 2009).

Yet another option available to older adults to defray the costs of health care is **Medigap** policies. These policies are designed to fill the gaps in health care not covered by standard Medicare. Medigap offers 10 different policy choices, which are offered through private insurance companies that set the regulations and costs for each plan. Thus, costs for plans can vary a great deal from company to company. Depending on the policy, Medigap can cover such things as deductibles for Medicare, outpatient copayments, mental health treatment, prescription drugs, and other services such as preventive care. Because of the complexity of Medicare and Medigap programs, seniors often need assistance in understanding the programs and wading through the policies, rules, and regulations for each one. Social workers can be very useful in helping older clients and their families to understand Medicare and Medigap programs and to help them choose plans that will meet their needs.

Although Judy has Medicare Part A, it is unlikely she has Part B or any Medigap policy. Even if she did, these policies would do little to help her in her current situation. Part A will help her should she need hospitalization or other types of rehabilitation, but it will not fund her long-term care needs.

Medicaid   The health care program for the poor that is administered jointly by federal and state entities, Medicaid was also enacted in 1965. Older adults who are poor can become eligible for Medicaid, even though they are already receiving Medicare benefits. Many older adults cannot afford to purchase extra coverage through Medicare Part B or Medigap policies; thus, they often find that their assets are depleted rapidly when they experience a lengthy or expensive illness. For many seniors, the cost of prescription drugs alone forces them to spend far beyond their means. Thus, many older adults rely on Medicaid to cover their health care costs.

Many elders find that they need Medicaid when they suffer a debilitating illness that requires them to spend time in a skilled nursing facility. Medicare covers only a limited number of days in skilled nursing care, and many older adults cannot afford to pay for the care on their own. Thus, many older adults find themselves "spending down" their assets, or impoverishing themselves, until they become poor enough to become eligible for Medicaid. Medicaid offers more liberal coverage than Medicare, and many older adults come to rely on it to pay for the expensive care that can come with chronic illness and disability. Some of the services covered by Medicaid that are excluded by Medicare include homemaker services, eye and hearing care, and prescription drugs.

Social workers can be instrumental in helping clients to understand the Medicaid program and navigate the application process. Debates on Medicaid, Medicare, and Social Security reform are also ever present. Changes in these programs will have a direct impact on elderly clients, as you have seen in Judy's case. Because laws and legislation can change rapidly, social workers need up-to-date information on these issues to support clients who might be grappling with services that depend on these programs.

Because Judy's care has been funded through Medicaid, she will not have any substantial income or assets to help her purchase alternative care. As mentioned earlier, you will need to help Judy find other ways to tap into Medicaid funds for her care needs.

End-of-Life Considerations

Many people argue that they would like to have some control over end-of-life decisions such as pain management, the ability to authorize the use of technology to extend life, the right to live with dignity, and the right to end life when pain and suffering outweigh the quality of life.

For many older adults who are terminally ill, the dying process is not necessarily hindered by physicians or modern technology. However, with advances in prolonging life, more and more means are available to keep people alive. The increasing availability of life-sustaining technology raises ethical questions concerning how far modern medicine should go in prolonging the dying process and whether we should be keeping people alive at all costs just because we have the capability to do so. It also raises questions for people as they age such as how much control they will have over illness and health and whether family members and health care professionals will respect their wishes regarding these issues.

One of the most hotly debated issues involves **euthanasia**, or assisted suicide. Euthanasia can be placed in two categories: active and passive. **Active euthanasia**, also known as mercy killing or assisted suicide, involves a physician, friend, or family member assisting someone in terminating her or his life. An example of active euthanasia is administering lethal doses of drugs to the dying person. **Passive euthanasia** is the omission of acts that prolong life, such as withholding medications or nutrition or respecting a Do Not Resuscitate (DNR) order (Gorman, 1999). The omission of these interventions ultimately leads to death.

Much of the current debate over assisted suicide involves active euthanasia; this debate is ongoing in the U.S. and other countries, where task forces of physicians, scholars, ethicists and other professionals are discussing definitions of euthanasia and physician-assisted suicide and the ethical issues associated with them (Materstvedt et al., 2003). For the most part, people in the United States have a right to refuse treatment if they are competent to make decisions. The courts agree that this right is constitutionally guaranteed (Pence, 1995). Indeed, for years, health care professionals have been allowing people to die through omission of treatment. However, active euthanasia is illegal in most states.

The debate over assisted suicide in the United States has been brought to the forefront by people such as Dr. Jack Kevorkian, who helped several people end their lives in the 1990s. At the crux of his actions is the question of whether physicians have a duty to end patients' suffering or to preserve life. Throughout the past decade, several landmark laws and court decisions have pushed this debate even further. In 1994, Oregon became the first state to legalize physician-assisted suicide. Opponents of this law have since attempted to challenge it in court but have been unsuccessful.

Other states have also pressed the issue, attempting to secure rights of individuals who wish to end their lives with the assistance of a physician. Courts have responded by arguing that determining whether a terminally ill individual is competent to make this decision is questionable at best. That is, there is a risk that people who are incompetent to make a life-and-death decision will be granted the right. Thus, through misuse of the law or through error, people who are not competent to make a decision on their own could die.

One way in which people can become active in planning for issues that may surface during an illness or hospital stay is through **advanced directives**. All states have legislation that allows patients to articulate in advance their wishes about the type of care they desire should they be admitted into a hospital. These directives can be written in a **living will**, which provides detailed instructions about such things as the use of respirators or other artificial means of life support. Living wills can also appoint someone to advocate on the patient's behalf. The Patient

Self-Determination Act requires all health providers who receive government funding to offer patients the opportunity to complete advanced directives (Cartwright & Steinberg, 1995).

Other countries use legal assisted suicide and have elaborate procedures to guide the process of determining whether or not a dying person is a candidate. For example, the Netherlands requires that a request to die be voluntary, that the patient be informed, that the patient consistently expresses the desire to die, and that at least two physicians agree that the person is competent to make the decision. In addition, several international organizations support assisted suicide and offer supports and referrals to people wishing to die. For example, the Hemlock Society, established in 1980, advocates for the rights of people to make end-of-life decisions and campaigns for assisted suicide laws.

Social workers, particularly those working in health care settings, need to be aware of local and national laws and policies that impact older adults. For example, because debates on and efforts to change assisted suicide laws change so rapidly, social workers need to find ways to stay informed about recent developments so that they can offer current information to their clients.

CONCLUSION

As you have seen, older age is a period in human development that can bring about many changes; however, the amount and type of change vary widely from individual to individual. And, like any point in human development, the aging process can be filled with rewards and challenges. The interplay of physical, psychological, familial, and social aspects of growing older can affect individuals personally and politically just as cultural expectations of aging can impact the way individuals interpret changes of age and how they react to them. The ways in which people develop throughout the life span also influence how they perceive and react to growing old.

As technological advances allow people to live longer, we will all face ethical and other challenges related to physical, spiritual, economical, psychological, and interpersonal well-being. Social workers need to be at the forefront of these challenges to help older adults work through issues that may impede development and to help them attain an acceptable quality of life.

MAIN POINTS

- Many physical, psychological, and social changes occur during the aging process; however, social workers need to be aware that these changes are different for each individual. Typical physical changes that occur as we age affect bone and muscle mass, hearing, eyesight, and reaction time.

- Some changes such as dementia and decreased sexual activity are not necessarily a normal part of the aging process; rather, they are the result of living longer than we have ever lived before and reacting to social stereotypes about what is expected for older adults. Gay, lesbian, bisexual, and transgendered older adults face a double stereotype: They are gay *and* old.

- Problems such as depression and suicide can be severe for people as they age, depending on many biopsychosocial factors such as illness, spirituality, social support, and other internal and external stressors.

- Three psychosocial theories on aging are disengagement theory, which posits that older people and the larger society gradually withdraw from each other; activity theory, which suggests that it is not necessarily normal for people to withdraw from life as they age; and continuity theory, which focuses on the stability of people's personalities and interactions with society as they age, which determine functionality in older age.

- Elisabeth Kübler-Ross developed five stages of death and dying: denial, anger, bargaining, depression, and acceptance. People also go through these processes in coping with loss.

- Increasingly, families are relying on grandparents as child-rearing resources. Many grandparents who are rearing their grandchildren are 65+ years of age and are living in poverty. In order to support these grandparents, social workers need to be aware of their social, legal, economic, and other needs.

- Adult children caring for aging parents is a major issue for many families. Social workers often play an important role in providing formal services that support caregivers and that prevent serious problems such as depression and health decline from occurring as a result of caregiving stress.

- Some of the most serious issues facing older adults are associated with advances in technology and health care that raise legal, ethical, and financial questions about long-term care. Poverty, which is inextricably linked with these issues, can be a permanent aspect of life for many older adults.

- Major government policies affecting older adults and their well-being are the Older Americans Act, Social Security, Medicare, and Medicaid. Social workers can be instrumental in helping clients understand and navigate these programs, as well as deal with end-of-life considerations such as living wills.

EXERCISES

1. Using the Sanchez Family interactive case (go to www.routledgesw.com/cases), review the major micro, mezzo, and macro issues involving the Sanchez parents.

After giving this information thorough review, answer the following questions:

a. What biological and psychological factors might influence the Sanchez parents' aging process and how?

b. What familial and community factors might impact their aging process and how?

c. What policies might the parents need to rely on as they grow into older age? What barriers might they face in accessing resources offered by these policies?

d. What theories or theoretical concepts might apply to the Sanchez parents with regard to conceptualizing their aging process?

2. Review the Carla Washburn interactive case (go to www.routledgesw.com/cases), and answer the following questions:

a. What physical and cognitive aspects might you want to assess with Carla and why?

b. Given what you know about Carla and her situation, which theory of aging would you say best represents Carla's progression into older adulthood? Why?

c. What information presented in this chapter might be useful in your work with Carla and why?

d. In what ways could you work with Carla to help her move toward aging well?

REFERENCES

AbouZahr, C., & Wardlaw, T. (2001). Maternal mortality at the end of a decade: Signs of progress? *Bulletin of the World Health Organization, 79*(6), 561–573.

Administration for Children and Families. (2008). *Head Start program fact sheet*. Washington, DC: Author.

Administration on Aging. (1998). The national elder abuse incidence study; final report. National Center on Elder Abuse, American Public Human Services Association. [Online]. Retrieved March 13, 2003, from http://www.aoa.dhhs.gov/abuse/report/Cexecsum.htm.

Administration on Aging. (2006). A layman's guide to the Older Americans Act. [Online]. Retrieved June 24, 2009, from http://www.aoa.gov/about/legbudg/oaa/laymans_guide/laymans_guide.asp.

Ahmad, K. (2000, September 23). Women suffer first from lack of health-care services. *Lancet, 356*(9235), 1085.

Ainsworth, M. D. S. (1979). Infant-mother attachment. *American Psychologist, 34*, 932–937.

Alexopoulos, G. S. (2000). Mood disorders. In B. J. Sadock & V. A. Sadock (Eds.), *Comprehensive textbook of psychiatry* (7th ed., pp. 1284–1440). Baltimore, MD: Williams and Wilkins.

Almeida, J., Johnson, R., Corliss, H., Molnar, B., & Azrael, D. (2009). Emotional distress among LGBT youth: The influence of perceived discrimination on sexual orientation. *Journal of Youth & Adolescence, 38*(7), 1001–1014.

Alzheimer's Association. (2002). Facts about Alzheimer's disease. [Online]. Retrieved March 11, 2003, from http://search.alz.org/ResourceCenter/FactSheets/FSalzheimerdisease.pdf.

Alzheimer's Association. (2009). *2009 Alzheimer's disease facts and figures*. [Online]. Retrieved June 30, 2009, from http://www.alz.org/national/documents/report_alzfactsfigures2009.pdf.

Amato, P. (2000). The consequences of divorce for adults and children. *Journal of Marriage and the Family, 62*(4), 1269–1287.

Amato, P. (2001). Children of divorce in the 1990s: An update of the Amato and Keith (1991) meta-analysis. *Journal of Family Psychology, 15*(3), 355–370.

Amato, P. R., & Sobolewski, J. M. (2001). The effects of divorce and marital discord on adult children's psychological well-being. *American Sociological Review, 66*, 900–921.

American Academy of Pediatrics. (2000). Prevention of sexual harassment in the workplace and educational settings. *Pediatrics, 106*, 1498–1499.

American Academy of Pediatrics. (2001, November). Media violence. *Pediatrics, 108*(5), 1222–1226.

American Academy of Pediatrics. (2002, February). Coparent or second-parent adoption by same-sex parents. *Pediatrics, 109*(2), 339–341.

American Association of Retired Persons. (2003). Facts about grandparents raising grandchildren. [Online]. Retrieved March 13, 2003, from http://www.aarp.org/confacts/grandparents/grandfacts.html.

American College of Obstetricians and Gynecologists. (1996). Maternal serum screening. *ACOG Technical Bulletin, 228*. Washington, DC: Author.

American Heart Association. (2001). Statistical fact sheet—populations. [Online]. Retrieved February 6, 2004, from http://www.americanheart.org/presenter.jhtml?identifier=2007.

American Heart Association. (2009). *Heart disease and stroke statistics*. Dallas, TX: American Heart Association.

American Psychiatric Association. (1998). *Psychiatric effects of media violence*. [Online]. Retrieved

September 8, 2003, from http://www.psych.org/public_info/media_violence.cfm.

American Psychiatric Association. (2000). *Diagnostic and statistical manual of mental disorders* (4th ed., Text Revision). Washington, DC: American Psychiatric Association.

Anderson, G. M. (2004). Making sense of rising caesarean section rates. *British Medical Journal, 329*(7468), 696–697.

Anderson, L. M., Shinn, C., Charles, J., Scrimshaw, S. C., Fielding, J. E., Normand, J., Sanchez-Way, R., Richardson, T., & Fullilove, M. T. (2002, February 1). Community interventions to promote healthy social environments: Early childhood development and family housing. *Morbidity & Mortality Weekly Report, 51*(4), 1–7.

Anderssen, N., Amlie, C., & Ytteroy, E. A. (2002). Outcomes for children with lesbian or gay parents. A review of studies from 1978 to 2000. *Scandinavian Journal of Psychology, 43*, 335–351.

Andreasen, N. C. (2001). *Brave new brain: Conquering mental illness in the era of the genome.* New York: Oxford University Press.

Ängarne-Lindberg, T., & Wadsby, M. (2009). Fifteen years after parental divorce: Mental health and experienced life-events. *Nordic Journal of Psychiatry, 63*(1), 32–43.

Angold, A., Costello, E. J., & Worthman, C. M. (1998). Puberty and depression: The roles of age, pubertal status and pubertal timing. *Psychological Medicine, 28*, 51–61.

Appleby, G. A., & Anastas, J. W. (1998). *Not just a passing phase: Social work with gay, lesbian, and bisexual people.* New York: Columbia University Press.

Arendt, R., Angelopouos, J., Salzaler, A., & Singer, L. (1999). Motor development of cocaine-exposed children at age two years. *Pediatrics, 103*, 86–92.

Aseltine, R. H., & Gore, S. L. (2000). The variable effects of stress on alcohol use from adolescence to early adulthood. *Substance Use and Misuse, 35*(5), 643–668.

Asthana, S., Bhasin, S., Butler, R. N., Fillit, H., Finkelstein, J., Harman, S. M., Holstein, L., Korenman, S. G., Matsumoto, A. M., Morley, J. E., Tsitouras, P., & Urban, R. (2004). Masculine vitality: Pros and cons of testosterone in treating andropause. *Journals of Gerontology Series A: Biological Sciences & Medical Sciences, 59A*(5), 461–465.

Atchley, R. C. (1989). A continuity theory of normal aging. *The Gerontologist, 29*, 183–190.

Atchley, R. C., & Barusch, A. (2004). *Social forces and aging* (10th ed.). Belmont, CA: Wadsworth.

Atkins, T. V., Jenkins, M. C., & Perkins, M. H. (1990–1991). Portrayal of persons in television commercials age 50 and older. *Psychology: A Journal of Human Behavior, 27*(4)–28(1), 30–37.

Autism Consortium. (2009). *Autism genome scan.* [Online]. Retrieved June 17, 2009, from http://www.autismconsortium.org/research-collaborations/autism-genome-scan-2.html.

Auyeung, B., Baron-Cohen, S., Ashwin, E., Knickmeyer, R., Taylor, K., & Hackett, G. (2009). Fetal testosterone and autistic traits. *British Journal of Psychology, 100*, 1–22.

Bachman, R., & Saltzman, L. E. (1995). *Violence against women: Estimates from the redesigned survey* (Bureau of Justice Statistics Special Report). Washington, DC: U.S. Department of Justice.

Bachrach, C. A., & Newcomer, S. (1999, Sept/Oct). Intended pregnancies and unintended pregnancies: Distinct categories or opposite ends of a continuum? *Family Planning Perspectives, 31*(5), 251–253.

Baillargeon, R. (1987). Object permanence in 3½–4½-month-old infants. *Developmental Psychology, 23*(5), 655–664.

Baldwin, S. A., & Hoffmann, J. P. (2002). The dynamics of self-esteem: A growth-curve analysis. *Journal of Youth and Adolescence, 31*(2), 101–113.

Ballard, K. D., Kuh, D. J., & Wadsworth, M. E. J. (2001). The role of the menopause in women's experiences of the "change of life." *Sociology of Health and Illness, 23*(4), 397–424.

Balogh, D. W., Kite, M. E., Pickel, K. L., Canel, D., & Schroeder, J. (2003). The effects of delayed report and motive for reporting on perceptions of sexual harassment. *Sex Roles, 48*(7/8), 337–348.

Bandura, A. (1965). Influence of models' reinforcement contingencies in the acquisition of imitative responses. *Journal of Personality and Social Psychology, 1*, 589–595.

Bandura, A. (1977). *Social learning theory.* Englewood Cliffs, NJ: Prentice Hall.

Bandura, A. (1997). *Self-efficacy*. New York: W. H. Freeman.

Barker, R. L. (2003). *The social work dictionary*. Washington, DC: NASW.

Barkley, R. A. (2002). Psychosocial treatments for attention-deficit/hyperactivity disorder in children. *Journal of Clinical Psychiatry*, *63*(12), 36–43.

Barr, H. M., & Streissguth, A. P. (2001). Identifying maternal self-reported alcohol use associated with fetal alcohol spectrum disorders. *Alcoholism: Clinical and Experimental Research*, *25*, 283–287.

Barrett, A. E., & White, H. R. (2002, December). Trajectories of gender role orientations in adolescence and early adulthood: A prospective study of the mental health effects of masculinity and femininity. *Journal of Health and Social Behavior*, *43*, 451–468.

Barry, R. A., Kochanska, G., & Philibert, R. A. (2008). G × E interaction in the organization of attachment: Mothers' responsiveness as a moderator of children's genotypes. *Journal of Child Psychology and Psychiatry*, *49*(12), 1313–1320.

Barusch, A. S., Rogers, A., & Abu-Bader, S. (1999). Depressive symptoms in the frail elderly: Physical and psycho-social correlates. *The International Journal of Aging and Human Development*, *49*(2), 107–125.

Bateson, G. (1972). *Steps to an ecology of mind*. New York: Ballentine.

Bateson, G. (1978, April 21). The double-bind theory—misunderstood? *Psychiatry News*, p. 40.

Bauer, C. R., Langer, J. C., Shankaran, S., Bada, H. A., Lester, B., Wright, L. L., Krause-Steinrauf, H., Smeriglio, V. L., Finnegan, L. P., Maza, P. L., & Verter, J. (2005). Acute neonatal effects of cocaine exposure during pregnancy. *Archives of Peidatrics and Adolescent Medicine*, *159*(9), 824–834.

Baumrind, D. (1968). Authoritarian vs. authoritative parental control. *Adolescence*, *3*(11), 255–272.

Baumrind, D. (1971). Current patterns of parental authority. *Developmental Psychology Monographs*, *4*(1, Pt. 2), 1–103.

Baumrind, D. (1994). The social context of child maltreatment. *Family Relations*, *43*(4), 360–368.

Beauvoir, Simone de. (1949). *The second sex*. New York: Knopf.

Beckett, J. O., & Johnson, H. C. (1995). Human development. In R. L. Edwards (Ed.), *Encyclopedia of social work* (19th ed., Vol. 2, pp. 1385–1405). Washington, DC: NASW Press.

Behavioral Health Treatment. (1997). APA passes resolution on homosexuality conversion therapy. *Behavioral Health Treatment*, *2*(9), 5.

Bell, J. (1992). In search of a discourse on aging: The elderly on television. *The Gerontologist*, *32*, 305–311.

Belle, D., & Doucet, J. (2003). Poverty, inequality, and discrimination as sources of depression among U. S. women. *Psychology of Women Quarterly*, *27*(2), 101–113.

Belsky, J. (2009). Classroom composition, childcare history and social development: Are childcare effects disappearing or spreading? *Social Development*, *18*(1), 230–238.

Belsky, J., & Braungart, J. M. (1991). Are insecure avoidant infants with extensive daycare experience less stressed by and more independent in the strange situation? *Child Development*, *62*, 567–571.

Bengtson, V., Horlacher, G., Putney, N., & Silverstein, M. (2008). *Growth and decline of religiosity across time and age*. Conference Papers—American Sociological Association, 2008 Annual Meeting.

Benjet, C., & Kazdin, A. E. (2003). Spanking children: The controversies, findings, and new directions. *Clinical Psychology Review*, *23*, 197–224.

Bergin, D. (1988). Stages of play development. In D. Bergin (Ed.), *Play as a medium for learning and development*. Portsmouth, NH: Heinemann.

Berkman, C. S., & Zinberg, G. (1997). Homophobia and heterosexism in social workers. *Social Work*, *42*, 319–332.

Berkowitz, L., & Walster, E. (1976). Equity theory: Toward a general theory of social interaction. In L. Berkowitz & E. Walster (Eds.), *Advances in Experimental Social Psychology* (Vol. 9, pp. 1–261). New York: Academic Press.

Berlin, L. J. (2001). Promoting early childhood development through comprehensive community initiatives. *Children's Services: Social Policy, Research, & Practice 4*(1), 1–23.

Berne, E. (1961). *Transactional analysis in psychotherapy.* New York: Grove Press.

Berry, M., Cavazos Dylla, D. J., Barth, R. P., & Needell, B. (1998). The role of open adoption in the adjustment of adopted children and their families. *Children and Youth Services Review, 20*(1–2), 151–171.

Bertalanffy, L. von. (1972). The history of general systems theory. In G. J. Klir (Ed.), *Trends in general systems theory* (pp. 21–41). New York: Wiley-Interscience.

Berwick, R. C. (2009). What genes can't learn about language. *Proceedings of the National Academy of Sciences, 106*(6), 1685–1686.

Bevan, E., & Higgins, D. J. (2002). Is domestic violence learned? The contribution of five forms of child maltreatment to men's violence and adjustment. *Journal of Family Violence, 17*(3), 223–243.

Bifulco, A., Moran, P. M., Ball, C., Jacobs, C., Baines, R., Bunn, A., & Cavagin, J. (2002). Childhood adversity, parental vulnerability and disorder: Examining intergenerational transmission of risk. *Journal of Child Psychology and Psychiatry, 43*(8), 1075–1086.

Billingsley, A., & Morrison-Rodriguez, B. (2007). The black family in the twenty-first century and the church as an action system. In L. A. Lee (Ed.), *Human behavior in the social environment from an African-American perspective* (2nd ed., pp. 31–48). New York: Haworth Press.

Bing, N. M., Nelson, W. M., & Wesolowski, K. L. (2009). Comparing the effects of amount of conflict on children's adjustment following parental divorce. *Journal of Divorce & Remarriage, 50*(3), 159–171.

Bishop, A. (1994). *Becoming an ally: Breaking the cycle of oppression.* Halifax, Canada: Fernwood.

Bitto, A., & Gray, R. H. (1997). Adverse outcomes of planned and unplanned pregnancies among users of natural family planning: A prospective study. *American Journal of Public Health, 87*(3), 338–343.

Bjerkedal, T., Kristensen, P., Skjeret, G. A., & Brevik, J. I. (2007). Intelligence test scores and birth order among young Norwegian men (conscripts) analyzed within and between families. *Intelligence, 35*(5), 503–514.

Blake, S. M., Kiely, M., Gard, C. C., El-Mohandes, A. A. E., & El-Khorazaty, N. (2007). Pregnancy intentions and happiness among pregnant black women at high risk for adverse infant health outcomes. *Perspectives on Sexual & Reproductive Health, 39*(4), 194–205.

Bleidorn, W., Kandler, C., Riemann, R., Angleitner, A., & Spinath, F. M. (2009). Patterns and sources of adult personality development: Growth curve analyses of the NEO PI-R scales in a longitudinal twin study. *Journal of Personality & Social Psychology, 97*(1), 142–155.

Bloom, B., & Cohen, R. A. (2007). Summary health statistics for U.S. children: National health interview survey, 2006. *National Center for Health Statistics. Vital Health Stat 10*(234), 1–12.

Blumer, H. (1969). *Symbolic interaction: Perspective and method.* Englewood Cliffs, NJ: Prentice-Hall.

Bolognini, M., Laget, J., Plancherel, B., Stephan, P., Corcos, M., & Halfon, O. (2002). Drug use and suicide attempts: The role of personality factors. *Substance Use and Misuse, 37*(3), 337–356.

Bowlby, J. (1969). *Attachment and loss* (Vol. I). London: Hogarth Press.

Bowlby, R. (2007). Babies and toddlers in non-parental daycare can avoid stress and anxiety if they develop a lasting secondary attachment bond with one carer who is consistently accessible to them. *Attachment & Human Development, 9*(4), 307–319.

Boyd, M. A. (2007). *Psychiatric nursing* (4th ed.). Baltimore, MD: Lippincott, Williams, & Wilkins.

Boye, B., Bentsen, H., & Malt, V. F. (2002). Does guilt proneness predict acute and long-term distress in relatives of patients with schizophrenia? *Acta Psychiatrica Scandinavica, 106*(5), 351–357.

Bradley, R. H., & Corwyn, R. F. (2002). Socioeconomic status and child development. *Annual Review of Psychology, 53*, 371–399.

Brandell, J. R. (Ed.). (1997). *Theory and practice in clinical social work.* New York: The Free Press.

Brandtjen, H., & Thomas, V. (2001). Short and long term effects on infants and toddlers in full time daycare centers. *Journal of Prenatal & Perinatal Psychology & Health, 15*(4), 239–286.

Bray, J., & Kelly, J. (1998). *Stepfamilies: Love, marriage, and parenting in the first decade.* New York: Broadway Books.

Brewis, A. A., Meyer, M. C., & Schmidt, K. L. (2002). Does school, compared to home, provide a unique adaptive context for children's ADHD-associated behaviors? A cross-cultural test. *Cross-Cultural Research, 36*(4), 303–320.

Brim, O. (1999). *The MacArthur Foundation study of midlife development.* Vero Beach, FL: MacArthur Foundation.

Brittan, A., & Maynard, M. (1984). *Sexism, racism, and oppression.* New York: Basil Blackwell Publisher.

Bronfenbrenner, U. (1979). *The ecology of human development.* Cambridge, MA: Harvard University Press.

Bronstein, P., & Clauson, J. (1993). Parenting behavior and children's social, psychological, and academic adjustment in diverse family structures. *Family Relations, 42*, 268–276.

Brooks, D., & Goldberg, S. (2001). Gay and lesbian adoptive and foster care placements: Can they meet the needs of waiting children? *Social Work, 46*(2), 147–157.

Brooks-Gunn, J., & Warren, M. P. (1989). The psychological significance of secondary sexual characteristics in 9- to 11-year-old girls. *Child Development, 59*, 161–169.

Brown, J. (1977). *Mind, brain, and consciousness.* New York: Academic Press.

Brown, T. H., & Warner, D. F. (2008). Divergent pathways? Racial/ethnic differences in older women's labor force withdrawal. *Journals of Gerontology Series B: Psychological Sciences & Social Sciences, 36B*(3), S122–S134.

Bryan, A., & Stallings, M. C. (2002). A case control study of adolescent risky sexual behavior and its relationship to personality dimensions, conduct disorder, and substance use. *Journal of Youth and Adolescence, 31*(5), 387–396.

Buhrmester, D., & Furman, W. (1987). The development of companionship and intimacy. *Child Development, 58*, 1101–1113.

Bureau of Justice Statistics. (2009). *Crime characteristics.* [Online]. Retrieved June 24, 2009, from http://www.ojp.usdoj.gov/bjs/cvict_c.htm#relate.

Burnette, D. (1998). Grandparents rearing grandchildren: A school-based small group intervention. *Research on Social Work Practice, 8*(1), 10–27.

Buzwell, S., & Rosenthal, D. (1996). Constructing a sexual self: Adolescents' sexual self-perceptions and sexual risk-taking. *Journal of Research on Adolescence, 6*, 489–513.

Cahill, K., Giandrea, M., & Quinn, J. (2006). Retirement patterns from career employment. *Gerontologist, 46*(4), 514–532.

Campbell, C. (2003). Anti-oppressive theory and practice as the organizing theme for social work education: The case in favour. *Canadian Social Work Review, 20*, 121–125.

Campbell, W. W., & Leidy, H. J. (2007). Dietary protein and resistance training effects on muscle and body composition in older persons. *Journal of the American College of Nutrition, 26*(6), 696S–703S.

Canda, E. R. (2008). Spiritual connections in social work: Boundary violations and transcendence. *Journal of Religion & Spirituality in Social Work, 27*(1–2), 25–40.

Cantor, J. (2000). Media violence. *Journal of Adolescent Health, 27*(2), 30–34.

Caputo, R. K. (2002). Discrimination and human capital: A challenge to economic theory and social justice. *Journal of Sociology and Social Welfare, 24*(2), 105–124.

Caputo, R. K. (2003). Head Start, other preschool programs, and life success in a youth cohort. *Journal of Sociology and Social Welfare, 30*(2), 105–126.

Carli, L. L., & Eagly, A. H. (2001). Gender, hierarchy, and leadership: An introduction. *Journal of Social Issues, 57*(4), 629–636.

Carroli, G., & Mignini, L. (2009). Episiotomy for vaginal birth. *PubMed, 21*(1). Retrieved June 17, 2009, from http://www.cochrane.org/reviews/en/ab000081.html.

Carter, C. S. (2002). Perinatal care for women who are addicted: Implications for empowerment. *Health and Social Work, 27*(3), 166–174.

Cartwright, C., & Steinberg, M. (1995). Decision-making in terminal care: Older people seek more involvement. *Social Alternatives, 14*(2), 7–10.

Cave, S., & Mitchell, D. (2001). *What your doctor may not tell you about children's vaccinations.* New York: Warner Books.

Centers for Disease Control and Prevention. (1995). Chorionic villus sampling and amniocentesis: Recommendations for prenatal counseling.

Morbidity and Mortality Weekly Report, 44(R-9). Atlanta, GA: Author.

Centers for Disease Control and Prevention. (1998). Trends in sexual risk behaviors among high school students—United States, 1991–1997. *MMWR Weekly, 47*(36), 749–752.

Centers for Disease Control and Prevention. (2000a). Youth risk behavior surveillance—United States 1999. *Morbidity and Moratlity Weekly Report, 49(SS-5)*.

Centers for Disease Control and Prevention. (2000b). *Tracking the hidden epidemics: Trends in STDs in the United States.* [Online]. Retrieved November 5, 2003, from http://www.cdc.gov/nchstp/dstd/Stats_Trends/Trends2000.pdf.

Centers for Disease Control and Prevention. (2001). *Data and statistics: Adolescent pregnancy.* Atlanta: Author.

Centers for Disease Control and Prevention. (2006). *Fetal alcohol spectrum disorders.* [Online]. Retrieved June 14, 2009, from http://www.cdc.gov/ncbddd/fas/fasask.htm.

Centers for Disease Control and Prevention. (2007a). *Chlamydia Fact Sheet.* [Online]. Retrieved June 22, 2009, from http://www.cdc.gov/std/chlamydia/STDFact-Chlamydia.htm.

Centers for Disease Control and Prevention. (2007b). *Gonorrhea Fact Sheet.* [Online]. Retrieved June 22, 2009, from http://www.cdc.gov/std/Gonorrhea/gonorrhea-fact-sheet.pdf.

Centers for Disease Control and Prevention. (2007c). *Herpes Fact Sheet.* [Online]. Retrieved June 22, 2009, from http://www.cdc.gov/std/Herpes/STDFact-Herpes.htm.

Centers for Disease Control and Prevention. (2007d). *Hepatitis Fact Sheet.* [Online]. Retrieved June 22, 2009, from http://www.cdc.gov/hepatitis/HBV/HBVfaq.htm#overview.

Centers for Disease Control and Prevention. (2007e). *Syphilis Fact Sheet.* [Online]. Retrieved June 22, 2009, from http://www.cdc.gov/std/syphilis/STDFact-Syphilis.htm.

Centers for Disease Control and Prevention. (2008a). *Autism information center.* [Online]. Retrieved June 18, 2009, from http://www.cdc.gov/ncbddd/autism/faq_prevalence.htm#whatisprevalence.

Centers for Disease Control and Prevention. (2008b).

HIV/AIDS among youth. [Online]. Retrieved June 22, 2009, from http://www.cdc.gov/hiv/resources/factsheets/youth.htm.

Centers for Disease Control and Prevention. (2008c). *Youth suicide.* [Online]. Retrieved June 23, 2009, from http://www.cdc.gov/ncipc/dvp/Suicide/youthsuicide.htm.

Centers for Disease Control and Prevention. (2009). Preventing teen pregnancy: An update in 2009. [Online]. Retrieved June 23, 2009, from http://www.cdc.gov/reproductivehealth/AdolescentReproHealth/AboutTP.htm.

Centers for Medicare and Medicaid Services. (2000). *Health and Human Services announces Medicare premium and deductible rates for 2001.* Press release, October 18, 2000. U.S. Department of Health and Human Services.

Centers for Medicare and Medicaid Services. (2002, August). Medicare current beneficiary survey. [Online]. Retrieved March 10, 2003, from http://www.cms.hhs.gov/mcbs/CMSsrc/1996/cp96appb.pdf.

Centers for Medicare and Medicaid Services. (2009). *Health and Human Services announces Medicare premium and deductible rates for 2009.* Washington, DC: U.S. Department of Health and Human Services.

Chanley, S. A., & Alozie, N. O. (2001). Policy for the "deserving," but politically weak: The 1996 welfare reform act and battered women. *Policy Studies Review 18*(2), 1–25.

Chatters, L. M., & Taylor, R. J. (1994). Religious involvement among older African-Americans. In J. S. Levin (Ed.), *Religion in aging and health* (pp. 196–230). Thousand Oaks, CA: Sage.

Chau, K. L. (Ed.). (1991). *Ethnicity and biculturalism.* New York: Haworth.

Cherlin, A. J., & Furstenberg, F. F. (1994). Stepfamilies in the United States: A reconsideration. In J. Blake & J. Hagen (Eds.), *Annual review of sociology* (pp. 359–381). Palo Alto, CA: Annual Reviews.

Chess, S., & Thomas, A. (1977). Temperamental individuality from childhood to adolescence. *Journal of Child Psychiatry, 16*, 218–226.

Chesson, H. W., Blandford, J. M., Gift, T. L., Tao, G., & Irwin, K. L. (2004). The estimated direct medical costs of sexually transmitted diseases among American youth, 2000. *Perspectives on Sexual and Reproductive Health*, *36*(1), 11–19.

Chickering, A. W., & Reisser, L. (1993). *Education and identity* (2nd ed.). San Francisco: Jossey-Bass.

Child Trends. (2001). *Trends among Hispanic children, youth, and families*. Washington, DC: Author.

Child Welfare Information Gateway. (2008). Long-term consequences of child abuse and neglect. U.S. Department of Health and Human Services. [Online]. Retrieved June 17, 2009, from http://www.childwelfare.gov/pubs/factsheets/long_term_consequences.cfm.

Children's Defense Fund. (2008). *The state of American's children: 2008 report of child health and health coverage*. Washington, DC: Author.

Children's Institute International. (1999). *Breaking the habit*. [Online]. Retrieved September 5, 2003, from http://www.childrensinstitute.org/press/spanking.html.

Chiriboga, C.A. (2003). Fetal alcohol and drug effects. *The Neurologist*, *9*(6), 267–279.

Chiriboga, C. A., Burst, J. C. M., Bateman, D., & Hauser, W. A. (1999). Dose-response effect of fetal cocaine exposure on newborn neurologic function. *Pediatrics*, *103*, 79–85.

Chomsky, N. (1975). *Reflections on language*. New York: Pantheon.

Chornesky, A. (1998). Multicultural perspectives on menopause and the climacteric. *Affilia*, *13*(1), 31–46.

Christakis, D. A., & Zimmerman, F. J. (2005). Violent television viewing during preschool is associated with antisocial behavior during school age. *Pediatrics*, *120*(5), 993–999.

Cianciotto, J., & Cahill, S. (2006). *Youth in the cross hairs: The third wave of ex-gay activism*. Washington, DC: National Gay and Lesbian Task Force Policy Institute.

Cicchetti, D., & Toth, S. L. (2005). Child maltreatment. *Annual Review of Clinical Psychology*, *1*, 409–438.

Cicirelli, V. G. (1994). Sibling relationships in crosscultural perspective. *Journal of Marriage and the Family*, *56*(1), 14–20.

Clark, E. (2000). Language acquisition. In A. Kazdin (Ed.), *Encyclopedia of psychology*. Washington, DC: American Psychological Association.

Clarkberg, M. (1999). The price of partnering: The role of economic well-being in young adults' first union experiences. *Social Forces*, *77*(3), 945–968.

Clocksin, B. D., Watson, D. L., & Ransdell, L. (2002). Understanding youth obesity and media use: Implications for future intervention programs. *Quest 54*, 259–275.

Coleman, P. K., & Karraker, K. H. (2003). Maternal self efficacy beliefs, competence, in parenting, and toddlers' behavior and developmental status. *Infant Mental Health Journal*, *24*(2), 126–148.

Coleman, R. A. (2002). A mediated model of social adjustment: Exploring the links between attachment security, social information processing, and prosocial behavior. *Dissertation Abstracts International: Section B: The Sciences and Engineering*, *63*(6–B), 3039.

Conlin, M. (2003, May 26). The new gender gap. *Business Week*, *3834*, 74–80.

Conwell, Y., Duberstein, P. R., Cox, C., Herrman, J., Forbes, N., & Caine, E. (1998). Age differences in behaviors leading to completed suicide. *American Journal of Geriatric Psychiatry*, *6*(2), 122–126.

Cooley, C. H. (1902). *Human nature and the social order*. New York: Scribner.

Corley, C. J., & Woods, A. Y. (1991). Socioeconomic, sociodemographic and attitudinal correlates of the tempo of divorce. *Journal of Divorce & Remarriage*, *16*(1–2), 47–68.

Correll, S. J., Benard, S., & Paik, I. (2007). Getting a job: Is there a motherhood penalty? *American Journal of Sociology*, *112*(5), 1297–1338.

Council on Social Work Education. (2008). *Educational policy and accreditation standards*. Alexandria, VA: Author.

Craig, A. P., & Beishuizen, J. J. (2002). Psychological testing in a multicultural society: Universal or particular competencies? *Intercultural Education*, *13*(2), 201–213.

Crawford, D. W., Houts, R. M., Huston, T. L., & George, L. J. (2002). Compatibility, leisure, and satisfaction in marital relationships. *Journal of Marriage and the Family*, *64*(2), 433–449.

Crockett, J. B., & Kauffman, J. M. (1999). *The least restrictive environment*. Mahwah, NJ: Erlbaum.

Crosnoe, R., Mistry, R. S., & Elder, G. H. (2002). Economic disadvantage, family dynamics, and adolescent enrollment in higher education. *Journal of Marriage and the Family, 64*(3), 690–702.

Crowley, B. J., Hayslip, B., & Hobdy, J. (2003). Psychological hardiness and adjustment to life events in adulthood. *Journal of Adult Development, 10*(4), 237–248.

Cumming, E., & Henry, W. (1961). *Growing old: The process of disengagement.* New York: Basic Books.

Curtis, G. B., & Schuler, J. (2004). *Your pregnancy week by week.* Cambridge, MA: Da Capo Press.

Dahrendorf, R. (1958). Toward a theory of social conflict. *Journal of Conflict Resolution, 2*(June), 170–183.

Daniel, S. S., Grzywacz, J. G., Leerkes, E., Tucker, J., & Han, W. J. (2009). Nonstandard maternal work schedules during infancy: Implications for children's early behavior problems. *Infant Behavior & Development, 32*(2), 195–207.

Danis, F. (2003). Social work response to domestic violence: Encouraging news from a new look. *Affilia, 18*(2), 177–191.

Darroch, J. E., Singh, S., & Frost, J. J. (2001). Developed countries: The roles of sexual activity and contraceptive use. *Family Planning Perspectives, 33*(5), 244–250.

Davidson, H. (1997). The legal aspects of corporal punishment in the home: When does physical discipline cross the line to become child abuse? *Children's Legal Rights Journal, 17,* 18–29.

Davis, J. M., & Watson, N. (2001). Where are the children's experiences? Analysing social and cultural exclusion in "special" and "mainstream" schools. *Disability & Society, 16*(5), 671–687.

Davitt, J. (2006). Policy to protect the rights of older adults. In B. Berkman (Ed.), *Handbook of social work in health and aging* (pp. 923–936). New York: Oxford University Press.

de Anda, D. (1984). Bicultural socialization: Factors affecting the minority experience. *Social Work, 29*(2), 101–107.

DeNavas-Walt, C., Proctor, B. D., & Smith, J. C. (2008). Income, poverty, and health insurance coverage in the United States: 2007. *Current Population Reports,* P60–P235. Washington, DC: U.S. Government Printing Office.

Denham, S. A. (1998). *Emotional development in young children.* New York: Guilford.

DeSouza, E., & Fansler, A. G. (2003). Contrapower sexual harassment: A survey of students and faculty members. *Sex Roles, 48*(11/12), 529–542.

DeVoe, J. E., Graham, A. S., Angier, H., Baez, A., & Krois, L. (2008). Obtaining health care services for low-income children: A hierarchy of needs. *Journal of Health Care for the Poor and Underserved, 19*(4), 1192–1211.

Digiovanna, A. G. (1994). *Human aging: Biological perspectives.* New York: McGraw-Hill.

Dodd, B., & Carr, A. (2003). Young children's letter-sound knowledge. *Language, speech, and hearing services in schools, 34,* 128–137.

Dominelli, L. (2002). Anti-oppressive practice in context. In R. Adams, L. Dominelli, & M. Payne (Eds.), *Social work: Themes, issues, and critical debates* (2nd ed., pp. 3–19). Houndmills, Basingstoke, UK: Palgrave Macmillan.

Donovan, J. (1994). *Feminist theory: The intellectual traditions of American feminism.* New York: Continuum.

Dorn, L. D., Kolko, D. J., Susman, E. J., Huang, B., Stein, H., Music, E., & Bukstein, O. G. (2009). Salivary gonadal and adrenal hormone differences in **boys** and girls with and without disruptive behavior disorders: Contextual variants. *Biological Psychology, 81*(1), 31–39.

Dowd, J. J. (1975). Aging as exchange: A preface to theory. *Journal of Gerontology, 30*(5), 584–594.

Dowd, J. J. (1980). Exchange rates and old people. *Journal of Gerontology, 35,* 596–602.

Du Bois, W. E. B. (1911). The girl nobody loved. *Social News, 2*(November), 3.

Du Bois, W. E. B. (1970). *The negro American family.* Cambridge, MA: MIT Press.

Dunlosky, J., Cavallini, E., Roth, H., McGuire, C. L., Vecchi, T., & Hertzog, C. (2007). Do self-monitoring interventions improve older adult learning? *Journals of Gerontology Series B: Psychological Sciences & Social Sciences, 62B,* 70–76.

Durkheim, E. (1933). *The division of labor in society.* New York: Free Press.

Durkheim, E. (1938). *The rules of the sociological method.* Chicago: The University of Chicago Press.

Early, T. J., & GlenMaye, L. F. (2000). Valuing families: Social work practice with families from a strengths perspective. *Social Work, 45*(2), 118–130.

Eckstein, D. (2000). Empirical studies indicating significant birth-order-related personality differences. *Journal of Individual Psychology, 56*(4), 481–494.

Ecojustice. (2008). *Aamjiwnaang Bucket Brigade discovers alarming levels of toxic chemicals in Sarnia.* Retrieved June 14, 2009, from http://www.ecojustice.ca/media-centre/press-releases/aamjiwnaang-bucket-brigade-discovers-alarming-levels-of-toxic-chemicals-in-sarnia.

Eisenberg, N., Chang, L., Ma, Y., & Huang, X. (2009). Relations of parenting style to Chinese children's effortful control, ego resilience, and maladjustment. *Development and Psychopathology, 21*(2), 455–477.

Eldar-Avidan, D., Haj-Yahia, M. M., & Greenbaum, C. W. (2009). Divorce is a part of my life . . . resilience, survival, and vulnerability: Young adults' perception of the implications of parental divorce. *Journal of Marital and Family Therapy, 35*(1), 30–46.

Elder, G. H., & Pavalko, E. K. (1993). Work careers in men's later years: Transitions, trajectories, and historical change. *Journal of Gerontology, 48,* S180–S191.

Erikson, E. (1950). *Childhood and society.* New York: W. W. Norton.

Esposito, N. W. (1999). Marginalized women's comparisons of their hospital and freestanding birth center experiences: A contrast of inner-city birthing systems. *Health Care for Women International, 20*(2), 111–126.

Evans, J. L. (2001). Eight is too late: Investment in early childhood development. *Journal of International Affairs, 55*(1), 91–109.

Evans, S. E., Davies, C., & DiLillo, D. (2008). Exposure to domestic violence: A meta-analysis of child and adolescent outcomes. *Aggression & Violent Behavior, 13*(2), 131–140.

Fairburn, C. G., & Harrison, P. J. (2003, February 1). Eating disorders. *Lancet, 361,* 407–416.

Family Caregiver Alliance. (2003). *Women and caregiving: Facts and figures.* San Francisco: Author.

Faraone, S. V., Brown, C. H., Glatt, S. J., & Ming, T. T. (2002). Preventing schizophrenia and psychotic behavior: Definitions and methodological issues. *Canadian Journal of Psychiatry, 47*(6), 527–537.

Fellin, P. (2000, Spring/Summer). Revisiting multiculturalism in social work. *Journal of Social Work Education, 36*(2), 261–278.

Fielding, R. A. (1995). The role of progressive resistance training and nutrition in the preservation of lean body mass in the elderly. *Journal of the American College of Nutrition, 14*(December), 87–94.

Fischer, J. (1981). The social work revolution. *Social Work, 26*(3), 199–207.

Fogg, P. (2003, April). The gap that won't go away. *The Chronicle of Higher Education, 49*(32), 12–15.

Fong, R., Spickard, P. R., & Ewalt, P. L. (1995). A multiracial reality: Issues for social work. *Social Work, 40*(6), 725–727.

Forness, S. R., & Kavale, K. A. (2001). ADHD and a return to the medical model of special education. *Education and Treatment of Children, 24*(3), 224–247.

Fouts, G., & Burggraf, K. (2000). Television situation comedies: Female weight, male negative comments, and audience reactions. *Sex Roles, 42* (9/10), 925–932.

Fowler, J. (1981). *Stages of faith: The psychology of human development and the quest for meaning.* San Francisco: Harper & Row.

Fowler, J. (1996). *Faithful change: The personal and public challenges of postmodern life.* Nashville, TN: Abingdon Press.

Frank, D. A., Augustyn, M., Knight, W. G., Pell, T., & Zuckerman, B. (2001) Growth, development, and behavior in early childhood following prenatal cocaine exposure. *The Journal of the American Medical Association, 285*(12), 1613–1625.

Freedle, R. (2006). How and why standardized tests systematically underestimate African-Americans' true verbal ability and what to do about it: Towards the promotion of two new theories with practical applications. *St. John's Law Review, 80*(1), 183–226.

Freud, S. (1909). *Selected papers on hysteria and other psychoneuroses.* New York: The Journal of Nervous and Mental Disease Publishing Company.

Freud, S. (1914). *The psychopathology of everyday life.* London: Adelphi Terrace.

Freud, S. (1920a). *A general introduction to psycho-analysis*. New York: Washington Square Press.

Freud, S. (1920b). *Three contributions to the theory of sex* (2nd ed.). New York: The Journal of Nervous and Mental Disease Publishing Company.

Fried, P. A., & Smith, A. M. (2001). A literature review of the consequences of prenatal marijuana exposure: An emerging theme of a deficiency in executive function. *Neurotoxicology and Teratology, 23*, 1–11.

Fried, P. A., & Watkinson, B. (1990). Thirty-six and forty-eight month neurobehavioral follow-up of children prenatally exposed to marijuana, cigarettes, and alcohol. *Developmental and Behavioral Pediatrics, 11*, 49–58.

Funk, J. B., Buchman, D. D., Jenks, J., & Bechtoldt, H. (2002, November). An evidence-based approach to examining the impact of playing violent video and computer games. *Simile, 2*(4), 1–11.

Gallup Organization. (1995). *Disciplining children in America: A Gallup poll report*. Princeton, NJ: Gallup Organization.

Gardella, J. R., & Hill, J. A. (2000). Environmental toxins associated with recurrent pregnancy loss. *Seminars in Reproductive Medicine, 18*, 407–424.

Gardner, H. (1983). *Frames of mind*. New York: Basic Books.

Garety, P. (1991). Reasoning and delusions. *British Journal of Psychiatry, 159*(suppl. 14), 14–18.

Garner, D. M., & Desai, J. J. (2001). Eating disorders in children and adolescents. In J. N. Stevenson, J. N. Hughes, A. M. La Greca, & J. C. Conoley (Eds.), *Handbook of psychological services for children and adolescents* (pp. 399–420). New York: Oxford University Press.

Garreau, J. (1992). *Edge city: Life on the new frontier*. New York: Anchor Books.

Gaten, D. R. (2009). Elementary school principals' perceptions of corporal punishment. *Dissertation Abstracts International Section A: Humanities and Social Sciences, 69*(7-A), 2542.

George, L. K. (1993). Depressive disorders and symptoms in later life. *Generations, Winter/Spring*, 35–38.

Gerety, M. B., & Farnett, L. (1995). Management of depression in the elderly. *Strategies in Geriatrics, 2*(6), 137–143.

Gershoff, E. T. (2002). Parental corporal punishment and associated child behaviors and experiences: A meta-analytic and theoretical review. *Psychological Bulletin, 128*, 539–579.

Gibelman, M. (2000). Affirmative action at the crossroads: A social justice perspective. *Journal of Sociology and Social Welfare, 27*(1), 153–174.

Gibelman, M. (2003). So how far have we come? Pestilent and persistent gender gap in pay. *Social Work, 48*(1), 22–32.

Gilligan, C. (1982). *In a different voice: Psychological theory and women's development*. Cambridge, MA: Harvard University Press.

Gilligan, C., & Attanucci, J. (1988). Two moral orientations. In C. Gilligan, J. V. Ward, J. M. Taylor, & B. Bardige (Eds.), *Mapping the moral domain* (pp. 73–86). Cambridge, MA: Harvard University Press.

Glazer, S. (1993, November 26). *Do current policies punish kids awaiting adoption*? The CQ Researcher [Online]. Available at http://0-library.cqpress.com.clark.up.edu/cqresearcher/document.php?id=cqresrre1993112607.

Global Community Monitor. (2007). *Canada: Aamji-wnaang First Nation: Toxic cocktail being tracked with buckets*. Retrieved June 14, 2009, from http://www.shellfacts.com/article.php?id=580.

Goffman, E. (1959). *The presentation of self in everyday life*. Garden City, NY: Anchor Books.

Gokcay, G. (2009). Breastfeeding for the sake of the Europe and the world: European society for social pediatrics and child health position statement. *Child: Care, Health, and Development, 35*(3), 293–297.

Goldberg, J., Holtz, D., Hyslop, T., & Tolosa, J. E. (2002). Has the use of routine episiotomy decreased? Examination of episiotomy rates from 1983 to 2000. *Obstetrics and Gynecology, 99*(3), 395–400.

Goldenberg, I., & Goldenberg, H. (2004). *Family therapy: An overview*. Belmont, CA: Brooks/Cole.

Goldsmith, H. H., Buss, K. A., & Lemery, K. S. (1997). Toddler and childhood temperament: Expanded content, stronger genetic evidence, new evidence for the importance of environment. *Developmental Psychology, 33*(6), 891–905.

Goldsmith, H. H., Lemery, K. S., Buss, K. A., & Campos, J. J. (1999). Genetic analyses of focal aspects of infant temperament. *Developmental Psychology, 35*(4), 972–985.

Goleman, D. (2006). *Emotional intelligence*. New York: Bantam Books.

Golombok, S. (2002). Adoption by lesbian couples. *British Medical Journal, 324*(7351), 1407–1409.

Gonzales, J. (2009). Prefamily counseling: Working with blended families. *Journal of Divorce & Remarriage, 50*(2), 148–157.

Goodman, A. H. (2000). Why genes don't count (for racial differences in health). *American Journal of Public Health, 90*(11), 1699–1702.

Gordon, W. (1969). Basic constructs for an integrative and generative conception of social work. In G. Hearn (Ed.), *The general systems approach: Contributions toward an holistic conception of social work*. New York: Council on Social Work Education.

Gorman, D. (1999). Active and passive euthanasia: The cases of Drs. Claudio Alberto de la Rocha and Nancy Morrison. *Canadian Medical Association Journal, 160*(6), 857–860.

Gottman, J. M., & Levenson, R. W. (2000). The timing of divorce: Predicting when a couple will divorce over a 14-year period. *Journal of Marriage and the Family, 62*, 737–745.

Gould, J. (2008). Non-standard assessment practices in the evaluation of communication in Australian Aboriginal children. *Clinical Linguistics & Phonetics, 22*(8), 643–657.

Grauerholz, E., & King, A. (1997). Prime time sexual harassment. *Violence Against Women, 3*, 129–148.

Grigorenko, E. L. (2001). Developmental dyslexia: An update on genes, brains, and environments. *Journal of Child Psychology and Psychiatry, 42*(1), 91–125.

Grimm, R., Spring, K., & Dietz, N. (2007). *The health benefits of volunteering: A review of recent research*. New York: Corporation for National and Community Service.

Grise-Owens, E. (2002). Sexism and the social work curriculum: A content analysis of the *Journal of Social Work Education*. *Affilia, 17*(2), 147–166.

Gross, H. E. (1993, May/June). Open adoption: A research-based literature review and new data. *Child Welfare, 72*(3), 269–285.

Gulli, C. (2009). Gay seniors get a place to call home. *Maclean's, 122*(14), 23.

Gurman, A. S. (1977). The patient's perception of the therapeutic relationship. In A. S. Gurman & A. M. Razin (Eds.), *Effective psychotherapy: A handbook of research* (pp. 503–543). Oxford: Pergamon.

Guthrie, M. L., & Bates, L. W. (2003). Sex education sources and attitudes toward sexual precautions across a decade. *Psychological Reports, 92*, 581–592.

Guttery, E. G., Friday, G. A., Field, S. S., Riggs, S. C., & Hagan, J. F. (2002, June). Coparent or second parent adoption by same-sex parents. *Pediatrics, 109*(6), 1192–1194.

Habermas, T., & Bluck, S. (2000). Getting a life: The emergence of the life story in adolescence. *Psychological Bulletin, 126*, 748–769.

Habicht J. P., Davanzo J., & Butz, W. P. (1986). Does breastfeeding really save lives, or are apparent benefits due to biases? *American Journal of Epidemiology, 123*, 279–290.

Hacker, A. (2003). *Mismatch: The growing gulf between women and men*. New York: Scribner.

Hagan, J. F. (2002, August). It's about their children. *Pediatrics, 110*(2), 408–410.

Haight, W. L., Kagle, J. D., & Black, J. E. (2003). Understanding and supporting parent–child relationships during foster care visits: Attachment theory and research. *Social Work, 48*(2), 195–209.

Hallahan, D. P., & Kauffman, J. M. (2000). *Exceptional learners: Introduction to special education* (8th ed.). Boston: Allyn & Bacon.

Hamilton, L., Cheng, S., & Powell, B. (2007). Adoptive parents, adaptive parents: Evaluating the importance of biological ties for parental investment. *American Sociological Review, 72*(1), 95–116.

Harkness, S. (1990). A cultural model for the acquisition of language: Implications for the innateness debate. *Developmental Psychobiology, 23*, 727–739.

Harlow, H. F., & Zimmerman, R. R. (1959). Affectional responses in the infant monkey. *Science, 130*, 421–432.

Harris, D. R., & Sim, J. J. (2002). Who is multiracial? Assessing the complexity of lived race. *American Sociological Review, 67*, 614–627.

Hart, B., & Risley, T. R. (1995). *Meaningful differences in the everyday experience of young American children*. Baltimore, MD: P. H. Brookes.

Harter, S. (1999). *The construction of self*. New York: Guilford.

Harvard Mental Health Letter. (2002, November). The spanking debate. *Harvard Mental Health Letter*, *19*(5), 1–3.

Hassold, T., & Patterson, D. (Eds.). (1998). *Down syndrome: A promising future together*. New York: Wiley Liss.

Havighurst, R. J., Neugarten, B. L., & Tobin, S. S. (1968). Disengagement and patterns of aging. In B. Neugarten (Ed.), *Middle age and aging: A reader in social psychology* (pp. 161–172). Chicago: University of Chicago Press.

Haws, W. A., & Mallinckrodt, B. (1998). Separation individuation from family of origin and marital adjustment of recently married couples. *American Journal of Family Therapy, 26*(4), 293–306.

Heilman, M. E. (2001). Description and prescription: How gender stereotypes prevent women's ascent up the organizational ladder. *Journal of Social Issues, 57*(4), 657–674.

Helsen, M., Vollebergh, W., & Meeus, W. (2000). Social support from parents and friends and emotional problems in adolescence. *Journal of Youth and Adolescence, 29*(3), 319–335.

Henry, W. (1963). The theory of intrinsic disengagement. In P. F. Hansen (Ed.), *Age with a future*. Copenhagen: Monksgaard.

Herek, G. M. (2001). On heterosexual masculinity: Some psychical consequences of the social construction of gender and sexuality. *American Behavioral Scientist, 29*(5), 563–577.

Herrera, N. C., Zajonc, R. B., Wieczorkowska, G., & Cichomski, B. (2003). Beliefs about birth rank and their reflection in reality. *Journal of Personality and Social Psychology, 85*(1), 142–150.

Hetherington, E. M. (2000). Divorce. In A. Kazdin (Ed.), *Encyclopedia of psychology* (pp. 61–65). Washington, DC: American Psychological Association.

Hetherington, E. M. (2003). Social support and the adjustment of children in divorced and remarried families. *Childhood, 10*(2), 217–236.

Heugten, K., & Wilson, E. (2008). Witnessing intimate partner violence: Review of the literature on coping in young persons. *Social Work Review, 20*(3), 52–62.

Hewagama, A., & Richardson, B. (2009). The genetics and epigenetics of autoimmune diseases. *Journal of Autoimmunity, 33*(1), 3–11.

Hildyard, K. L., & Wolfe, D. A. (2002). Child neglect: Developmental issues and outcomes. *Child Abuse and Neglect, 26*, 679–695.

Hillier, S., & Barrow, G. M. (2006). *Aging, the individual, and society* (8th ed.). Belmont, CA: Wadsworth.

Hobbins, J. C. (1997). Alpha-fetoprotein screening for neural tube defects. *Contemporary Ob/Gyn*, 160–161.

Hodges, E. V. E., & Card, N. A. (Eds.). (2003). *Enemies and the darker side of peer relations*. San Francisco: Jossey-Bass.

Hoek, H. W. (2006). Incidence, prevalence, and mortality of anorexia nervosa and other eating disorders. *Current Opinion in Psychiatry, 19*(4), 389–394.

Hoff, E. (2003). The specificity of environmental influence: Socioeconomic status affects early vocabulary development via maternal speech. *Child Development, 74*(5), 1368–1378.

Hoffman, L. (1981). *Foundations of family therapy*. New York: Basic Books.

Hollenshead, C. S., & Miller, J. E. (2001). *Diversity workshops: Gender equity—a closer look*. [Online]. Retrieved January 21, 2004, from http//www.diversityweb.org/Digest/Sp01/research2.html.

Homan, M. S. (1999). *Promoting community change: Making it happen* (2nd ed.). Pacific Grove, CA: Brooks/Cole.

Homans, G. C. (1967). *The nature of social science*. New York: Harcourt, Brace & World.

Hopper, R., & Naremore, R. (1978). *Children's speech: A practical introduction to communication development*. New York: Harper & Row.

Howie, P. W., Forsyth, J. S., Ogston, S. A., Clark, A., Du, V., & Florey, C. (1990). Protective effect of breast feeding against infection. *British Journal of Medicine, 300*, 1–11.

Huang, Z. J., Yu, S. M., Liu, X. W., Young, D., & Wong, F. Y. (2009). Beyond medical insurance: Delayed or forgone care among children in Chinese immigrant families. *Journal of Health Care for the Poor and Underserved, 20*(2), 364–377.

Huesmann, L. R., Moise-Titus, J., Podolski, C., & Eron, L. D. (2003). Longitudinal relations between children's exposure to TV violence and their aggressive and violent behavior in young adulthood: 1977–1992. *Developmental Psychology, 39*(2), 201–221.

Hulsey, T. M., Laken, M., Miller, V., & Ager, J. (2000). The influence of attitudes about unintended pregnancy on use of prenatal and postpartum care. *Journal of Perinatology, 20*, 513–519.

Humphreys, C., Lowe, P., & Williams, S. (2009). Sleep disruption and domestic violence: Exploring the interconnections between mothers and children. *Child & Family Social Work, 14*(1), 6–14.

Hunter College Women's Studies Collective (1995). *Women's realities, women's choices: An introduction to women's studies*. New York: Oxford University Press.

Hybels, C. F., & Blazer, D. G. (2003). Epidemiology of late-life mental disorders. *Clinics in Geriatric Medicinee, 19*, 663–696.

Inomata, K., Aoto, T., Binh, N. T., Okamoto, N., Tanimura, S., Wakayama, T., Iseki, S., Hara, E., Masunaga, T., Shimizu, H., & Nishimura, E. K. (2009). Genotoxic stress abrogates renewal of melanocyte stem cells by triggering their differentiation. *Cell, 137*(6), 1088–1099.

Institute of Medicine. (1997). *The hidden epidemic*. Washington, DC: National Academy Press.

International Women's Health Coalition. (1997, May 21). *A women's lens on foreign policy: A symposium*. [Online]. Conference proceedings retrieved July 15, 2003, from http://www.iwhc.org/uploads/womenslens.pdf.

Isidori, A. (2008). Myths and reality of male andropause. *Sexologies, 17*(1), S24–S25.

Izard, C. E. (1982). *Measuring emotions in infants and young children*. New York: Cambridge University Press.

Izard, C. E. (1991). *The psychology of emotions*. New York: Plenum Press.

Jackson, D. D. (1957). The question of family homeostasis. *Psychiatric Quarterly Supplement, 31*, 79–90.

Jacobsen, S. W., Jacobson, J. L., Sokol, R. J., Martier, S. S., & Ager, J. W. (1993). Prenatal alcohol exposure and infant information processing ability. *Child Development, 64*, 1706–1721.

Jacobson, L. (2003, May 28). Head Start bill jump-starts debate on program's future. *Education Week, 22*(38), 20.

Jensen, R., & Burgess, H. (1997). Mythmaking: How introductory psychology texts present B. F. Skinner's analysis of cognition. *Psychological Record, 47*(2), 221–231.

Johnson, C. C., & Johnson, K. A. (2000). High-risk behavior among gay adolescents: Implications for treatment and support. *Adolescence, 35*(140), 619–637.

Johnson, H. C., Atkins, S. P., Battle, S. F., Hernandez-Arata, L., Hesselbrock, M., Libassi, M. F., & Parish, M. S. (1990). Strengthening the "bio" in the biopsychosocial paradigm. *Journal of Social Work Education, 26*(2), 109–123.

Johnston, L. D., O'Malley, P. M., & Bachman, J. G. (2001). *Monitoring the future: 2001*. Ann Arbor, MI: Institute for Social Research.

Jones, M. C. (1965). Psychological correlates of somatic development. *Child Development, 36*, 899–911.

Jones, M. C., & Bayley, N. (1950). Physical maturing among boys as related to behavior. *Journal of Educational Psychology, 41*, 129–148.

Jones, T. (2007). Examining potential determinants of parental self-efficacy. *Dissertation Abstracts International: Section B: The Sciences and Engineering, 67*(9-B), 5383.

Joyce, T., & Kaestner, R. (2000). The effect of pregnancy intention on child development. *Demography, 37*(1), 83–94.

Joyce, T., Kaestner, R., & Korenman, S. (2000). The stability of pregnancy intentions and pregnancy-related maternal behaviors. *Maternal & Child Health Journal, 4*(3), 171–178.

Kahana, E., & Kahana, B. (1996). Conceptual and empirical advances in understanding aging well through proactive adaptation. In V. Bengtson (Ed.), *Adulthood and aging: Research on continuities and discontinuities* (pp. 124–145). New York: Springer Publishing.

Kahana, E., & Kahana, B. (2003). Contextualizing successful aging: New directions in an age-old search. In R. Settersten, Jr. (Ed.), *Invitation to the life course: A new look at old age*. Amityville, NY: Baywood Publishing.

Kahana, E., Kahana, B., & Kercher, K. (2003). Emerging lifestyles and proactive options for successful aging. *Ageing International*, *28*(2), 155–180.

Kaiser Family Foundation (2005a). *Media multi-tasking changing the amount and nature of young people's media use*. [Online]. Retrieved June 21, 2009, from http://www.kff.org/entmedia/ entmedia030905nr.cfm.

Kaiser Family Foundation. (2005b). *Inaugural health education research disparities summit: Health disparities and social inequities: Plenary II—Framing solutions for the elimination of health disparities*. August 8, 2005.

Katz, A. H. (1983). Deficiencies in the status quo. *Social Work*, *28*(1), 71.

Kauffman, J. M., & Hallahan, D. P. (2005). *The illusion of full inclusion* (2nd ed.). Austin, TX: Pro-Ed Publishers.

Kausler, D. H., Kausler, B. C., & Krupsaw, J. A. (2007). *The essential guide to aging in the twenty-first century*. Columbia, MO: University of Missouri Press.

Keating, D. P. (1990). Adolescent thinking. In S. S. Feldman & R. Elliott (Eds.), *At the threshold: The developing adolescent* (pp. 54–92). Cambridge, MA: Harvard University Press.

Kelley, B. T., Thornberry, T. P., & Smith, C. A. (1997). *In the wake of childhood violence*. Washington, DC: National Institute of Justice.

Kendall, K. (2003, Summer). Lesbian and gay parents in child custody and visitation disputes. *Human Rights: Journal of the Section of Individual Rights and Responsibilities*, *30*(3), 8–10.

Keyes, C., & Ryff, C. (1999). Psychological well-being in midlife. In S. L. Willis & J. D. Reid (Eds.), *Life in the middle* (pp. 161–178). San Diego, CA: Academic Press.

Kim, C. J. (2004). Unyielding positions: A critique of the "race" debate. *Ethnicities* (9/1/2004), 337–355.

Kimble, M. A. (2001). Beyond the biomedical paradigm: Generating a spiritual vision of ageing. *Journal of Religious Gerontology*, *12*(3/4), 31–41.

Kinsley, M. (1995). The spoils of victimhood: The case against the case against affirmative action. *New Yorker*, 62–69.

Klaus, M. H., & Fanaroff, A. A. (Eds.) (2001). *Care of the high-risk neonate*. Philadelphia: Saunders.

Kling, K. C., Hyde, J. S., Showers, C. J., & Buswell, B. N. (1999). Gender differences in self-esteem: A meta-analysis. *Psychological Bulletin*, *125*(4), 470–500.

Koenig, H. G. (1995). *Aging and God: Spiritual pathways to mental health in midlife and later years*. New York: Haworth Pastoral Press.

Kohlberg, L. (1969). *Stages in the development of moral thought and action*. New York: Holt, Rinehart, & Winston.

Kohlberg, L. (1976). Moral stages and moralization: The cognitive-developmental approach. In T. Lickona (Ed.), *Moral development and behavior*. New York: Holt, Rinehart, & Winston.

Kohlberg, L. (1978). Revisions in the theory and practice of moral development. *New Directions for Child Development*, *2*.

Kohlberg, L. (1981). *The philosophy of moral development*. New York: Harper & Row.

Kools, S. M. (1997). Adolescent identity development in foster care. *Family Relations*, *46*(3), 263.

Kornblum, W., & Julian, J. (2001). *Social problems* (10th ed.). Upper Saddle River, NJ: Prentice-Hall.

Koropeckyj-Cox, T. (2002). Beyond parental status: Psychological well-being in middle and old age. *Journal of Marriage and the Family*, *64*(4), 957–971.

Korvatska, E., Van de Water, J., Anders, T. F., & Gershwin, M. E. (2002). Genetic and immunologic considerations in autism. *Neurobiology of Disease*, *9*(2), 107–125.

Kost, K., Landry, D. J., & Darroch, J. (1998). The effects of pregnancy planning status on birth outcomes and infant care. *Family Planning Perspectives*, *30*(5), 223–230.

Kosterman, R., Graham, J. W., Hawkins, J. D., Catalano, R. F., & Herrenkohl, T. I. (2001). Childhood risk factors for persistence of violence in the transition to adulthood: A social development perspective. *Violence and Victims*, *16*(4), 355–369.

Krisberg, K. (2003, Dec/Jan). Deaths due to unintended pregnancies on the rise. *Nation's Health*, *32*(10), 12.

Kruk, E. (1994). Grandparent visitation disputes: Multi-generational approaches to family mediation. *Mediation Quarterly*, *12*(1), 37–53.

Kübler-Ross, E. (1969). *On death and dying*. New York: Macmillan.

Kübler-Ross, E. (1971). Stages of dying. In R. H. Davis (Ed.), *Confrontation with dying*. Los Angeles: Gerontology Center, University of Southern California.

Kuhl, P. (1993). Infant speech perception: A window on psycholinguistic development. *International Journal of Psycholinguistics*, *9*, 33–56.

Kuhn, D. (2008). Formal operations from a twenty-first century perspective. *Human Development*, *51*, 48–55.

Kuhn, D., & Pease, M. (2006). Do children and adults learn differently? *Journal of Cognition and Development*, *7*, 279–293.

Kurdek, L. A. (2001). Differences between heterosexual-nonparent couples and gay, lesbian, and hetero-sexual-parent couples. *Journal of Family Issues*, *22*(6), 728–755.

Kurdek, L. A. (2002). Predicting the timing of separation and marital satisfaction: An eight-year prospective longitudinal study. *Journal of Marriage and the Family*, *64*(1), 163–179.

Kwalombota, M. (2002). The effect of pregnancy in HIV-infected women. *AIDS Care*, *14*(3), 431–433.

Lancet. (2003, July 5). A victory for affirmative action. *Lancet*, *362*(9377), 1.

Langford, J., Bohensky, M., Koppel, S., & Newstead, S. (2008). Do older drivers pose a risk to other road users? *Traffic Injury Prevention*, *9*(3), 181–189.

Lanphear, B. P., Vorhees, C. V., & Bellinger, D. C. (2005). Protecting children from environmental toxins. *PLoS Medicine*, *2*(3), e61.

Lansford, J. E., & Dodge, K. A. (2008). Cultural norms for adult corporal punishment of children and societal rates of endorsement and use of violence. *Parenting: Science and Practice*, *8*(3), 257–270.

LaRochebrochard, E., & Thonneau, P. (2002). Paternal age and maternal age are risk factors for miscarriage: Results of a multicentre European study. *Human Reproduction*, *17*(6), 1649–1656.

Laumann, E. O., Leitsch, S. A., & Waite, L. J. (2008). Elder mistreatment in the United States: Prevalence estimates from a nationally representative study. *Journals of Gerontology Series B: Psychological Sciences & Social Sciences*, *63B*(4), S248–S254.

Lawrence, R. C., Felson, D. T., Helmick, C. G., Arnold, L. M., Choi, H., Deyo, R. A., Gabriel, S., Hirsch, R., Hochberg, M. C., Hunder, G. G., Jordan, J. M., Katz, J. N., Kremers, H. M., & Wolfe, F. (2008). Estimates of the prevalence of arthritis and other rheumatic conditions in the United States. Part II. *Arthritis and Rheumatism*, *58*(1), 26–35.

Lefebvre, H. (1968). *The sociology of Marx*. New York: Columbia University Press.

Lemery, K. S., Goldsmith, H. H., Klinnert, M. D., & Mrazek, D. A. (1999). Developmental models of infant and childhood temperament. *Developmental Psychology*, *35*(1), 189–204.

Lenski, G. (1988). Rethinking macrosociological theory. *American Sociological Review*, *53*, 163–171.

Leon, K. (2003). Risk and protective factors in young children's adjustment to parental divorce: A review of the research. *Family Relations*, *52*, 258–270.

Levinson, D. J. (1978). *The seasons of a man's life*. New York: Knopf.

Levinson, D. J., & Levinson, J. D. (1996). *The seasons of a woman's life*. New York: Knopf.

Lindau, S. T., Schumm, L. P., Laumann, E. O., Levinson, W., O'Muircheartaigh, C. A., & Waite, L. J. (2007). A study of sexuality and health among older adults in the United States. *New England Journal of Medicine*, *357*(8), 762–774.

Lindberg, L. D., Boggs, S., Porter, L., & Williams, S. (2000). *Teen risk-taking: A statistical report*. Washington, DC: Urban Institute.

Liu, H. M., Kuhl, P. K., & Tsao, F. M. (2003). An association between mothers' speech clarity and infants' speech discrimination skills. *Developmental Science*, *6*(3), 1–9.

Lorenz, K. Z. (1965). *Evolution and the modification of behavior*. Chicago: University of Chicago Press.

Loughran, D. S., Seabury, S. A., & Zakaras, L. (2007). Regulating older drivers. Are new policies needed? [Online]. Retrieved July 1, 2009, from http://www.rand.org/pubs/occasional_papers/2007/RAND_OP189.pdf.

Lowis, M. J., Edwards, A. C., & Burton, M. (2009). Coping with retirement: Well-being, health, and religion. *Journal of Psychology*, *143*(4), 427–448.

Lum, D. (1995). Cultural values and minority people of color. *Journal of Sociology and Social Welfare*, *22*(1), 59–74.

Lupton, C. (2003). *The financial impact of fetal alcohol syndrome*. SAMHSA Fetal Alcohol Spectrum Disorders Center for Excellence. [Online]. Retrieved June 14, 2009, from http://www.fasdcenter.samhsa.gov/publications/cost.cfm.

Luxton, D. D. (2008). The effects of inconsistent parenting on the development of uncertain self-esteem and depression vulnerability. *Dissertation Abstracts International: Section B: The Sciences and Engineering, 69*(4-B), 2631.

MacKinlay, E. (2001). Ageing and isolation: Is the issue social isolation or is it lack of meaning in life? *Journal of Religious Gerontology, 12*(3/4), 89–99.

Macular Degeneration Foundation. (2002). Adult macular degeneration. [Online]. Retrieved March 11, 2003, from http://www.eyesight.org/Adult/adult.html.

Maier, W., Gansicke, M., Freyberger, H. J., Linz, M., Heun, R., & Lecrubier, Y. (2000). Generalized anxiety disorder (ICD-10) in primary care from a cross-cultural perspective: A valid diagnostic entity? *Acta Psychiatrica Scandinavica, 101*(1), 29–36.

Malinosky-Rummell, R., & Hansen, D. J. (1993). Long-term consequences of childhood physical abuse. *Psychological Bulletin, 114*, 68–79.

Mangione-Smith, R., DeCristofaro, A. H., Setodji, C. M., Keesey, J., Klein, D. J., Adams, J. L., Schuster, M. A., & McGlynn, E. A. (2007). The quality of ambulatory care delivered to children in the United States. *New England Journal of Medicine, 357*(15), 1515–1523.

March of Dimes. (2009). *Quick references and fact sheets*. [Online]. Retrieved June 14, 2009, from http://search.marchofdimes.com/cgi-bin/MsmGo.exe?grab_id=6&page_id=10027264&query=birth+defects&hiword=BIRTHED+BIRTHING+BIRTHS+DEFECT+DEFECTIVE+DEFECTOS+birth+defects+.

Martin, S. K., & Lindsey, D. (2003). The impact of welfare reform on children: An introduction. *Children and Youth Services Review, 25*(1/2), 1–15.

Martin, S. L., Kupper, L. L., Mackie, L., Clark, K. A., Buescher, P. A., & Halpern, C. (2001). Are abused women more or less likely to use health care services during pregnancy? *Paediatric and Perinatal Epidemiology, 15*, A1–A38.

Martorell, R., Mendoza, F., & Castillo, F. (1988). Poverty and stature in children. In J. C. Waterlow (Ed.), *Linear growth retardation in less developed countries*. New York: Raven.

Marx, K. (1973). *On society and social change*. Chicago: University of Chicago Press.

Marx, K. (1987). *Das Kapital*. Washington, DC: Regnery Gateway.

Marx, K. (1994). Classes in capitalism and pre-capitalism. In D. B. Grusky (Ed.), *Social stratification: Class, race, and gender in sociological perspective* (pp. 69–78). San Francisco: Westview Press.

Marx, K., & Engels, F. (1977). *The communist manifesto*. Mattituck, NY: Amereon House.

Maslow, A. H. (1954). *Motivation and personality*. New York: Harper & Brothers.

Materstvedt, L. J., Clark, D., Ellershaw, J., Forde, R., Gravgaard, A. B., Muller-Busch, H. C., Sales, J. P., & Rapin, C. H. (2003). Euthanasia and physician-assisted suicide: A view from an EAPC ethics task force. *Palliative Medicine, 17*, 97–101.

Mather, J. H., & Lager, P. B. (2000). *Child welfare: A unifying model of practice*. Belmont, CA: Wadsworth.

Mathers, C. D., & Loncar, D. (2006). Projections of global mortality and burden of disease from 2002 to 2030. *PLoS Medicine, 3*(11), 2011–2203.

Matsumoto, A. M. (2002). Clinical implications of the decline in serum testosterone levels with aging in men. *The Journals of Gerontology, 57A*(2), M76–M99.

Maynard, R. (1996). *Kids having kids: Robin Hood Foundation special report on the costs of adolescent childbearing*. New York: Robin Hood Foundation.

McAdam, D., McCarthy, J., & Zald, M. (Eds.). (1996). *Comparative perspectives on social movements*. New York: Cambridge University Press.

McCluskey, C. P., Krohn, M. D., Lizotte, A. J., & Rodriguez, M. L. (2002). Early substance use and school achievement: An examination of Latino, White, and African American youth. *Journal of Drug Issues, 32*(3), 921–943.

McCrae, R. R., & Costa, P. T. (1990). *Personality in adulthood*. New York: Guilford.

McCrae, R. R., Costa, P. T., Pederoso de Lima, M., Simões, A., Ostendorf, F., Angleitner, A., Marušić, I., Bratko, D., Caprara, G. V., Barbaranelli, C., Chae, J-H., & Piedmont, R. L. (1999). Age differences in personality across the adult life span: Parallels in five cultures. *Developmental Psychology*, *35*(2), 466–477.

McCullough, P. K. (1991, October). Geriatric depression: Atypical presentations, hidden meanings. *Geriatrics*, *46*, 72–76.

McElwain, N. L., & Booth-LaForce, C. (2006). Maternal sensitivity to infant distress and nondistress as predictors of infant–mother attachment security. *Journal of Family Psychology*, *20*(2), 247–255.

McElwain, N. L., Booth-LaForce, C., Lansford, J. E., Wu, X., & Dyer, W. J. (2008). A process model of attachment-friend linkages: Hostile attribution biases, language ability, and mother–child affective mutuality as intervening mechanisms. *Child Development*, *79*(6), 1891–1906.

McKnight, A. J. (2000, Winter). Too old to drive? *Issues in Science and Technology*, *17*(2), 1–11.

Mead, G. H. (1934). *Mind, self, and society from the standpoint of a social behaviorist.* Chicago: University of Chicago Press.

Mead, G. H. (1956). *On social psychology.* Chicago: University of Chicago Press.

Media Report to Women. (1999). Women 40 and older underrepresented in acting jobs, Screen Actors Guild says. *Media Report to Women*, *27*(2), 3.

Media Report to Women. (2001). SAG: Women still underrepresented on screen: Ageism, role prominence factors. *Media Report to Women*, *29*(1), 1.

Media Report to Women. (2009). Industry statistics. [Online]. Retrieved June 25, 2009, from http://www.mediareporttowomen.com/statistics.htm.

Mellor, J. (2000). Filling the gaps in long-term care insurance. In M. H. Meyer (Ed.), *Care work* (pp. 202–216). New York: Routledge.

Menkes, J. H., & Till, K. (1995). Malformations of the central nervous system. In J. H. Menkes (Ed.), *Textbook of child neurology* (5th ed.). Baltimore, MD: Williams & Wilkins.

Merton, R. K. (1968). *Social theory and social structure.* New York: Free Press.

Mills, C. W. (1959). *The sociological imagination.* London: Oxford University Press.

Mills, C. W. (1994). The power elite. In D. B. Grusky (Ed.), *Social stratification: Class, race, and gender in sociological perspective* (pp. 161–170). San Francisco: Westview Press.

Minuchin, P. (1985). Families and individual development: Provocations from the field of family therapy. *Child Development*, *56*, 289–302.

Minuchin, S. (1974). *Families and family therapy.* Cambridge, MA: Harvard University Press.

Mitchell, B. D., Kammerer, C. M., Reinhart, L. J., & Stern, M. P. (1994, June). NIDDM in Mexican American families: Heterogeneity by age of onset. *Diabetes Care*, *17*(6), 567–573.

MMWR. (2005). Mental health in the United States: Prevalence of diagnosis and medication treatment for attention-deficit/hyperactivity disorder—United States, 2003. [Online]. Retrieved June 21, 2009, from http://www.cdc.gov/mmwr/preview/mmwrhtml/mm5434a2.htm.

Mock, S. (2001). Retirement intentions of same-sex couples. *Journal of Gay and Lesbian Social Services*, *13*(4), 81–86.

Moen, P., & Wethington, E. (1999). Midlife development in a life course context. In S. L. Willis & J. D. Reid (Eds.), *Life in the middle: Psychological and social development in middle age* (pp. 1–18). San Diego, CA: Academic Press.

Molino, A. C. (2007). Characteristics of help-seeking street youth and non-street youth. In D. Dennis, G. Locke, & J. Khadduri (Eds.), *National Symposium on Homelessness Research.* Retrieved July 20, 2008, from http://aspe.hhs.gov/hsp/homelessness/symposium07/molino/index.htm.

Montague, A. (1964). *Man's most dangerous myth: The fallacy of race* (4th ed.). Cleveland: World.

Montemurro, B. (2003). Not a laughing matter: Sexual harassment as "material" on workplace-based situation comedies. *Sex Roles*, *48*(9/10), 433–445.

Montgomery, K. S. (2001). Planned adolescent pregnancy: What they needed. *Issues in Comprehensive Pediatric Nursing*, *24*, 19–29.

Montgomery, S. M., Ehlin, A., & Sacker, A. (2006). Breastfeeding and resilience against psychosocial stress. *Archives of Disease in Childhood*, *91*(12), 990–994.

Moolchan, E. T., & Mermelstein, R. (2002). Research on tobacco use among teenagers: Ethical challenges. *Journal of Adolescent Health*, *30*, 409–417.

Moore, K. L., & Persaud, T. V. N. (1998). *The developing human*. Philadelphia: W. B. Saunders.

Moore, M. L., & Piland, W. E. (1994). Impact of the campus physical environment on older adult learners. *Educational Gerontology, 20*(2), 129–138.

Morris, L. A., Ulmer, C., & Chimnani, J. (2003). A role for community healthcorps members in youth HIV/AIDS prevention education. *Journal of School Health, 73*(4), 138–142.

Moster, D., Lie, R. T., & Markestad, T. (2008). Long-term medical and social consequences of preterm birth. *New England Journal of Medicine, 359*(3), 262–273.

Moxnes, K. (2003). Risk factors in divorce. *Childhood, 10*(2), 131–146.

Mullaly, B. (1997). *Structural social work: Ideology, theory and practice* (2nd ed.). Toronto, Canada: Oxford University Press.

Mumme, D. L., Fernald, A., & Herrera, C. (1996). Infants' responses to facial and vocal emotional signals in a social referencing paradigm. *Child Development, 67*, 2319–2337.

Murkoff, H., & Mazel, S. (2008). *What to expect when you're expecting* (4th ed.). New York: Workman Publishing.

Murphy, D. (2007). Theory of mind functioning in mentally disordered offenders detained in high security psychiatric care: Its relationship to clinical outcome, need and risk. *Criminal Behaviour and Mental Health, 17*, 300–311.

Muth, J. L., & Cash, T. F. (1997). Body-image attitudes: What difference does gender make? *Journal of Applied Social Psychology, 27*, 1438–1452.

Narang, A., & Jain, N. (2001). Haemolytic disease of newborns. *Indian Journal of Pediatrics, 58*, 167–172.

Nash, R. (2001). Class, ability, and attainment: A problem for the sociology of education. *British Journal of Sociology of Education, 22*(2), 189–202.

National Alliance for Caregiving. (2007). *Evercare study of family caregivers: What they spend, what they sacrifice*. Bethesda, MD: Author.

National Association for Down Syndrome. (2009). *Facts about Down syndrome*. Retrieved June 15, 2009, from http://www.nads.org/pages_new/facts.html.

National Association of Social Workers. (1987). *Encyclopedia of social work* (18th ed., 2 vols.). Silver Spring, MD: Author.

National Association of Social Workers. (approved 1996, revised 2008). *Code of ethics*. Washington, DC: NASW.

National Association of Social Workers. (2001). *NASW standards for cultural competence in social work practice*. Washington, DC: NASW.

National Autism Association. (2009). *Autism is treatable*. [Online]. Retrieved June 17, 2009 at http://www.nationalautismassociation.org/psa.php.

National Center for Health Statistics (2000). *Health United States, 2000, with adolescent health chartbook*. Bethesda, MD: Department of Health and Human Services.

National Center for Health Statistics. (2008a). *Health, United States, 2008*. Hyattsville, MD: Author.

National Center for Health Statistics (2008b). Understanding school violence. [Online]. Retrieved June 23, 2009, from http://www.cdc.gov/Violence Prevention/pdf/SchoolViolence_FactSheet-a.pdf.

National Coalition for the Homeless. (2008). *Homeless youth: NCH Fact sheet #13*. [Online]. Retrieved June 23, 2009, from http://www.nationalhomeless.org/factsheets/youth.html.

National Diabetes Information Clearinghouse. (2008). *Prevalence of diagnosed and undiagnosed diabetes among people 20+, U.S., 2007*. Bethesda, MD: Author.

National Down Syndrome Society. (2009). *About Down syndrome*. New York: Author.

National Institute of Child Health and Human Development. (2008). *Autism spectrum disorders*. National Institutes of Health. [Online]. Retrieved June 17, 2009, from http://www.nichd.nih.gov/health/topics/asd.cfm.

National Institute of Environmental Health. (2008). *Smoking*. Washington, DC: National Institutes of Health.

National Institute of Mental Health. (2009). Older adults: Depression and suicide facts. [Online]. Retrieved June 30, 2009, from http://www.nimh.nih.gov/health/publications/older-adults-depression-and-suicide-facts-fact-sheet/index.shtml.

National Institutes of Health. (2001). NIH consensus statement: Osteoporosis prevention, diagnosis, and therapy. *JAMA, 285*(6), 785–795.

National Institutes of Health. (2009). *Bone health and osteoporosis: A guide for Asian women age 50 and older*. [Online]. Retrieved June 30, 2009, from http://www.niams.nih.gov/Health_Info/Bone/Osteoporosis/Background/asian_women_guide.pdf.

National Institute on Drug Abuse. (2001). *Marijuana*. Washington, DC: National Institutes of Health.

National Institute on Drug Abuse (2008). Behavioral problems related to maternal smoking during pregnancy manifest early in childhood. *NIDA Notes, 21*(6). [Online]. Retrieved June 14, 2009, from http://drugabuse.gov/NIDA_notes/NNvol21N6/behavioral.html.

National Osteoporosis Foundation. (2008). *Fast facts on osteoporosis*. [Online]. Retrieved June 29, 2009, from http://www.nof.org/osteoporosis/diseasefacts.htm.

National Vital Statistics Reports. (2005). Trends in cesarean rates for first births and repeat cesarean rates for low-risk women: United States, 1990–2003. [Online]. Retrieved June 23, 2009, from http://www.cdc.gov/nchs/data/nvsr/nvsr54/nvsr54_04.pdf.

National Women's Health Information Center. (2006). *Infertility*. [Online]. Retrieved June 14, 2009, from http://www.womenshealth.gov/faq/infertility.pdf.

National Women's Law Center. (2008). *Poverty among women and families, 2000–2007: Getting worse even before the downturn*. Washington, DC: Author.

Neiss, M. B., Stevenson, J., Legrand, L. N., Iacono, W. G., & Sedikides, C. (2009). Self-esteem, negative emotionality, and depression as a common temperamental core: A study of mid-adolescent twin girls. *Journal of Personality, 77*(2), 327–346.

Neisser, U., Boodoo, G., Bouchard, T. J., Boykin, A. W., Brody, N., Ceci, S. J., Halpern, D. F., Loehlin, J. C., Perloff, R., Sternberg, R. J., & Urbina, S. (1996). Intelligence: Knowns and unknowns. *American Psychologist, 51*, 77–101.

Nelson-Becker, H., & Canda, E. R. (2008). Spirituality, religion, and aging research in social work: State of the art and future possibilities. *Journal of Religion, Spirituality, and Aging, 20*(3), 177–193.

Neugarten, B., & Weinstein, K. (1964). The changing American grandparent. *Journal of Marriage and the Family, 26*, 199–205.

Newacheck, P., Hung, Y., Hochstein, M., & Halfon, N. (2002). Access to health care for disadvantaged young children. *Journal of Early Intervention, 25*(1), 1–11.

Newman, W. (1973). *American pluralism: A study of minority groups and social theory*. New York: Harper & Row.

Nguyen, T. V., Kelly, P. J., Sambrook, C., Gilbert, N. A., Pocock, N. A., & Eisman, J. A. (1994). Lifestyle factors and bone density in the elderly: Implications for osteoporosis prevention. *Journal of Bone Mineral Research, 9*, 1339–1346.

Nixon, E., Mansfield, P. K., Kittell, L. A., & Faulkner, S. L. (2001). "Staying strong": How low-income rural African American women manage their menopausal changes. *Women & Health, 34*(2), 81–95.

North American Menopause Society. (2006). *Menopause guidebook: Helping women make informed healthcare decisions through perimenopause and beyond*. Cleveland, OH: Author.

Norton, D. (1978). *The dual perspective: Inclusion of ethnic minority content in the social work curriculum*. Washington, DC: Council on Social Work Education.

NUA Internet Surveys. (2002). *IM programs draw US kids and teens online*. [Online]. Retrieved September 9, 2003, from http://www.nua.ie/surveys/index.cgi.

Nuba, H., Searson, M., & Sheiman, D. L. (Eds.). (1994). *Resources for early childhood: A handbook*. New York: Garland Publishers.

Nybo Andersen, A. M., Hansen, K. D., Andersen, P. K., & Smith, D. (2004). Advanced paternal age and risk of fetal death: A cohort study. *American Journal of Epidemiology, 160*, 1214–1222.

O'Connor, M. J., Kogan, N., & Findlay, R. (2002). Prenatal alcohol exposure and attachment behavior in children. *Alcoholism: Clinical and Experimental Research, 26*(10), 1592–1602.

O'Connor, T. P., Hoge, D. R., & Alexander, E. (2002). The relative influence of youth and adult experiences on personal spirituality and church involvement. *Journal for the Scientific Study of Religion, 41*(4), 723–733.

Oddy, W. H. (2002). The impact of breastmilk on infant and child health. *Breastfeeding Review, 10*(3), 5–18.

O'Donohue, W., & Caselles, C. E. (1993). Homophobia: Conceptual, definitional, and value issues. *Journal of Psychopathology and Behavioral Assessment, 15*(3), 177–195.

O'Laughlin, E. M. (2001). Perceptions of parenthood among young adults: Implications for career and family planning. *American Journal of Family Therapy, 29*(2), 95–108.

Olfson, M., Gameroff, M. J., Marcus, S. C., & Jensen, P. S. (2003). National trends in the treatment of attention deficit hyperactivity disorder. *American Journal of Psychiatry, 160*(6), 1071–1077.

Omar, H. A., Fowler, A., & McClanahan, K. K. (2008) Significant reduction of repeat teen pregnancy in a comprehensive young parent program. *Journal of Pediatric & Adolescent Gynecology, 21*(5), 283–287.

Orbuch, T. L., House, J. S., Mero, R. P., & Webster, P. S. (1996). Marital quality over the life course. *Social Psychology Quarterly, 59*, 162–171.

Orlinsky, D. E., & Howard, K. I. (1986). Process and outcome in psychotherapy. In S. L. Garfield & A. E. Bergin (Eds.), *Handbook of psychotherapy and behavior change* (3rd ed., pp. 311–381). New York: John Wiley.

Osgood, N. J. (1991). Prevention of suicide in the elderly. *Journal of Geriatric Psychiatry, 24*(2), 293–306.

Osmond, J., & O'Connor, I. (2006). Use of research and theory in social work practice: Implications for knowledge-based practice. *Australian Social Work, 59*(1), 5–19.

Owen, M. T. (2002). NICHD study of early child care. In J. G. Borkowski, S. L. Ramey, & M. Bristol- Power (Eds.), *Parenting and the child's world: Influences on academic, intellectual, and social-emotional development* (pp. 99–124). Mahwah, NJ: Lawrence Erlbaum Associates.

Paloutzian, R. (2000). *Invitation to the psychology of religion* (3rd ed.). Boston: Allyn & Bacon.

Papalia, D. E., Olds, S. W., & Feldman, R. D. (2001). *Human development* (8th ed.). Boston: McGraw-Hill.

Papalia, D. E., Olds, S. W., & Feldman, R. D. (2003). *Human development* (9th ed.). Boston: McGraw-Hill.

Parker, J. G., Rubin, K. H., Erath, S., Wojslawowicz, J. C., & Buskirk, A. (2006). Peer relationships, child development, and adjustment: A developmental psychopathology perspective. In D. Cicchetti (Ed.), *Developmental psychopathology*: Vol. 2: *Risk, disorder, and adaptation*. New York: Wiley.

Parsons, T. (1951). *The social system*. New York: Free Press.

Parsons, T. (1994). Equality and inequality in modern society, or social stratification revisited. In D. B. Grusky (Ed.), *Social stratification: Class, race, and gender in sociological perspective* (pp. 670–685). San Francisco: Westview Press.

Partamian, C. M. (2009). The impact of child adjustment to preschool on maternal separation anxiety. *Dissertation Abstracts International: Section B: The Sciences and Engineering, 69*(8-B), 5046.

Parten, M. (1932). Social play among preschool children. *Journal of Abnormal and Social Psychology, 27*, 243–269.

Parton, N. (2000). Some thoughts on the relationship between theory and practice in and for social work. *British Journal of Social Work, 30*(4), 449–464.

Pasterski, V., Hindmarsh, P., Geffner, M., Brook, C., Brain, C., & Hines, M. (2007). Increased aggression and activity level in 3- to 11-year-old girls with congenital adrenal hyperplasia (CAH). *Hormones & Behavior, 52*(3), 368–374.

Pastor, P. N., & Reuben, C. A. (2008). Diagnosed attention deficit hyperactivity disorder and learning disability: United States, 2004–2006. National Center for Health Statistics. *Vital Health Stat 10*(237), 1–13.

Patterson, C. H. (1984). Empathy, warmth, and genuineness in psychotherapy: A review of reviews. *Psychotherapy, 21*, 431–438.

Patterson, W. M., Dohn, H. H., Bird, J., & Patterson, G. A. (1983). Evaluation of suicidal patients: The SAD PERSONS scale. *Psychosomatics, 24*(4), 343–345.

Paul, J. P., Catania, J., Pollack, L., Moskowitz, J., Canchola, J., Binson, D., Mills, T., & Stall, R. (2002). Suicide attempts among gay and bisexual men: Lifetime prevalence and antecedents. *American Journal of Public Health, 92*(8), 1338–1345.

Pauls, B. S., & Daniels, T. (2000). Relationship among family, peer networks, and bulimic symptomatology in college women. *Canadian Journal of Counseling, 34*, 260–272.

Pavlov, I. P. (1927). *Conditioned reflexes: An investigation of the physiological activity of the cerebral cortex*. New York: Dover Publications.

Payne, M. S. (1997). *Modern social work theory* (2nd ed.). Chicago: Lyceum Books.

Pearson, J. L., & Conwell, Y. (1995). Suicide in late life: Challenges and opportunities for research. *International Psychogeriatrics, 7*, 131–135.

Pelkonen, M., Marttunen, M., Kaprio, J., Huurre, T., & Aro, H. (2008). Adolescent risk factors for episodic and persistent depression in adulthood. A 16-year prospective follow-up study of adolescents. *Journal of Affective Disorders, 106*(1/2), 123–131.

Pence, G. E. (1995). *Classical cases in medical ethics*. New York: McGraw-Hill.

Perkins, D. F., & Hartless, G. (2002). An ecological risk factor examination of suicide ideation and behavior of adolescents. *Journal of Adolescent Research, 17*(1), 3–26.

Perloff, J., & Buckner, J. (1996). Fathers of children on welfare: Their impact on child well-being. *American Journal of Orthopsychiatry, 66*, 557–571.

Perls, F., Hefferline, R. F., & Goodman, P. (1973). *Gestalt therapy: Excitement and growth in the human personality*. Harmondsworth, Middlesex: Penguin Books.

Perrin, E. C. (2002, February). Technical report: Co-parent or second-parent adoption by same-sex parents. *Pediatrics, 109*(2), 341–344.

Philliber, S., Kaye, J. W., Herrling, S., & West, E. (2002). Preventing pregnancy and improving health care access among teenagers: An evaluation of the children's aid society-Carrera program. *Perspectives on Sexual and Reproductive Health, 34*(5), 244–251.

Piaget, J. (1952). *The origins of intelligence in children*. New York: International Universities Press.

Piaget, J. (1972). Intellectual evolution from adolescence to adulthood. *Human Development, 15*(1), 1–12.

Piaget, J., & Inhelder, B. (1969). *The psychology of the child*. New York: Basic Books.

Pickens, J. (1998). Formal and informal care of people with psychiatric disorders: Historical perspectives and current trends. *Journal of Psychosocial Nursing, 36*(1), 37–43.

Pierce, J. L. (2003). Racing for innocence: Whiteness, corporate culture, and the backlash against affirmative action. *Qualitative Sociology, 26*(1), 53–70.

Plöderl, M., & Fartacek, R. (2009). Childhood gender nonconformity and harassment as predictors of suicidality among gay, lesbian, bisexual, and heterosexual Austrians. *Archives of Sexual Behavior, 38*(3), 400–410.

Plowfield, L. A., Raymond, J. E., & Blevins, C. (2000). Holism for aging families: Meeting needs of caregivers. *Holistic Nursing Practice, 14*(4), 51–59.

Pluess, M., & Belsky, J. (2009). Differential susceptibility to rearing experience: The case of childcare. *Journal of Child Psychology and Psychiatry, 50*(4), 396–404.

Polce-Lynch, M., Myers, B. J., Kliewer, W., & Kilmartin, C. (2001). Adolescent self-esteem and gender: Exploring relations to sexual harassment, body image, media influence, and emotional expression. *Journal of Youth and Adolescence, 30*(2), 225–243.

Polenski, T. A. (2002). Child characteristics and relations in the family as predictors of peer relationships. *Dissertation Abstracts International: Section B: The Sciences and Engineering, 63*(5-B), 2624.

Popper, K. R. (1959). *The logic of scientific discovery*. London: Hutchinson.

Potera, C. (2008). Comprehensive sex education reduces teen pregnancies. *American Journal of Nursing, 108*(7), 18.

Prigoff, A. W. (2003). Social justice framework. In J. Anderson & R. W. Carter (Eds.), *Diversity perspectives for social work practice*. Boston: Allyn & Bacon.

Pruger, R., & Specht, H. (1969). Assessing theoretical models of community organization practice: Alinsky as a case in point. *The Social Service Review, 43*(2), 123–135.

Quadagno, J. (2008). *Aging and the life course* (4th ed.). Boston: McGraw-Hill.

Quick, H., & Moen, P. (1998). Gender employment and retirement quality: A life course approach to the differential experiences of men and women. *Journal of Occupational Health Psychology, 3*(1), 44–64.

Quinn, J., & Kozy, M. (1996). The role of bridge jobs in the retirement transition: Gender, race and ethnicity. *The Gerontologist, 36*, 363–372.

Raman, P., Harwood, J., Weis, D., Anderson, J. L., & Miller, G. (2008). Portrayals of older adults in U.S. and Indian magazine advertisements: A cross-cultural comparison. *Howard Journal of Communications, 19*(3), 221–240.

Ramirez, A. G. (1996). Hypertension in Hispanic Americans: Overview of the population. *Public Health Report, 111*(2), 25–26.

Rapport, M. D., Bolden, J., Kofler, M. J., Sarver, D. E., Raiker, J. S., & Alderson, R. M. (2009). Hyperactivity in boys with attention-deficit/hyperactivity disorder (ADHD): A ubiquitous core symptom or manifestation of working memory deficits? *Journal of Abnormal Child Psychology, 37*(4), 521–534.

Ravdin, P. M., Cronin, K. A., Howlader, N., Berg, C. D., Chlebowski, R. T., Feuer, E. J., Edwards, B. K., & Berry, D. A. (2007). The decrease in breast cancer incidence in 2003 in the United States. *New England Journal of Medicine, 356*(16), 1670–1674.

Rawls, J. (1971). *A theory of justice.* Cambridge, MA: Harvard University Press.

Reardon, L. E., Leen-Feldner, E. W., & Hayward, C. (2009). A critical review of the empirical literature on the relation between anxiety and puberty. *Clinical Psychology Review, 29*(1), 1–23.

Reinharz, S. (1992). *Feminist methods in social research.* New York: Oxford University Press.

Reinisch, J. M. (1990). *The Kinsey Institute new report on sex.* New York: St. Martin's Press.

Reitzes, D. C., Mutran, E., & Pope, H. (1991). Location and well-being among retired men. *Journal of Gerontology, 46,* 195–203.

Remafedi, G., French, S., Story, M., Resnick, M. D., & Blum, R. (1998). The relationship between suicide risk and sexual orientation: Results of a population-based study. *American Journal of Public Health, 88,* 57–60.

Rende, R. (2000). Emotion and behavior genetics. In M. Lewis & J. M. Haviland-Jones (Eds.), *Handbook of emotions* (2nd ed.). New York: Guilford Press.

Richardson, G. A., Ryan, C., Willford, J., Day, N. L., & Goldschmidt, L. (2002). Prenatal alcohol and marijuana exposure: Effects on neuropsychological outcomes at 10 years. *Neurotoxicology and Teratology, 24*(3), 309–320.

Richmond, M. (1920). *Social diagnosis.* New York: Russell Sage Foundation.

Rickman, J. (1957). *A general selection from the works of Sigmund Freud.* New York: Doubleday & Company.

Ritter, J., Stewart, M., Bernet, C., Coe, M., & Brown, S. A. (2002). Effects of childhood exposure to familial alcoholism and family violence on adolescent substance use, conduct problems, and self-esteem. *Journal of Traumatic Stress, 15*(2), 113–122.

Robbins, J. M., Bird, T. M., Tilford, J. M., Cleves, M. A., Hobbs, C. A., Grosse, S. D., & Correa, A. (2007). Hospital stays, hospital charges, and in-hospital deaths among infants with selected birth defects—United States, 2003. *Journal of the American Medical Association, 297*(8), 802–803.

Robbins, S. P. (1984). Anglo concepts and Indian reality: A study of juvenile delinquency. *Social Casework, 65*(4), 235–241.

Roberts, R. N. (2002). Stating the obvious: Why do we care about access to health care? *Journal of Early Intervention, 25*(1), 12–14.

Robinson, T., & Anderson, C. (2006). Older characters in children's animated television programs: A content analysis of their portrayal. *Journal of Broadcasting & Electronic Media, 50*(2), 287–304.

Robinson, T., Callister, M., Magoffin, D., & Moore, J. (2007). The portrayal of older characters in Disney animated films. *Journal of Aging Studies, 21*(3), 203–213.

Röcke, C., & Lachman, M. E. (2008). Perceived trajectories of life satisfaction across past, present, and future: Profiles and correlates of subjective change in young, middle-aged, and older adults. *Psychology & Aging, 23*(4), 833–847.

Rogers, A. T. (1999). Factors associated with depression and low life satisfaction in the low-income, frail elderly. *Journal of Gerontological Social Work, 31*(1/2), 167–194.

Rogers, C. R. (1951). *Client-centered therapy: Its current practice, implications, and theory.* Boston: Houghton Mifflin.

Rosenbaum, J. E. (2009). Patient teenagers? A comparison of the sexual behavior of virginity pledgers and matched nonpledgers. *Pediatrics, 123*(1), 110–120.

Rosenblum, L. P., & Corn, A. L. (2002). Experiences of older adults who stopped driving because of their visual impairments: Part 3. *Journal of Visual Impairment & Blindness*, *96*(10), 701–710.

Rothenberg, A., & Weissman, A. (2002). The development of programs for pregnant and parenting teens. *Social Work in Health Care*, *35*(3), 65–83.

Rothman, J. (1995). Approaches to community intervention. In J. Rothman, J. L. Erich, & J. E. Tropman (Eds.), *Strategies of community intervention* (5th ed.). Itasca, IL: F. E. Peacock Publishers.

Rowe, J. W., & Kahn, R. L. (1987). Human aging: Usual and successful. *Science*, *237*(4811), 143–149.

Rowe, J. W., & Kahn, R. L. (1997). Successful aging. *Gerontologist*, *37*(4), 433–440.

Ruschena, E., Prior, M., Sanson, A., & Smart, S. (2005). A longitudinal study of adolescent adjustment following family transitions. *Journal of Child Psychology and Psychiatry*, *46*(4), 353–363.

Russell, S. T., & Joyner, K. (2001). Adolescent sexual orientation and suicide risk: Evidence from a national study. *American Journal of Public Health*, *91*, 1276–1281.

Ruth, J. E., & Coleman, P. (1996). Personality and aging: Coping and management of the self in later life. In J. Birren and K. W. Schaie (Eds.), *Handbook of the psychology of aging* (pp. 308–322). San Diego, CA: Academic Press.

Ryan, C., Huebner, D., Diaz, R. M., & Sanchez, J. (2009). Family rejection as a predictor of negative health outcomes in White and Latino lesbian, gay, and bisexual young adults. *Pediatrics*, *123*(1), 346–352.

Rymer, J., Wilson, R., & Ballard, K. (2003). Making decisions about hormone replacement therapy. *British Journal of Nursing*, *326*, 322–326.

Saha, S., Barnett, A. G., Foldi, C., Burne, T. H., Eyles, D. W., Buka, S. L., & McGrath, J. J. (2009). Advanced paternal age is associated with impaired neurocognitive outcomes during infancy and childhood. *PLoS Medicine*, *6*(3), e1000040.

Saleebey, D. (1992). *The strengths perspective in social work practice*. New York: Longman.

Salter, M. D. (1940). *An evaluation of adjustment based upon the concept of security*. Toronto: University of Toronto Press.

Saltman, J. E. (2002). Theory and practice in social work: Two perspectives on reality. *Arete*, *26*(part 2), 84–99.

Saltman, J. E., & Greene, R. R. (1993). Social workers' perceived knowledge and use of human behavior theory. *Journal of Social Work Education*, *20*(1), 88–98.

Samuels, G. M. (2009). Being raised by White people: Navigating racial difference among adopted multiracial adults. *Journal of Marriage & Family*, *71*(1), 80–94.

Santos-Reboucas, C. B., Correa, J. C., Bonomo, A., Fintelman-Rodrigues, N., Moura, K. C. V., Rogrigues, C. S. C., Santos, J. M., & Pimentel, M. M. G. (2009). The impact of folate pathway polymorphisms combined to nutritional deficiency as a maternal predisposition factor for Down syndrome. *Disease Markers*, *25*(3), 149–157.

Sarigiani, P. A., & Petersen, A. C. (2000). Adolescence: Puberty and biological maturation. In A. Kazdin (Ed.), *Encyclopedia of psychology* (pp. 39–46). Washington, DC: American Psychological Association.

Sayer, D. (1989). *Readings from Karl Marx*. New York: Routledge.

Schaefer, R. T. (2001). *Sociology* (7th ed.). New York: McGraw-Hill Companies.

Schaie, K. W., & Willis, S. L. (2000). A stage theory model of adult development revisited. In R. Rubinstein, M. Moss, & M. Kleban (Eds.), *The many dimensions of aging: Essays in honor of M. Powell Lawton*. New York: Springer.

Scharlach, A. (1994). Caregiving and employment: Results of an employee survey. *The Gerontologist*, *29*, 382–387.

Scher, A., & Mayseless, O. (2000). Mothers of anxious/ambivalent infants: Maternal characteristics and child-care context. *Child Development*, *71*(6), 1629–1639.

Schiffman, J., Abrahamson, A., Cannon, T., LaBrie, J., Parnas, J., Schulsinger, F., & Mednick, S. (2001). Early rearing factors in schizophrenia. *International Journal of Mental Health*, *30*(1), 3–16.

Schiffman, J., LaBrie, J., Carter, J., Cannon, T., Schulsinger, F., Parnas, J., & Mednick, S. (2002). Perception of parent–child relationships in high-risk families, and adult schizophrenic outcome of offspring. *Journal of Psychiatric Research*, *36*(1), 41–47.

Schmitt, M., Kliegal, M., & Shapiro, A. (2007). Marital interaction in middle and old age: A predictor of marital satisfaction? *International Journal of Aging and Human Development, 65*(4), 283–300.

Schneider, B. H., Atkinson, L., & Tardif, C. (2001). Child–parent attachment and children's peer relations: A qualitative review. *Developmental Psychology, 37*, 86–100.

Schoen, J. (2000). Reconceiving abortion: Medical practice, women's access, and feminist politics before and after Roe v. Wade. *Feminist Studies, 26*(2), 349–376.

Schoendorf, K. C., & Kiely, J. L. (1992). Relationship of sudden infant death syndrome to maternal smoking during and after pregnancy. *Pediatrics, 90*, 905–908.

Schope, R. (2005). Who's afraid of growing older? Gay and lesbian perceptions of aging. *Journal of Gerontological Social Work, 45*(4), 23–38.

Schrag, S. G., & Dixon, R. L. (1985). Occupational exposure associated with male reproductive dysfunction. *Annual Review of Pharmacology and Toxicology, 25*, 467–592.

Scott, G., & Ni, H. (2004). Access to health care among Hispanic/Latino children: United States, 1998–2001. *Advance Data, 344*, 1–20.

Sedgh, G., Henshaw, S., Singh, S., Ahman, E., & Shah, I. H. (2007). Induced abortion: Estimated rates and trends worldwide. *Lancet, 370*(9595), 1338–1345.

Segraves, R. T., & Segraves, K. B. (1995). Human sexuality and aging. *Journal of Sex Education and Therapy, 21*, 88–102.

Semba, R. D., Blaum, C. S., Bartali, B., Xue, O. L., Ricks, M. O., Guralnik, J. M., & Fried, L. P. (2006). Denture use, malnutrition fraility, and mortality among older women living in the community. *The Journal of Nutrition, Health, and Aging, 10*(2), 161–167.

Shansky, J. (2002). Negative effects of divorce on child and adolescent psychosocial adjustment. *Journal of Pastoral Counseling, 37*, 73–87.

Shapiro, J., & Applegate, J. S. (2002). Child care as a relational context for early development: Research in neurobiology and emerging roles for social work. *Child and Adolescent Social Work Journal, 19*(2), 97–114.

Shepard, M. (1992). Child visiting and domestic abuse. *Child Welfare, 71*, 357–367.

Sheppard, M. (1998). Practice validity, reflexivity, and knowledge for social work. *British Journal of Social Work, 28*(5), 763–781.

Shidlo, A., & Schroeder, M. (2002). Changing sexual orientation: A consumer's report. *Professional Psychology: Research and Practice, 33*(2), 249–259.

Shih, M., & Sanchez, D. T. (2009). When race becomes more complex: Towards understanding the landscape of multiracial identity and experiences. *Journal of Social Issues, 65*(1), 1–11.

Shpancer, N., Bowden, J. M., Ferrell, M. A., Pavlik, S. F., Robinson, M. N., Schwind, J. L., Volpe, E. K., Williams, L. M., & Young, J. N. (2002). The gap: Parental knowledge about daycare. *Early Child Development and Care, 172*, 635–642.

Sigelman, C. K., & Rider, E. A. (2005). *Life-span human development* (5th ed.). Belmont, CA: Wadsworth Publishing.

Simmons, R. G., & Blyth, D. A. (1987). *Moving into adolescence*. Hawthorne, NY: Aldine.

Simon, B., & Thyer, B. (1994). Are theories for practice necessary? Yes/No! *Journal of Social Work Education, 30*(2), 144–153.

Skinner, B. F. (1938). *The behavior of organisms: An experimental analysis*. New York: Appleton-Century-Crofts.

Slicker, E. K. (1998). Relationship of parenting style to behavioral adjustment in graduating high school seniors. *Journal of Youth and Adolescence, 27*(3), 345–372.

Smith, L., Yonekura, M. L., Wallace, T., Berman, N., Kuo, J., & Berkowitz, C. (2003) Effects of prenatal methamphetamine exposure on fetal growth and drug withdrawal symptoms in infants born at term. *Journal of Developmental & Behavioral Pediatrics, 24*(1), 17–23.

Smith, R., Ashford, L., Gribble, J., & Clifton, D. (2009). *Family planning saves lives* (4th ed). Washington, DC: Population Reference Bureau.

Snow, C. E. (1999). Social perspectives on the emergence of language. In B. MacWhinney (Ed.), *The emergence of language*. Mahwah, NJ: Lawrence Erlbaum Associates.

Solomon, B. B. (1976). *Black empowerment: Social work in oppressed communities*. New York: Columbia University Press.

Sommer, B. (2001). Menopause. In J. Worell (Ed.), *Encyclopedia of women and gender* (pp. 729–738). San Diego, CA: Academic Press.

Sontag, L. M., Graber, J. A., Brooks-Gunn, J., & Warren, M. P. (2008). Coping with social stress: Implications for psychopathology in young adolescent girls. *Journal of Abnormal Child Psychology, 36*(8), 1159–1174.

Sorrell, J. M. (2009). Aging toward happiness. *Journal of Psychological Nursing, 47*(3), 23–26.

Spence, A. P. (1999). *Biology of human aging* (2nd ed.). Englewood Cliffs, NJ: Prentice Hall.

Spencer, K., Spencer, C. E., Power, M., Dawson, C., & Nicolaides, K. H. (2003). Screening for chromosomal abnormalities in the first trimester using ultrasound and maternal serum biochemistry in a one-stop clinic. *BJOG: An International Journal of Obstetrics & Gynaecology, 110*(3), 281–286.

Spina Bifida Association. (2008). *Spotlight on spina bifida*. Washington, DC: Author.

Starck, M. (1993). *Women's medicine ways*. Freedom, CA: Crossing Press.

Stark, R. (1998). *Sociology* (7th ed.). Belmont, CA: Wadsworth.

Stattin, H., & Magnusson, D. (1990). *Pubertal maturation in female development: Paths through life* (Vol. 2). Hillsdale, NJ: Erlbaum.

Steelman, L. C., Powell, B., Werum, R., & Carter, S. (2002). Reconsidering the effects of sibling configuration: Recent advances and challenges. *Annual Review of Sociology, 28*, 243–269.

Stephens, C., Budge, R. C., & Carryer, J. (2002). What is this thing called hormone replacement therapy? Discursive construction of medication in situated practice. *Qualitative Health Research, 12*(3), 347–359.

Sternberg, R. J. (1977). *Intelligence, information processing, and analogical reasoning: The componential analysis of human abilities*. New York: John Wiley & Sons.

Sternberg, R. J. (1985). *Beyond IQ: A triarchic theory of human intelligence*. New York: Cambridge University Press.

Sternberg, R. J. (1988). Triangulating love. In R. J. Sternberg & M. L. Barnes (Eds.), *The psychology of love*. New Haven, CT: Yale University Press.

Stevens-Ratchford, R., & Krause, A. (2004). Visually impaired older adults and home-based leisure activities: The effects of person-environment congruence. *Journal of Visual Impairment & Blindness, 98*(1), 14–27.

Stolzenberg, R. M., Blair-Roy, M., & Waite, L. J. (1995). Religious participation in early adulthood: Age and family life cycle effects on church membership. *American Sociological Review, 60*, 84–103.

Strasburger, V., & Grossman, D. (2001). How many more Columbines? What can pediatricians do about school and media violence? *Pediatric Annals, 30*(2), 87–94.

Stratton, K., Howe, C., & Battaglia, F. (Eds.). (1996). *Fetal alcohol syndrome: Diagnosis, epidemiology, prevention, and treatment*. Washington, DC: National Academy Press.

Straus, M. A. (2001). *Beating the devil out of them: Corporal punishment in American families and its effects on children*. New Brunswick, NJ: Transaction Publishers.

Straus, M. A. (2008). The special issue on prevention of violence ignores the primordial violence. *Journal of Interpersonal Violence, 23*(9), 1314–1320.

Striegel-Moore, R. H., Rosselli, F., Perrin, N., DeBar, L., Wilson, G. T., May, A., & Kraemer, H. C. (2009). Gender difference in the prevalence of eating disorder symptoms. *International Journal of Eating Disorders, 42*(5), 471–474.

Striegel-Moore, R. H., Silberstein, L. R., & Rodin, J. (1993). The social self in bulimia nervosa: Public self-consciousness, social anxiety, and perceived fraudulence. *Journal of Abnormal Psychology, 102*, 297–303.

Strong, B., DeVault, C., Sayad, B. W., & Yarber, W. L. (2002). *Human sexuality: Diversity in contemporary America* (4th ed.). Boston: McGraw-Hill.

Studd, J. (2009). Estrogens as first-choice therapy for osteoporosis prevention and treatment in women under 60. *Climacteric, 12*(3), 206–209.

Sullivan, M., & Wodarski, J. S. (2002). Social alienation in gay youth. *Journal of Human Behavior in the Social Environment, 5*(1), 1–17.

Sun, Y., & Li, Y. (2002, May). Children's well-being during parents' marital disruption process: A pooled time-series analysis. *Journal of Marriage and the Family, 64*, 472–488.

Sun, Y., & Li, Y. (2009). Parental divorce, sibship size, family resources, and children's academic performance. *Social Science Research, 38*(3), 622–634.

Swann, J. (2009). Learning: An evolutionary analysis. *Educational Philosophy & Theory, 41*(3), 256–269.

Swenson, C. R. (1998). Clinical social work's contribution to a social justice perspective. *Social Work, 43*(6), 527–537.

Takahashi, P. Y., Okhravi, H. R., Lim, L. S., & Kasten, M. J. (2004). Preventive health care in the elderly population: A guide for practicing physicians. *Mayo Clinic Proceedings, 79,* 416–427.

Tanne, J. H. (2009). Obama diverts funds from abstinence-only sex education. *British Medical Journal, 338*(7705), 1232.

Tarrow, S. (1994). *Power in movement: Social movements, collective action, and politics.* New York: Cambridge University Press.

Tasker, F. (2005). Lesbian mothers, gay fathers, and their children: A review. *Journal of Developmental & Behavioral Pediatrics, 26*(3), 224–240.

Tesser, A. (2000). Self-esteem. In A. Kazdin (Ed.), *Encyclopedia of psychology* (pp. 213–216). Washington, DC: American Psychological Association.

Thackray, H., & Tifft, C. (2001). Fetal alcohol syndrome. *Pediatric Review, 22,* 47–55.

Thompson, R. A. (2000). Early experience and socialization. In A. Kazdin (Ed.), *Encyclopedia of psychology.* Washington DC: American Psychological Association and Oxford University Press.

Tickle, J. J., Heatherton, T. F., & Wittenberg, L. G. (2001). Can personality change? In W. J. Livesley (Ed.), *Handbook of personality disorders* (pp. 242–258). New York: Guilford Press.

Tiggemann, M. (2001). The impact of adolescent girls' life concerns and leisure activities on body dissatisfaction, disordered eating, and self-esteem. *Journal of Genetic Psychology, 162*(2), 133–142.

Timins, J. K. (2001). Radiation during pregnancy. *New Jersey Medicine, 98,* 23–33.

Tjaden, P., & Thoennes, N. (1998). *Prevalence, incidence, and consequences of violence against women: Findings from the National Violence against Women Survey.* Washington, DC: National Institute for Justice and Centers for Disease Control and Prevention.

Tucker, J. S., Kressin, N. R., Spiro, A., & Ruscio, J. (1998). Intrapersonal characteristics and the timing of divorce: A prospective investigation. *Journal of Social & Personal Relationships, 15*(2), 211–225.

Turner, J. H. (1998). *The structure of sociological theory.* New York: Wadsworth.

Tutty, L., & Wagar, J. (1994). The evolution of a group for young children who have witnessed family violence. *Social Work with Groups, 17*(1/2), 89–104.

Uhlenberg, P. I. (1996). Mortality decline over the twentieth century and supply of kin over the life course. *Gerontologist, 36,* 681–685.

UNICEF. (2004). *Low birth weight: Country, regional, and global estimates.* New York: UNICEF.

U.S. Bureau of Labor Statistics. (2002). *2002 National occupational employment and wage estimates.* Washington, DC: Author.

U.S. Bureau of Labor Statistics. (2009). *Usual weekly earnings of wage and salary workers news release.* Washington, DC: Author.

U.S. Census Bureau. (2001). *Households and families: 2000.* Washington, DC: U.S. Department of Commerce.

U.S. Census Bureau. (2003). *Marital status: 2000.* Washington, DC: U.S. Department of Commerce.

U.S. Census Bureau. (2006). *American community survey.* Washington, DC: U.S. Department of Commerce.

U.S. Census Bureau. (2008). *Household income rises, poverty rates unchanged, number of uninsured down.* Washington, DC: Department of Commerce.

U.S. Department of Health and Human Services. (2003). *Prevention pays: The costs of not preventing child abuse and neglect.* Washington, DC: Government Printing Office.

U.S. Department of Health and Human Services. (2004). *Literacy and health outcomes summary.* Washington, DC: U.S. Department of Health and Human Services, Agency for Healthcare Research and Quality.

U.S. Department of Health and Human Services. (2007a). *Child maltreatment 2007.* Washington, DC: Government Printing Office.

U.S. Department of Health and Human Services. (2007b). *Economic costs of injuries among children and adolescents*. Washington, DC: National Center for Injury Prevention and Control.

U.S. Department of Labor. (2007). Labor force characteristics by race and ethnicity. [Online]. Retrieved June 25, 2009, from http://www.bls.gov/cps/cpsrace2007.pdf.

U.S. Department of Labor. (2008). Report of the taskforce on the aging of the American workforce. [Online]. Retrieved June 25, 2009, from http://www.doleta.gov/reports/FINAL_Taskforce_Report_2_27_08.pdf.

U.S. Department of Labor. (2009). *Family and Medical Leave Act*. [Online]. Retrieved June 15, 2009, from http://www.dol.gov/esa/whd/fmla/.

U.S. Office of Personnel Management. (1993). *Federal employee entitlements under the Family and Medical Leave Act of 1993*. [Online]. Retrieved July 15, 2003, from http://www.opm.gov/compconf/Postconf00/leave/Herzbrg1.htm.

U.S. Office of Personnel Management (1997, April 11). *Memorandum for the heads of executive departments and agencies*. [Online]. Retrieved July 15, 2003, from http://www.opm.gov/oca/leave/html/fampres.htm.

Vaish, A., & Striano, T. (2004). Is visual reference necessary? Contributions of facial versus vocal cues in 12-month-olds' social referencing behavior. *Developmental Science, 7*(3), 261–269.

Van Den Bergh, N., & Cooper, L. B. (Eds.). (1986). *Feminist visions for social work*. Silver Springs, MD: National Association of Social Workers.

Vanderplasschen, W., Wolf, J., Rapp, R. C., & Broekaert, E. (2007). Effectiveness of different models of case management for substance-abusing populations. *Journal of Psychoactive Drugs, 39*(1), 81–95.

Van Goozen, S. H. M., Matthys, W., Cohen-Kettenis, P. T., Thisjssen, J. H. H., & Van Engeland, H. (1998). Adrenal androgens and aggression in conduct disorder among prepubertal boys and normal controls. *Biological Psychiatry, 43*, 156–158.

Van Soest, D. (1994). Strange bedfellows: A call for reordering national priorities from three social justice perspectives. *Social Work, 39*(6), 710–717.

Vartanian, L. R., Giant, C. L., & Passino, R. M. (2001). "Ally McBeal vs. Arnold Schwarzenegger": Comparing mass media, interpersonal feedback and gender as predictors of satisfaction with body thinness and muscularity. *Social Behavior and Personality, 29*, 711–723.

Vermeulen, A. (1994). Adropause, fact or fiction? In G. Berg & M. Hammar (Eds.), *The modern management of the menopause* (pp. 567–577). New York: The Parthenon Publishing Group.

Vermeulen, A., & Kaufman, J. M. (1995). Ageing of the hypthalamo-pituitary-testicular axis in men. *Hormone Research, 43*, 25–28.

Vestergaard, M., Mork, A., Madsen, K. M., & Olsen, J. (2005). Paternal age and epilepsy in the offspring. *European Journal of Epidemiology, 20*, 1003–1005.

Viadero, D. (2003, June 18). Researcher insists NYC vouchers benefit black students. *Education Week, 22*(41), 16.

Waite, L. J., & Gallagher, M. (2000). *The case for marriage*. New York: Doubleday.

Wakefield, A. J., Murch, S. H., Anthony, A., Linnell, J., Casson, D. M., Malik, M., Berelowitz, M., Dhillon, A. P., Thomson, M. A., Harvey, P., Valentine, A., Davies, S. E., & Walker-Smith, J. A. (1998). Illeal-lymphoid-nodular hyperplasia, non-specific colitis, and pervasive developmental disorder in children. *Lancet, 351*, 637–641.

Waldfogel, J. (2001). *The future of child protection*. Cambridge, MA: Harvard University Press.

Waldman, M., Nicholson, S., Adilov, N., & Williams, J. (2008). Autism prevalence and precipitation rates in California, Oregon, and Washington Counties. *Archives of Pediatric and Adolescent Medicine, 162*(11), 1026–1034.

Walker, H. (1998, May 31). Youth violence: Society's problem. *Eugene Register Guard*, 1C.

Waller, M. R., & Bitler, M. P. (2008). The link between couples' pregnancy intentions and behavior: Does it matter who is asked? *Perspectives on Sexual & Reproductive Health, 40*(4), 194–201.

Wang, H., & Amato, P. (2000). Predictors of divorce adjustment: Stressors, resources, and definitions. *Journal of Marriage and the Family, 62*(3), 655–668.

Ward, R. A. (1993). Marital happiness and household equity in later life. *Journal of Marriage and the Family, 55*, 427–438.

Ward, R. A., & Spitze, G. D. (2004). Marital implications of parent–adult child coresidence: A longitudinal view. *Journals of Gerontology: Series B, 59B*(1), S2–S8.

Watkins, D. R. (2009). Spiritual formation of older persons. *Journal of Religion, Spirituality, and Aging, 21*(1–2), 7–16.

Watson, J. B. (1925). *Behaviorism.* New York: W. W. Norton.

Webb, M. B., & Harden, B. J. (2003). Beyond child protection: Promoting mental health for children and families in the child welfare system. *Journal of Emotional and Behavioral Disorders, 11*(1), 49–58.

Weber, M. (1957). *The theory of social and economic organization.* New York: The Free Press of Glencoe.

Weber, M. (1958). *The Protestant ethic and the spirit of capitalism.* Translated by Talcott Parsons. New York: Scribner.

Weber, M. (1968). *Economy and society.* Translated by Guenther Roth and Claus Wittich. New York: Bedminster Press.

Weber, M. (1994). Class, status, party. In D. B. Grusky (Ed.), *Social stratification: Class, race, and gender in sociological perspective* (pp. 113–122). San Francisco: Westview Press.

Weick, A., Rapp, C., Sullivan, W. P., & Kisthardt, W. (1989). A strengths perspective for social work practice. *Social Work, 34*(4), 350–354.

Weinstein, L. B. (2000). Mothers and methadone. *American Journal of Nursing, 100,* 13–40.

Weitzman, M., Gortmaker, S., & Sobol, A. (1992). Maternal smoking and behavior problems of children. *Pediatrics, 90*(3), 342–349.

Wespes, E., & Schulman, C. C. (2002). Male andropause: Myth, reality, and treatment. *International Journal of Impotence Research, 14*(1), 93–98.

Westheimer, R. K., & Lopater, S. (2004). *Human sexuality.* Baltimore, MD: Lippincott Williams & Wilkins.

Whaley, A. L. (2000). Differential risk perceptions for unintended pregnancy, STDs, and HIV/AIDS among urban adolescents: Some preliminary findings. *Journal of Genetic Psychology, 161*(4), 435–452.

White, P. (2002). Access to health care: Health insurance considerations for young adults with special health care needs/disabilities. *Pediatrics, 110*(6), 1328–1335.

Whitebeck, L. B., & Hoyt, D. R. (1999). *Nowhere to grow: Homeless and runaway adolescents and their families.* New York: Aldine de Gruyter.

Whiting, B. B., & Edwards, C. P. (1988). *Children of different worlds.* Cambridge, MA: Harvard University Press.

Wilcox, S. (1997). Age and gender in relation to body attitudes: Is there a double standard of aging? *Psychology of Women Quarterly, 21,* 549–565.

Williams, N. R., Lindsey, E. W., Kurtz, P. D., & Jarvis, S. (2001). From trauma to resiliency: Lessons from former runaway and homeless youth. *Journal of Youth Studies, 4*(2), 233–253.

Wink, P., & Dillon, M. (2002). Spiritual development across the adult life course: Findings from a longitudinal study. *Journal of Adult Development, 9,* 79–94.

Wink, P., Dillon, M., & Prettyman, A. (2007). Religion as moderator of the sense of control—health connection: Gender differences. *Journal of Religion, Spirituality & Aging, 19*(4), 21–41.

Winterbottom, J., Smyth, R., Jacoby, A., & Baker, G. (2009). The effectiveness of preconception counseling to reduce adverse pregnancy outcome in women with epilepsy: What's the evidence? *Epilepsy & Behavior, 14*(2), 273–279.

Wintre, M. G., & Vallance, D. D. (1994). A developmental sequence in the comprehension of emotions: Intensity, multiple emotions, and valence. *Developmental Psychology, 39,* 509–514.

Women's International Network News. (1997). Teen pregnancy a major problem in the U.S. *Women's International Network News, 23*(3), 69–70.

Women's International Network News. (1998). Making pregnancy and childbirth safer. *Women's International Network News, 24*(4), 19.

World Bank. (1999). *World development indicators 1999.* New York: Oxford University Press.

World Health Organization. (2000). *The World Health Report.* Geneva: Author.

World Health Organization. (2003). *Family planning.* [Online]. Retrieved July 15, 2003, from http://www.who.int/reproductive-health/family_planning.

Wrosch, C., & Heckhausen, J. (1999). Control processes before and after passing a developmental deadline: Activation and deactivation of intimate relationship goals. *Journal of Personality & Social Psychology, 77*(2), 415–427.

Yoon, D. P., & Lee, E. K. (2007). The impact of religiousness, spirituality, and social support on psychological well-being among older adults in rural areas. *Journal of Gerontological Social Work, 48*(3–4), 281–298.

Zabin, L., Hirsch, M. B., Smith, B. A., & Hardy, J. B. (1986). Evaluation of a pregnancy prevention program for urban teenagers. *Family Planning Perspectives, 18*(3), 119–126.

Zaider, T. I., Johnson, J. G., & Cockell, S. J. (2002). Psychiatric disorders associated with the onset and persistence of bulimia nervosa and binge eating disorder during adolescence. *Journal of Youth and Adolescence, 31*(5), 319–329.

Zald, M., & McCarthy, J. (1987). *Social movements in an organizational society*. New Brunswick, NJ: Transaction.

Ziegler, J. C., & Goswami, U. (2005). Reading acquisition, developmental dyslexia, and skilled reading across languages: A psycholinguistic brain size theory. *Psychological Bulletin, 131*(1), 3–29.

Zill, N., Morrison, D. R., & Coiro, M. J. (1993). Long-term effects of parental divorce on parent–child relationships, adjustment, and achievement in young adulthood. *Journal of Family Psychology, 7*, 91–103.

Zimmerman, P. (2004). Attachment representations and characteristics of friendship relations during adolescence. *Journal of Experimental Child Psychology, 88*(1), 83–101.

CREDITS

Box 3.1: From the *Diagnostic and Statistical Manual of Mental Disorders, Fourth Edition, Text Revision*, in Psychopharmacology. Copyright © 2000. Reprinted with permission from the *Diagnostic and Statistical Manual of Mental Health Disorders*, Copyright 2000. American Psychiatric Association.

Table 9.2: From the *Diagnostic and Statistical Manual of Mental Disorders, Fourth Edition, Text Revision*, in Psychopharmacology. Copyright © 2000. Reprinted with permission from the *Diagnostic and Statistical Manual of Mental Health Disorders*, Copyright 2000. American Psychiatric Association.

Box 9.3: From *Not Just a Passing Phase: Social Work with Lesbian, Gay, and Bisexual People*, by G. A. Appleby and J. Anastas. Copyright © 1998 Columbia University Press. Reprinted by permission.

Table 10.3: From *Mismatch: The Growing Gulf Between Women and Men*, by Andrew Hacker. Copyright © 2003 by Andrew Hacker. Adapted with the permission of Scribner, an imprint of Simon & Schuster Adult Publishing Group.

Table 10.4: From *Mismatch: The Growing Gulf Between Women and Men*, by Andrew Hacker. Copyright © 2003 by Andrew Hacker. Adapted with the permis-

sion of Scribner, an imprint of Simon & Schuster Adult Publishing Group.

Exhibit 11.1: From *The Psychology of Love*, by R. J. Sternberg and M. L. Barnes (Eds.). Copyright © 1988 Yale University Press. Reprinted with permission.

Photo Credits:

Exhibit 2.3: Scott Vandehey

Exhibit 3.1: C Squared Studios/Getty Images

Exhibit 4.1: Royalty-Free/Corbis

Exhibit 5.1: Getty (Digital Vision)

Exhibit 6.1: S. Pearce/PhotoLink/Getty Images

Exhibit 6.2: PhotoDisc/Getty Images

Exhibit 7.1: Jack Star/PhotoLink/Getty Images

Exhibit 7.2: Scott T. Baxter/Getty Images

Exhibit 8.1: Ryan McVay/Getty Images

Exhibit 8.2: Escobar Studios

Exhibit 9.1: Jack Star/PhotoLink/Getty Images

Exhibit 10.1: M. Freeman/PhotoLink/Getty Images

Exhibit 11.1: Keith Brofsky/Getty Images

Exhibit 12.1: Mel Curtis/Getty Images

GLOSSARY/INDEX

Note: page numbers followed by *e* denote references to exhibits; page numbers followed by *t* denote references to tables.